Armies
of the
Napoleonic Era

Armies of the Napoleonic Era

Otto von Pivka

DAVID & CHARLES
Newton Abbot Devon

Pivka, Otto von
  Armies of the Napoleonic Era.
  1. France. Armée – History
  2. France – History, Military – 1789–1815
  I. Title
  355′.00944   UA702
  ISBN 0–7153–7766–3

Set in 10 on 11pt Times by Trade Linotype Limited
Birmingham
and printed in Great Britain
by Biddles Limited, Guildford
for David & Charles (Publishers) Limited
Brunel House Newton Abbot Devon

Contents

Acknowledgements

My sincere thanks are due to the following who have helped me in the preparation of this book: the directors and staff of the museums and archives in Berlin (Lipperheide Kostumsammlung—Frau Doktor Gretel Wagner), London, Vienna and Leiden; the Librarian and staff of the Ministry of Defence Library (Mr Andrews, Mr Potts, Miss Glover) and the Zentral Bibliothek der Bundeswehr, Düsseldorf; Mr F. Feather of Leigh-on-Sea and my wife.

Otto von Pivka
December 1978

Introduction

Comprehensive works of reference on Napoleonic land forces have been produced in the past, but not in the English language. Perhaps the best known of these are Professor Richard Knötel's *Handbuch der Uniform Kunde*, first published in Hamburg in 1937 by H. G. Schulz, and Lienhart and Humbert's *Les Uniformes de l'Armee Française depuis 1690 jusq'à nos Jours*, five volumes, published in Leipzig from 1895–1906. As their titles suggest, both books concentrate on details of military costume, although both contain certain data on the organisational side of life including the dates of the raising and disbandment of some units.

Recently there has been a wealth of uniform data published, including much repetitive work on France, Britain and Prussia. Unfortunately, a large proportion of this work is based on sources which at best must be described as of doubtful authenticity, many merely distorting the original and causing confusion to the unfortunate reader.

While a considerable part of this book is devoted to the study of the uniforms of the period 1792–1815, care has been taken to select in each case the best sources available, thus very few modern works have been used for reference although many were consulted.

Lack of space has forced economy of words and thus, where feasible, individual regimental details such as facings, badges and button colours have had to be refined into extremely abbreviated forms which however, preserve coherence.

Due to this restricted space, no militia or colonial regiments have been included in the book and similarly palace troops, who fulfilled only ritual and parade functions, have also had to be excluded. Apart from uniforms, the book deals with other aspects of the various Napoleonic armies, which normally receive scant mention if any (except in very restricted specialist periodicals). These include the characteristics of the weapons used by the infantry, cavalry and artillery of the armies of the period and a brief look at some basic tactics.

It will be noted that Hanoverian musketry experiments resulted in about three-quarters of the shots fired at a representative infantry target finding their mark at 100 paces with a rapid falling off of hits scored as range increased. These results were achieved under 'laboratory' conditions, however, and the target was a wood and cloth frame about 6ft high and 100ft long, meant to represent a company of enemy infantry deployed in time. Under battlefield conditions, with confusion, smoke, excitement, fatigue and terror affecting the firers, with a certain number of casualties (and others absent for whatever reason) and a proportion of misfires from the firearms also to be considered, it must be assumed that the total of hits scored would be less than half of the laboratory level, particularly when it is remembered that many balls falling into the theoretical target area would pass between the files of men anyway.

It is thus not surprising to learn that even as late as the Vietnam war, the proportion of men killed by enemy action during an extended campaign was far less than those who died from disease. The losses of the Napoleonic British and French regiments serving in their respective colonies in the West and East Indies and the terrible losses of Napoleon's Grande Armée in Russia in the summer of 1812 are other cases in point.

A word now as to the nature of European armies as they were in 1792.

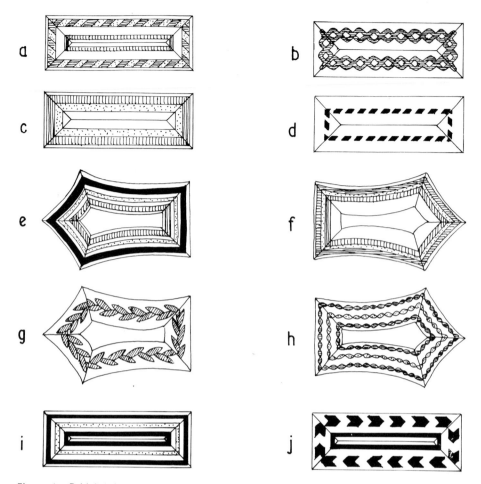

Figure 1   British Infantry Regimental Lace
a   34th Foot: white, a narrow red stripe and a wide yellow and blue stripe
b   1st Foot: white with blue lozenges
c   37th Foot: white with wide red and yellow stripes
d   70th Foot: white with black dotted line
e   12th Foot: white, bastion-ended, with black, yellow and red stripes
f   25th Foot: white, bastion-ended, with blue, yellow and red stripes
g   45th Foot: white, bastion--ended, with green leaves
h   29th Foot: white, bastion-ended, with blue, yellow and blue 'chains'
i   28th Foot: white with black, yellow and black stripes
j   32nd Foot: white with black chevrons and a black stripe

Military conflict within Europe had been relatively low-key since the end of the Seven Years' War in 1763. Armies which had then achieved high martial reputations (such as the Prussian) were still highly regarded thirty years later, although their actual military value had often changed considerably in the meantime. Tactics, dress, doctrine and weaponry had changed little from 1763 and it was generally only the Russian and Austrian armies which had widely spread current combat experience as they defended their borders against repeated Turkish inroads. Britain and France had also squabbled continuously in colonies all over the world.

The War of American Independence had brought out the value of light troops, suitably clad, equipped and armed, and both Britain and France, as well as many minor German states, had raised light troops (Chasseurs or

8

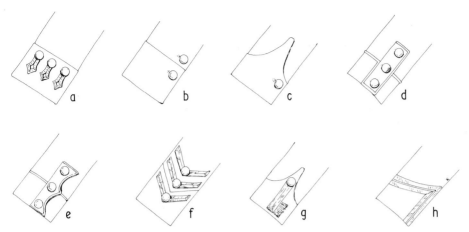

Figure 2   Various Cuff Patterns
a Swedish or round—here British infantry pattern with bastion-ended lace
b Swedish
c Polish (or pointed); lancer kurtkas and hussar dolmans always had this style of cuff
d Brandenburg with rectangular cuff flap
e French with scalloped cuff flap
f British heavy cavalry c1795; Bavarian Chevau Légers had a similar cuff in the 1790s but without the lace and buttons shown here
g Polish cuff of Hungarian infantry
h British heavy cavalry cuff c1812

Jägers) and armed a proportion of them with rifles so that more accurate fire could be brought to bear by these chosen marksmen. Jägers were not entirely new, however, and during the Seven Years' War they were frequently employed as light troops (equipped with rifles) by Prussia, Austria and Hanover. Their lack of use in the relatively peaceful years following this conflict had caused them to fade into the background somewhat and few commanders had exhibited sufficient interest in these riflemen to develop the best tactics required.

Military affairs had stagnated for many years and the condition of European armies reflected this. They were all professional bodies, that is to say soldiers were recruited and signed up for very long periods, frequently for life. Dress was expensive, elaborate, complex and impracticable for field use and great emphasis was laid on the soldier's daily impeccable parade ground appearance, while sabres and muskets were allowed to lapse into unserviceable condition as long as they were well polished. A soldier's daily toilet took hours and involved pomading, curling, plaiting and powdering his hair, pipeclaying his belts, blacking and polishing his cartridge pouch and shoes and polishing his buttons (and helmet plate if he was a grenadier or fusilier wearing such a cap). That was the infantryman's lot; a cavalry trooper had, in addition, all his harness and a horse to keep in tip-top condition and perhaps a Kürass to polish as well.

Punishments for the slightest infringements of the high standards of parade cleanliness were Draconian and included flogging, imprisonment, 'Krumm-schliessen' (being chained right hand to left foot for long periods) and 'riding the wooden horse' which involved being forced to sit astride a sharp ridge of wood for hours with no support for the feet.

Physical violence was the accepted method whereby officers and non-

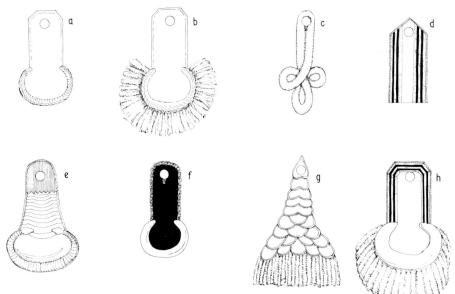

Figure 3 Epaulettes
a Contre-epaulette
b French grenadier and Voltigeur pattern
c French trefoil
d Prussian 1806–1812—captain with black and silver lace stripes
e Bavarian Chevau Légers metal-scale type 1800–1815
f Bavarian c1790
g Portuguese officer 1808–1815
h Prussian field officer 1813–1814

commissioned officers (NCOs) instructed their men in the highly complex arms drill and tactical evolutions which were practised daily and battlefield manoeuvres were correspondingly ponderous and slow. Occasional isolated voices in the military world were raised against this pointless charade of fancy dress and 'military Minuettes' (such as the Russian General Potemkin in April 1786) but they were few and far between and even Potemkin's excellent reforms were negated ten years later when the new Tsar, Paul I, put the clock back and reintroduced all the impractical pomp of a bygone age to plague the soldiers.

Apart from the disadvantages of boring, grinding daily routine, harsh discipline and no prospects of changing the way of life, the pay was low, accommodation bad and to this was added the rather evil 'Beurlaubungs' system common in many armies whereby about half the enlisted men would be sent off on unpaid leave during the late autumn, winter and spring months and recalled to the colours only for the summer weeks when they would be ruthlessly drilled to achieve a high standard of parade ground drill for the annual manoeuvres which would be held in front of the reigning monarch.

All these disadvantages made soldiering a 'career which appealed mainly to those who were unable or unwilling to earn their livelihood by other means. Tradesmen, farmers, state officials and clerics were almost always excused military service even when conscription was introduced. The rate of desertion was high even though the penalty for that offence was death and many soldiers moved from state to state, enlisting for the proffered

10

bounty and then absconding after a few months complete with weapons and equipment which they would then sell. As modern Germany was then a complex patchwork of tiny, independent states, each of which regarded the other as 'foreign', such mobility was easily achieved and chances of detection were very low. This led to a situation in which many armies grew completely apart from the civil population of their countries and became a sort of sink into which society's less-favoured members fell and were there mixed with undesirable foreigners and fugitive criminals. Like a savage guard dog an army was generally regarded as a necessary evil, to be kept under careful control and given only the minimum of freedom.

It was also a well established practice that officers' positions were sold to the highest bidder and advancement in rank depended firstly on a man's pocket, secondly on his influence with higher officials and only to a third and minor degree on his martial efficiency. Regiments would be 'sold' to generals or to members of domestic or foreign nobility and would thence carry the name of their 'Colonel-in-Chief' or 'Chef'. In former times the Chef had considerable powers concerning the dress of his regiment and the colours they carried but by 1792 these had largely been done away with. The regiments would be arranged in line of battle from the right according to the seniority of their Chefs and when a regiment changed Chefs its title and its position in the line of battle also altered. This constant changing of titles makes the task of tracing the genealogy of continental regiments extremely difficult.

At lower military levels, companies were 'sold' to their commanders who then received from the state annual financial grants based on the strength of the company. The company commander was at liberty to make as much money from his command as he could and it was a common malpractice to falsify parade states to claim greater allowances. The state countered this by 'reviewing' regiments physically and counting the number of men present, comparing their findings with the figures submitted by the officers to support their claims. As the company commander was generally the man who paid for powder and ball used on musketry practice in peace time, it is not suprising that live firing was a rare event, usually taking place only once a year. It was a realisation of the underlying evils of this system which led to its gradual abolition in the 1790s and the direct taking over by the state of all expenses of the maintenance of their armies.

Being professional armies, there were no great numbers of trained soldiers available among the civilian populations to form reserves in the case of mobilisation; there were no reserves there to replenish the ranks of the armies and to make good the losses of any campaign. It took time to train recruits, particularly those of the artillery and cavalry and thus it can easily be seen that any military commander of the period would be loath to risk his army and to incur casualties. This led to the practice of elaborate manoeuvring instead of head-on conflict and of regular exchanges of prisoners of war during a campaign. An army of the late eighteenth century was far too precious and rare to be squandered in a battle!

Change came to this situation by violent means in the form of the French Revolution. The main immediate effects of this event (initially on the French army, later spreading gradually to almost all others) were six fold: firstly, corporal punishment for minor military crimes was abolished and replaced by varying terms and degrees of arrest and imprisonment. Secondly, the relationship between officers and men was greatly changed and became much closer with vastly increased opportunities for soldiers to be promoted

11

to commissioned ranks by merit alone. Thirdly, the purchasing of commissions, and of higher military office was abolished in many armies, although it persisted in the British army until much later. Fourthly, the army and the nation became much more closely integrated, particularly when Lazare Nicolas Marguerite Carnot (13 May 1753–3 August 1823) called the levée en masse with his army reorganisations of 1793 and 1794 and the reputation of this now-popular army rose accordingly in the eyes of the nation at large. This was later followed by the conscription system whereby military service liability was extended to almost all male adults (certain trades and classes of people were excluded and Jews were encouraged to buy their immunity with suitably large sums). Fifthly, there was a massive degree of political interference in daily military affairs at all levels and 'People's Representatives' were attached to all commanders' staffs and gave 'advice' on almost all matters, military and otherwise. During the Terror (1793–1794) over eighty French generals were guillotined as a result of incurring the displeasure of the People's Representatives. This was a forerunner of the Political Commissar system which was to cause such similar damage to the Red Army in the earlier stages of World War II. Finally, the numbers of recruits needed within a short time by Revolutionary France to defend her borders against her monarchical foes and later to carry the Revolutionary Message into other lands was so vast that there was no time to train them perfectly in the demanding rituals of the old linear tactics.

The Revolutionary French armies were incapable of carrying out these complex manoeuvres and so a new, simpler, more flexible tactical system had to be devised. This was the birth of the famous Napoleonic column. Instead of a long line of three men deep on a battalion frontage advancing over broken terrain, the French infantry formed columns usually on the frontage of one company (ie only one-sixth so wide as a battalion) with the other companies ranged behind either in close order—at about three paces distance one from another—or in open order, that is at one company's length from each other. The first company in the column was the grenadier company and it was followed by the four centre or fusilier companies. In the advance towards the enemy the column was preceded by the Voltigeur company well ahead of it and in extended, or skirmishing order.

Napoleon's great tactical art was combining all arms of his army into a careful assault at a chosen spot in the enemy's line. This selected spot would be subjected to a preparatory barrage of artillery from various batteries concentrated to fire at the one target. After sufficient preparation, the infantry assault columns would advance on the point, preceded by their skirmishers who would unsettle the enemy line with armed fire from positions of cover. Conventional vollies from the enemy infantry caused little harm to these skirmishers and they were immune to artillery fire. Cavalry was the only thing which would scare them off but they were usually well supported by their own cavalry and so suffered little. When the assaulting column had closed up to within about a hundred paces from the chosen point of contact in the enemy line, the Voltigeur skirmishers would fall back to the sides and form into a closed company at the rear of the column. Within a few moments the relentless, imposing phalanx would impact on the already shaken troops in the area well ripped by artillery fire and their numerical superiority at that point would usually bring a quick decision and the weakened line would break. Once the line was broken, it would be rolled up to left and right of the gap, French cavalry would pour through and attack the rear of the line and usually the route of the enemy was assured.

12

This system was so successful that it was aped by all Napoleon's vassal states although it must be stressed that column itself was a formation which had commonly been used for many years for certain situations by all armies of the period. It was column combined with artillery preparation, advanced skirmishers and supporting cavalry that brought success. Column had its disadvantages, however, the main ones being that it formed an excellent target for enemy artillery and musket fire and that its fire-power was limited to the first three ranks (one-sixth of its total strength if skirmishers were in rear).

The army which beat column repeatedly from the Maida (4 July 1806) to Waterloo was the British and this fact remains, surprisingly, almost totally unrecognised on the Continent of Europe today. Having deduced that the success of column depended upon effective artillery preparation and the cloud of advanced skirmishers, the British countered these by having their line lay down or be deployed in cover to escape the worst of the artillery fire and by deploying greater numbers of their own skirmishers in advance of the line to shoot down the opposing Voltigeurs. Once the protective Voltigeurs were disposed of, the column was subject to harassing fire by the British skirmishers in its further advance and when close to the line was given a volley by the British line which usually tore away the leading grenadier company, the following ranks stumbled over their fallen comrades and momentum was lost at which point the British line mounted a bayonet charge which usually won the day. Another great factor in this victory over column was that the British army had not been subject to a period of years of repeated defeats at French hands—just the reverse, they had beaten the French in all the colonies and thus morally they were totally unimpressed with the poor tactical logic of the column as it lumbered towards them.

Logically poor as it was, the French column was adopted by many other European armies as were the French conscription system, military discipline code, rank badges, organisation and higher formation levels such as corps and divisions; the requisition system (which did away with the existing magazine ration resupply system for bread, biscuit and flour) and the reduced military baggage train.

It will be clear that the numerically limited professional armies of France's foes were unable to stand against the French nation in arms once it had perfected a winning battlefield system. The pipeclay and boot-polish forces of over-aged warriors soon melted away under the hammer blows of their younger, more numerous and enthusiastic enemies and by 1806 conscription (the 'Tax of Blood' as it was called by the Germans) was providing the young recruits needed to keep Napoleon's insatiable war machine operating. Dress and accoutrements were generally simplified and made more functional, most armies cut off their pigtails and stopped pomading and powdering hair by 1806 and the general standards of efficiency of weapons increased greatly as defective weapons of local manufacture were thrown away to be replaced by the French M1777 musket. Of course the recipients had to pay France for all these benefits but within a few years Napoleon had raised the equivalent of the present-day Warsaw Pact – a group of armies in which policy, language, staff duties, strategy, tactics, uniform detail (badges of rank and function), weapons, administration, resupply and recruiting were all standardised and controlled from one headquarters and directed towards one end.

Napoleon's interference in the affairs of his vassal states of the Confederation of the Rhine (which included all territories covered by both the present

13

day German states and much of present day Poland) extended far beyond the purely military and encompassed the legal systems, the social structure and weights and measures. Having opened the Pandora's box of social reform and change in these states, it was impossible to reverse the process at the touch of a switch in 1815 when Napoleon was finally exiled to St. Helena. Revolutionary movements grew in many states, including Russia, in the years after 1815 and in 1848 a rash of upheavals occurred which the authorities were hard put to suppress.

Some of the most far-reaching and successful tactical and logistic developments which came about in the period were born of desperate necessity. When Carnot took over the French army in 1793 it was so disorganised after the upheaval of the Revolution that its professional expertise in drill and manoeuvre was negligible and the logistic system had ceased to function. The magazines contained no flour, there was no ration resupply for the army in the field and no transport existed to move the supplies from base to forward troops. To combat the lack of tactical expertise Carnot developed the column into a viable assault formation. As the problems of reviving a logistic system were too daunting, he introduced requisitioning whereby the commissary officials with the forward troops were empowered to demand from the local populace rations sufficient for the needs of their men. At a stroke he had done away with a large proportion of the cumbersome and slow waggon trains of food which otherwise dogged the steps of the fighting troops of all armies of the period and thus increased enormously the mobility of the remainder. The commodities taken by the army were paid for (much in arrears if at all) by the French government on receipt of a duly signed requisition note which the commissary was supposed to give to the unfortunate and unwilling donor.

Requisitioning was a system which obviously would only succeed if there were supplies to be had in the immediate area of the army. It thus worked reasonably well (as far as the army was concerned) in fertile, well developed farming lands but had its limitation in unpopulated, or sparsely populated areas or if the army remained in one spot for any length of time.

In the Revolutionary wars and in the central European campaigns of 1805 and 1809, where the country was rich or the duration of the wars short, requisitioning was ideal. In Spain from 1808 to 1813 and in Russia in 1812, however, there were only very limited supplies initially available and these were jealously guarded by the hostile inhabitants.

Requisitioning soon became naked pillage, detachments of troops had to be sent further and further afield to gather food, convoys of unofficial vehicles were 'acquired' to carry the food over the long distances, escorts had to be provided to protect the gathered supplies from guerrilla attack, military strength was expended and dissipated and the whole process was counter-productive in the long term. Added to this is the fact that the civil population rapidly became alienated and hostile to the requisitioning army and its worthless paper receipts and the full disadvantages of Carnot's quick, easy solution to his logistic problems can be appreciated. The next problem which the French army 'solved' was that of the extensive baggage train full of tents for officers and men. To do away with yet more of the tails of their armies they abolished tents for all but the top commanders and resorted to billeting their soldiers on the populace in the area of operations. The limitations which applied to requisitioning are equally valid here.

It was usually the case that the advanced guard of any large formation on the move lived and ate to excess, squandering what food and drink they could not at once consume and often destroying accommodation by fires neglectfully or maliciously started while their following comrades lived under increasingly deprived conditions the closer to the rearguard that they marched.

Requisitioning and billeting made the French army cordially hated throughout Europe and unpopular even within France itself. Armies that were better disciplined, had efficient logistic systems and paid cash for anything that they wanted from the local market were much more favourably regarded even as in the case of Wellington's army in southern France in 1814.

It is hoped that this book will provide an insight into the capabilities and limitations of the armies of the Napoleonic era and will give general information on their uniforms.

The reference material given here is comprehensive but by no means exhaustive; the serious student will doubtless further his researches into his selected area of interest and if this book serves as a spur then its aim has been achieved.

Part One
Weapons, Equipment and Tactics

Artillery

Weapons and Equipment

Measurements used in Napoleonic times were not standardised and varied considerably between states.

The Pace

Hanover	—	2⅔ Calenburgischen Fuss	—	346 Parisian Line*	=	935.93 mm
France	—	2½ to a *Toise*	—	345 Parisian Line	=	933.23 mm
Prussia	—	2¼ Rheinländischen Fuss	—	347 Parisian Line	=	938.64 mm
Saxony	—	1¼ Saxon Elle	—	314 Parisian Line	=	849.37 mm
Denmark	—	2½ Danish Fuss	—	347 Parisian Line	=	938.64 mm
England	—	measurement in yards (expressed in this chapter as Hanoverian paces) 1 yard=900 mm				
Bückeburg	—	*Toisen* (expressed as French paces)				

*1 Parisian Line=2.705 mm

Dimensions of Field Artillery Pieces in the Napoleonic Era

Artillery pieces included cannon, howitzers and mortars and differed in their construction as follows: a cannon's barrel length was sixteen to twenty-four times as long as the inner diameter of the barrel (the calibre); a howitzer was four-and-a-half to six calibres long and a mortar three to four calibres long. The projectile trajectory of a cannon was almost horizontal, a howitzer could vary its trajectory from horizontal to a high arch and a mortar threw its projectile only in a high arch. Early howitzers and mortars had a special chamber at the end of the barrel to accommodate the charge but during the Napoleonic era it became the custom to cast them just like cannon, ie without this chamber.

Cannon

A cannon was categorised in accordance with the weight of shot that it fired, the weight being expressed in pounds.

The individual parts of a cannon barrel are shown in Figure 4a: a=endpiece; a–d=the trunnion piece or spigot; b=touchhole; c=the soul, its centre line (along the barrel) is the soul axis. To the rear it is closed by the 'floor' or butt plate and the rear end of the barrel is thus called the 'Bodenstück' or endpiece; d=the band; e=forward band; f=the trunnions on which the barrel rests on the carriage; g=the grape; h=the middle band; i=the head; l=the muzzle; m=the dolphins (for lifting the barrel with block and tackle).

In early times it was the practice to make the walls of the barrel at the rear equal to the calibre of the piece, reducing at the muzzle to half a calibre. As casting techniques improved, the barrel thickness was reduced at the rear.

Until 1810 the French and Saxon artillery had 4, 8 and 12 pdr field cannon whereas all other European states had 3, 6 and 12 pdrs. Following the 1809 campaign (against Austria), Napoleon completely reorganised his artillery based only on the 6 and 12 pdrs. The Saxons did the same but preferred long, light barrels to short, heavy (and less accurate) ones.

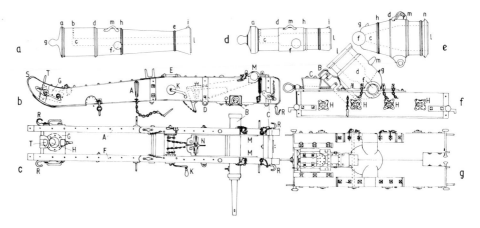

Figure 4   Artillery Weapons and Equipment
a Cannon barrel
b Cannon trails, side view
c Gun carriage, plan view
d Howitzer barrel
e Hanging mortar
f Standing mortar and bed, side view
g Standing mortar bed, plan view

The Weight of Cannons

Within any calibre, weights of barrels (and thus of carriages) varied in accordance with the charge and length. This was usually expressed in terms of the ball thrown; it was usual for a cannon to weigh 150 to 200 lb for each pound of the cannon ball thrown, eg a 3 pdr would weigh 450 to 600 lb. In general terms field artillery pieces had the following weights:

DIMENSIONS OF ARTILLERY PIECES OF VARIOUS ARMIES 1815

Country	Calibre (lb)	Charge (as a fraction of projectile weight)	Charge in pounds	Barrel length in calibres	Weight of piece for each pound of projectile weight	Weight of whole piece (lb)
PRUSSIA						
Medium	12	$\frac{1}{3}$	4	18	154	1,847
Heavy	6	$\frac{3}{8}$	$2\frac{1}{4}$	22	269	1,617
Light	6	$\frac{3}{8}$	$2\frac{1}{4}$	18	156	935
AUSTRIA						
	12	$\frac{1}{4}$	3	16	134	1,618
	6	$\frac{1}{4}$	$1\frac{1}{2}$	16	137	824
	3	$\frac{7}{24}$	$\frac{7}{8}$	16	160	480
DENMARK						
	12	$\frac{1}{3}$	4	22	200	2,400
	6	$\frac{5}{12}$	$2\frac{1}{2}$	22	200	1,200
Heavy	3	$\frac{1}{2}$	$1\frac{1}{2}$	22	200	600
Regimental	3	$\frac{1}{3}$	1	16	135	406

20

SAXONY (Old)					
Heavy	12	$\frac{5}{12}$	5	16	200	2,410
Light	12	$\frac{1}{3}$	4	16	141	1,700
Heavy	8	$\frac{13}{32}$	$3\frac{1}{4}$	16	200	1,600
Light	8	$\frac{3}{8}$	3	16	140	1,120
Heavy	4	$\frac{1}{2}$	2	21	222	900
Light	4	$\frac{3}{16}$	$1\frac{1}{4}$	16	167	670
BRITAIN					
Medium	12	$\frac{1}{3}$	4	16	150	1,800
Light	12	$\frac{1}{4}$	4	13	100	1,200
Medium	6	$\frac{1}{3}$	2	18	146	875
Belford's	6	$\frac{1}{4}$	$1\frac{1}{2}$	16	92	550
Light	6	$\frac{1}{4}$	$1\frac{1}{2}$	14	53	500
RUSSIA					
	12	$\frac{1}{3}$	4	18	173	2,080
	6	$\frac{1}{3}$	2	18	147	880
FRANCE					
Field guns	12	$\frac{1}{3}$	4	18	150	1,800
	8	$\frac{5}{16}$	$2\frac{1}{2}$	18	150	1,200
	4	$\frac{3}{8}$	$1\frac{1}{2}$	18	150	600

Field Gun Carriages (Figure 4b and c)

The carriage consisted of the two walls A and F (between which the barrel lay), the axle B and three or four strengthening bolts holding the walls together (C, D, G). Through G is hole H through which the limber pin fits. In order to assist in loading, the Saxon artillery made bolt D (under the rear of the barrel) removable so that the barrel could be elevated to an extreme angle. On top of the carriage walls were the trunnion rests MM. The barrel spigots rested here when the gun was in action and thus caused the centre of gravity of the piece to be in front of the carriage axle. This eased the limbering and unlimbering of the gun without causing the tail S to lift from the ground when the gun was fired. A cranking handle K operated the elevating screw N.

When on the march, however, the French 8 and 12 pdrs had a system whereby the barrel was moved backwards about four calibres so that the weight was more evenly distributed between carriage and limber.

The length of the carriage was in proportion to the length of the barrel, the height of the wheels and the strength of the charge used. Generally they were 10 to 12 ft long for a 12 pdr, 9 to 10 ft for a 6 pdr and 8 to 9 ft for a 3 pdr. Carriage walls were usually one calibre thick and three to four high. They were covered by hooks, chains and attachments to take tools, equipment and forage during the march. A handspike was put through the trail ring T to assist manoeuvring the piece for re-aiming when in the firing position or in steering it when it was being relocated by the gun team towing it about by means of their tow ropes fastened to hooks 'R' (see section on Gun Crews p 32).

The Limber (Figure 5)

This consisted of a wheeled axle C supporting the trail arms and on which, in most armies, an ammunition chest M sat. Behind this chest was the limber pin N which took the gun carriage trail when on the march. The British artillery had replaced this with a hook, shutter and slide arrangement which fitted through a ring in the gun carriage trails and made limbering and unlimbering easier. The French artillery (and those modelled on it) had no

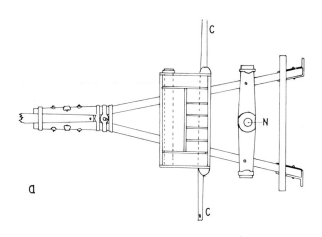

a

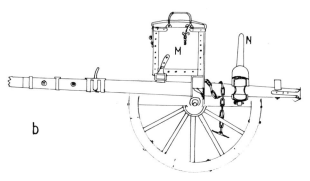

b

Figure 5 Artillery Weapons and Equipment
a Gun limber with ammunition chest, plan view
b Gun limber with ammunition chest, side view

ammunition chest on the limber but carried their immediate ammunition requirements ('First Line' supplies) in a small chest on the gun carriage trails. This had two disadvantages, firstly the ammunition thus carried was very limited and secondly limbering and unlimbering were complicated by the need to remove and replace the chest. 'Second Line' ammunition supplies were carried in purpose-built ammunition waggons.

The diameter of gun wheels was generally 5 or 6 ft regardless of calibre; limber wheels were $4\frac{1}{2}$ to 5 ft in diameter. The distance between the wheels was generally dictated by the nature of the country of origin; a flat, open country produced widely tracked pieces, a mountainous land narrow pieces to fit on the narrow tracks.

Most artillery equipment was made of oak, but lack of this hardwood forced some nations (eg Saxony) to use pine or fir. As long as sufficiently strong timber was used, it proved to be no disadvantage and the following ratios of fir to oak were established:

| Calibre | Cross-section of carriage walls at trunnion point | |
	French (oak) carriages	Fir carriages
12 pdr	45.00 sq in	65.00 sq in
8 pdr	35.75 sq in	51.62 sq in
4 pdr	24.75 sq in	28.38 sq in

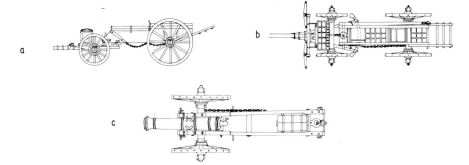

Figure 6 *Württemberg Artillery Equipment 1806–1815*
a & **b** Side view and plan (with open top) of M1808 artillery ammunition waggon using a gun limber as forepart. This arrangement ensured that spare limbers were always available in emergencies so that the ammunition waggon could be abandoned and a gun brought away instead. The plan view shows the compartments in which the individual cartridges were stored. The rack at the rear was used to carry hay for the draught horses
c 12 pdr cannon
During the Napoleonic Wars Württemberg's artillery equipment was of Austrian pattern. Note the small ammunition chest on the trails

WEIGHTS OF GUN CARRIAGES OF VARIOUS NATIONS

Calibre	Carriage Weight (lb)	Limber (lb)	Barrel (lb)	Charge (lb)	Total Weight (Barrel, Carriage and Limber)
PRUSSIA					
12 pdr	1,811	562	1,847	4	4,220
6 pdr	1,132	810	935	$2\frac{1}{4}$	2,877
SAXONY					
Old 12 pdr	1,627	387	2,410	5	4,424
New 12 pdr	1,408	354	1,700	4	3,462
Old 8 pdr	1,173	550	1,600	$3\frac{1}{4}$	3,323
New 8 pdr	1,019	524	1,120	3	2,663
BRITAIN					
Light 18 pdr	1,649	770	1,980	6	4,399
Medium 12 pdr	1,649	770	1,800	4	4,219
Light 12 pdr	1,295	658	1,200	4	3,153
Desnaulieres' 6 pdr	1,064	1,061	1,200	2	3,325
Belford's 6 pdr	1,046	985	660	$1\frac{1}{2}$	2,691
RUSSIA					
12 pdr	2,160	—	2,080	4	4,240
6 pdr	1,280	—	880	2	2,160
DENMARK					
12 pdr	2,100	1,100	2,400	4	5,600
6 pdr	1,200	1,100	1,200	$2\frac{1}{2}$	3,500
FRANCE					
12 pdr	1,433	787	1,800	4	4,020
8 pdr	1,167	787	1,200	$2\frac{1}{2}$	3,154
4 pdr	757	591	600	$1\frac{1}{2}$	1,948

Mortars and Howitzers (Figure 4d and e)

The 7 pdr howitzer or mortar threw a 7 lb stone ball but their shells weighed 14 or 15 lb; the bomb of a 30 pdr mortar weighed 60 lb. It was also the custom to grade these guns by their calibre ('six inch' etc). The external parts of mortars and howitzers were given the same names as those of cannon; within the barrel the rear part, reserved for the charge, was called the 'chamber' (c—d on Figure 4d). Mortars were subdivided into 'hanging' or 'standing' according to whether their trunnions were in the middle of the barrel (as on a cannon) or at the base end (Figure 4f). The hanging mortar in Figure 4e has a conical chamber c—d. In front of the chamber was the 'load' (d) and in front of this the 'flight' or 'kettle' (d—l). Externally (on mortars) g was the sight, h—f the chamberpiece, d—m the reinforcement and m—n the flight or muzzle piece.

The length of a howitzer was graded according to the length of a man's arm and experience showed that if the flight was up to $2\frac{1}{4}$ ft long a gunner could still easily set the cartridge in the chamber.

The 7 pdr was four-and-a-half calibres to the chamber (and six calibres in all) long; the 10 pdr was five-and-a-half calibres and the 30 pdr three calibres long. Greater length gave greater range and accuracy but it complicated correct loading.

Mortars were shorter than howitzers, usually three calibres long. Originally mortars and howitzers had smaller chambers than their calibres because they were used with varying charges but experiments in Berlin in 1792 showed that by making them with uniform inner dimensions a far greater range could be achieved for the same charge of powder. It was also established that by setting howitzer shells in a sabot, like a cannon shot, a tighter fit in the barrel and thus greater range and accuracy was possible. Howitzers with conically shaped barrels, like the Russian 'Unicorn' (see Figure 7), had the disadvantage that the cartridges were difficult to make and tended to lose their shape when transported for long in the field.

The weight of howitzers and mortars was in proportion of calibre to charge; with a charge $\frac{1}{8}$ the weight of the bomb, a howitzer's weight would be 50 times that of the bomb; with a $\frac{1}{20}$ charge, 35 times the bomb weight.
A 7 pdr howitzer using a 2 lb charge weighed 50 x 15 = 750 lb.
A 30 pdr howitzer using a 3 lb charge weighed 60 x 35 = 2,100 lb.

WEIGHTS AND CHARGES OF VARIOUS HOWITZERS

Calibre	Weight (lb)	Charge (lb)
PRUSSIA		
7 pdr	572	2
10 pdr	1,370	$2\frac{3}{4}$
SAXONY		
4 pdr	695	$1\frac{3}{8}$
8 pdr	705	$1\frac{1}{2}$
16 pdr	1,390	2
AUSTRIA		
7pdr	563	$1\frac{1}{4}$
10 pdr	824	2
RUSSIA		
10 pdr (Unicorn)	920	2
20 pdr	1,680	4

BRITAIN		
$5\frac{1}{2}$ in	450	1
8 in	1,428	$3\frac{1}{2}$
10 in	2,860	$6\frac{1}{2}$
FRANCE		
6 in	650	$1\frac{1}{16}$
8 in	1,120	$1\frac{3}{4}$

Mortars

Using a charge $\frac{1}{40}$th the weight of the bomb, a mortar would weight 15 times the bomb weight; using a $\frac{1}{24}$th charge it would weigh 20 times the bomb weight or 900 lb and 1,200 lb respectively.

WEIGHTS AND CHARGES OF VARIOUS MORTARS

Calibre	Weight (lb)	Charge (lb)
SAXONY		
48 pdr	2,103	5
32 pdr	1,560	$4\frac{1}{2}$
24 pdr	1,183	$2\frac{1}{2}$
16 pdr	433	2
AUSTRIA		
100 pdr	2,318	7
60 pdr	2,020	$4\frac{1}{2}$
30 pdr	1,011	$2\frac{1}{4}$
BRITAIN		
13 in	2,810	$9\frac{1}{2}$
10 in	1,173	$4\frac{1}{2}$
8 in	484	2
FRANCE		
10 in	2,050	$6\frac{1}{2}$
10 in	1,600	$3\frac{1}{2}$
8 in	550	$1\frac{1}{4}$

Carriages of Howitzers and Mortars

Howitzer carriages were built as for those of field cannon with the exception that they were heavier and stronger for similar weight of barrel due to the need to absorb more shock when firing high trajectory shots.

Mortar carriages were as heavy again as the weapon itself. The hanging mortar had by now been replaced by the standing mortar for ease of aiming.

WEIGHT OF MORTAR BEDS AND MORTARS

		Weight of Mortar (lb)	Weight of Bed (lb)
FRANCE	12 in	3,150	3,000
	10 in	2,050	2,616
	10 in	1,600	1,739
	8 in	550	820
BRITAIN	12 in	2,500	2,000
	10 in	1,068	1,400
	8 in	420	800

SAXONY	48 pdr	4,103	1,971
	32 pdr	1,560	1,635
	25 pdr	1,140	1,087

Mortars were transported, like the barrels of 24 pdr cannon, on 'saddle waggons'.

Aiming devices

When resting on the carriage, the barrels of cannon and howiters lay at an angle of elevation of $+10°$ to $+15°$. In order to be able to use them for horizontal or depression shots, they had to be fitted with appropriate regulating devices. This could be done simply by lifting the rear of the barrel with hand spikes and chocking it up with wedges but this method was slow, cumbersome and always demanded two men and by 1815 was completely replaced by better 'aiming machines' enabling one man to set the cannon at any desired angle of elevation or depression within a given range and for this setting to be undisturbed by the repeated firing of that gun. Prussian, British, French and Spanish artillery all introduced the vertical aiming screw, while the Russians, Austrians and Saxons used horizontal screws which moved wedges forwards or backwards under the rear of the barrel. The latter method was slower and required more strength than the former.

A similar device was used on mortars (see Figure 4f, points C and B).

Tolerances in barrel and shot calibre

French field artillery shot had a clearance of 1 Parisian Line (2.705 mm) within the bore of the cannon; Hannoverian guns had a clearance of $\frac{1}{30}$th of the bore, Prussian guns $\frac{1}{24}$th. Spanish guns' clearance was 1 Line (2.705 mm), the Dutch $\frac{1}{24}$th and the Saxon $\frac{1}{25}$th of the calibre. If the clearance was in excess of $\frac{1}{20}$th calibre, the range of the shot was seriously reduced as was the accuracy.

There was a system whereby newly cast shot was wrought between a concave hammer and concave anvil to give a denser and smoother outer skin. This process reduced barrel wear, gave much better ricochet performance and inhibited rust formation on the shot. It was however so expensive that it was not generally introduced.

Canister or Grapeshot

Canister (or grape) was originally a collection of small lead balls fired instead of a solid, full calibre shot. The disadvantage of lead balls was that, if propelled with a full charge, they tended to distort. This was reduced if a wooden disc was placed between charge and balls.

The weight of canister balls varied between nations but was generally half as many ounces as the gun's shot had pounds. In order to achieve greater effective range, canister balls were increased in weight to one-sixteenth or one-twelfth of the calibre and iron replaced lead as a material.

These balls were contained in either canvas sacks (grape) or tin cylinders (canister) but the latter caused increased damage to the bore of the cannon and the remains of the tin had to be removed with a 'corkscrew' after each firing.

Powder

Gunpowder for field gun use was a mixture of saltpetre, sulphur and charcoal made from limewood. (Erlenholz or Schiessbeerenholz was also used.)

26

PERCENTAGE COMPOSITION OF GUNPOWDERS USED BY VARIOUS NATIONS

	Saltpetre	Charcoal	Sulphur
FRANCE			
Artillery (normal)	75	12.5	12.5
'Berne round'	76	14	10
As ordered by the Welfare	76	15	9
	77	17	7
Committee (after Champy)	80	15	5
Chaptal's Mixture	77	14	9
HARBURG (HANOVER)	75	15	15
SPAIN	78	13	11
BRITAIN	75	15	10
SWEDEN	75	15	10
SAXONY			
Fine	76	12	10
Artillery	75	16	8

The most effective powder was made in the ratios 76:15:9 but usually weaker powders were used so that, with the larger quantities needed, inaccuracies of measurement would have less damaging effects on gun, crew and range.

When loading with loose powder, it was placed in the chamber by the loading shovel and tamped down with straw so that the ignition spark would spread fire in the powder much more quickly and thus give a more efficient propellent effect. On top of this went the ball.

Loading with loose powder was a slow and hazardous affair and the use of cartridges was rapidly developed. Cartridges were sacks of serge, flannel or parchment, filled with powder in an arsenal and tied at the top. They were placed in the barrel of the gun with the knotted end towards the muzzle. The ball was either rammed home on a wad of straw or was fitted into a wooden shoe or sabot and pushed on to the sacked charge. As this 'separated' ammunition involved two ramming operations to load the gun and thus reduced the rate of fire, field gun ammunition was made up into cartridges containing charge, sabot and shot all in one.

Parchment charge cases had the disadvantage that after being fired, smouldering pieces (particularly of the rear end) remained in the chamber and often caused the next inserted cartridge to explode prematurely and many loaders lost their arms when rapid fire was required. To avoid this, loaders used jointed 'flails' to ram home the cartridge and were less likely to be injured by prematures as their arms would not be directly in front of the muzzle. The Saxon artillery avoided this danger in the 4 pdr by dropping the rear of the cannon to reload it and the cartridge would then slide to the bottom of the chamber on its own.

The Austrian artillery sought to reduce both premature ignition risk and the deformation of the cartridge during transport by painting the sacking with a mixture of $1\frac{1}{2}$ oz vermouth, 80 lb coloquinten, $\frac{1}{2}$ l barley flour, $\frac{7}{8}$ oz bolus which was boiled in water. When dry, the cartridge was again brushed over with a mixture of $\frac{1}{2}$ Maas linseed oil, $\frac{5}{16}$ oz pine oil, $\frac{3}{4}$ oz litharge and $1\frac{1}{4}$ lb of lead carbonate. This treatment, and the parchment cartridges had the disadvantage that by prolonged fire they tended to block up the touchhole so that it had to be periodically drilled clear.

The British artillery used parchment cartridges with bottoms made of gauze or serge to reduce the risk of premature detonation. By 1815 woollen cartridge cases were gaining in popularity although the Russians still used tin.

PROPERTIES OF CANISTER ROUNDS OF VARIOUS STATES

	Calibre of the pieces	*Balls in each cartridge*	*Weight of the balls (oz)*	*Powder charge (lb)*
PRUSSIA				
	12 pdr	$\left\{\begin{array}{l}41\\170\end{array}\right.$	$\begin{array}{l}6\\1\frac{1}{2}\end{array}$	$\begin{array}{l}4\\4\end{array}$
	6 pdr	41	3	$2\frac{1}{4}$
SAXONY (Old)	12 pdr	40	4	5
(Old)	8 pdr	28	4	$3\frac{1}{2}$
(Old)	4 pdr	27	2	$1\frac{1}{4}$
(New)	12 pdr	48	4	4
(New)	6 pdr	41	3	2
AUSTRIA	24 pdr	$\left\{\begin{array}{l}38\\114\end{array}\right.$	$\begin{array}{l}12\\3\end{array}$	$\begin{array}{l}7\\7\end{array}$
	12 pdr	$\left\{\begin{array}{l}12\\28\end{array}\right.$	$\begin{array}{l}16\\6\end{array}$	$\begin{array}{l}3\frac{1}{2}\\3\frac{1}{2}\end{array}$
	6 pdr	$\left\{\begin{array}{l}28\\60\end{array}\right.$	$\begin{array}{l}3\\1\frac{1}{2}\end{array}$	$\begin{array}{l}2\\2\end{array}$
RUSSIA	12 pdr	36	6	3
	6 pdr	36	3	$1\frac{1}{2}$
BRITAIN Medium	12 pdr	42	6	$3\frac{1}{2}$
Medium	6 pdr	42	$3\frac{1}{2}$	$2\frac{1}{4}$
Light	12 pdr	34	6	$3\frac{1}{2}$
Light	6 pdr	34	$3\frac{1}{2}$	$2\frac{1}{4}$
DENMARK	12 pdr	100	2	5
	6 pdr	100	1	3
	3 pdr	100	$\frac{1}{2}$	$1\frac{1}{4}$
FRANCE	12 pdr	$\left\{\begin{array}{l}41\\112\end{array}\right.$	$\begin{array}{l}6\\2\text{--}3\end{array}$	$\begin{array}{l}4\frac{1}{4}\\4\frac{1}{4}\end{array}$
	8 pdr	$\left\{\begin{array}{l}41\\112\end{array}\right.$	$\begin{array}{l}4\\1\text{--}2\end{array}$	$\begin{array}{l}2\frac{3}{4}\\2\frac{3}{4}\end{array}$
	4 pdr	63	$\frac{3}{4}\text{--}2$	$1\frac{3}{4}$

Shells

Mortars and howitzers were often used to shoot hollow iron spheres filled with gunpowder and called bombs if full calibre, or grenades if small, so that several were fired at once.

Bombs for a 7 pdr howitzer weighed 14 to 15 lb; for a 30 pdr, 60 lb etc. Most bombs were filled with a gunpowder charge through the touchhole but Saxon bombs had a separate filling hole, about a quarter of a diameter from the touchhole and $\frac{3}{8}$ in wide, plugged with a birch or limewood plug. This enabled the sensitive fuse to be inserted into the bomb before it was filled and thus obviated accidental explosions caused by the fuse igniting while being pushed into the charged bomb. This fuse ignited when the bomb was fired and was designed to detonate the charge when the bomb had reached the enemy. In Britain howitzer shells were filled with gunpowder and small lead balls which became known as 'shrapnel' after their inventor.

Fuses

These wooden tubes were made of ash, birch, poplar, lime or beechwood, were one-eighth to one-sixth shorter than the diameter of the bomb and wider at the outer end than the diameter of the hole into which they were fitted. The hole inside the tube was about one-third of the total diameter. The Saxon artillery did not put the fuse mixture directly into the tube but put it first into a double paper funnel wound with hemp and painted with a special glue consisting of 1 lb of clear iron oxide, 1½ lb of clear iron filings, 1 lb of unslaked lime, 1½ lb of clear 'gebeutelten' brickdust, 1 lb of barley flour, all mixed up with thin limewater and made into a paste.

The fuse mixture could be made up into various grades as shown:

FUSES

	Flour powder	Saltpetre	Sulphur	Fine corn powder	Colophony	Antimony
No 1	4½ lb	5 lb	7 lb	½ lb	— lb	— lb
No 2	4½	6	2½	½	—	—
No 3	4	8	4	—	¼	—
No 4	4	16	8	—	—	—
No 5	4	8	3	—	—	—
No 6	3	8	3½	—	—	—
No 7	2	10⅔	4	—	—	1
No 8	—	4	5⅓	—	—	2
No 9	4	¾	1	—	—	—
No 10	4	8	2	—	—	—

A No 3 fuse, 6 in long would burn for 22 seconds, No 4 for 31 seconds. Nos 1, 2 and 3 burned most fiercely, Nos 4 and 5 had a very fierce spark due to the inclusion of camphor. No 6 tended to lead to misfires.

The mixture was packed tightly into the wooden fuse tube and at the outer end some twists of thread included so that ignition at time of firing was ensured. Ambient humidity affected the efficiency of these fuses.

Loading of Bombs

Before filling the bomb with powder, it was lined with liquid pitch to seal up any undiscovered holes. When the powder was in, the fuse tube was inserted (the bottom end having been cut off at an angle first). The joint between tube and hole was tightly filled with oakum and painted with 'glue' so that there was no possibility of the charge within the bomb igniting at time of being fired.

Flares and Incendiaries

If it was desired to illuminate an area by means of artillery fire, then special flares were used. These were shells with three or four extra holes, each 3 in in diameter, bored around the filling hole. They were filled with an incendiary mixture as shown below.

ILLUMINATING FLARE MIXTURES

	No 1	No 2	No 3	No 4
Flour powder	— lb	1 lb	1¼ lb	6 lb
Saltpetre	16⅓	10	4½	12

29

Sulphur	10	$4\frac{1}{2}$	$2\frac{1}{2}$	6
Antimony	$1\frac{1}{4}$	1	$\frac{3}{8}$	—
Sawdust	—	—	$\frac{3}{8}$	—
Corn powder	—	—	$\frac{9}{16}$	—
Melted mixture	10	—	—	—
Saltpetre 'Griefen'	2	—	—	—

Of these Nos 2 and 4 gave the brightest flares; Nos 1 and 3 were best for incendiary purposes. The mixtures were stuffed into drill sacks and attached to cannon-balls by means of sabots and twine. Both devices were set with booby traps to dissuade people from trying to extinguish them. These consisted of 3 in long sections of musket barrel, closed at one end and loaded with powder and ball. Several would be set in each device and designed to fire at irregular intervals; when the incendiary charge was almost finished, the final touch would be given by the explosion of a grenade, built in to the base of the compound.

Matches

During slow firing the weapon was discharged by firstly poking a hole in the cartridge case through the touchhole with a picker, filling the touchhole with powder and igniting it with a match. The match consisted of a length of oakum, about finger thick (flax or hemp was also used), boiled for four or five hours in a lye of beech ash. It took 50 lb of ash and 25 lb of unslaked lime to produce 100 lb of match. A match in good condition should have burned at 1 ft in $2\frac{1}{2}$ hours and 25 ft of match weighed a pound. For rapid fire 'Stopinen' or 'speedtubes' were used; these consisted of tin tubes or reeds filled with fuse mixture. The lower ends were pointed and the fuse mixture consisted of three cotton threads which had been soaked in a mixture of brandy, gunpowder and camphor. The top of the tube was sealed with paper which was torn off at time of use.

Smoke bombs

To hide a movement from the enemy, or to drive him out of mine galleries, smoke bombs were used. These were made of straw or paper and filled with a suitable mixture such as 4 parts of powder, 8 of sulphur, 6 of turpentine, 4 of hemp oakum, 18 of coal tar, 36 of pitch and 48 of tallow.

Incendiaries could not be used with cannon but the British artillery had developed a type of modified incendiary for these weapons consisting of a sub-calibre ball wound around with layers of burning compound.

FIRE BOMB MIXTURES

	No 1	No 2	No 3	No 4	No 5	No 6
Flour powder	4 lb	— lb	10 lb	4 lb	15 lb	1 lb
Saltpetre	8	16	6	2	2	—
Sulphur	2	4	3	1	1	—
Charcoal	1	3	—	—	—	—
Camphor	—	—	—	$\frac{1}{2}$	$\frac{1}{16}$	—
Ashes	—	—	—	—	—	1

Six inches of No 3 burned for 22 seconds; No 4 for 31 seconds. Nos 1, 2 and 3 burned most fiercely; Nos 4 and 5 burned longest and hottest due to the camphor.

	No 1	No 2	No 3	No 4
Coarse powder	6 lb	$4\frac{3}{4}$ lb	30 lb	— lb
Fine powder	7	—	—	—
Sulphur	—	7	—	$12\frac{1}{2}$
Saltpetre	—	14	—	25
Pitch	4	$5\frac{3}{4}$	10	$2\frac{1}{2}$
Resin	$1\frac{1}{2}$	$1\frac{1}{4}$	10	4
Colophony	1	—	5	—
Antimony	—	$2\frac{1}{2}$	—	$2\frac{1}{2}$
Fine (corn) powder	6	—	—·	—
Turpentine	1	—	—	—
Tallow	$\frac{1}{4}$	$\frac{1}{3}$	2	—
Oakum	$\frac{1}{4}$	$1\frac{1}{4}$	$1\frac{1}{2}$	—

Nos 2 and 4 gave the brightest and purest flames.

Red Hot Shot

These had to be prepared in specially dug ovens and required about 18 cu ft of soft wood or 6 cwt of charcoal burning for an hour to bring the balls to the necessary cherry red heat in a further thirty minutes. The red hot shot was set into the gun with a steel spoon and firing continued as before, a wet cloth having been inserted between ball and cartridge.

Rockets

These consisted of paper tubes filled with incendiary compounds. They were used for signalling and also for setting fire to villages etc. Their diameter was used to indicate calibre in that if it was the same size as a 6 oz ball, they were called '6 oz', if the diameter of a 3 pdr cannonball '3 pdr' etc. The paper cartridges were set into wooden tubes nine calibres long. Composition of the rocket propellant was as follows:

ROCKET PROPULSION CHARGES

	No 1	No 2	No 3	No 4
Saltpetre	1 lb	1 lb	$1\frac{5}{8}$ lb	$4\frac{1}{4}$ lb
Sulphur	$\frac{3}{8}$	—	$\frac{3}{8}$	$\frac{3}{4}$
Charcoal	$\frac{1}{2}$	$\frac{5}{16}$	$\frac{3}{8}$	2
Flour powder	1	—	$\frac{3}{4}$	—

For fierce, bright flames rockets were filled with the following mixtures:

	$\frac{1}{2}$–1 pdr	2 pdr	4 pdr
Flour powder	2 lb	2 lb	3 lb
Saltpetre	2	2	2
Sulphur	$\frac{3}{4}$	$\frac{3}{4}$	$\frac{1}{2}$
Charcoal	$\frac{11}{16}$	$\frac{7}{8}$	1
Iron Filings			
No 1	$\frac{3}{8}$	$\frac{3}{8}$	$\frac{3}{8}$
No 2	$\frac{1}{2}$	$\frac{1}{2}$	$\frac{1}{2}$
No 3	$\frac{5}{8}$	$\frac{5}{8}$	$\frac{1}{2}$
No 4	—	—	$\frac{3}{8}$

Rocket Calibre	Diameter (in)	Length (in)	Height of the mixture from the end (in)	Length of mixture (in)	Powder Content (oz)
4 oz	1.04	10.5	6.5	3.5	$\frac{1}{4}$
6 oz	1.19	12.0	7.25	4.5	$\frac{5}{8}$
8 oz	1.309	13.25	8.0	4.75	$\frac{3}{4}$
1 lb	1.64	15.0	9.0	5.5	$1\frac{1}{4}$
2 lb	2.07	17.5	10.5	6.5	$2\frac{1}{4}$
4 lb	2.60	21.0	12.25	7.5	$3\frac{1}{8}$

No 1 was used by the Saxon artillery, No 2 by the French and Nos 3 and 4 by the British.

The rocket tubes were now fixed to sticks seven times as long as the tube and so heavy that the resulting centre of gravity was 2 or 3 in below the tube. These sticks were about ½ calibre at the rocket end and dwindled to ⅙ at the far end.

Experiments in Hanover in October 1786 established the following average performances of various rockets: 1 pdr—5,688 ft, ¾ pdr—3,482 ft, ½ pdr—3,915 ft, 5 oz—2,679 ft.

Congreve's British rockets were modelled on those found in the army of Hyder Ali in India. They weighed 20 lb with heads made of tin 28 in long and 4 in in diameter. The stick was 18 to 22 ft long. They were first employed against Copenhagen in 1801 but did not achieve impressive results due to lack of reliability in their trajectory. They were also expensive to produce.

The Strength of Field Artillery
Cannon taken into the field ranged in this period in size from 1 to 12 lb while howitzers extended from 7 to 10 lb. Each battalion usually had two 4 or 6 pdr cannon (battalion pieces) with it. The Prussians and Austrians tended to have more pieces of heavier calibre than other armies. The heavier guns (usually about twice as many guns as battalions) were called the 'park' or 'position pieces'.

Bonaparte did away with battalion pieces (largely due to lack of guns) in the late 1790s and formed the lighter field pieces into batteries with a ratio of 3 guns per 1,000 men—a relatively low figure for that time. After his defeat at Aspern-Essling in 1809, however, he increased his artillery, reintroduced battalion pieces and directed that the park should consist of only 6 pdr and 12 pdr guns; these heavy guns were now grouped into batteries to achieve more effective fire. The practice of attaching howitzers to cannon batteries had the disadvantage that they were no longer used only for long range work, falling silent when the enemy was closer and the cannon could be better used, but tended to fire at all ranges and thus to use more ammunition.

Gun Crews
Any field gun could be crewed by six men and by only five if it weighed less than 300 lb. In order to achieve high rates of fire however, it had been found necessary to allot 12–16 men to the heavy guns and 8–10 men to the

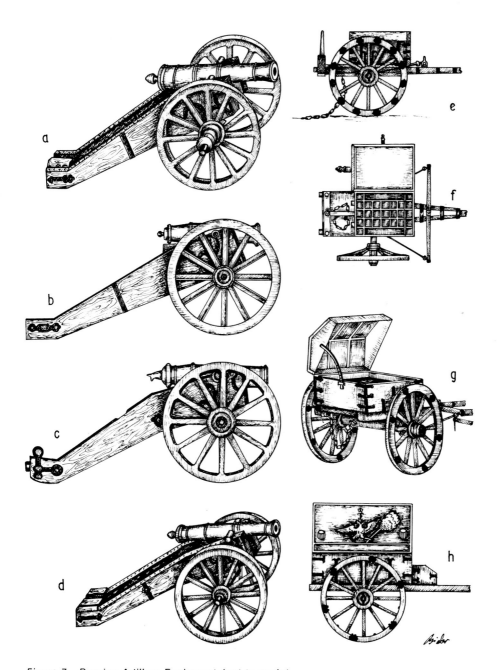

Figure 7   Russian Artillery Equipment (not to scale)
a 3 pdr field artillery 1760–1797
b 3 pdr gun, regimental artillery 1760–1800
c 1 pud (16.38 kg) Unicorn 1752–1805
d 3 pdr Unicorn 1760–1838
e Artillery limber with ammunition chest 1768–1845—side view
f Artillery limber with ammunition chest 1768–1845—plan view
g Field artillery limber with ammunition chest 1805–1825
h Infantry cartridge cart 1795

light ones. Each gun had an NCO in command and an officer was in charge of anything from two to four guns.

The French 4 pdr (600 lb) had a crew of 8, the 8 pdr (1,200 lb) had 11, the 12 pdr (1,800 lb) 15 men.

The Prussian 3 pdr (600 lb) had 8 men, the 6 pdr (900 lb) 12 and the 7 pdr howitzer (800 lb) 12 men.

The Austrian 3 pdr (400 lb) had 6 men, the 6 pdr had 8 men and a horse to move it and the 12 pdr was moved in the field by 12 men and a horse.

The Danish 12 pdr (2,400 lb) and the 3 pdr (600 lb) each had 12 man crews.

Duties of the Gun Crew (Figure 8)

Gun crews were required to carry out the following tasks in the field: unlimber the gun (separate carriage from limber); load, aim and fire the piece; move the piece on its carriage around the battlefield without the limber and team; limber the cannon (reunite carriage and limber); move with the gun on the march, defend the gun.

The basic needs of loading, aiming and firing could be covered by three men (see Figure 8a), the first (No 1) who stood to the right of the muzzle

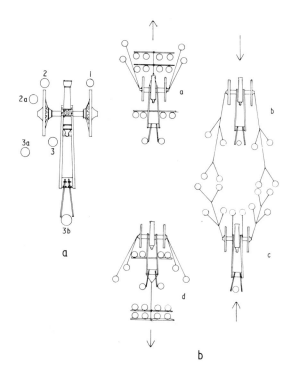

Figure 8   Gun Crews
a Duties of the gun crew:
   1 Mop out and ram home charge and cartridge
   2 Insert charge and cartridge
   2a Carry cartridges to cannon
   3 Aim and fire cannon
   3a Hold match, clean touch hole
   3b Adjust alignment of cannon in accordance with instructions given by 3
b Various methods of moving cannon and howitzers short distances across country using manpower, tow ropes and beams only

mopped out the barrel and rammed home the cartridge; the second (No 2) who stood on the left of the muzzle and inserted into it the cartridge and No 3 who was at the rear of the piece and who aimed the cannon, set the fuse in the touchhole and fired it. No 3 was always the most experienced man in the crew. Other men were added to the crew to help No 2 in keeping a steady supply of cartridges ready (2a) and to help No 3 in keeping matches burning and touchholes clear (3a) as well as repositioning the gun carriage trails to reset the aim after each shot (3b)—the recoil of the shot would shift the piece back from its original position. There was also an observer to report on where the shot struck as well as someone in charge of the ammunition waggon and another (one or two depending on the overall size of the gun crew) to hold the riding horses of mounted crew members.

Movement of an Artillery Piece by Manpower (see Figure 8b)
This was achieved by means of pulling the piece with tow ropes attached to leather bandoliers which the crew wore and tied to hooks on the carriage and by lifting and pushing the piece with beams. The usual scale of men was one per 100 lb deadweight of the piece over flat, firm heathland for short distances. For distances greater than 1,000 paces, or in soft or sandy soil or over hills, the number of men required doubled. It was usual practice to fit a small wheel under the carriage trail so that friction was reduced as much as possible. One man, usually the NCO, steered the gun by means of the two hand spikes inserted in the carriage trail.

Changing the Barrel Stance from March Position to Action Position and Back
Supposing the gun was in the firing position; to put it into the march position a beam was inserted in the muzzle, the muzzle depressed and the aiming device removed and replaced by a short roller which lay under the breech, across the carriage. The muzzle of the gun was now lifted by six to eight men using the muzzle extension beam and a transverse beam, a second roller inserted under the barrel and the whole then rolled backwards into the march position, the rollers removed and the barrel secured. The reverse process was carried out to bring the barrel forward into the firing position.

Limbering and Unlimbering
If gun and limber were married and were to be disconnected, the tail of the gun carriage was lifted by two to six men using a beam while the trail pole of the limber was also lifted, thus lowering the trail post which fitted into the hole in the carriage trail. Limbering was a similar process.

Gun movement with two or three horses
If a gun was to be moved and the distance or going was beyond the capabilities of the available men, one or more horses would be harnessed to an evener and the evener connected to the gun carriage axle with a rope or chain. The Saxons attached chains from the evener to the two hooks at the front of the carriage walls and towed the gun very well that way. With this mode of transport one should reckon one horse to every 600 lb of gun in level, firm terrain, two horses if in uneven or sandy, boggy ground.

Tools
The following tools were needed for the serving of guns in the field: beams (hand spikes) 5 to 8 ft long; block and tackle for lifting barrels; ropes; tripod beams with which to build a crane.

Removal of the barrel of a damaged cannon

If a carriage was damaged and it was desired to recover the intact barrel, this could be done in a number of ways. Firstly, the broken carriage could be patched up with a beam and towed away. Secondly, the barrel could be taken from the carriage and tied beneath a limber and towed away (this was only possible with the lighter barrels). Thirdly, the barrel (if too heavy for a limber) would be placed in an emptied ammunition waggon and removed.

If it was only a wheel damaged on a carriage, then a limber wheel or a matching waggon wheel would be put in its place. It was often possible to repair broken spokes or fellows on the wooden wheels or to fix badly damaged wheels so that an intact segment dragged along instead of the wheel rotating.

If a cannon overturned on the march it could be righted again by use of block and tackle, as a complete piece if of small calibre and in two separate operations (first the carriage alone and then reset the barrel) if over 12 pdr calibre.

Guns in Batteries or in Field Work

This situation presupposed that a long term struggle was taking place and that firing would continue for days at a relatively slower rate than during a battle in the open field. The ground under the guns would have been levelled and strengthened to give a firm firing platform and it was possible to work a gun in these conditions quite adequately with a much reduced crew, eg four men for a 12 pdr.

The recoil would usually roll the piece far enough back to allow mopping out and loading within the ramparts but if not then Nos 1 and 2 of the crew inserted their spikes through the wheel spokes towards the trail and under the carriage and pressed down on the outer ends; Nos 3 and 4 put their spikes under the flank hooks at the trail, jammed the ends against the ground and levered upwards. It was thus possible for four men to move the gun backwards.

To bring the piece forwards for firing, Nos 1 and 2 put their spikes through the spokes (towards the muzzle) and under the carriage and pressed down; Nos 3 and 4 put their spikes under the trail from the rear and levered upwards and thus forwards.

Loading and Aiming

No 1 mopped out the gun with the wet sponge end of the rammer; if a metal cartridge case had been used the debris would be removed with the 'double corkscrew' tool on the rammer. No 2 would bring the powder or cartridge, No 3 the hay inserts which were put in after the powder or cartridge and ball and No 4 blocked the touchhole with his thumb during the mopping operation (to prevent it being blocked with debris) and carried the cannon ball.

As soon as the barrel was mopped out, No 2 inserted the cartridge, No 1 rammed it home with the butt of the rammer and both rammed it well home with three blows of the rammer. No 3 inserted the hay twist and it was rammed home by No 1, No 4 inserted the ball, No 1 rammed it home.

If the ball was already in a wooden sabot (which increased accuracy of shot) then no hay inserts were needed and loading was that much quicker. Loading with loose powder was awkward and dangerous and only resorted to if no cartridges were available.

The loaded cannon was run forward into the embrasure; No 1 stood by the carriage to aim the piece, Nos 2 and 3 put their spikes into the trail end hooks, ready to move the piece from side to side to aim it, and No 4 stood ready with the match.

No 1 signalled to Nos 2 and 3 which way to move the trail; this done, Nos 2 and 3 put their spikes under the rear of the barrel so that No 1 could set the required elevation. This done, No 1 mounted the earthworks to observe the fall of the shot; No 4 gave No 2 the match and he fired the piece. If a piece had an elevating device under the breech, then No 1 could adjust it himself.

A 24 pdr gun could be adequately crewed in battery conditions as described above by six men. A 6 pdr needed only three men.

A 30 pdr mortar needed a crew of three men. After having been fired, the piece was rebedded using hand spikes and re-aimed using a pendulum, set up behind the weapon and aligning the target with the centre line of the barrel of the piece.

If the mortar was in an earthwork or behind an obstacle and thus the target could not be seen, a point would be painted on the inside of the earthwork, in line with the target, and this aiming mark used instead. Having established direction, range would be given by use of a quadrant and pendant. The quadrant was set on the top of the central portion of the barrel; the barrel was then raised or lowered on the wedges by means of a beam inserted in the muzzle until the pendant showed the right range. The position of the mortar carriage on the ground would now be marked, the weapon loaded and fired and the fall of the shot noted. If a hit was scored, the mortar would once again be set back on to the marked position for refiring; if not, the position of the weapon could be altered with reference to the marked line.

In order to ensure that the bombs burst at point of impact and not either too soon or too late, at the point of firing the mortar a similar fuse to that in the bomb would also be lit and when the bomb reached the target the then point of burning would be marked on the test fuse and all other fuses used against that target would have holes bored in them at that point so that they would explode at roughly the same time. Mortars could be loaded with paper cartridges or, if having a conical barrel, with loose powder.

When firing illuminating flares and stone balls, the powder charge was reduced and a wooden disc inserted between charge and projectile because these items were easily smashed by the shock of a full charge.

Gun Horse Teams and Ammunition Waggon Teams

The necessary horse teams for artillery equipments were reckoned at one horse per 200–300 lb of gun weight or 400–600 lb of ammunition. The heavier the load, the less weight could be apportioned to each horse. In France the 4 pdr cannon (600 lb and 15 shot in the trail chest) had three or four horses; the 8 pdr cannon (1,200 lb and 18 shot) had four, the 12 pdr (1,800 lb) had six, the 12 pdr ammunition waggon (2,337 lb) and the 4 pdr ammunition waggons had four horses each.

The Russian 6 pdr cannon was pulled by four horses as was the 10 pdr Unicorn; the 12 pdr cannon and the 20 pdr Unicorn were each pulled by eight horses while the ammunition cart for a cannon had two horses and that for a Unicorn had three horses in 'troika' fashion.

In the British artillery the 6 pdr cannon (2,702 lb) and the 5 in howitzer each had four horses while the 12 pdr horse artillery gun (45 cwt, 14 lb) had six.

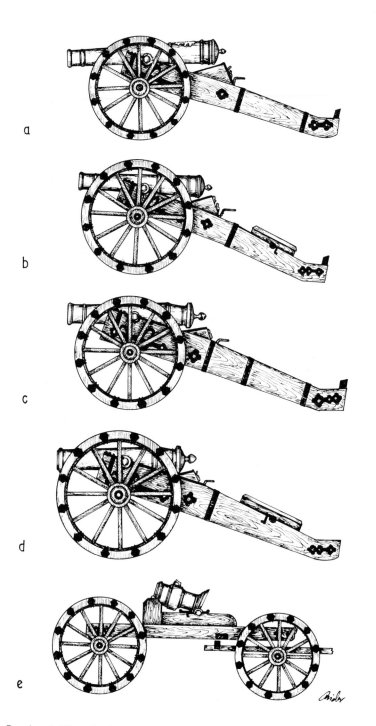

Figure 9 Russian Artillery Equipment 1796–1825 (not to scale)
a Medium 12 pdr cannon. In 1805 the limbers of the various pieces were made lighter to improve mobility; this weapon was a 'positions piece'
b Short 12 pdr cannon; note ammunition chest on trails
c $\frac{1}{2}$ pud Unicorn (8.18 kg); as a 'positions piece' no ammunition was carried on the trails
d $\frac{1}{4}$ pud Unicorn (4.09 kg); note ammunition chest on trails
e 2 pud (32.76 kg) standing mortar on travelling carriage

The Danish artillery were relatively lavish in their use of horses: the 12 pdr (2,400 lb) had ten, the 6 pdr (1,200) six, the heavy 3 pdr (600 lb) four and the light 3 pdr (400 lb) two horses.

Prussian artillery pieces were relatively conventionally teamed: the 3 pdr cannon (600 lb and 40 shot in the trail chest) had four horses, the 6 pdr (900 lb and 40 shot) six and the 7 pdr howitzer (800 lb and 40 shot) had six horses.

Ammunition Scales

For each gun about 200–300 rounds were taken into the field and of these one-quarter to one-third consisted of canister or grape. The national details were as follows:

Austrian Foot Artillery

The 3 pdr cannon: 200 rounds including 20 canister and 12 ball on the limber and 24 canister and 144 ball in the ammunition waggon. The 6 pdr cannon: 212 rounds; 28 canister on the limber, 160 ball and 16 canister (sic) in the waggon. The 12 pdr cannon: 12 canister on the limber; 20 canister and 86 ball in the waggon. The 7 pdr howitzer: 16 canister, 80 shell and 3 firebombs.

Austrian Horse Artillery (The 'Würst' or sausage batteries)

The 6 pdr cannon: 14 canister on the gun carriage trails; 28 canister and 146 ball either on packhorses or in the reserve ammunition waggons. The 7 pdr howitzer: 71 shell, 11 firebombs and 3 canister.

Prussian Artillery

The 3 pdr regimental cannon: 100 ball and 20 canister. The 6 pdr cannon: 80 ball and 20 canister. The 7 pdr howitzer: 60 shell, 18 canister, 3 fire-bombs, 2 illuminating bombs and 2 'Rebhühnergranaten'. The 12 pdr cannon: 20 canister and 130 ball. The 6 pdr: 30 canister and 150 ball.

British Artillery

The 12 pdr cannon: 6 ball and 6 canister on the limber; 114 ball and 18 canister in the waggon. The heavy 6 pdr cannon: 36 ball and 14 canister on the limber; 84 ball and 6 canister in the waggon. The light 6 pdr cannon: 34 ball and 16 canister in the limber; 154 ball and 52 canister in the waggon.

Danish Artillery

The 12 pdr cannon: 44 canister and 128 ball. The 6 pdr cannon: 166 ball and 53 canister. The 3 pdr cannon: 58 canister and 176 ball. The 10 pdr howitzer: 25 canister, 76 shell and 12 firebombs.

Russian Artillery

The 12 pdr cannon: 8 rounds in the limber and 3 ammunition carts each with 90 ball and 30 canister. The 6 pdr cannon: 20 rounds on the limber and 2 ammuntion carts each with 90 ball and 30 canister. The Unicorn ammunition carts contained 80 shell, 30 canister and 10 firebombs each.

French Artillery

Each 12 pdr cannon had 9 rounds on the gun carriage and 3 ammunition waggons each carrying 68 rounds. Each 8 pdr cannon had 15 rounds on the gun carriage and 184 rounds carried in two ammunition waggons.

The Saxon Artillery

The new (from 1810) 12 pdr cannon: 12 rounds on the limber and a further 60 ball and 15 canister on the ammunition waggon. The new 6 pdr cannon: 18 rounds in the limber and 120 ball and 30 canister in the ammunition waggon.

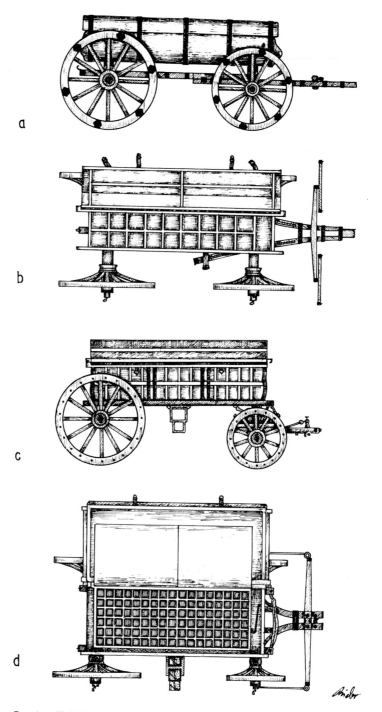

Figure 10   Russian Field Artillery Vehicles 1803–1825
a Mortar ammunition waggon, side view
b Mortar ammunition waggon, plan view; note the individual compartments for each round of ammunition to prevent shifting of the load in transit
c Cannon ammunition waggon, side view
d Cannon ammunition waggon, plan view

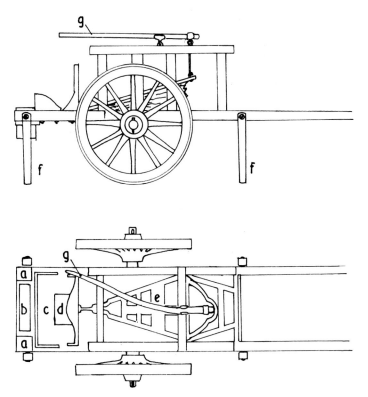

Figure 11   British Artillery Field Forge
The device is shown with supports extended and thus in the working position
a Tool boxes
b Water trough
c Fireplace
d Iron hearth
e Bellows
f Supports
g Bellows handle

Other Field Artillery Equipment

To facilitate rapid replacement of damaged gun carriages on the battlefield, a certain number of spare gun carriages were taken on campaign. The scale varied from 1 spare to every 16 cannon to 1 spare per 4 cannon according to army. Apart from these, spare gun carriage parts, loading equipment, wheels, axles, spokes, fellows and iron tyres were also taken along in vehicles specially built for the purpose. Portable forges and wheelwrights' machines were also necessary: forges were at a scale of one per sixteen guns and these again required an accompanying waggon to carry charcoal, iron and tools. A forge would have a two-horse team, the charcoal waggon 4 or 6. For each 8 or 16 guns there would also be a waggon with grease for lubricating the vehicles' axles and one with equipment for preparing red hot shot; each of these had a four or six-horse team.

Further vehicles were needed to carry the lifting gear required to move the heavy gun barrels between their carriages and the saddle waggons. Others would carry gunpowder and laboratory equipment, infantry and cavalry cartridges (one 4-horse waggon could carry 20,000 cartridges), bridging stores, pontoons, mining and entrenching equipment. One 4-horse waggon would carry 224 shovels and spades, 133 pickaxes, 8 machetes, 8 saws and

41

20 axes, and these stores would be scaled to supply four battalions of labourers.

Bridging Equipment

In order to cross a river 500 or 600 ft wide, 45 pontoons were needed each on its own six-horse waggon and in addition there would be 4 six-horse equipment waggons, 4 four-horse tool waggons and 2 waggons for the forge and charcoal. Light, portable infantry bridges (1 per six-horse waggon) were also included so that smaller streams could rapidly be crossed.

Horse Artillery

In the late eighteenth century some guns were made specially lighter and given lighter limbers and carriages and more horses in their teams so that their mobility was greatly increased. The crews of these pieces either rode on the gun team horses, the gun trails (Austria, Württemberg and Bavaria), the limbers (Britain) or on extra horses especially provided for the purpose. The task of this horse artillery was not exclusively to accompany cavalry but to provide the commander with a fast, powerful force which he could move rapidly to a desired point to achieve a decision. The horse artillery thus often formed part of the reserve on the battlefield or would be attached to the advanced guard or rearguard.

Experience had shown that it was better to limber up a piece to move it on the battlefield rather than to move it on its own by means of manpower alone. Horse artillery achieved the following times for the distances shown (limbering, moving, unlimbering and firing one shot in each case): 300 paces—1 minute; 1,100 paces—3 minutes; 3,500 paces—9½ minutes; 6,000 paces—22 minutes.

The Prussian horse artillery was organised in batteries or brigades each of two 7 pdr howitzers and eight 6 pdr cannon of normal construction but with eight-horse teams in each case. The limbers had large ammunition chests carrying between 60 and 100 rounds for a cannon and from 30 to 50 for a howitzer. The mounted crews were: howitzer, one NCO and eight men; the cannon, one NCO and six men.

The Russian horse artillery battery was equipped with eight light 6 pdr cannon and four 8 pdr Unicorns. Each gun had a twelve man crew riding either on the gun horses or on the 160 chargers. The limber chests carried 20 rounds for each 6 pdr.

The British, Saxon and Bavarian horse artillery were similarly organised. The Bavarians used the Austrian 12 pdr Würst guns where some of the crew sat on the cushioned top of the trail ammunition box in which were 6 ball and 8 canister rounds; 4 packhorses carried a total of 80 further rounds. A two-horse ammunition cart held 64 ball and 32 canister for two cannon. The 7 pdr howitzer Würst held 2 shells, 4 canister and all powder; on the four packhorses were a further 40 shell and in the ammunition waggon 22 shell, 2 firebombs and 5 canister. The light 12 pdr cannon of the British horse artillery had a six-horse team and carried 16 rounds and 2 gunners on the limber.

The Siege Artillery

This consisted of 12 pdr and 24 pdr cannon, 7 pdr and 10 pdr howitzers and 20 to 60 pdr mortars. While the 12 pdr cannon travelled on its carriage and was drawn by eight horses, the barrel of the 24 pdr moved on a saddle-waggon pulled by twelve horses while its carriage was pulled by four. The

7 pdr howitzer had a four-horse team, the 10 pdr a six-horse team and mortars were pulled by eight horses. There then followed the usual ammunition train, laboratory and tool vehicles, lifting devices, tools and forges.

Obstacle Crossings on the March

The river was reconnoitered to find flat, firm, shallow spots and the horses were unhitched and either walked or swum across. The trail arm was removed from the limber and a rope slung across the river and attached to the limber itself. Other tow ropes were then attached to the cannon dolphins and to the carriage axle and the gun teams then towed the limber (and cannon) across with a long tow rope. If the carriage capsized or the barrel broke loose in the crossing then they would be recovered with the previously attached ropes.

To cross trenches and hollow ways the banks would be cut out with shovels and the spoil thrown into the ditch to create a smoother path. If a river or trench was even deeper, then a causeway would be constructed out of fascines (bundles of logs). Nearby houses and villages would be demolished to provide suitable materials.

To bridge narrow rivers, trees would be felled at either side of the chosen crossing point so that they crossed in the middle. Planks or narrow diameter logs would then be laid crossways and a bridge thus constructed.

On the march the heaviest and most cumbersome pieces would go first so that they enjoyed the better going. The lighter pieces could better negotiate the broken ways in their wake.

The Effects of Artillery Projectiles

Trajectory

A projectile tended initally to follow the axis of the barrel of the piece from which it was fired and then, sooner or later according to charge used and weight of projectile, wind resistance etc, it would fall to earth and bounce to a standstill in a series of ever-decreasing hops (provided that the firing took place on firm, level ground).

If a Hanoverian 3 pdr was fired with the barrel at 0° elevation (horizontal) with normal charge, the shot would strike (level) ground at about 400 paces for the first time. With a 6 pdr and a 12 pdr this would be about 500 paces.

With variations of elevation from 1° to 3° the following table could be established:

Weapon	Elevation			
	+1°	+2°	+3°	
3 pdr	700	950	1150	
6 pdr	750	1050	1310	range of first fall shot in paces
12 pdr	800	1150	1460	

A field piece was capable of being elevated to a maximum of about 10° and thus the maximum ranges which could be achieved without special arrangements were about 2,390 paces for a 3 pdr and 3,200 for a 12 pdr.

French cannon had an elevation sight affixed to the breech (Figure 12a) whereby the estimated range of a target could be translated into extension of the notched top of the rod 'A' and the foresight on the muzzle brought into line with the top of the notch by use of the elevating devices. This gave a rough range setting but took no account of whether the gun axle was horiontal or not. If the gun was leaning to one side, then the resultant misalignment of the barrel could cause the shot to miss the apparent aiming

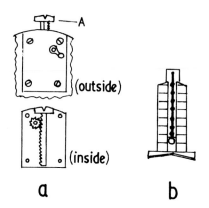

Figure 12 Artillery Equipment
a French cannon sight
b Saxon cannon sight with plumbline

point by about 27 ft at 1,200 paces if barrel error was only 2 in. To combat this the Saxon artillery elevation sights had a plumb line incorporated in them (Figure 12b) but these had the disadvantage of being fragile and easily damaged.

It will be readily seen that cannon balls were liable to cause more casualties in a deep formation of enemy than if the enemy were extended across the front in only one or two lines. Thus it was that the linear formation came to be adopted when close to the enemy, while column could be used when further away. It also followed that cavalry (being about 9 ft tall when mounted) presented a better target than infantry in the same formation.

Allowing for the inaccuracy of the cannon at that time, the following table of probability of hit (assuming that range had been accurately assessed and set) could be constructed:

Elevation in degrees	Range in paces to first strike			Proportion of shots *which hit		Paces of target depth* covered	
	3 pdr	6 pdr	12 pdr	Infantry	Cavalry	Infantry	Cavalry
1	750	900	950	$\frac{1}{2}$	$\frac{3}{4}$	135	200
2	1,080	1,300	1,390	$\frac{1}{4}$	$\frac{3}{5}$	67	100
3	1,350	1,630	1,770	$\frac{1}{6}$	$\frac{3}{12}$	45	66
4	1,570	1,900	2,100	$\frac{1}{8}$	$\frac{3}{16}$	34	50
5	1,750	2,120	2,380	$\frac{1}{10}$	$\frac{3}{20}$	27	40
10	2,280	2,680	3,680	$\frac{1}{20}$	$\frac{3}{40}$	14	20

(*in hard ground)

Strike of shot of a 3 pdr cannon at varying degrees of elevation are shown below:

	1st	2nd	3rd	4th	5th	strikes
0°	400	900	1,150	1,275	1,345	paces
1°	750	1,200	1,425	1,525	1,575	paces
2°	1,050	1,400	1,575	1,620	1,665	paces

Given that a cannon with a barrel eighteen calibres long, loaded with a charge half the weight of the shot, was fired at a mass of infantry marching each 2 ft apart, then the following casualties could be caused unless the projectile was stopped by the resistance of the bodies through which it passed:

Cannon	At 400 paces	At 800 paces
12 pdr	48 men	36 men
6 pdr	39 men	28 men
3 pdr	30 men	19 men

Casualties to cavalry under similar conditions would be about half those quoted above.

When used against freshly made earthworks cannon balls had the following penetrative effects if the cannon was twenty calibres long and a charge of $\frac{5}{12}$ the weight of shot was used. (Prussian artillery experiment, 1802)

Cannon	400 paces range	600 paces	800 paces
24 pdr	7–12 ft	3–7 ft	2.5–6 ft
12 pdr	4–7 ft	3–6 ft	2–5 ft
6 pdr	2.5–4.5 ft	2.5–3.5 ft	1–5 ft
3 pdr	3–6 ft	2.5–8 ft	1–2.5 ft

Howitzers
The 7 pdr howitzer achieved the following ranges and ricochets on level heathland:
1. With 1 lb or $\frac{1}{15}$ bombweight charge
    $2\frac{1}{2}°$ elevation ... 288, 468, 550, 753, 983 paces
    $2\frac{1}{2}°$ elevation ... 301, 590, 681, 780, 900 paces
    $4\frac{1}{2}°$ elevation ... 420, 560, 800, 865, 938 paces
    $5\frac{1}{2}°$ elevation ... 500, 738, 810, 915 — paces
    $5\frac{1}{2}°$ elevation ... 580, 780, 887, 1,008 — paces
    $5\frac{1}{2}°$ elevation ... 847, 1,056, 1,246 — — paces
2. With $1\frac{1}{2}$ lb or $\frac{1}{10}$ bombweight charge
    $2°$ elevation ... 500 paces first strike; 1,300 paces last strike
    $2°$ elevation ... 570 paces first strike; 1,400 paces last strike
3. With 2 lb or $\frac{1}{7}$ bombweight charge
    $2°$ elevation ... 700 and 1,600 paces (first and last)
    $3°$ elevation ... 900 and 1,800 paces (first and last)
    $4°$ elevation ... 1,100 and 1,900 paces (first and last)
    As a general rule, the Napoleonic gunners tried to get their cannon-balls to hit the enemy ranks after the third ricochet at 0° elevation and after the second with 3° or more elevation. It was under these conditions that greatest damage could be caused and the desired effect was achieved by varying the powder charge used.

It is now also obvious that the destructive effect of a cannon-ball was in inverse proportion to the range, it being a kinetic energy projectile. With a howitzer shell, however, the effect was not dependent upon range as it was the explosion of the charge in the shell and the dispersal of the shell fragments which caused the major damage. Howitzers were thus best used to engage the enemy at long range and cannon for the closer combat.
Canister
This was a close combat anti-infantry and anti-cavalry weapon with the

following characteristics for a 12 pdr cannon:

Powder charge
⅓ to ½
canister weight

{
7½ oz balls—1,000 paces effective range
4 oz balls— 800 paces effective range
2 oz balls— 600 paces effective range
1 oz balls— 300 paces effective range
}

However, not all canister balls discharged reached the quoted ranges, they dispersed both horizontally and vertically from the gun muzzle and gave an oval shaped beaten zone which varied in length according to charge, ball weight and gun elevation. The width of spread of canister balls can be indicated by the following data: at 100 paces, with ⅓ canister weight charge and small balls, the spread was 20 to 24 ft; with large balls 15 to 18 ft. In some armies canister balls came in two weights for each piece. The canister balls used in a 6 pdr cannon were 3½ and 4½ oz; in a 3 pdr 1¾ and 2 oz and in a 12 pdr 7½ and 9 oz. These gave the following effective ranges:

Heavy grade 12 pdr—1,000 paces; 6 pdr—800; 3 pdr—600.
Light grade 12 pdr—600 paces; 6 pdr—400.

The following table gives an idea of the effectiveness of canister at varying ranges, expressed as fractions of the total number of canister balls fired which would hit the target:

Range in paces	Large balls against		Small balls against	
	Cavalry	Infantry	Cavalry	Infantry
100	$\frac{11}{16}$	$\frac{1}{2}$	$\frac{1}{2}$	$\frac{1}{3}$
200	$\frac{1}{3}$	$\frac{2}{9}$	$\frac{1}{4}$	$\frac{1}{6}$
300	$\frac{1}{4}$	$\frac{1}{6}$	$\frac{1}{6}$	$\frac{1}{9}$
400	$\frac{1}{6}$	$\frac{1}{9}$	$\frac{1}{8}$	$\frac{1}{12}$
500	$\frac{1}{8}$	$\frac{1}{12}$	$\frac{1}{9}$	$\frac{1}{14}$
600	$\frac{1}{9}$	$\frac{1}{14}$	$\frac{1}{11}$	$\frac{1}{17}$

Rates of Fire

At long ranges, where care had to be taken to aim the shots exactly, a 3 pdr cannon could fire 2 shots per minute, a 12 pdr and a 7 pdr howitzer 2 shots in 3 minutes.

At close ranges, using grape, the 3 pdr and 6 pdr could shoot twice a minute, the 12 pdr cannon and the 7 pdr howitzer 3 shots in 2 minutes. If the rate of fire was raised above this level, safety regulations were being neglected and the consequences could be disastrous.

Experience showed that it took the following times in battle to shoot twenty rounds from the undermentioned pieces: heavy 12 pdr—15½ minutes; medium 12 pdr—20 minutes; heavy 6 pdr—13 minutes; light 6 pdr—12 minutes; 3 pdr—9 minutes.

Ranges, Charges and Elevation of Mortars and Howitzers

For a given charge the greatest range could be achieved at an angle of 45° elevation. The following ranges could be arrived at with the combinations of charge and elevation shown:

Range in in paces	Howitzers		Mortars with cylindrical chambers	
	Charge in bomb weight	Elevation in degrees	Charge in bomb weight	Elevation in degrees
500	$\frac{1}{16}$	4	—	—
	$\frac{1}{38}$	8	$\frac{1}{30}$	8
	$\frac{1}{72}$	15	$\frac{1}{60}$	15
	$\frac{1}{40}$	24	$\frac{1}{80}$	24
	$\frac{1}{144}$	45	$\frac{1}{120}$	45
1,000	$\frac{1}{20}$	8	—	—
	$\frac{1}{40}$	15	$\frac{1}{30}$	15
	$\frac{1}{53}$	24	$\frac{1}{40}$	24
	$\frac{1}{80}$	45	$\frac{1}{60}$	45
1,800	$\frac{1}{20}$	15	—	—
	$\frac{1}{27}$	24	$\frac{1}{20}$	24
	$\frac{1}{40}$	45	$\frac{1}{30}$	45
2,600	$\frac{1}{27}$	45	$\frac{1}{22}$	45
3,200	$\frac{1}{20}$	45	$\frac{1}{19}$	45
3,500	—	—	$\frac{1}{17}$	45
4,100	—	—	$\frac{1}{13}$	45
4,400	—	—	$\frac{1}{11}$	45
5,800	—	—	$\frac{1}{7}$	45

Howitzers

The Prussian 25 pdr howitzer (cylindrical chamber and 54 lb bomb) had a range of 2,000 paces at 18° with a 3½ lb charge; the Danish 18 pdr (36 lb bomb, cylindrical chamber) reached 2,600 paces at 45° with a 2 lb charge; the Saxon 16 pdr howitzer, 2 lb charge, reached 2,000 paces at 30°; the Hanoverian 30 pdr (61 lb bomb, cylindrical chamber) reached 631 paces with 15° and a 1 lb charge; the British 8 in (23 pdr) howitzer threw a 46 lb 4 oz bomb 2,350 paces at 45° with a 3½ lb charge.

The lighter field pieces had the following characteristics: the British light 5½ in howitzer (15½ lb bomb) with a 1 lb charge at 5° threw the bomb 1,100 yd; at 11° it reached 770 yd at first strike, rolling to a final distance of 1,400 yd. The British heavy 5½ in howitzer (15½ lb bomb, 2 lb charge, 5°) threw the bomb 1,000 yd to first strike, final distance 1,400 yd. With a 3 lb charge at 5° the bomb first struck at 1,325 yd, bouncing to 1,900 yd.

The French 6 in howitzer with a 23 lb bomb, 1¾ lb charge at 45° threw the bomb 1,200 *Toisen*. The French 8 in howitzer (43 lb bomb, 1 lb 12 oz charge, 45°) threw it 1,600 yd.

The Danish 10 pdr howitzer (20 lb bomb, cylindrical chamber, 12 oz charge, 5 in elevation) threw the bomb 1,100 paces to first strike, total distance 1,600 paces.

Mortars

1 *Prussia.* The 50 pdr (116 lb bomb, 30°, 1 lb charge) threw its projectile 492 paces with a flight time of 7½ seconds; at 45° (1 lb charge) first strike was 586 paces with a flight time of 11 seconds. The 25 pdr (62¾ lb bomb, 30°, 1¼ lb charge) threw 1,296 paces in 12.9 seconds. At 45° (1¼ lb charge) it was 1,470 paces in 16 seconds. The 10 pdr (25½ lb bomb, 30°, 1 lb charge) threw 1,907 paces in 17 seconds; with 45° elevation (1 lb charge) it threw 2,005 paces in 22 seconds.

47

2 *Saxony.* 48 pdr mortar, conical chamber, 100 lb bomb, 20°, 1 lb 4 oz charge, 443 *Dresden Elles* (301 m) in 12½ seconds. At 45° (1 lb 4 oz charge) it was 605 *Dresden Elles* (411 m) in 8⅙ seconds. The 32 pdr mortar (conical chamber, 66 lb bomb, 20°, 2 lb charge) threw 846 *Dresden Elles* (574.85 m) in 15⅔ seconds and at 45° (same elevation and charge) it was 1,221 *Dresden Elles* (829.66 m) in 11⅚ seconds. The 24 pdr (conical chamber, 58 lb bomb, 20°, 2 lb 9 oz charge) threw 1,362 *Dresden Elles* (925.47 m) in 21½ seconds. At 45° (2 lb 1 oz charge) it threw 1,739 *Dresden Elles* (1,189.64 m) in 12⅔ seconds.

3 *British* (all elevations 45°)

	Bomb weight	Charge	Range (paces)	
13 in (100 pdr)	198 lb	9 lb	2,450	2293.03 m
10 in (45 pdr)	91 lb	3½ lb	2,200	2059.05 m
8 in (23 pdr)	26 lb	2 lb	1,840	1722.11 m
5½ in (8 pdr)	15 lb 12 oz	9 oz	1,400	1310.30 m
4½ in (4 pdr)	4 lb 8 oz	5 oz	1,150	1076.32 m

4 *French* (all elevations 45°)

	Bomb weight	Charge	Range (metres)	Charge	Range (metres)
12 in	147 lb	1 lb	182.91	3 lb	595.4
10 in (heavy)	100 lb	1 lb	212.78	3 lb	718.59
10 in (light	100 lb	1 lb	289.30	3 lb	743.78
8 in	43 lb	5 oz	153.98	1 lb 4 oz	598.2

The French also had a 15 in stone mortar weighing 1,000 lb and having a conical chamber; it threw the stone a maximum of 250 paces (233.3075 m) with a 2 lb 8 oz charge.

Accuracy of Howitzers and Mortars
At a range of 1,000 paces, with 25° elevation and always using the same charge, half of the projectiles fired from such a weapon fell within a rectangle 25 paces wide by 50 paces long. Reducing the rectangle to 12 by 25 paces, one-eighth of the projectiles fired landed in it.

Destructive Effects of Bursting Bombs and Shells
A shell filled with a gunpowder charge one-thirtieth of its weight would burst into about twenty to thirty pieces on exploding and each piece would be thrown about 100–200 paces. With larger explosive charges the bomb would burst into far fewer fragments (maximum ten) which would be thrown 400–800 paces.

Artillery on the March
There were two general methods of moving artillery on campaign, either in its own convoy or with the batteries distributed and each attached to its own infantry or cavalry brigade. In the second case the park column would still form its own, considerable convoy. When close to the enemy each pair of guns was given an ammunition waggon.

Artillery was always given the best and firmest ground to march over and the batteries moved in several columns in line abreast with the heaviest guns leading, the lightest vehicles at the rear. At the head of the column would be vehicles carrying digging tools, beams, planks and ropes so that obstacles could be bridged. For rivers or other obstacles over 20 ft wide, bridges would have to be built and thus some of the bridging vehicles would also have to be near the front of the convoy. Waggons loaded with powder were dangerous and marched in a column of their own, away from other vehicles. One man marched ahead of each gun team to point out to the mounted driver any potholes into which the horses might fall.

When moving down a steep hill, only the two rearmost horses were left harnessed to the limber and they functioned as a brake with their rear breeching (harness). The gunners would attach their tow ropes to the gun carriage and slow it down as it rolled down the hill.

When marching up steep hills it was often necessary to unhitch the teams from some vehicles to increase the number of horses available to pull each piece up the hill. The teams would then be taken down the hill again to repeat the process with the other vehicles.

Periodically the convoy would halt to rest the horses and to feed them. If a long, steep hill were encountered after the column had been marching for some time, it would halt at its foot for an hour while the horses were watered and fed so that they might tackle the hill refreshed and with new strength.

In very general terms, an artillery team in good condition, moving over firm, flat terrain could cover 4.9 km in one hour, 9.88 km in 4 hours and 19.8 km in 10 hours. This could easily be reduced to 15 km in 10 hours if the horses were weak, the loads heavy or the going mediocre.

Tactics

Gun Emplacements

Where possible each gun was dug into a large pit about 18 in deep and with the spoil thrown up towards the enemy so that the barrel of the piece just cleared it. Hedges, walls and ditches were also used to give cover from enemy fire.

When placing cannon to cover a defile, they should not have been more than 300 paces from it so that they could rake it effectively with grape but be behind the obstacle, thus safe from being cut off or outflanked by the enemy.

When defending a village the artillery was usually set to one side or behind it (if there was a suitable hill which overlooked the place). Very rarely were the guns set in the village because of the danger of the wooden buildings catching fire and thus endangering the ammunition. Churchyards or other walled places were most favoured as gun emplacements provided that the pieces could quickly be evacuated if needed.

The heaviest calibre pieces were given the best field of fire on the battlefield so that they could cover the weakest spots without changing position and could make most use of their long range (up to 2,500 paces). The lighter pieces were used to occupy forward positions, to support sudden crises and to cover the flanks. It was common practice to mix cannon and howitzers in all batteries so that effective long range fire could be maintained using the explosive howitzer shells.

Batteries were not to be more than 900 paces apart or mutual fire support became impossible and enemy troops could pass unscathed between them.

An interval of 600 paces was considered best.

Infantry or cavalry were always attached to the artillery in the field to protect the guns and crews from sudden enemy rush attacks or from close range sniping by sharpshooters.

An artillery reserve was always to be maintained by each corps and the highly mobile horse artillery batteries were best suited to this purpose. They could rapidly be deployed wherever and whenever the commander deemed best.

Deployment of ammunition waggons occurred in two halves: one with the limbers (if these had no ammunition chests), ie 25–50 paces behind the guns and to one side and the rest a few hundred paces to the rear in a place covered from enemy fire. If the limbers had ammunition chests, all the ammunition waggons would be in the rear. When half the limbers were empty they would gallop back to the ammunition waggons, refill and return to a position behind the guns. The waggons were to be 25–30 paces apart to minimise the danger of fire and explosion spreading from one to another.

When marching in an area likely to be under enemy attack, the guns were loaded (the lighter ones with grape) and two matches kept burning for each piece. For each two guns four men would be detached 100 or 200 paces to the threatened flank, with muskets to act as guard. If the enemy encountered by this outpost were too strong to be frightened off with a few shots, some light pieces would be sent to the flank, unlimber and engage the enemy with grape.

If awaiting an enemy attack, it was customary to hold the artillery (or most of it) concealed until their troops had closed to about 1,200 paces. The guns would then be directed to advance to the most advantageous sites to engage them. It was considered undesirable to unlimber in view of the enemy due to the confusion which could easily be caused at that time by well aimed enemy fire. Unlimbering was thus ideally carried out in cover and the guns then dragged into position by one or two horses attached to the piece by chains around the axle.

If unlimbering in view of the enemy and under fire was unavoidable, then the guns were unlimbered with the teams still facing the enemy, then the detached teams would turn and move to the rear with the limbers. The most favoured method of entering a chosen battery site with limbered cannon was from the flank so that the enemy was presented with only a thin line target. Incorrectly judged range thus meant that the enemy shot would more easily miss their intended target. Cannon were ideally set 20 paces one from another in line in a battery.

Opening Fire

In flat, open country a battery would unlimber so as to open fire on advancing enemy at a range of 2,000 paces, in broken country at 1,500 and in all cases certainly by 1,200 paces as at this range 30 per cent of the shots fired would hit and at 900 paces 50 per cent. The best targets were enemy batteries or columns of infantry and cavalry and full charge was to be used to obtain maximum effect of ricochet at this long range.

When awaiting an enemy assault in a prepared position, the gun commanders should previously have measured ranges to certain obvious landmarks to their front (trees, hedges, houses, bridges etc) so that when the enemy reached them accurate fire could be brought to bear. Where no landmarks existed, stakes were set up at desired ranges.

Firing was by rotation, one gun after the other so that each crew had ample time to load and the target could be kept under a rate of fire of one shot every four seconds (if the battery had eight guns). The fall of every shot was carefully observed but corrections were not made until at least five shots.had been fired, otherwise the effect would have been too erratic.

To guard against night attacks on a battery position, the guns would be set at horizontal in daylight so that they could fire to best effect with canister in the dark. The positions of gun wheels and trail would be marked by planks fixed to the ground.

When faced with numerically superior enemy guns it was recommended that a battery be split into two or three detachments which would dash forward (with the guns already loaded with grape) to predetermined points, unlimber and bombard the opposing battery from close range, thus killing or wounding as many gunners as possible. After one or two rounds the battery would then limber up again and retire behind cover.

Special attention was given to throwing the enemy cavalry into disorder, thus crippling his prime offensive weapon. If the enemy cavalry was over-thrown by one's own, the artillery should at once have advanced on the enemy battery and place it under close range fire to prevent it from attacking one's own victorious cavalry in flank as they swept past in pursuit. Conversely the artillery's main task if one's own cavalry were put to flight was to turn the guns a quarter to the side and to rake the pursuing enemy cavalry with flanking fire.

Concurrent activity of several batteries against one selected target was highly recommended. Oblique fire against the enemy infantry in line was very effective especially in flat, open terrain.

Economy of ammunition supplies was vital and fire should never have been opened unless worthwhile targets could effectively be engaged. Each gun was ordered to keep at least four canister rounds as a last reserve to use against enemy infantry or cavalry at close range.

When the point in a battle came for one's own infantry to advance on the enemy, the guns advanced with them (half firing, half moving, turn and turn about), the pieces being unlimbered and pulled by the gunners. At 1,200 paces from the enemy line the guns were trotted out 100 paces ahead of the advancing infantry and opened fire. This 100-pace advanced position was maintained until 400 paces from the enemy line when the guns would await infantry support. If no effective enemy countering artillery fire was experienced, the guns fired on the enemy infantry; if however enemy artillery fire became a serious hazard to one's own battery, they would concentrate on silencing the artillery first.

In cases where regimental pieces and battery pieces were engaged together in an advance against the enemy as described above, the light regimental pieces would engage the infantry and the battery pieces the artillery.

If the enemy had begun to withdraw (and thus was formed partially in column) the artillery were to advance as quickly as possible and to bring them under aimed shot at about 500 paces. This was more destructive in these conditions than grape.

When being advanced upon by enemy infantry the artillery was to fire on the enemy artillery until their infantry had closed to 400 paces and then change aim to engage the infantry.

If one's own troops were forced to withdraw, it was the task of the artillery to keep firing until they could no longer be of use to our own troops. The battery then withdrew using fire and movement as before described. If horses (or wheels) were in short supply, then ammunition waggons would be abandoned in preference to cannon. Abandoned ammunition waggons would be left with a burning fuse inside them so that they would blow up rather than fall into enemy hands.

If a cannon had to be abandoned it would first be 'spiked' that is, a metal spike would be hammered into the touchhole, thus making further use impossible until the piece had been overhauled by a workshop.

Cavalry

Cavalry Tactics

Spacings
Each horse occupied a frontage of 1 pace (about 75 cm) and a depth of 3 paces. A squadron of 60 files deployed in line thus measured 60 paces wide and had an interval to the next squadron of 12 paces. Two ranks deep gave it a depth of 7 paces. If deployed in closed column of troops (frontage of $\frac{1}{4}$ squadron) it was 15 paces wide and 37 paces deep including the 6-pace interval behind it to the next squadron.

Sixteen squadrons deployed in a close column on squadron frontage measured 60 paces wide by 202 paces deep (assuming a 6-pace inter-squadron interval).

Deployment
A squadron commander (with his trumpeter beside him) stood before the centre of his squadron (if deployed in line) with two officers behind him; the NCOs were on either flank and the remaining officers were behind the second rank. All changes of formation were carried out at the trot or gallop.

Speed
Cavalry moved at the following speeds per minute: walk—120, trot—240, gallop—480, charge—600.

Methods of Attack Against Cavalry
There were three main formations of using closed squadrons (Figure 13a, b and c): first—in one line with 12–24 pace intervals between squadrons; second—in two lines 'en echiquier' where the squadrons in the second line coincided with the gaps in the first line; third—in echelon from one flank or the other. In this formation the leading squadron(s) advanced 100 paces before the next squadron(s) started to advance and so on.

The pace would be increased to a gallop only 200 paces from the intended point of impact, ie about 400 paces from enemy cavalry advancing to meet one's own assault. A squadron which was kept at a gallop for more than 200 paces would lose momentum as the horses became blown.

The second rank of riders in a charge would keep about 3 paces from the front rank until about 50 paces from the point of impact when they would move forward if possible and fill up any gaps in the front rank. It was recommended that a single line of 12–20 men should be detached to cover the inter-squadron gaps and to act as skirmishers if opportunity arose.

A second line of cavalry squadrons was best deployed 250–300 paces behind the first (but never at a gallop) and with squadron-wide spacings

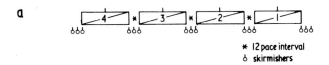

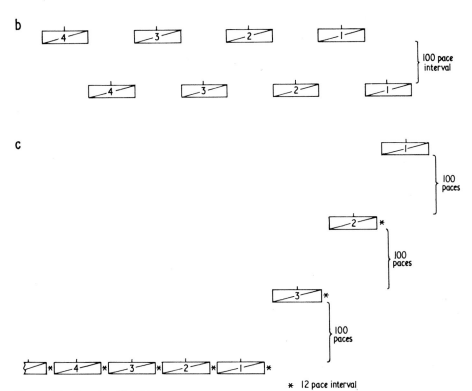

Figure 13 Cavalry Tactics
a A regiment of four squadrons in line
b Two regiments attacking 'en echiquier'
c Two regiments attacking in echelon, right flank leading

between their own squadrons so that the first line could fall back through them to reform if they had been repelled by the enemy. In this event the second line was to assault the enemy again as soon as the withdrawing first line had fallen back through them. If the first rank overthrew the enemy cavalry, part of the second rank would follow up in support, the rest were to take the enemy infantry in flank.

If the enemy cavalry was overthrown, the trumpeters would sound recall and a slow advance would be made while gathering in the dispersed troopers. Hussars were not used for these shock tactics but were kept in reserve behind the line and sent in to pursue and harry a broken enemy.

If a charge was unsuccessful, the officers' duty was to rally some men, form a rank and collect to them all other troopers.

Methods of Attack Against Infantry
Wherever possible infantry was to be attacked in flanks or in rear and

53

infantry squares were to be attacked at the corners (where the regimental guns would be). Experience showed that steady infantry could always repel a frontal cavalry charge; successful cavalry action was only possible if the infantry had previously been subject to adequate artillery fire or if their morale was shaky.

When attacking infantry, the squadrons would break into a trot as soon as they came under cannon fire (about 600 paces) and into a gallop when within canister fire range; the riders bent low over their horses' necks to reduce the risk of being hit. It was usual to attack with units in echelon as previously described for assault against cavalry but with 150 pace intervals between units. If one unit broke the enemy line, all others would at once converge on the gap.

Cavalry Withdrawal

Cavalry in withdrawal behaved as described for infantry (see p 75); the alternate squadron withdrawal distance was about 100 paces.

Withdrawal Through a Defile

If a line of cavalry or infantry was hard pressed by the enemy, it would withdraw through a defile with the flanks moving first and setting up another line (in the same order) on the other side of the defile to stop the enemy advance. If danger of pursuit was not great, the line would pass through the defile with the centre companies first, the flanks last.

Infantry

Muskets, Pistols and Cavalry Carbines

Muskets

The musket consisted of the following main parts: barrel, stock, lock and ramrod.

The Barrel

At the rear of the barrel was the chamber for the gunpowder, at the front was the muzzle. The rear of the chamber was closed by the tail screw and the diameter of the inside of the barrel was the calibre of the weapon; the barrel was made of iron. At the right side of the chamber was the touchhole, of conical shape, the larger end at the inside of the barrel and the smaller leading out into the pan.

This conical hole was a relatively new development and speeded up the loading process as once the man had poured gunpowder down the barrel and into the chamber he had only to tip the weapon sideways and give it a tap and a quantity of powder poured into the pan. Previously it was necessary to bite open the cartridge, open the pan, pour a little powder in the pan, close it and then pour the rest down the barrel. On the top of the muzzle was the foresight and on top of the chamber the rear sight.

The Stock

The butt was that lower part of the stock which was put against the shoulder when aiming and firing; the end was covered by a metal plate called the

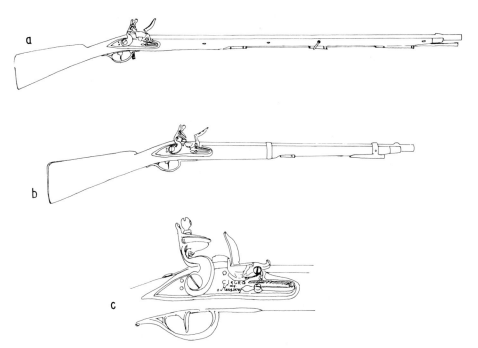

Figure 14
a Hanoverian musket, pre-1803; brass fittings, walnut stock, length 149 cm, barrel length 108.5 cm, calibre 16.8 cm
b Hanoverian cavalry carbine, pre-1803
c Detail of lock of pre-1803 Hanoverian cavalry carbine

butt plate. The 'small' of the butt was then held in the right hand and the forefinger of the right hand activated the trigger. The wood of the stock ran under the barrel and had along its length a hollow in which the ramrod was carried. It was held to the barrel with metal clips, rings or screws called the fittings.

Around the trigger was a metal arch, the triggerguard, to which was also fitted the lower sling swivel which held the musket sling at one end, the other being at the top band and being called the upper sling swivel.

In addition to these parts, a cavalry carbine (a short-barrelled musket) would have a bar and ring along the side of the stock into which the trooper's carbine hook would clip.

The Lock
This was the firing mechanism and was mounted on a large iron plate on the right side of the chamber. It had a cocking handle holding the flint, a pan to hold the igniting powder charge, pan cover and springs to hold the pan cover firm. On the inside of the plate were two springs, one (the larger) the trigger spring which rested with a hook against the concave part of the nut. The nut had two cutouts and above it was the cover.

The Ramrod
This was cylindrical (originally it had been conical in shape), of wood or iron and at each end it terminated in a truncated cone. It was used to push the powder, paper wad and bullets into the chamber.

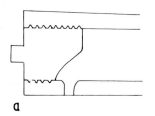 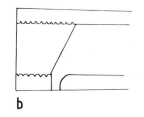 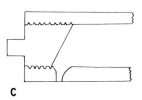

Figure 15   Musket touch-holes
a Prussian infantry musket 1780
b Hanoverian infantry musket 1790
c Hanoverian Freytag rifle 1756–1763

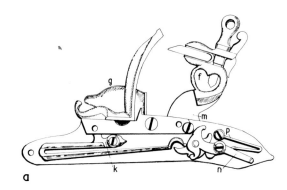

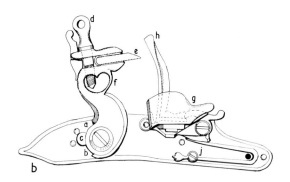

Figure 16   Austrian infantry musket 1800–1815
a Inside of lock-plate, shown in half-cocked position
    g Fireshield on pan
    k Main spring
    m Flattened inside of cocking handle
    n Trigger lever
    p Trigger spring
b Outside of lock-plate
    a, b Stops to prevent damage to mechanism by overstraining cocking handle
    c Fixed stud locking in stops a and b
    d Tightening screw to jaws holding flint
    e Flint
    f Cutout in cocking handle
    g Fireshield on pan
    h Striking piece of pan-cover
    j Pan-cover spring

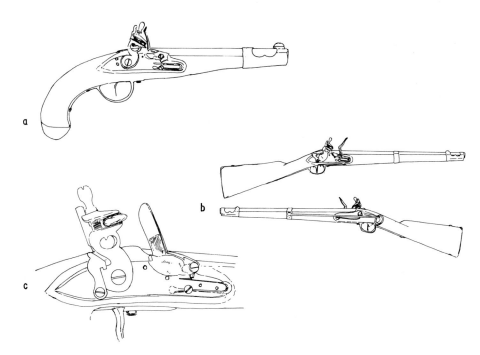

Figure 17

a Austrian cavalry pistol M1798; length 47.5 cm, barrel length 29 cm, calibe 17.8 mm, weight 1.5 kg

b Two views of Austrian cavalry carbine M1798; length 85.2 cm, barrel length 47 cm, calibre 17.58 mm, weight 2.5 kg; note the bar and ring for the hook of the carbine bandolier

c Detail of lock-plate of b; note the safety catch holding the cocking handle

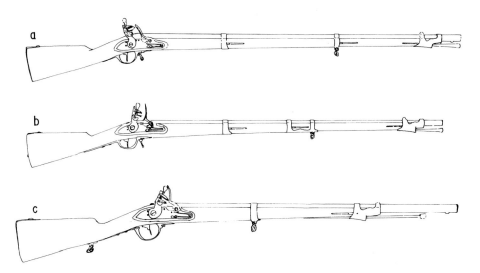

Figure 18   French Infantry and Cavalry Weapons

a Musket M1777; iron fittings, length 146.5 cm (186.5 cm with bayonet), barrel length 108.4 cm

b Voltigeur musket; brass fittings, length 141.5 cm, barrel length 103 cm

c Cavalry carbine An IX; brass fittings, length 113 cm, barrel length 75.5 cm

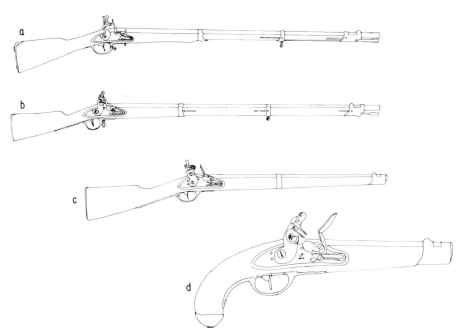

Figure 19   Bavarian Firearms
a Infantry musket, pre-1804, made in Fortschau in Oberpfalz; walnut stock, iron fittings, conical ramrod; length 143.5 cm, barrel length 104 cm, calibre 18 mm
b 'Manson' musket M1804, made in Amberg; brass fittings, length 148 cm, barrel length 109.7 cm
c Chevau Léger 'Manson' carbine M1804; walnut stock, iron fittings, barrel length 57.5 cm, calibre 17.5 mm
d Chevau Léger 'Manson' pistol; barrel length 22.5 cm, calibre 17.5 mm

Operation of the Musket

The flintlock musket worked in the following fashion: when powder and ball were rammed home in the chamber and some powder was in the pan and the pan cover closed, the cocking handle was pulled back into the fully cocked position and the trigger pulled. This released the cocking handle which was pulled forward by the trigger spring, the flint struck the steel pan cover generating a spark (directed into the pan), knocked the pan cover open and allowed the spark into the powder. This small quantity of powder exploded and sent a flame through the touchhole into the main charge in the chamber. The main charge exploded driving the ball out of the weapon. Due to damp powder, blocked touchholes and worn flints, misfires were a frequent occurrence.

Musket Balls

These came in three sizes for each calibre: small (or loose fitting)—these could be fired four or six at a time against enemy at close range and were a type of canister; up to calibre but with a small clearance and called 'calibre balls' and full calibre size with no clearance—these had to be forced into the barrel and were called 'fitting balls'.

Most muskets were about 5 ft 2 in to 5 ft 6 in long. They could not be shorter or it would have been impossible for the rear rank of three to fire without endangering their front rank companions. If they were over the above mentioned length, they were difficult to load and the centre of gravity was so far forward that when the man fired his aim was too shaky.

58

Weight

There was a direct relationship between the weight of the weapon and the charge of gunpowder used; with a ½ oz charge (and a 1 oz ball) the weapon weighed about 12 lb; with a ⅜ oz charge (and a ¾ oz ball) it was about 10 lb. Lightening the weapon increased the recoil which the firer had to absorb with his body.

The barrel length was found to be optimal (when using a powder charge half the ball weight and a ball of up to 1 oz) if set at 3.75 ft times the calibre in inches. Expressed another way, this meant a barrel length of 45 calibres.

The butt had to be set at a certain vertical angle to the barrel in order that the firer could squint along the barrel (if no sights were provided) so as to be able to aim the weapon. The Prussian muskets at this time had practically no such angle and thus aimed fire was unknown for the line infantry of that nation. This had been deliberately done in order to speed up the rate of fire.

Aiming

A Hanoverian musket of 1790 used a ball weighing ¾ oz, a charge of ⅜ oz and at a range of 100–150 paces it placed the ball 1 ft higher than the point aimed at. At 200 paces the aiming point and the point of impact coincided; at 250 paces the ball would strike 3 to 6 ft lower than the aiming point. Translated into practical terms, this meant that to hit an enemy infantryman at the waistline a soldier would aim at his knees at 100–150 paces range, at his belt at 200 paces and over his head at 250 paces.

As the thickness of the barrel decreased from touchhole to muzzle (and these dimensions were more or less standard for all barrel lengths), it will be seen that the shorter the barrel the greater its angle of elevation for aimed fire at any given point—if the top of the barrel was the only 'sight' used. This explains why short barrelled weapons carried further than longer weapons, all other factors being equal. Aiming with a bayonet fixed shortened the achieved range as the muzzle of the weapon became effectively thicker.

Effective Range

For a given calibre of weapon the range achieved was a direct function of the charge used, the barrel length and the amount of play which the ball had in the barrel. The relatively slow burning rate of the powder used meant that in a short weapon not all of it would have ignited by the time the ball left the muzzle. Experiments conducted in Hanover established that a musket barrel length of 45 in was needed in order that a charge of ½ oz could be completely consumed in the time it took for the ball to reach the muzzle. The shape of the charge also affected its burning rate and thus it was that larger calibre weapons (eg cannon) could use greater charges to full effect with relatively short barrels.

The following ranges were achieved under experimental conditions: (Antoni. *Physikalisch-Mathematische Grundsätze der Artillerie*)

1. Rifle with 3 ft barrel, ¾ oz ball, ⅜ oz charge + 15° elevation—2,396 ft; + 24°—2,492 ft; + 45°—2,360 ft.

2. Musket with 3 ft 3 in barrel, 1 oz ball, ⅜ oz charge + 7½° elevation—2,520 ft; + 15°—3,510 ft; + 24°—3,564 ft; + 45°—3,090 ft.

3. Musketoon with 5 ft 2 in barrel, 3 oz ball, 1¼ oz charge + 15° elevation—5,244 ft; + 24°—4,602 ft; + 45°—4,540 ft; with a 3½ oz ball and a 1¼ oz charge at + 15° the range was 4,506 ft.

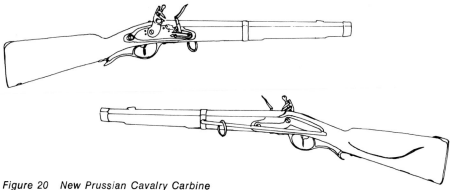

Figure 20   New Prussian Cavalry Carbine
Made in Potsdam; beechwood stock, brass fittings, length 81 cm, barrel length 43 cm, calibre 15.7 mm

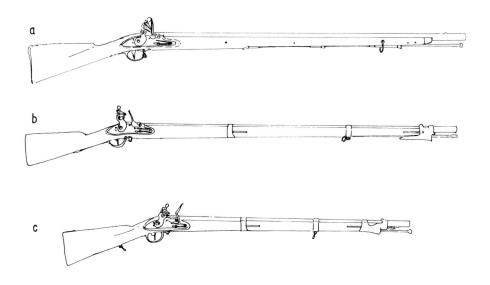

Figure 21
a British 'India Pattern' musket M1794 ('Brown Bess'); brass fittings, length 139 cm
, (the light infantry version was 96.5 cm long, the artillery weapon was 83.8 cm long), barrel length 99 cm, calibre 19.2 mm; the previous 'Brown Bess' model was 106.7 cm long
b Austrian infantry musket M1798, brass fittings, length 150 cm (198 cm with bayonet), barrel length 112.5 cm
c Jäger carbine M1807; length 123 cm (170 cm with bayonet), barrel length 85 cm, calibre 17.58 mm, weight 3.5 kg

It will be seen that the rifle had no greater range than the musket, but its greater accuracy gave rise to the fallacy of increased power.

Probability of Hit
Hanoverian experiments in 1790 showed that when fired at various ranges against a representative target (a placard 6 ft high and up to 50 yd long for infantry, 8 ft 6 in high for cavalry) the following results were achieved at the ranges shown: 100 paces—$\frac{3}{4}$ of all shots fired hit the infantry target, $\frac{5}{6}$ hit the cavalry target. 200 paces—$\frac{3}{8}$ hit the infantry, $\frac{1}{2}$ the cavalry. 300 paces—$\frac{1}{3}$ hit the infantry, $\frac{3}{8}$ the cavalry. The weapon used was an infantry musket firing a $\frac{3}{4}$ oz ball and the firers were able to aim each shot.

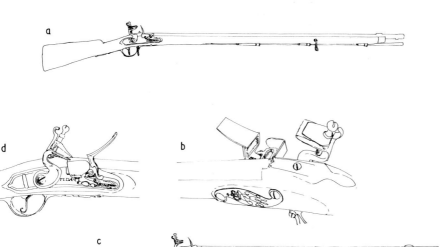

Figure 22   Prussian Infantry Weapons
a Nothardt musket M1801; length 144.5 cm, barrel length 105 cm, calibre 15.5 mm
b Detail of lock of a; note swan-necked cocking handle, simple fireshield round pan, hollowed-out roof of pan-cover and royal cypher on opposing side-plate
c Musket M1782; length 148 cm, barrel length 105.2 cm
d Lock of c; partially obscured by the cocking handle is the arsenal designation 'POTZDAM MAGAZ'

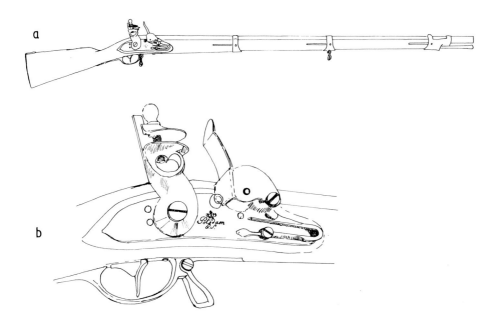

Figure 23   New Prussian or 'Scharnhorst' Musket M1809
a General view: brass fittings, length 143.5 cm (193.5 cm with bayonet), barrel length 104.5 cm, calibre 18.57 mm
b Detail of lock; the flint is not shown; note arsenal marking 'Potsdam G.S.'

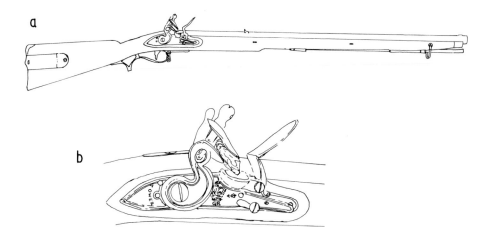

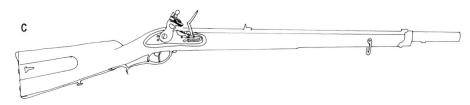

Figure 24

a British Army rifle; walnut stock, brass fittings, length 116.3 cm, barrel length 77.6 cm, calibre 15.9/16.5 mm; the barrel was browned with seven grooves

b Detail of lock-plate of a; note absence of fire shield

c Austrian Jäger rifle M1807; walnut stock, brass fittings, length 103.5 cm (171 cm with sword bayonet), barrel length 66.6 cm, calibre 14.2/13.7 mm; note backsight and foresight and patch box in the butt

Causes of Inaccuracy of Musket Fire

It was established that the major causes of inaccurate fire were: too great a playroom between ball and barrel and the imperfect roundness of the musket ball which allowed the air pressure to deflect the shot in a random fashion. This explained why a rifle (with its low playroom and its property of spinning the projectile in flight) achieved greater accuracy than the smooth-bore musket. Barrel length was also directly related to accuracy. As the experiments which led to these conclusions were conducted with weapons fired from fixed clamps, irregularity of powder burn and the shock of the recoil could be excluded from the causes as they affected both muskets and rifles.

The lesson to be learned was that a perfectly rounded, tightly fitting ball would give best results whether in a smoothbore or a rifled weapon.

Effects of Bullets

Using a 1 oz or ¾ oz ball, it was established that at point blank range, the projectile would be stopped by 5 in of oak or 6½ in of pine. At 300 paces it was stopped by 3 in of oak or 4½ in of pine.

Hard-packed earth 1½ ft thick or loose earth 2½ ft thick would also stop a musket ball and no great difference was noted in the effectiveness of the 1 oz or ¾ oz balls.

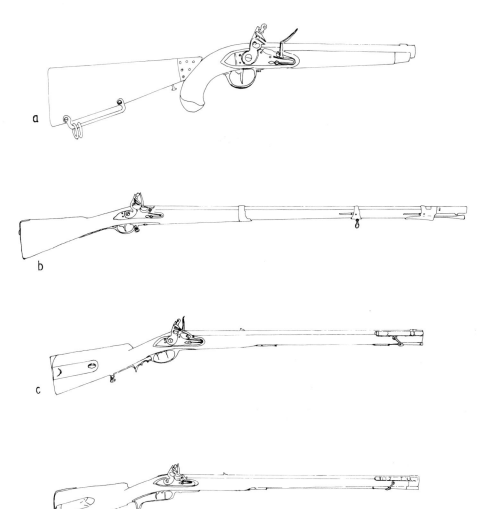

Figure 25

a Hanoverian cavalry pistol with detachable butt; produced prior to 1803, this weapon was of remarkably modern concept; length 70 cm (45 cm without butt), barrel length 28.5 cm, calibre 15.8/16.3 mm; the weapon had a rifled barrel, a rear sight, walnut stock and brass fittings. The butt was attached by a stud and was removed by a twist and pull, the butt being carried on the carbine bandolier hook; its use was limited

b Saxon 'Alt Sühler' infantry musket M1778; walnut stock, iron fittings, backsight (obscured by cocking handle), length 145 cm, barrel length 106.5 cm, calibre 17.2 mm. In 1804 the Sühl arsenal produced a new light infantry weapon, length 146.5 cm, barrel length 106.9 cm, calibre 16.5 mm

c Westfalian Jäger rifle from Schmalkalden arsenal; walnut stock, brass fittings, length 107 cm (160.5 cm with fixed 'Hirschfanger' or sword bayonet), barrel length 70 cm, calibre 15/16 mm with seven grooves

d Hessen-Kassel Jäger rifle, pre-1803; walnut stock, brass fittings, length 117 cm, barrel length 79.5 cm, calibre 15.5/16.5 mm with seven grooves; note patch box on butt

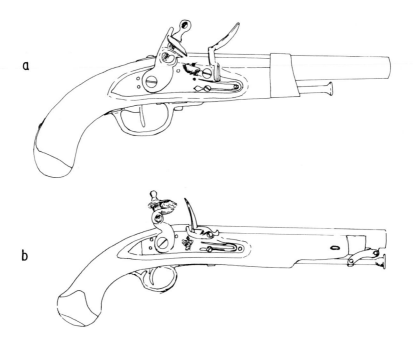

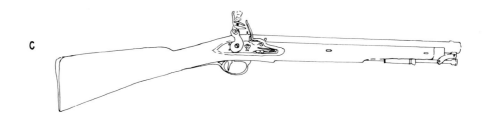

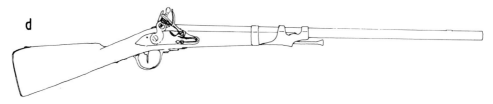

Figure 26
a French cavalry pistol An XIII made in Essen (then in Grand Duchy of Berg); **brass** fittings, length 34 cm, barrel length 21 cm
b British light dragoon pistol M1800; brass fittings, length 40 cm, barrel length 23 cm, calibre 17 mm; note the 'stirrup' under the muzzle which held the ramrod so that it could not be lost
c British light dragoon carbine M1800; brass fittings, length 78 cm, barrel length 40 cm, calibre 17 mm; note ramrod retaining stirrup as in b
d French light cavalry carbine M1786; iron fittings except for brass forepart, length 105 cm, barrel length 69.5 cm

Variations in Different Muskets

The Prussian muskets were equipped with conical touchholes (see Figure 15a) from about 1780 and were the first of the Napoleonic era to be so made. Conical touchholes were however known during the eighteenth century and were mentioned in Geisler's *Artillerie* as being a special secret. The Hanoverian Freytag Jägers used rifles with conical touchholes in the Seven Years' War. The Prussian touchhole was larger (2 Rheinländischen Lines [5.5 mm]) than any other at this time; the Hanoverian was 1½ Rh. Lines (4.13 mm) (Figure 15b) and the Austrian was also less than the Prussian. The Freytag rifle had a touchhole not quite 1½ Calenbergischen Lines in diameter (4.13 mm) (Figure 15c).

The muskets of other nations at this time (1790) had parallel touchholes all about 1 Line (2.75 mm) in diameter. The advantage of the conical touchhole was that it obviated the need to put powder into the pan in a separate operation. As the touchhole diameter reduced, so the powder used had to be ground finer. Constant musket drill tended to lead to damage to the base screw being caused by the ramrod being banged down an empty barrel and the Prussian base screw design with its flat facial area was intended to reduce wear. The inner face of the Austrian base screw was wholly concave.

Ramrods

These varied only in their weight, the Prussian being the heaviest, the Austrian the lightest. The introduction of cylindrical ramrods (to replace the conical type) was attributed to the Hanoverian General von Freytag.

Bayonets

Generally these were triangular or 'reed' shaped in cross section, the Hanoverian model had a flat, two-edged blade like that of a sword. They were fixed to the muzzle of the weapon either by rings, studs or springs.

The Flintlock

This was undoubtedly the heart and soul of any weapon and generally was so badly designed and constructed that it was responsible for the high rate of misfires in action. The most reliable model was generally reckoned to be the Austrian (see Figure 16) which had the following advantages over those of other weapons:

1 The parts were heavier and more robust—especially the springs.
2 The cocking piece had a cutout from a to b and stud c which prevented the cocking spring being strained or overtensioned.
3 When being fired, it often happened that a stream of flame and sparks would shoot out of the touchhole, across the pan and into the face of the mand standing on the right of the firer. The metal fireshield g around the pan was designed to prevent this.
4 The pan-cover was contoured on its underside so that it made a water resistant seal around the edges of the pan.
5 The Hanoverian lock differed from others in that it had fewer screws and thus required less frequent attention. Studs took the place of screws.

Pistols

Pistol barrels were between 1¼ and 1½ ft long, very limited in accuracy and rarely used in combat. Their ballistic and mechanical properties were as described for muskets. The British cavalry pistols (and carbines) had a small, mobile 'stirrup' arrangement under the muzzle through which the ramrod was held captive. This meant that it could not be dropped and lost and it was easy for the man to locate the ramrod in the muzzle.

Carbines
Carbine barrels were between 2½ and 2⅔ ft long and fired a ball of about ¾ oz; properties of lock, butt and balance were all as for muskets. The carbine was designed for easy loading when mounted but barrel length had to be maintained in order to give the required accuracy at longer ranges. The rear top of the barrel was 4 'lines', about 10 cm) higher than the foresight so as to give the customary aiming characteristics. As cavalry rarely used their firearms, the weapons were not equipped with conical touchholes—an economy measure.

Infantry Tactics

The infantry formations used on the battlefield in the eighteenth century were designed so that each man could use his firearm or sidearm (sabre) effectively in any situation. The Napoleonic column, with its phalanx-like shape, was a departure from this principle and was a measure borne of necessity during the French Revolutionary wars, when the half-trained French recruits were not capable of carrying out the demanding evolutions in line without falling into disorder and confusion.

The tactics used in any age are dictated by the weapons available and this is as true today as it was in Roman times. The rate of fire and the effective ranges of muskets, cannon and howitzers in the eighteenth century led logically to the development of line as the normal infantry combat posture. If a line was two or three ranks deep then all ranks could fire their weapons at the enemy; thicker lines meant that the fourth and subsequent ranks could not fire and thus stood uselessly there, presenting merely a better potential target for enemy fire. As movement in line was difficult to control, units marched on to and between battlefields in column, ie usually with a frontage of only three men. Frontages of a platoon, or a company were commonly used by Napoleon. Column however presented enemy artillery and muskets with a dense target in which dreadful carnage could be wrought by even one cannonball. To protect his vulnerable columns on the battlefield from musket fire, Napoleon set out ahead of them a cloud of skirmishers (the light companies or Voltigeurs) who fired and moved individually against the enemy line and harassed them. When the assaulting column approached the chosen spot in the enemy infantry line, the skirmishers fell back and joined the rear of their column. Columns were only directed at infantry lines which had previously been weakened at the intended point of impact by prolonged, concentrated artillery fire. This usually ensured that the column would pierce the line and the broken enemy would flee. Although this system worked well against all Napoleon's continental foes, it was never successful against British infantry—a fact still almost unknown on the Continent today.

The effects of the enemy artillery fire were often reduced by having the men in line lay down until the assaulting column came into musket range. Recognising the fallacy of column formation on the battlefield, and realising the vital role played by the protective skirmishers, the British countered this with a stronger skirmishing force which shot down the Voltigeurs and left their own line free to pour crashing and extremely destructive vollies into the heads of the columns as they neared the intended point of impact. The

TABLE OF MUSKETS AND CARBINES 1792

Weapon	Lengths (cm)				Calibre (cm)	Weights (kg)				Woodwork and Fittings	Total (kg)
	Barrel	Butt	Overall	Bayonet		Barrel	Ramrod	Lock	Bayonet		
British infantry musket	116.6	38.9	155.5	53.5	2	2.31	.27	.53	.34	1.76†	5.21
Prussian musket*	102.1	38.9	141.0	43.7	1.9	2.22	.47	.54	.34	1.59†	5.16
Austrian musket*	111.8	41.3	153.1	43.7	1.9	1.79	.38	.51	.33	1.69‡	4.70
Saxon musket	104.4	36.45	140.85	53.5	2	2.2	.28	.53	.48	1.38‡	4.89
New Hanoverian musket*	106.8	41.3	148.1	38.9	1.75	2.12	.47	.58	.34	1.53‡	5.04
Old Hanoverian musket	109.4	38.9	148.3	46.2	2	2.60	.26	.48	.33	1.31†	4.98
Hanoverian dragoon musket	99.6	36.45	136.05	41.3	1.75	2.04	.21	.44	.33	1.19†	4.21
Hanoverian cavalry carbine	94.8	36.45	131.25	—	1.75	1.95	.19	.44	—	1.14†	3.72
Hanoverian light dragoon carbine	77.8	36.45	114.25	—	1.75	1.39	.19	.45	—	1.19†	3.22

* = with cylindrical ramrod and conical touchhole
† = pins
‡ = rings

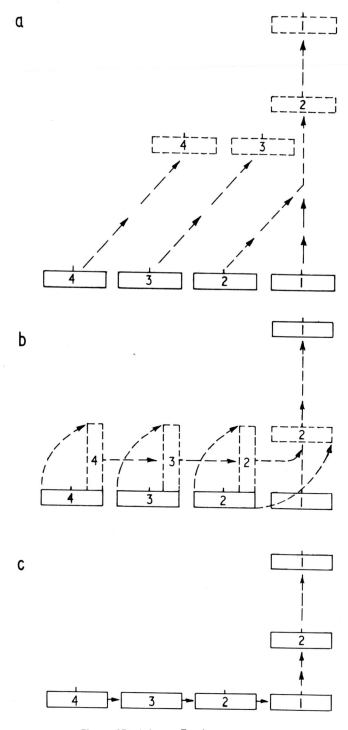

Figure 27 Infantry Tactics
Formation of open column from line:
a Diagonal marching
b Forming
c Turnings

column wavered, held up by the piles of its own dead and dying, the vollies poured in, no one in the column could fire back and a bayonet charge usually decided the day in favour of the logically superior line.

When several battalions were deployed in line abreast, they were separated by intervals of 20 paces in which the regimental artillery was deployed. If no artillery was available, inter-battalion spaces were reduced to 12 paces.

Definitions

A file   A series of men deployed one behind the other. This was normally two or perhaps three deep.

Rank   A series of men deployed alongside one another. The number of men in a rank is referred to as its frontage.

Battalion   This was the normal tactical infantry unit and consisted of about 600 men. It was subdivided into companies and platoons. A battalion consisted of about 200 files.

Company (or *Division*)   An infantry sub-unit consisting of about 120 men or 40 files, or ¼ or ⅕ of a battalion.

Platoon   Half or one-third of a company; 6–9 files.

Spacings

It was reckoned that each man occupied a frontage of 2 ft and that the depth (including the interval between ranks) was also 2 ft. Thus a battalion of 600 men, deployed in three ranks, had a frontage of 400 ft and a depth of 6 ft, including the supernumerary officers and NCOs who stood behind the third rank.

Marching Pace

There were generally two speeds of marching, first the normal pace at about 75 to the minute and this was used for evolutions in line but out of contact with the enemy. The second, and faster, pace was the double pace of 108–120 to the minute used when deploying before the enemy (often referred to as 'Dublir' or 'Deplojir' pace.

The Prussians used a speed of 76 paces per minute (1 pace=2 ft 4 in Rheinisch) for normal drill and a Dublir-pace of 100 per minute. In 1788 the French army had two rates of marching (76 and 110 per minute) and three lengths of pace (1 ft, 2 ft and 2 ft 6 in). In Saxony in 1789 they used a normal pace of 1 Elle (58.4 cm) at 75 per minute and a Dublir pace of 140 per minute, later modified to 110 per minute at 1 Dresden Elle with the normal pace at 75 per minute with a coverage of ½ Dresden Elle (29.2 cm).

Formation of Column

Movement on the battlefield was only rarely carried out in line due to the difficulty of controlling the manoeuvre; changes of position (apart from the charge) were thus carried out in column.

Column could be formed on frontages of a file (three men), a platoon, company or (rarely) a battalion and was achieved in various ways. Firstly, diagonal march (Figure 27a): the right hand unit marched straight forward, the 2nd and subsequently units marched diagonally to the right front until they were directly behind the first unit. Secondly, the forming by platoons/companies to right or left (Figure 27b). The right (or left) hand platoon marched straight forward, the others formed to the right, marched to the right and then formed left (or right) in succession as soon as they came in

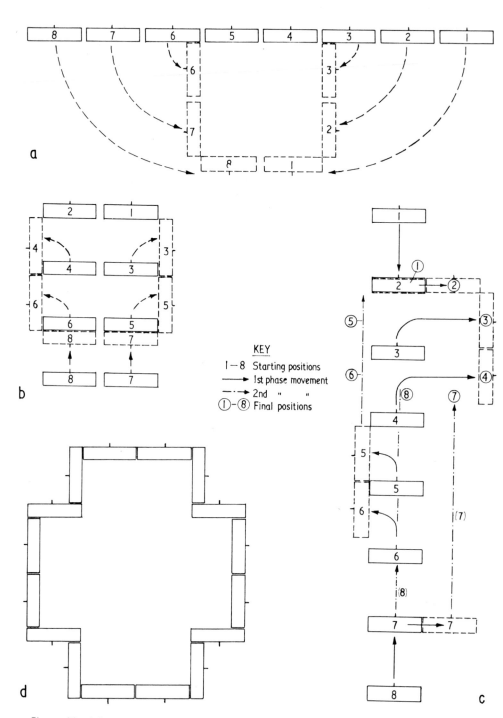

Figure 28   Infantry Tactics
a Formation of battalion square from line of eight companies
b Formation of battalion square from open column of four divisions (eight companies)
c Formation of square by a battalion originally deployed in open column of eight
platoons
d Prussian battalion of sixteen platoons in 'eight-sided' square

line with the left (or right) hand end of the first platoon. Figure 27b shows a company in column of platoons formed on the right. Thirdly, by turnings (Figure 27c): the first (right hand) platoon marched straight ahead, the others turned right, marched until directly behind the first, turned left and advanced behind them.

These columns so formed were termed 'open columns' due to the large intervals (usually the length of the frontage of the units within a column) between the units. If the column's units decreased these intervals to two paces, with officers and NCOs at either flank, this was called 'close column'.

Formation of Square

Square was a formation adopted by infantry when subjected to threat of cavalry attack with exposed flanks and rear, ie when in open terrain. As this situation could arise with the infantry either in line or in column, there were two main methods of forming square, one from each original formation. If the flank of an infantry line were in open country, it could be protected by having a battalion form square at the extremity; another method would be to have battalions in column at the threatened point.

Formation of Square from Line (Figure 28)

In a battalion consisting of eight companies, the two centre companies in the line remained steady and the three on either flank fell back to form the sides and rear of the square. This could be done in eight sub-variations. Square could be formed not only from one battalion but from several battalions. Frederick the Great regularly had his troops exercise formation and movement of multi-battalion squares.

It must be stated here that, contrary to popular modern belief, square was not just a static formation but was as mobile as any other. Regiments regularly practised movement when so deployed and the only limitations on the square were that it had to march in a direction perpendicular to one of its faces and that its progress could be impeded by a defile. In order to march 'diagonally', a square would have moved in a series of horizontal and perpendicular movements and there are several recorded examples of such evolutions carried out under fire (eg the Saxons in the Battle of Jena – 14 October 1806).

If regimental cannon (or other artillery pieces) were present, they would be stationed at the corners of the squares; the troops would be in the normal two or three ranks, the officers, colours and bands and drums in the centre.

Formation of battalion square from column occurred in at least three ways with the column usually in company frontage before the evolution took place. The leading two companies (a division) would halt, the second division divide to left and right to form flanks, the third division divide in a similar manner and the last division close up to form the rear flank of the square (Figure 28b).

Another method was for the column of platoons to break in half, the first half to halt, the second half to march to the left and then forward to line up with the first half when platoons 1 and 5 formed the leading face, 2 and 3 the right, 6 and 7 the left and 8 and 4 the rear.

The third, and more complex, method is shown in (Figure 28c). The system went as follows: the 1st and 2nd platoons halted, the 1st turned about and marched to the rear to occupy the place originally held by the 2nd which had by then marched to the right to make room for it. The 3rd and 4th platoons formed to the right and marched out in that direction to a point in line with the extreme right of the repositioned 2nd platoon. The 5th and 6th platoons formed left and were thus at the extreme left of the original column frontage; the 7th platoon turned right and marched one platoon's width to the right, the 8th marched forward to fill its place. The two right angles of the square were now formed and the rear marched forward to close up with the front or vice versa as dictated by the tactical situation.

The Prussians had also developed a so-called 'eight-cornered square' (Figure 28d) which looked in plan like a cross but was extremely difficult to form and offered limited tactical advantages.

Methods of Firing

Firing could be either in a series of controlled fashions or could be at will but the latter method had so many disadvantages (loss of control by the officers, waste of ammunition, disorganisation) that it was never recommended.

Regulated fire was always delivered by sub-units or by ranks, the former being known as firing by files, platoons, divisions, half battalions or battalions; the latter as rank fire.

If individual platoons fired in sequence this was called 'platoon fire'; if individual files within a platoon fired in sequence this was called 'firing by files'.

Rate of Fire

Experience showed that using the average infantry musket with conical ramrod (ie which had to be reversed during the loading sequence) and conventional or tubular touchhole (which meant that the gunpowder had to be poured into the pan in a separate operation) it took 11 seconds to load.

Using muskets with cylindrical ramrods and conical touchholes this could be reduced to 8–9 seconds. Aiming and firing took another 3 seconds in each case. A unit could thus fire only 4–4½ times per minute with the old muskets and 5–6 times with the new weapons. This speed could however not be maintained for long before dirt accumulated in the barrel and touchhole and slowed down the sequence. Realistic rates of fire for the old muskets were thus about 4 per minute and with the new muskets about 5 per minute.

A 3-second interval occurred between fire being given by subsequent detachments due to the fact that the noise of the first firers had to die away before the officer commanding the next detachment could command 'Aim' and 'Fire'.

A unit equipped with new pattern muskets (cylindrical ramrods and conical touchholes) was best divided into four sub-units so that a continuous and steady rate of fire could be maintained. This allowed each sub-unit ample time to reload and fire at 12-second intervals and the enemy could be subject to fire once every 3 seconds. It was not usual for a whole battalion to fire as a single unit unless threatened with an imminent attack by cavalry or infantry. Any prolonged fire fight would be carried out as described above in sub-units.

Using old muskets; a regular series of sub-unit vollies could be maintained at 3-second intervals if five sub-units were formed. As firing by ranks imposed a maximum of three 'sub-units', the prolonged rate of fire was slower than other methods and more difficult to control with a large unit due to the limitations of the commander's voice amid the other battlefield noises.

Experiments were carried out in which infantrymen were encouraged to aim their muskets as hunters would intead of just pointing it roughly ahead and pulling the trigger. The results of two groups (one trained to aim, the other not) were then compared after each had fired 1,000 rounds at each of the ranges shown below; the target was representing a line of cavalry:

Range (paces)	Aimed shots hits (%)	Unaimed shots hits (%)
100	53.4	40.3
200	31.8	18.3
300	23.4	14.9
400	13.0	6.5

The firing methods of various infantry formations in 1792 were as follows:

Austria
Each battalion had three divisions each of eight platoons. Sequence of firing within each division started with the right wing platoon, and then alternated between the wings ending in the centre. The three divisional right wing platoons all fired at one command etc.

Prussia and Hanover
Alternate platoons fired, from the right, in the following sequence: 1, 3, 5, 7 and then from the right again 2, 4, 6, 8.

France
Firing began with the 1st Platoons of the two central divisions, then the 1st Platoons of the next flanking divisions and finally the 1st Platoons of the outer divisions. The 2nd Platoons of the six divisions then repeated the process in the same sequence.

Saxony
Each battalion had four divisions each of four platoons; as in the Austrian army, firing sequence within each division went from the flanks to the centre.

Fire and movement
A peculiarity of the Austrian army was a system whereby the first rank did not fire and the second and third ranks fired at will (but as ranks). The fire of the first rank was held in reserve for crisis situations and the battalion formation remained under control. This system was however wasteful of one-third of the available fire power. When contact with the enemy was imminent, battalion fire would be used as this (at the correct, close range) would have the greatest physical and psychological effect on them.

The principle of 'fire and movement' was already well established in the infantry regulations of 1789 and it was strongly recommended that any force required to move in the presence of the enemy did so in two halves, the one moving, the other firing and then vice versa.

Due to the established inaccuracy of musket fire in the Napoleonic era it was no wonder that the regulations taught that commanders should only open fire on enemy infantry at 40–80 paces—and this a battalion volley—and then at once mount a bayonet charge.

Fire above these ranges would be relatively ineffective, but if a good, well aimed volley could be poured into the enemy close to, *before* he had chance to fire, it was likely that the retaliatory volley would be confused, diminished

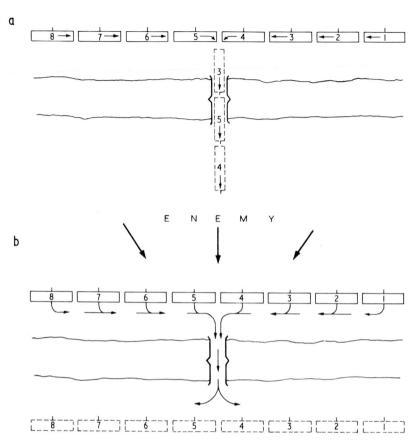

Figure 29   Infantry Withdrawal
a Withdrawal through a defile with no enemy purusuit
b Withdrawal through a defile under threat of enemy attack

and scattered due to casualties and shock. Continuous volley firing was also of limited effectiveness because of the large amount of smoke generated, the decreasing carefulness of the men, the increasing fouling in barrels and touchholes, the misfire rate and the casualty rate.

The use of cover from artillery fire on the battlefield was also recommended to commanders but examples of its use are rarely mentioned in historical battle accounts except in those dealing with British regiments. Napoleon and many other continental commanders were notoriously generous with the lives of their soldiers and perhaps the most extreme example of this was the Battle of Borodino in 1812 where Russian casualties were magnified by the very deep formations adopted. Many units of the Grande Armée also spent several hours exposed to harrowing Russian artillery fire without being able to take cover of any sort.

The Prussians had developed fire and movement to such a degree in 1790 that when an infantry battalion mounted an assault, it advanced at a short, slow pace of 1 ft at 76 per minute; the uneven-numbered platoons took 3 large, rapid paces forward, aimed, fired and then reloaded while the rest of the battalion caught up. The even-numbered platoons then marched 3 large, rapid paces forward, fired and reloaded and so on. Estimated total advance between salvoes was about 10 paces.

Another method of reducing casualties on the battlefield was widely employed by infantry when subject to long range cannon fire. As the cannon-ball bounced ever more slowly towards them, the files would open left and right of the apparent trajectory so that it would pass harmlessly between them.

When confronted with charging cavalry, infantry were recommended to hold their fire until the horsemen were only 40 paces away and then to greet them with a battalion volley. It was certainly not unknown for steady infantry, in the open, in line, to repel and shatter cavalry charges with such tactics. Even if charging cavalry reached a steady infantry line intact, it was difficult for the troopers to urge their mounts into a threatening array of bayonets—cavalry was not necessarily always victorious as soon as it appeared although its effect on broken, fleeing infantry was of course tremendous.

Infantry Withdrawal

This was, and is, undoubtedly the most vulnerable movement on the field of battle. Should this be necessary, it was critical that the greatest control over the withdrawing infantry should be maintained or the movement would rapidly degenerate into a route with disastrous consequences.

With infantry in line (ie not under threat of cavalry attack) one of the best and most easily controlled methods was to have alternate units (battalions or companies) march a specified distance to the rear, halt, turn about and make ready to fire while the remaining units held the enemy in check. When the rearward line was formed, the forward, alternate units would turn about, march back to (or through) them and the process would be repeated. This method made use of the principles of fire and movement. The distances withdrawn at each movement varied in relation to the size of units chosen to move; with divisions it was 30 paces, with battalions 50–100.

If a line of infantry was forced to withdraw in the presence of enemy cavalry in open ground, it would form battalion squares which would then withdraw about 400 paces at a time, first the evenly numbered squares (2, 4, 6 etc) in the line and then the unevenly numbered ones. The static squares kept the enemy under fire. Whenever possible, skirmishers would be deployed between withdrawing troops and the enemy to slow down his pursuit.

Part Two
National Sections

Anhalt-Bernburg, Anhalt-Dessau, Anhalt-Köthen

(Cockade green)

The first standing troops of these principalities was the Jäger-Corps raised in 1795—bicorn with green plume, dark green coat with white epaulettes, buttons and turnbacks, green cuffs, red collar, white belts and small clothes, white gaiters.

From 1807 to 1813 the three states together provided one infantry battalion (1st Battalion, 5th Regiment of the Confederation of the Rhine). The uniform was shako with white metal shield bearing the Anhalt crest, white chinscales, company distinctions and rank badges as in the French army; green, single-breasted tunic, pink collar, shoulder straps and piping, green cuffs, white buttons, black belts, grey breeches and black gaiters. In 1813 Napoleon demanded that a regiment of Chasseurs à Cheval also be raised; uniform as for the infantry but with pointed, pink cuffs, white shako cords, white metal shoulder scales, grey overalls piped pink.

Battle History

1807—in Prussia with the French at the siege of Glogau; 1809—Tyrol; 1809–1811—Spain as part of the German Division; 1812—Russia as part of 1st Brigade of the 'Division Princiere'; 1813 (infantry)—besieged in Danzig; Chasseurs à Cheval—captured by the allies almost as soon as they took the field.

THE

Austrian Empire

1792 – 1815

(Unless otherwise stated, all rosettes, pompons and cockades were black within yellow and all plumes one-third black over two-thirds yellow; in 1805 the pigtail was abandoned.)

Rank Badges

Generals
Bicorn with wide gold edging, dark green drooping feather plume, wide gold loop and button, black within gold hat tassels, bearing the imperial cypher ('F II' up to 1806 then 'F I') in gold. White, long skirted coat with red collar and Swedish cuffs, these and the front of the coat and the pocket flaps covered in wide gold lace according to rank. Red waistcoat edged in gold braid, red breeches, cuffed boots. Gold and black silk waist sash

and sword knot, the tassels of the latter embroidered on one side with the imperial cypher, on the other with the double eagle. Brown cane with gold knob, cords and tassels.

Field officers (colonel to major)
Bicorn as above but no plume, black and yellow hat tassels, black within yellow pompon with imperial cypher in gold. Plain white coat with wide gold lace to top and back of cuffs, regimental buttons, white breeches, short boots. Black and yellow worsted waist sash, sword knot as above (up to 1805 it had been in the button colour), cane with gold and black cords.

If the helmet was worn the crest was of black silk and gold thread and the combe was covered with decorated gold plate—initially leaf patterns, later with a lion and snake motif—gilt front plate and fittings.

If the shako was worn the peak and neck flap were covered in gold wire and the top was circled with three gold/silver bands in the button colour.

Junior officers
As for senior officers but no cuff lace; helmet crest black and yellow silk. shako top bands – captain two, subaltern one.

NCOs
Stabs – Feldwebel—short skirted coat, two yellow shako top bands, cane with gold knob and black and yellow tassels; black and yellow sabre knot. Feldwebel—as above but one shako top band. Corporal—as above but narrow yellow shako lace, hazelnut stick with white strap. Gefreiter—yellow shako top band.

Infantry

Throughout its history the uniform of the Austrian army has been characterised by its relative simplicity coupled with 'good taste'.

Encompassing many nations as it did, the Austrian Empire gave expression to the identity of certain of these in the uniforms of certain regiments. Hungarian infantry regiments wore Polish cuffs decorated with white lace and tassels (called Bärentatzen—bear's claws) and light blue, ankle length breeches with black and yellow thigh knots and side piping and ankle boots as opposed to the 'German' infantry's white knee breeches, black gaiters and shoes. (The Hungarian cavalry or hussars wore national costume as did the Polish lancers.)

Each battalion of infantry was subdivided into grenadier (elite) companies and fusiliers. There were no organic light troops but (for a time) there were light infantry battalions and there were also the famous Jägers and the Border Infantry of the nowadays Yugoslavian, Rumanian and Bulgarian areas which fulfilled this role.

In 1792 the infantryman wore the peakless kasket of black leather with raised front plate edged in white lace and bearing a brass plate with the imperial cypher. On the top left side of the crown was a rosette and a plume. The tunic was white, single breasted with nine buttons, Swedish cuffs for the German infantry, Polish for the Hungarian infantry. The short tunic

Plate 1   Austrian Empire: Hungarian Infantry 1806–1815
(*l to r*) Fusilier private, grenadier private, private sharpshooter Grenz-Infanterie-Regiment Kreutzer No 64 (later No 5) – the absence of Bear's Claws on the cuff is unexplained, drummer of fusiliers (reclining), officer of grenadiers, officer of fusiliers (rear view), officer of fusiliers in the dark grey Überrock, senior officer of fusiliers, sergeant of fusiliers (rear view) – the double eagle pouch badge is not standard, various privates in fatigue dress. A contemporary plate by T. Weigl, Vienna

skirts were turned back only at the front and in the rear of the tails were two vertical pipings in the facing colour which were also shown on collar, cuffs, turnbacks and the edging to the white shoulder strap. For German regiments the breeches were white and the long black gaiters were closed with black leather buttons. The pack was of brown calfskin; belts were white and the black pouch lid bore an oval brass plate with the imperial cypher. The water bottle was round and of light brown wood. Hungarian regiments wore long, light blue breeches decorated with black and yellow cord. Privates were armed with muskets and bayonets; NCOs and grenadiers had brass hilted sabres in brown leather sheaths.

In 1800 the antique style black leather helmet with front and neck peak, black leather combe topped by a black over yellow woollen crest and with wide brass front plate bearing 'F II' was introduced but did not reach all regiments before being superseded by the black felt shako with front and rear peaks, button, loop, cockade and large pompon at the top. This headgear underwent several changes of style before 1815.

The cut of the tunic was altered in 1805 and 1813 but the differences in each case were minor. Officers' coats had long skirts with white lining and turnbacks and they often wore grey Litewkas instead to protect these expensive garments. They wore boots and yellow and black waist sashes tied on the left and carried swords if German fusiliers, sabres if Hungarian or grenadiers.

Grenadiers wore the high fronted bearskin cap with brass plate bearing

81

the Austrian crest within trophies of arms and flanked by the cypher 'F II'. It had a backing in the facing colour decorated with white tape and a pompon on the right side of the frontal fur. It was fitted with a peak and black chinstrap. On their cross belts grenadiers has a brass grenade badge.

In 1806 the imperial cypher on all appointments was changed from 'F II' to 'F I' when Kaiser Franz renounced the throne of the Holy Roman Empire and became 'Franz I' of Austria.

Drummers wore swallows' nests in the facing colour edged in white lace and with a circle of white lace in the centre; drums were brass with black and yellow striped hoops. Their collars and cuffs were also edged in wavy white lace.

Line Infantry

NUMBERS, TITLES, FACINGS AND BUTTONS OF THE AUSTRIAN LINE INFANTRY
1792–1815 (* = HUNGARIAN REGIMENT)
As at 1792, unless otherwise stated.

		a (facings)	b (buttons)
1	Kaiser	a purple	b yellow
*2	Erzherzog Ferdinand	a sulphur yellow	b yellow
3	Erzherzog Carl	a sky blue	b white
4	Hoch und Deutschmeister	a light blue	b yellow
5	1st Garrison	a dark blue	b white
	1807 converted to 1st and 2nd Garrison Battalions		
6	2nd Garrison	a black	b white
	1807 converted to 3rd and 4th Garrison Battalions		
7	Carl Schröder	a light blue	b yellow
	1798	a dark brown	b white
8	Huff	a poppy red	b white
	1798		b yellow
9	Clerfayt	a light green	b yellow
10	Kheul	a black	b white
	1798	a poplar green	
11	Michael Wallis	a pink	b yellow
	1798		b white
12	Khevenhüller	a dark brown	b yellow
	1809 Manfreddini		
13	Reisky	a grass green	b yellow
14	Klebeck	a black	b yellow
15	d'Alton	a madder red	b yellow
	1798 Oranien		
16	Terzi	a violet	b white
	1798		b yellow
17	Hohenlohe	a sulphur yellow	b yellow
	1798	a light brown	
	1801 Reuss-Plauen		
18	Stuart	a purple	b white
	1809 d'Aspre then Reuss-Greitz		
19	Alvinczy	a black	b white
	1798	a sky blue	b yellow
20	Kaunitz	a lobster red	b yellow
	1798		b white
21	Gemmingen	a sea green	b white
	1798		b yellow
22	Lacy	a light blue	b white
	1798	a emperor yellow	
23	Grossherzog Ferdinand	a poppy red	b yellow
	1798		b white
	1809 Disbanded		

24	Preiss	*a* dark blue	*b* yellow
	1798		*b* white
	1801 Auersperg		
	1808 Strauch		
25	Brechainville	*a* sea green	*b* yellow
	1798		*b* white
	1801 Spork then de Vaux		
26	Wilhelm Schröder	*a* poplar green	*b* yellow
	1803 Hohenlohe – Bartenstein		
27	Strassoldo	*a* emperor yellow	*b* white
	1798		*b* yellow
	1809 Chasteler		
28	Wartensleben	*a* emperor yellow	*b* yellow
	1798	*a* grass green	*b* white
	1799 Frelich		
29	Olivier Wallis	*a* grass green	*b* yellow
	1798	*a* light blue	*b* white
	1803 Lindenau		
30	de Ligne	*a* pike grey	*b* white
	1798		*b* yellow
*31	Orosz	*a* light blue	*b* white
	1798 Benjowsky		
		a emperor yellow	*b* white
*32	Gyulai	*a* dark green	*b* white
	1798	*a* sky blue	*b* yellow
*33	Sztaray	*a* dark blue	*b* white
	1804 Colloredo		
*34	Kray	*a* light green	*b* white
	1798	*a* madder red	
	1804 Davidovich		
35	Brentano	*a* black	*b* yellow
	1798 Wenkheim		
		a lobster red	
	1809 Erzherzog Max then Argenteau		
36	Ulrich Kinsky	*a* pink	*b* white
	1798 Fürstenberg		
	1801 Kolowrat		
*37	de Vins	*a* poppy red	*b* white
	1798		*b* yellow
	1802 Auffenberg		
	1808 Weidenfeld		
38	Württemberg	*a* madder red	*b* yellow
	1798	*a* pink	
*39	Nadasdy	*a* crimson	*b* white
	1798	*a* poppy red	
	1803 Duka		
40	Mittrowsky	*a* crimson	*b* white
	1809 Württemberg		
41	Bender	*a* light brown	*b* yellow
	1798	*a* sulphur yellow	*b* white
	1805 Sachsen – Hildburghausen		
	1808 Kottulinksy		
42	Matheson	*a* orange	*b* yellow
	1798 Erbach	*b* white	
43	Thurn	*a* sulphur yellow	*b* white
	1798		*b* yellow
	1806 Simbschen		
44	Belgiojoso	*a* pink	*b* white
	1798	*a* madder red	
	1801 Bellegarde		
45	Latterman	*a* poplar green	*b* yellow
	1798	*a* crimson	
	1809 de Vaux		
46	Neugebauer	*a* dark blue	*b* yellow
	1809 Chasteler		

47	Fr. Kinsky	a steel green		b white
	1805 Vogelsang			
*48	Caprara	a light green		b white
	1798 Vukassovich		b yellow	
49	Pellegrini	a pike grey		b white
	1797 Kerpen			
50	Stain	a violet		b white
*51	Splény	a poplar green		b white
	1798	a dark blue		b yellow
*52	Erzherzog Anton			
	Victor	a pink		b white
	1798	a purple		b yellow
	1804 Franz Carl			
*53	Jellachich	a purple		b white
54	Callenberg	a apple green		b white
	1805 Froon			
55	Murray	a light blue		b white
	1795			b yellow
	1803 Reuss Greitz			
56	Wenzel Colloredo	a steel green		b yellow
57	Joseph Colloredo	a pink		b yellow
58	Vierset	a lobster red		b white
	1798 Beaulieu			
		a black		
59	Jordis	a orange		b yellow

Light Infantry

Border Infantry (Grenz Regiments)

These tough troops from the areas of the Empire adjacent to the Ottoman Turks fulfilled the role of light infantry in all Austrian campaigns. They wore the Kasket, then the shako, white or tobacco brown coat of Hungarian style, light blue Hungarian breeches and black belts.

In 1809 the regiments 1–4, 10 and 11 were taken into French service when Austria was robbed of her Adriatic seaboard and returned to the Empire in 1813.

In 1798 they were removed from the line numbering and given the numbers shown below:

1792		1798–1815		a (facings)	b (buttons)
60	Liccaner	1		a violet	b yellow
61	Ottocaner	2	in French	a violet	b white
62	Oguliner	3	Service	a orange	b yellow
63	Szluiner	4	1809/1813	a orange	b white
64	Kreutzer	5		a lobster red	b yellow
65	St. Georges	6		a lobster red	b white
66	Brooder	7		a pink	b yellow
67	Gradiscaner	8		a pink	b white
68	Peterwardeiner	9		a grey	b yellow
69	1st Banal	10	in French	a crimson	b yellow
70	2nd Banal	11	Service	a crimson	b white
71	Deutschbanater	12	1809/1813	a dark grey	b white
72	Wallachisch-Illyrisches	13		a light grey	b white
73	1st Szeckler	14		a pink	b yellow
74	2nd Szeckler	15		a pink	b white
75	1st Wallachisches	16		a poplar green	b yellow
76	2nd Wallachisches	17		a poplar green	b white
77	3rd Garrison				

Plate 2   Austrian Empire: Infantry, Artillery and Technical Services 1806–1815
(*l to r*) Pontonnier, German fusilier in antique helmet, German grenadier, Jäger, artilleryman; (*central group*) Pontonnier officer, fusilier officer, mineur officer, fusilier officer (seated), artillery officer, mineur officer, officer of the general staff (dark green coat, black facings, yellow buttons), mineur officer, officer of the train (grey coat, yellow facings, white buttons). A contemporary plate by T. Weigl, Vienna.

In 1798 three new Hungarian and a German line infantry regiments were raised:

*	Ignaz Gyulai	60	*a* steel green	*b* white
*	St. Julien	61	*a* grass green	*b* yellow
*	Franz Jellačic	62	*a* grass green	*b* white
	Erzherzog Franz Joseph	63	*a* light brown	*b* yellow

Light Infantry Battalions 1798–1801

German fusilier helmet but no brass front plate; just brass initials 'F II'; the Italian battalions (*) wore German coats and trousers, the others wore Hungarian style cuffs and long light blue breeches trimmed black and yellow; white belts.

They were disbanded in 1801, having been raised from various Freikorps.

	a (facings)	*b (buttons)*		*a (facings)*	*b (buttons)*
1	*a* madder red	*b* yellow	* 2	*a* madder red	*b* white
* 3	*a* brick red	*b* yellow	* 4	*a* brick red	*b* white
5	*a* orange	*b* yellow	6	*a* orange	*b* white
7	*a* steel green	*b* white	8	*a* sulphur yellow	*b* white
9	*a* crimson	*b* yellow	10	*a* dark blue	*b* white
*11	*a* dark blue	*b* yellow	12	*a* steel green	*b* white
13	*a* sulphur yellow	*b* yellow	*14	*a* black	*b* white
15	*a* black	*b* yellow			

Jägers

The oldest standing Jäger battalions were raised in 1798. Initially they wore the antique helmet with white cypher 'F II' and dark green crest, pike grey coat of German infantry cut and German breeches, grass green facings, white buttons, black belts and gaiters. In 1805 the helmet was replaced by the 'Corsican' hat with large left hand brim upturned and extending above the crown, pompon and green plume.

Buglers wore green swallows' nests edged white with white ring in the centre, brass horns, dark green cords and tassels, white edging to collar and cuffs. About half the Jägers were armed with rifles and sword bayonets, the others with smooth bore muskets.

Artillery

1792–1815. Bicorn with loop, button and pompon, deer brown coat of German infantry style, red facings, yellow buttons, white belt and breeches, boots. In 1800 some units were issued with the antique helmet with red crest and brass front plate bearing a horizontal cannon barrel but this was withdrawn soon after.

Engineers

Kasket, grey coat of German infantry cut, grass green facings, white buttons, breeches and belts. Later the Corsican hat was worn with pompon and plume.

Pontoniers

Kasket, dark blue German tunic and breeches, red facings, white buttons and belts, boots. Later the Corsican hat was worn with pompon and plume.

Mineurs

Kasket, grey German tunic with crimson facings and yellow buttons. Later the Corsican hat was worn with pompon and plume.

Cavalry

The Austrian cavalry were classified as German (Kürassiers, dragoons, Chevau Légers and Jäger zu Pferde) and National (hussars and lancers).

German Cavalry

Until 1798 the large bicorn with button, loop and plume (and with white/yellow edging for Kürassiers) was worn, in that year it was replaced by the antique helmet which was then retained, with occasional modifications, until well into the 1860s.

They wore German infantry style tunics, but with short white skirts turned over at front and back and edged in the facing colour; white breeches, short straight-topped boots and white belts.

Saddle furniture was red and edged in black/yellow/black lace with the imperial cypher in the rear corners. The round red portmanteau was plain. A white sheepskin saddle cloth with red edging covered saddle and holsters. Officers had black fur saddle skins edged red. Harness was black with brass fittings.

Trumpeters wore red crests, swallows' nests in the facing colour edged in white tape with a ring of white tape in the centre. Trumpets were brass with black and yellow cords and tassels; they rode greys.

Plate 3   Austrian Empire: Officer of Jäger zu Pferde 1798–1801
Yellow helmet fittings (cypher 'F II') – note oak leaf sprig in chinstrap boss; pike
grey coat and breeches, grass green facings, yellow buttons; red saddle furniture
edged and piped black and yellow; rear cypher – crowned 'FII'. A contemporary plate
from Vienna.

Plate 4   Austrian Empire: Trooper, 11th Chevau Légers, 'La Tour' 1800
Facings purple, buttons yellow, dark green coat, red saddle furniture edged and piped black and yellow, helmet and shabracque cyphers 'F II'. A contemporary plate from Vienna.

Weapons were a heavy, straight-bladed, steel-hilted sword in steel sheath, carbine and pistols. Troopers had white leather sabre straps.

Kürassiers

Apart from the above mentioned generalities their particular uniform features were: white collar with facings shown only on small patches, 'Paroli', each with a regimental button in the rear corner. Only the front plate of the black Kürass was worn, it was edged in white leather for men, red velvet for officers and was held by white cross straps armoured with square black metal plates for men, with red velvet covered straps studded with gold plates for officers.

Junior officers had a short gilt point extending down the Kürass from the neck, field officers had long gold peaks. Trumpeters wore no Kürass. Kürassiers carried no carbines and their shabracque were short and of rectangular shape.

Kürassiers 1798–1815

		a (facings)	b (buttons)	
1	Kaiser	a purple	b white	
2	Erzherzog Franz	a black	b white	
3	Herzog Albert	a purple	b yellow	
4	Czartoryski	a dark blue	b yellow	Disbanded 1801
5	Zeschwitz	a grass green	b yellow	Disbanded 1801
6	Melas	a light blue	b yellow	Converted to dragoons (No 6) in 1801
7	Carl Lothringen	a dark blue	b white	
8	Hohenzollern-Hechingen	a scarlet	b yellow	
9	Nassau-Usingen	a light blue	b white	1801 No 5 1805 Sommariva
10	Mack	a black	b yellow	1801 No 6 1805 Liechtenstein
11	Anspach	a scarlet	b white	Disbanded 1801
12	Kavanagh	a grass green	b white	1801 Erzherzog Ferdinand No 4

Dragoons and Chevau Légers

During the period 1792–1815 there were repeated reorganisations between these two arms with the coats of some regiments changing from white (dragoons) to dark green (Chevau Légers or light dragoons) and back again. For these regiments the entire collar was in the facing colour. Until 1798 the dragoons wore the plain bicorn with button, loop and plume while the Chevau Légers wore the infantry style Kasket. From this date on both wore the antique helmet. From 1798–1801 both arms were converted to light dragoons with dark green coats.

From 1798–1802 the dragoons and Chevaux Légers regiments were all combined, titled Light Dragoons and numbered consecutively. In 1802 they were once more separated into their respective arms and given their own numbering systems. Their arm from 1792 appears in brackets after their 1798 Light Dragoon title.

Dragoons and Chevau Légers 1798

	a (coat)	c (buttons)	b (facings)
1st Light Dragoons 'Kaiser'	a white	c yellow	b dark red
(Dragoons) 1802 1st Chevaux Légers			
	1807 a dark green	c yellow	b red

	a	b	c
2nd 'Erzherzog Ferdinand' (Chevaux Légers) 1801 disbanded	white	emperor yellow	white
3rd 'Erzherzog Johann' (Dragoons) 1801 1st Dragoons	white	orange	yellow
	white	black	white
4th 'Karaczay' (Chevaux Légers) 1801 'Hohenzollern' 1802 2nd Chevaux Légers	dark green	scarlet	white
	white	dark green	yellow
1807	dark green	scarlet	white
5th 'Modena' (Chevaux Légers) 1801 disbanded	dark green	orange	white
6th 'Coburg' (Chevaux Légers) 1801 disbanded	dark green	pink	white
7th 'Waldeck' (Chevaux Légers) 1801 Hohenlohe 1802 2nd Dragoons	dark green	sulphur yellow	white
	white	dark blue	white
8th 'Württemberg' (Dragoons) 1802 3rd Dragoons	dark green	pink	yellow
	white	purple	white
9th 'Liechtenstein' (Chevaux Légers) 1801 disbanded	dark green	black	white
10th 'Lobkowitz' (Chevaux Légers) 1802 3rd Chevaux Légers	dark green	sky blue	white
	white	sky blue	yellow
11th 'La Tour' (Chevaux Légers) 1802 4th Chevaux Légers	dark green	pompadour	yellow
	white	dark blue	yellow
1807	dark green	pompadour	yellow
12th 'Kinsky' (Dragoons) 1802 5th Chevaux Légers	dark green	sky blue	yellow
	white	dark blue	yellow
13th vacant 1802 6th Chevaux Légers 'Rosenberg'	dark green	pompadour	white
	white	black	yellow
1806	white	pompadour	yellow
14th 'Levenehr' (Dragoons) 1802 4th Dragoons	dark green	emperor yellow	yellow
	white	light red	white
15th 'Savoy' (Dragoons) 1802 5th Dragoons	dark green	black	yellow
	white	dark green	white

In 1802 the Kürassier Regiment 'Melas' was converted to the 6th Dragoons

	white	light blue	yellow

In 1814 the 7th Chevaux Légers was raised

	white	crimson	white

Jäger zu Pferde

Green helmet, crest, yellow front cypher 'F II', pike grey coat, grass green facings, yellow buttons, black belts. This regiment was raised in 1798 and disbanded in 1801.

The National Cavalry

This catagory of light cavalry included the Hungarian hussars and the Galician (Polish) lancers; both arms wore uniforms closely related to their national costume. Saddle furniture was as for the German cavalry but with long rear corners. Arms were a steel-hilted sabre in steel sheath, pistols and carbines (or lances for the first rank of these regiments).

Hussars

In 1792 they wore a peakless shako with cockade, pompon and plume at the front centre, black and yellow cords and flounders tied around the top. This developed front and rear peaks (the latter turned up and purely decorative) and was in different colours for various regiments. Traditional hussar costume of dolman, pelisse, breeches and short boots was worn, all lace for non-commissioned ranks was black and yellow; for officers it was in the button colour. The barrel sash was black and yellow for all regiments and the sabretasche was red with black and yellow edging and crowned imperial cypher. For junior officers this decoration was gold and for field officers the cypher was couched within trophies of arms.

Hussars 1798–1815

		a (shako)	b (buttons)	c (dolman)	d (breeches)
1	Kaiser	a black	b yellow	c dark blue	d dark blue
2	Erzherzog Joseph	a madder red	b yellow	c light blue	d light blue
3	Erzherzog Ferdinand	a pike grey	b yellow	c dark blue	d dark blue
4	Vecsey	a light blue	b white	c poplar green	d poppy red
5	(newly raised)	a madder red	b white	c dark green	d crimson
6	Blankenstein	a black	b yellow	c light blue	d light blue
7	(newly raised)	a grass green	b white	c light blue	d light blue
8	Wurmser	a black	b yellow	c poplar green	d poppy red
9	Erdödy	a black	b yellow	c dark green	d crimson
10	Meszaros	a grass green	b yellow	c light blue	d light blue
11	Széckler (Grenz)	a black	b white	c dark blue	d dark blue
12	Slavonisch	a black	b white	c pike grey	d light blue
		1801 disbanded			

A new 12th regiment (formerly the Palatinal Hussars) was raised in 1807.

In 1802 all dolmans, pelisse and breeches became light blue, lace black and yellow, buttons yellow and the shako was left in the regimental colour: 1 purple; 2 poppy red; 3 grey; 4 light blue; 5 (Ott.) emperor yellow; 6 violet; 7 (Liechtenstein) dark green; 8 (Kienmayer) orange; 9 white; 10 (Stipsics) light green; 11 black; 12 dark blue.

Lancers

In 1792 there were two regiments of this arm. Both wore low, yellow-topped czapkas, grass green kurtka, red facings and yellow buttons, white breeches and short boots. The czapka gradually grew taller and stiffer and was fitted with a black peak, a pompon and plume, green overalls with a red side stripe and black booting replaced the white breeches, and yellow woollen epaulettes were adopted. Around the waist was worn a yellow 'Passgürtel' with two black stripes. Belts were white and the lance pennants were black over yellow.

In 1809 regiments were distinguished by the coloured tops to the czapka: 1st Merveldt—emperor yellow; 2nd Schwarzenberg—grass green. In 1812 the 3rd regiment 'Erzherzog Karl' wore dark green kurtka and trousers, red facings, yellow buttons and red czapka tops. The 4th regiment, raised in 1813, had the same uniform as the 3rd but with white czapka tops.

91

GRAND DUCHY OF

Baden

(Cockade red within yellow)

Rank Badges

Prior to July 1806 rank badges and inter-company distinctions were as in Prussia. When Baden joined the Confederation of the Rhine in that year the French rank badge system was adopted.

Officers wore silver, red and yellow sashes and sabre knots, gold gorgets with gold cyphers ('CF') on dark blue enamelled ground.

Infantry 1790

Leib-regiment

This regiment's uniform was apparently a direct copy of that of the Prussian Infantry Regiment 'Garde' (No 15): musketeers a small, white-edged bicorn with red pompon; grenadiers a brass fronted mitre cap bearing the crowned cypher 'CF', red backing and blue headband; dark blue coat, red collar, lapels, turnbacks and round cuffs, white buttons, buttonholes, small clothes and belts; white grenades and crowned oval plate pouch badge, long white gaiters for parades, otherwise black.

Füsilier-Bataillon 'Erbprinz'

As above but fusiliers had yellow metal plates and blue backing to their mitre caps (which were shorter than grenadier caps and had a domed head-piece instead of joining up with the front plate). Their coats were single breasted with yellow facings and buttons.

In 1793 officers' spontoons were abandoned and subalterns (who had previously worn gaiters) received boots. In 1803 the coat was closed to the waist with straight lapels and in 1806 the pigtail was abolished.

Leib-grenadier Battalion

This battalion received a new uniform in October 1806: bearskin bonnet with white plate bearing a crowned oval enclosing the red and yellow Baden crest (but the colours indicated by hatchings), red and white cords, white over red plume, red top patch with white grenade. Dark blue, single-breasted tunic with red collar, cuffs and turnbacks, dark blue cuff flaps, white buttons, edging to collar and cuffs and nine white lace bars across the chest. White breeches and belts, black, short gaiters.

Line Infantry 1806–1815

The four line infantry regiments had low-crowned, black leather helmets with black, round crest on a leather combe which was covered by red and yellow fringes. The front of the combe was covered by a lion's head and under this was an eight-pointed star for the 1st (Leibregiment) and a crowned oval plate bearing 'CF' for the other three regiments; across the front of the helmet was a metal band with the regimental designation. The red and yellow cockade was mounted over the left hand chinstrap boss. Helmet fittings were white for the Leibregiment and for the 3rd regiment (Graf Wilhelm von Hochberg), yellow for the 2nd (vacant Erbgrossherzog) and 4th (vacant). The dark blue coat had red collar, shoulder straps, cuffs and turnbacks, dark blue cuff flaps (Leibregiment had two white lace bars to each side of the collar, three on each cuff flap). Crowned oval pouch badge, white belts, buttons and breeches.

Officers wore bicorns with black plumes and silver epaulettes. Grenadiers wore a white plume on the left side of the helmet. Drummers' sleeves were edged in special white lace with red and yellow stripes; six chevrons (point up) were on each sleeve and they had dark blue swallows' nests edged in the lace.

Jäger-Bataillon
Bavarian-style Raupenhelm with green woollen crest, green plume, brass crowned 'CF' front badge, brass chinstrap bosses. Dark green, double-breasted coat, black collar, cuffs and turnbacks, white piping to facings and front of jacket, white buttons, green epaulettes. Black leatherwork and gaiters, grey breeches.

Foot Artillery
Up to 1806 bicorn, dark blue coat, black facings, yellow buttons, red turn-backs. After this Bavarian Raupenhelm with black crest, yellow plate bearing the crowned crest of Baden, red piping added to black collar, lapels and round cuffs; white breeches, black belts and gaiters.

Horse Artillery
As for foot artillery but white belts and plume, no red piping to facings; boots.

Train
As for artillery but grey coats and trousers, light blue facings, white buttons.

Cavalry

Garde du Corps squadron
Bicorn with silver loop and brooch, white over red plume, white tunics, red collar, cuffs and turnbacks, red waist sash, red and white lace to hooked front, white belts, breeches and high boots. Red sabretasches with white crowned 'CF' and white edging. In 1806 the bicorn was replaced by a black leather helmet with black combe, white plume, front plate and fittings and the tunic became double-breasted with two rows of buttons. In 1813 white guards lace was added to collar and cuffs.

Hussars
One regiment was raised in 1806. Shako with black plume (red tip for NCOs, red base for officers), yellow/gold top band loop and button, cockade, brass chin chains. Dark green dolman and pelisse, red collar and cuffs, yellow lace and buttons, red breeches with yellow Hungarian lacing and hussar boots for parades otherwise grey button overalls. Pelisse fur was black for the men, white for officers. White belts, green sabretasches edged yellow bearing yellow crowned 'CF'. Dark green shabraque edged yellow. Trumpeters had red plumes and wore reversed colours. The regiment was destroyed in Russia in 1812.

Plate 5   *Grand Duchy of Baden: 1807 Cavalry*
(*l to r*)   Troopers, Garde du Corps (red facings; sabretasche and saddle furniture, red waist sash and plume base), hussar officer (dark green plume with red base, dark green dolman and pelisse, red collar and breeches, gold lace and buttons), officer, Garde du Corps (as above but with silver, red and yellow sash), hussar trooper (as above but black fur to pelisse). After *Charackteristiche Darstellung der vorzuglichsten europaischen Militars* by J. M. Voltz, referred to as the *Augsburger Bilder.*

Leichtes Dragoner-Regiment

Raised in 1800 from a squadron of Bavarian Chevaux Légers. Original uniform in Baden's service—bicorns, white plumes, light blue tunics with red collar, cuffs, lapels and turnbacks, white buttons, lace, breeches and

94

Plate 6   Grand Duchy of Baden: 1807 Artillery
(*l to r*)   Officer, rear view (gilt helmet fittings, black crest, dark blue coat, black facings edged red, red turnbacks, gold buttons, sabre and sheath), two gunners (as above). *Augsburger Bilder.*

belts; high, cuffed boots. In 1805 the men were issued with Bavarian cavalry-style Raupenhelm with white fittings (crowned oval plate with 'CF'), black crest, white plume. Officers also adopted the helmet in 1808 when also the white lace to collar, lapels and cuffs was abandoned. Grey overalls were worn off parades. In 1810 the lapels were removed and the coat had two rows of white buttons on the front.

Battle History

1806—Küstrin and Stettin; 1807—⚔ Friedland (with 2nd Division X Corps); 1808–1813—the 4th Infantry Regiment in Spain as part of the 'German Division'; 1809—with the Grande Armée (part of 1st Division, IV Corps) in Vorarlberg, ⚔ Aspern; ⚔ Raab; ⚔ Wagram and ⚔ Znaim; 1812—in Russia as part of 26th Division, IX Corps, destroyed at the Beresina crossing; 1813 —in Saxony with Ney's Corps.

Bavaria

Electorate until 1806 thence kingdom

(Cockade light blue within white)

Rank Badges 1789

Generals
Cocked hat with cockade, gold brooch, loop, button and cords. Rank shown by number of lapel buttons each with matching gold/silver buttonholes and tassels. 'Inhabers' (Colonels-in-Chief of regiments) also had embroidered buttonholes to sides of collars. General—five lapel buttons with embroidery, silver and light blue sash and sword knot, high boots. Lieutenant-general—as above but four buttons and buttonholes, coat tails knee length; facings shown on turnbacks. Major-general—as above but three lapel buttons and buttonholes. All carried gold topped canes.

Field officers
Rumford Kasket (see below) with regimental hair crest; cane and sabre knot as above. Colonel—five lapel buttons with matching buttonholes but no tassels. Lieutenant-colonel—four; Major—three.

Junior officers
Captain—as above but five lapel buttons with buttonholes embroidered in silk in the lapel colour. Lieutenant—four; Second lieutenant—three.

NCOs
Short coat skirts turned over only at the front; five lapel buttons, rank being shown by the number of embroidered buttonholes. Sergeant-major—five white embroidered buttonholes, white and light blue sabre strap with red wreath, gold topped cane. Quartermaster—the top four buttonholes embroidered, white and light blue sabre strap, cane. Sergeant—the top three, cane and white and light blue sabre strap. Corporal—the top two, hazelnut stick, white and blue sabre strap. Private—plain buttonholes. Until 1793 the hair was still powdered.

Line Infantry

Black leather 'Rumford Kasket' with low crown, leather crest, brass front plate terminating at the sides in round chinstrap bosses and at the top front of the combe in a lion's head and bearing the Bavarian crest, horizontal black peak extending all around the head, long in front, narrow at sides and rear. The drooping, horse hair plume was white for grenadiers, black for fusiliers and garrison regiments.

Short-skirted white tunic with half lapels, standing collar, cut away front and false white waistcoat, round cuffs and skirts turned back only at the front. Facings were shown on collar, lapel, cuffs and turnbacks. On the shoulders were black, fringeless epaulettes with brass half moon and brass chain around the strap. Grey Hungarian breeches with hussar style black

Plate 7   *Kingdom of Bavaria: 1806 Infantry Regiment 'Herzog Karl'*
(*l to r*)   Lieutenant of fusiliers (cornflower blue coat, red facings, yellow buttons, white piping, silver and light blue sash), grenadiers (red plumes, otherwise as above). *Augsburger Bilder*.

gaiters (permanently attached), closing with black leather buttons. White belts, black pouches, calfskin packs.

Drummers' facings were edged with a diced light blue and silver lace; the Drum Major's top lapel buttonhole was embroidered in white silk. The facings and buttons were as follows:

97

	a (facings)	b (buttons)
1st Grenadier and Lieb-Infanterie-Regiment	a light blue	b white
2nd Grenadier-Regiment (Kurprinz)	a light blue	b yellow
3rd Grenadier-Regiment (Graf Ysenburg)	a dark blue	b white
4th Grenadier-Regiment (Baaden)	a dark blue	b yellow
1st Füsilier-Regiment (Herzog von Zweibrücken)	a red	b white
2nd Füsilier-Regiment (Prinz Wilhelm von Birkenfeld)	a red	b yellow
3rd Füsilier-Regiment (Rodenhausen)	a brick red	b white
4th Füsilier-Regiment (de la Motte)	a brick red	b yellow
5th Füsilier-Regiment (von Wahl)	a yellow	b white
6th Füsilier-Regiment (Pfalzgraf Max)	a yellow	b yellow
7th Füsilier-Regiment (von Zedtwitz)	a green	b white
8th Füsilier-Regiment (von Rambaldi)	a green	b yellow
9th Füsilier-Regiment (von Weichs)	a peach red	b white
10th Füsilier-Regiment (Joseph Hohenhausen)	a peach red	b yellow
11th Füsilier-Regiment (von Preysing)	a crimson	b white
12th Füsilier-Regiment (von Belderbusch)	a crimson	b yellow
13th Füsilier-Regiment (Moritz von Isenburg)	a black	b white
14th Füsilier-Regiment (von Kling)	a black	b yellow

In 1799 this impractical economy uniform was abandoned and the new, more conventional coat reverted to the traditional Bavarian cornflower blue. The Rumford Kasket was replaced by an equally impractical, very high crowned black leather helmet (Raupenhelm) with 'sausage' crest (of black wool for privates and corporals, bearskin for senior NCOs and officers). The oval brass front plate bore the electoral cypher 'MJ' and was topped with an

Plate 8 Kingdom of Bavaria: 1806 Foot Artillery
Red plumes, dark blue coats, red facings and piping, yellow buttons and shoulder scales. *Augsburger Bilder.*

electoral cap. Over the peak was a brass band with a star in the centre; it terminated in the brass chinstrap bosses holding the black leather chinstrap edged in fine brass chains. There was an eye and neck shield. Small clothes were white, gaiters black.

Until 1805 officers wore cocked hats with cockade, brooch button and loop, thence a finer version of the Raupenhelm described above. From 1800–1812 they wore silver and light blue waist sashes. In 1803 the Grenadier company of each battalion adopted a short red plume above the cockade over the left hand chinstrap boss.

Fusiliers had a small, woollen tuft in the following company colours: 1st—white; 2nd—white and yellow; 3rd—green; 4th—green and yellow. In 1804 the light companies were given a short green plume worn as for grenadiers.

Drummers' facings were edged in wide lace in the button colour as were their red swallows' nest which bore the electoral crest. On each sleeve were four yellow chevrons point up and the sleeve seams were also edged in yellow tape. They wore large red plumes. Drums were brass, hoops light blue and white.

Plate 9   Kingdom of Bavaria: 1806 Chevau Légers and Dragoons
(*l to r*) Officer of unidentified regiment drinking, trooper, 2nd Chevau Légers Regiment 'König' (white plume, light green coat, red facings, yellow buttons), trooper, 1st Dragoons 'Minucci' (red facings, white buttons). *Augsburger Bilder.*

Plate 10   Kingdom of Bavaria: 1806 Chevau Légers and Dragoons
(*l to r*) Trooper, 4th Chevau Légers (light green coat, black facings edged red, white buttons and shoulder scales), rittmeister (captain), 2nd Chevau Légers 'König' (light green coat, red facings, yellow buttons, silver and light blue waist sash and bandolier), lieutenant, 1st Dragoons 'Minucci' (red facings, white buttons, sash and bandolier as before). *Augsburger Bilder.*

The infantry regiments were allotted numbers in 1806 and these may be seen in the following table of facings (valid from 1800–1806). Facings were worn on collar, cuffs and lapels, turnbacks were red.

		a (facings)	b (buttons)
1	Leib-regiment	a black (red from 1802) with wide white buttonhole laces	b white
2	Kurprinz	a black (red from 1802) with wide yellow buttonhole laces	b yellow
3	Herzog Karl	a red	b yellow
4	von Weichs	a sulphur yellow	b white
5	von Preysing	a pink with red edging	b white
6	Herzog Wilhelm	a red	b white
7	von Morawitzky	a white	b yellow
8	Herzog Pius	a sulphur yellow	b yellow
9	Graf von Ysenburg	a scarlet	b yellow
10	von Junker	a crimson	b white
11	von Kinkel*	a black	b yellow

*In 1806 this regiment was transferred to the Grand Duchy of Berg; a new 11th was raised in 1807, disbanded in 1811 and yet another 11th (Kinkel) was raised in 1813.

A new system of rank badges was introduced; for infantry and cavalry officers and cavalry NCOs it consisted of laces and edgings to the collar, canes and sword knots. Officers wore sashes as before. Colonel—bicorn, broad gold or silver lace edging to top and front of collar (button colour) and three gold/silver stripes to each side. Lieutenant-colonel—as above but two stripes; Major—as above, one stripe. Captain—Raupenhelm with bearskin crest and gilt fittings; no collar edging but three stripes. Lieutenant—as for Captain but two stripes. Second lieutenant—one stripe. NCOs—as before but bearskin helmet crests.

In 1806 infantry facings changed as shown below:

1st	as before	
2nd	as before	
3rd	white piping added to facings	
4th	red piping added to facings	
5th	as before	
6th	white piping added to facings	
7th	a—pink	
8th	red piping added to facings	
9th	collar poppy red, lapels and cuffs yellow, red piping added to facings	
10th	a—collar poppy red, lapels and cuffs yellow, red piping added to facings	
11th	(1807–1811) a—collar poppy red, lapels and cuffs green, red piping added to facings	b white
12th	disbanded in 1806 very shortly after having been raised	
13th	a—black, red piping added to facings (collar red from 1806)	b—white
14th	a—red collar, black lapels and cuffs, red piping added to facings	b—yellow

In 1811 the 13th Regiment was renumbered 11th and the 14th became the 13th. On 15 April 1812 officers discarded the sash and adopted the golden gorget with silver crest as a sign of office. In 1814 all regiments received red facings and were distinguished only by their number on the brass buttons.

In 1814 new 12th and 14th Regiments were raised as was the Garde-Grenadiere. This latter unit wore bearskin bonnets with brass plate, white cords, red top patch with white cross, white and light blue plumes. Coat as for the Line but with white lace buttonholes, white grenades in the turnback corners and white buttons bearing a grenade. At this point the 1st and 2nd Line regiments lost their distinctive buttonhole decoration.

Light Infantry 1790–1799

Light green coats, black crest to helmet, otherwise as for the Line infantry.
1st Feldjäger-Regiment (von Schweicheldt) a (facings)—black b (buttons)—white.
2nd Feldjäger-Regiment (Fürst Ysenburg) a—black b—yellow.

In 1799 the 'Rumford' uniform was abandoned and the style of coat was as for the line infantry but in light green (changed to dark green in 1809) with the high leather Raupenhelm. Lapels and cuffs were black piped red, turnbacks red, breeches were grey. The elite company had green plumes on the left side of the Raupenhelm, the small pompon badges of the other companies were: 1st—white; 2nd—green; 3rd—red; 4th—blue; 5th—yellow. In 1811 Karabinier companies were raised which wore red plumes.

The new Light Battalions' title changes were as follows:
1 1801 Metzen: raised from 2nd Feldjägers; 1804 1st Leichte Infanterie Bataillon 'Metzen' a (collar)—red b (buttons)—yellow. 1807 Habermann. 1809 1st Gedoni. 1811 Hertling then Fick. 1815 Fortis.
2 1801 Clossmann: raised from 1st Feldjägers, 1804 2nd Vicenti a—red b—yellow; 1805 Ditfurth; 1808 Wreden; 1811 Treuberg then Merz; 1815 Sebus.
3 1801 1st Salern: raised from 2nd Feldjägers; 1804 3rd Preysing a—black edged red b—white; 1808 Bernclau; 1811 Scherer; 1813 used to form the new 12th Line Infantry Regiment together with the 1st and 2nd Battalions of the Würzburg Infantry Regiment.
4 1801 2nd Salern: raised from 2nd Feld jägers; 1804 4th Stengel a—black edged red b—yellow; 1806 Zoller; 1807 Wreden; 1809 Donnersperg; 1810 Theobald; 1813 Cronegg; 1815 used to form the new 1st Battalion, 16th Line Infantry Regiment.
5 1803 de la Motte; a—crimson (crimson lapels and cuffs until 1806 when they became black edged red) b—white. 1806 the battalion absorbed the disbanded infantry battalion of the Reichstadt Nürnberg; 1807 Dalwigk; 1808 Buttler; 1812 Herrmann; 1814 Treuberg. In 1815 this unit became 2nd Battalion 16th Line Infantry Regiment.
6 1803 Lessel; 1804 6th Lessel then Weinbach; 1806 Taxis. Initially all facings crimson but later in 1806 the collar became lemon yellow edged red, cuffs and lapels black edged red, buttons yellow. 1809 La Roche; 1812 Palm; 1814 Flad. The unit was then used to form the new 14th Line Infantry Regiment together with the 1st and 2nd Battalions of the Frankfurt Infantry Regiment.
7 1808 7th Günter a—light blue edged red b—white.
8 1807 A Tyroler Jäger-Bataillon was raised; it wore black shako with cockade loop and button, dark green coat and lining, no lapels, light blue collar and cuffs edged dark green, white buttons, grey breeches, black belts, dark green shoulder straps edged light blue.

Artillery 1790
Line infantry uniform with black helmet crest, dark blue coat, black facings and yellow buttons. 1799 changes as for the line infantry, black facings, yellow buttons.

Engineers
As for artillery.

Train
Uniform 1800 Raupenhelm, grey, single-breasted tunic and breeches, light blue facings, white buttons, black bandoliers.

Cavalry

The 1790 uniform was of infantry cut with white helmet crest, white coats and collars for Kürassiers and dragoons with facings on lapels, round cuffs and on turnback edgings; light green coat and collar and cuffs cut out at an angle across the top for Chevau Légers. White waistcoats and belts, breeches grey for Chevau Légers, yellow for Kürassiers and dragoons. Saddle furniture was red for Kürassiers and dragoons edged in light blue and white dicing; grey edged white for Chevau Légers. Kürassiers wore no Kürass.

In 1800 they received the new high-crowned Raupenhelm of infantry pattern but with two brass reinforcing struts to either side, cockade and white plume. New style coat but in white with white collar; facings on lapels, cuffs and turnback edging; white metal scale epaulettes. Weapons were curved sabre with steel hilt and brown leather sheath, pistols and a carbine. Kürassiers and dragoons had German saddles and harness, Chevau Légers Hungarian all in black with white fittings. Officers' bandoliers and sabre slings were silver edged in the facing colour.

In November 1809 the Chevau Légers' coat changed from light green to dark green; in the green turnback corners were white crowns and rampant lions. Breeches were white and worn in below-knee, straight-lopped boots. Long, grey buttoned overalls were often worn over these items.

In 1804 the last remaining Kürassier Regiment was converted to dragoons, in 1811 the two dragoon regiments were converted to Chevau Légers (thus making six regiments in all). The National Chevau Légers was raised in spring 1813, became the 7th Chevau Légers, 'Prinz Karl von Bayern' on 12 August that year and in 1815 was converted to the 1st Kürassier-Regiment.

Also in 1813 a lancer regiment was raised and in 1814 it absorbed the Würzburg Chevau Légers Division and the Frankfurt-Aschaffenburg hussars.

The National Chevau Légers wore a shako with cockade loop and button, single-breasted dark green tunic with light blue collar, cuffs and piping, white buttons. As Kürassiers they wore steel helmets with combe and peaks, black crest, brown fur turban, steel Kürasses of French pattern with red cuff trimmed white, cornflower blue tunics, red facings, white buttons, steel contre-epaulettes.

The 2nd Kürassiers wore the same but with yellow buttons and the Garde du Corps (raised 1814) had a uniform as for the 1st Kürassiers but with brass helmet and Kürass.

The lancers wore uniform of Austrian (Polish) pattern with yellow top and white plume to czapka, dark green kurtka with light blue facings and piping (changed to red in 1814), white buttons and shoulder scales, white and cornflower blue striped waist sash, green overalls with light blue (later red) side stripes, black leather booting. Lance pennant white over cornflower blue.

The hussars (raised December 1813) wore traditional Hungarian costume and in 1815 the regiment was split into two. The 1st wore black shakos, the new 2nd red—both had cornflower blue dolmans, pelisse and breeches, white lace and buttons, blue and white barrel sashes, black fur, white belts, black sabretasche with white crowned cypher 'MJK'. Shabraque light blue edged white, black Hungarian harness with white fittings. Shako plumes were white over light blue, cords white.

Bavarian Cavalry Regiments and their History 1790–1815

1   1790 1st Kürassier-Regiment Minucci; 1804 converted to 1st Dragoner-Regiment Minucci; 1811 1st Chevau Légers-Regiment.
2   1790 2nd Kürassier-Regiment Winckelhausen; 1799 converted to 4th Chevau Légers-Regiment then to 1st Chevau Légers-Regiment Kurfürst; 1804 renumbered 2nd Regiment; 1806 title changed to König; 1811 4th Chevau Légers-Regiment König.
3   1790 1st Dragoner-Regiment (Leibdragoner); 1801 vacant; disbanded 1803.
4   1790 2nd Dragoner-Regiment (Taxis); 1806 absorbed the Nürnberg cavalry and the Prussian Husaren-Bataillon von Bila; 1811 converted to 2nd Chevau Légers-Regiment Taxis.
5   1790 1st Chevau Légers-Regiment Prinz Leiningen; 1799 renumbered 4th; 1804 renumbered 3rd; 1811 renumbered 5th.
6   1790 2nd Chevau Légers-Regiment La Rosee; 1799 3rd Chevau Légers-Regiment vacant Fürst Bretzenheim; disbanded 1801, men transferred to 2nd Chevau Légers (Fugger).
7   1790 3rd Chevau Légers-Regiment Wahl; 1799 2nd Chevau Légers-Regiment Fugger; 1804 1st Chevau Légers-Regiment Kurprinz; 1806 title changed to Kronprinz; 1811 renumbered 3rd Chevau Légers.
8   1803 4th Chevau Légers-Regiment Bubenhofen raised from the Würzburg Dragoner-Regiment Bubenhofen and the Würzburg Husaren-Kompagnie two squadrons of Bamberg-Dragoner and the Bamberg-Husaren-Eskadron; 1811 renumbered 6th.

Bavarian Cavalry Regimental Facings 1790–1815

			a (facings)	b (buttons)
1	1st Kürassiers	1790	a scarlet, collar in the coat colour	b white (retained until 1815)
2	2nd Kürassiers	1790	a scarlet, collar in the coat colour	b yellow (retained these until 1815)
3	Leibdragoner 1803 disbanded	1790	a black, collar in the coat colour	b white
4	2nd Dragoner Taxis	1790	a black, collar as for lapels, cuffs and turnback edgings	b yellow
		1811	a red	b yellow
5	1st Chevau Légers Leiningen	1790	a black, collar in the coat colour	b white
		1811	a red, collar as for lapels, cuffs and turnback edgings	b yellow
6	2nd Chevau Légers La Rosee 1811 disbanded	1790	a black	b yellow
7	3rd Chevau Légers Wahl	1790	a apple green, collar in the coat colour	b white
		1811	a black edged red, collar as for lapels, cuffs and turnback edgings	b yellow
8	4th Chevau Légers	1803	a black edged red, collar as for lapels, cuffs and turnback edgings	b white

Battle History

1800—⚔ Hohenlinden (against France); 1805—in Bavaria (with France against Austria); 1806—against Prussia; 1809—Tyrol; ⚔ Aspern, ⚔ Wagram VIII Corps Grande Armée; 1812—Russia as VI Corps Grande Armée; 1813 —Saxony as VI Corps until the Armistice thence with the Allies against as France ⚔ Hanau; 1814—France; 1815—France.

DUCHY OF

Brunswick

(Cockade black)

The uniforms of Brunswick's troops until 1806 were entirely Prussian; in that year there were two infantry regiments in bicorns, dark blue coats, white belts, small clothes, black gaiters. The 1st Regiment 'Warmstedt' had red facings, white lace and yellow buttons; the 2nd 'Griesheim' had red facings, lapels edged in white lace having a blue worm and white buttons. Grenadiers wore fur caps with plates in the button colour and backing in the facing colour edged in the button colour.

Following the French victories at Jena and Auerstädt on 14 October 1806, Brunswick was dissolved and incorporated into the new Kingdom of Westfalia until late in 1813.

When Austria again took up arms against Napoleon in 1809 the dispossessed Duke Friedrich Wilhelm of Brunswick raised a legion of all arms in Bohemia under Austrian patronage and invaded Westfalia, subsequently making his way to England where his corps was taken into British service until 1815. The 1809 uniforms were as follows.

Infantry Regiment (three battalions)
Black Austrian shako with tall drooping black horsehair plume and white metal skull and crossbones badge, black chinstrap (some had white metal chinscales), black, single-breasted Litewka with full, knee-length skirts, light blue collar, seven rows of black cord frogging on the chest, black glass buttons, black trousers and belts. Rank badges seemed to have been limited to silver and yellow sabre straps; officers carried sabres in black and steel sheaths on black slings. Drummers had black swallows' nests edged gold; brass drums with light blue and yellow hoops.

Scharfschützen-Kompagnie (Sharpshooter Company)
Black Corsican hat with the left hand brim turned up, green edging, headband and loop, dark green, double-breasted tunic of Prussian style with red collar, shoulder straps, turnbacks and round cuffs, yellow buttons, black belts, white (or grey) trousers. This unit was armed with rifles. Officers wore shakos as for the infantry regiment but with black cock feather plumes and had a gold aiguillette on the right shoulder.

Hussar Regiment

Infantry shako but with brass chinscales, black dolman with black lace and five rows of black buttons, light blue collar and cuffs, light blue and yellow sash, black button overalls, belts and sabretasche. Black saddle furniture with light blue edging and white skull and bones badge, black harness with brass fittings. Trumpeters had black swallows' nests trimmed gold and blue and gold trumpet cords.

Lancer Squadron

Austrian uniform, ie yellow topped czapka, with small white skull and bones badge on the front of the black lower half, dark green kurtka and overalls faced red with yellow buttons. Black belts, lance pennant yellow over red.

Artillery Battery

As for the infantry but with short-skirted tunics with black lace and buttons and light blue collar, cuffs, shoulder straps and turnbacks.

In British service (1809–15) the uniforms remained basically the same but British rank badges were adopted and the Litewka gave way to a short-skirted black tunic with black lace frogging and buttons. NCOs wore crimson and light blue waist sashes, officers crimson. Hussars adopted light blue and crimson waist sashes (gold and crimson for officers). The Sharpshooter company discarded the Corsican hat in favour of the infantry shako and changed their facings from red to light blue.

In 1814 the Duke re-entered his homeland and raised a new army; by 1815 it consisted of the following units.

Light Infantry

Avantgarde

Including two companies of Gelernte Jäger—black Corsican hat with green headband, binding, loop and plume, white metal springing horse badge on upturned left brim-side; grey, single-breasted coat with dark green collar, shoulder straps, round cuffs and turnbacks, white buttons bearing the springing horse badge, grey trousers, black belts. Officers had silver hat edging and drooping green cock feather plume, silver edging to collar and cuffs, no shoulder straps. Black bandolier, silver and yellow sabre knot and waist sash.

Two companies of light infantry—uniform as above except white hat trim and white hunting horn badge, black dolman with dark green collar, shoulder straps and Polish cuffs, black buttons and frogging, black trousers with green stripe.

Leib-Bataillon

1809 pattern shako, black dolman with light blue collar and shoulder straps, black frogging and buttons (three rows), black trousers and belts. NCOs wore British rank chevrons in silver and light blue and yellow waist sashes and sabre knots. Officers had feather plumes, black embroidery to collars and five rows of buttons on the chest; majors and above had black bandoliers with silver picker equipment and silver 'FW' to the black pouch lid. Drummers had swallows' nest in black trimmed and edged in the facing colour, drums as before.

1st–3rd Light Battalions

Shako with yellow over light blue, pear-shaped pompon, black cockade, white stringed bugle horn 'hanging' from an oval plate bearing the battalion number, black leather chinscales. Black, waist length tunic as for the Leib-Bataillon but with facings as follows: 1st Battalion—buff (red from 1 July 1815); 2nd—yellow; 3rd—orange. Black belts and trousers.

Line Infantry

1st—3rd Line Infantry Battalions

Uniform as for the three light battalions except: shako pompon light blue over yellow, half round white metal shako plate bearing the springing horse under the motto 'nunquam retrorsum' under an oval with the battalion number. Facings: 1st Battalion—red; 2nd—green; 3rd—white.

Reserve Infantry

1st–5th Battalions—a Landwehr formation.

Cavalry

Hussar Regiment
Uniform as in 1809.

Lancer Squadron
Light blue czapka top, black kurtka and breeches faced light blue, white buttons and small skull and bones badge to front of czapka.

Artillery

Horse Artillery Battery
As for hussars except: brass grenade under skull and bones shako badge, black collars and cuffs edged yellow, yellow trouser side stripes.

Foot Artillery Battery
As for horse artillery except: no white skull and bones badge to shako, yellow pompon (plume for officers), infantry style tunics with black collar and cuffs outlined yellow.

Foot Artillery Train
Foot artillery shako, dark grey tunic and breeches, black collar and cuffs edged yellow; black belts.

Horse Artillery Train
Horse artillery shako but with brass grenade badge, yellow lace decoration to collar and cuffs, yellow grenades on black turnbacks; black bandolier and pouch with brass grenade badge.

Battle History

1806—✗ Jena; 1809—invasion of Westfalia; 1810–13 Spain ✗ Fuentes d'Oñoro, ✗ Vittoria, ✗ Maya, ✗ Roncesvalles, ✗ Sorauren (1st and 2nd); ✗ Nive, ✗ Orthez; 1815— ✗ Quatre-Bras, ✗ Waterloo.

Danzig

Established by Napoleon on 28 October 1807, absorbed into Prussian Poland in November 1813.

Troops consisted of a battalion in dark blue coats and breeches, white facings, belts and buttons, black gaiters; grenadiers wore bearskins with red top patches having a white central spot, musketeers wore French shakos.

Battle History

Siege of Danzig, January–November 1813.

KINGDOM OF

Denmark

1792 – 1815

Until 1814 Norway belonged to Denmark and its troops are listed below up to that point, from 1814 on there was a personal union between Norway and Sweden which lasted until 1905.

Generals wore large bicorns trimmed gold, red coats, faced light blue with gold buttons and embroidery to collar, lapels and cuffs. White small clothes, gold and crimson waist sash and sword knot.

Infantry

Black 'top hat' with left-hand brim turned up, held by regimental button with a regimental loop extending to the top of the crown where there was a white plume. Red tunic of Russian 1792 pattern with facings shown on collar, straight lapels, cuffs, red cuff flaps, small white turnbacks to front of short skirts, white belts and waistcoats. Summer legwear was a light grey combined trouser-gaiter as in Russia. Grenadiers wore Prussian-style caps with black leather front plate trimmed with a white crest from ear to ear, pointed brass front band, black peak. On the left side was a white plume with a coloured tip and a bag in the facing colour hung to the rear.

Officers wore more conventional, long-skirted tunics with lapels which widened out at the tops; small bicorns with white plumes; gold and crimson waist sashes and sword knots, white waistcoat and breeches, boots.

Regimental distinctions in 1800 were as follows.

	a (collar, cuffs and lapels)	b (piping to facings)	c (buttons)
Garde	a light blue (no lapels)	b none	c white
Danish Leib-Regiment	a light yellow	b none	c white
Norwegian Leib-Regiment	a light yellow	b white	c white
König	a light blue	b none	c white
Königin	a light blue	b none	c yellow
Kronprinz	a light blue	b white	c white

Erbprinz Friedrich	*a* green	*b* none	*c* white
Fünen	*a* white	*b* none	*c* white
Seeland	*a* green	*b* white	*c* white
1st Jutland	*a* black	*b* white	*c* yellow
2nd Jutland	*a* white	*b* none	*c* yellow
3rd Jutland	*a* black	*b* white	*c* white
Oldenburg	*a* green	*b* none	*c* white
Schleswig	a light blue	*b* white	*c* yellow
Holstein	*a* green	*b* white	*c* yellow

Grenadier and sharpshooter companies of the line regiments were equipped with sabres, the centre companies only had bayonets.

In 1807 the Garde had bearskins and by 1813 a French-style shako with pompon, cockade, loop, button and white cords was worn by the line regiments. The cuffs on their tunics were now in the pointed, Polish style without flaps and dark grey breeches and black gaiters were worn.

The Jäger regiments wore line infantry uniforms but in dark green with black facings piped white. Their elite companies (Grenadier-Jäger) wore the grenadier cap but with black crest, green bag and red-tipped green plume. Jäger coat turnbacks were white, belts black.

They were armed partially with rifles (elite companies), partially with muskets.

Artillery

Line infantry uniform with dark blue facings, turnbacks and breeches and high black gaiters; buttons were yellow and there was no piping to the facings.

Cavalry

Guards Cavalry

Leibgarde til Hest—black, British-style light dragoon helmet with black crest, red and silver turban, white plumes with red tip to left side of helmet. Yellow, single-breasted tunic with red collar and cuffs and silver lace edging; yellow breeches, high boots. Black belts, red sabretasche edged silver and bearing the crowned royal cypher 'C7' (Christian VII).

Heavy Cavalry

Large bicorn with loop, button, corner tassels and white plume, red tunic of infantry cut, yellow turnbacks, regimental facings and buttons, buff leather breeches and Hungarian boots. For everyday wear these were replaced by dark blue button overalls. White belts and gauntlets; heavy, straight sword with brass hilt in black and yellow sheath, carbines, red shabrack edged white, black harness. Officers' coat skirts were long.

In 1801 the facings were as follows (all buttons were white):

	a (collar, cuffs and lapels)	*b (piping to facings)*
Leib-reiterregiment	*a* yellow	*b* none
Seeland	*a* dark blue	*b* none
Schleswig	*a* light blue	*b* none
Holstein	*a* light green	*b* yellow

Light Dragoons

Helmet as for the guards cavalry but with turban in the facing colour

Plate 11   Kingdom of Denmark: Infantry 1801
(*l to r*) Private, Regiment Kronprinz (red coat, light blue facings, white buttons, piping and turnbacks), officer, Regiment Seeland (red coat, green facings, white piping, buttons and turnbacks), private, 1st Jutland Regiment (seated), (red coat, black facings, white piping and turnbacks, yellow buttons), private, Danish Leib-regiment (seated), (red coat, buff facings, white cuff flap piping, turnbacks and buttons). *Augsburger Bilder*.

(the Leib-regiment had a red turban), red tunic of infantry cut but with officer-style lapels (widening out at the tops), yellow skirt turnbacks, white belts and gauntlets, white breeches and hussar boots or dark blue button overalls, carbines and curved sabres in black and steel sheath, pistols. Red shabrack trimmed white, black harness.

109

Plate 12   Kingdom of Denmark: Cavalry 1801
(*l to r*) Trooper, Holstein Heavy Cavalry (red coat, light green facings, white
buttons, yellow piping and turnbacks, red tip to plume), trooper (standing) Leibgarde
(yellow tunic, red facings, turban, plume tip and sabretasche inner ground, silver
lace), hussar trooper (obscured), (black Mirliton withm white trim, light blue
dolman with crimson collar and cuffs, white lace and buttons, crimson pelisse, white
breeches, crimson Scharawaden trimmed white, sabretasche as before). *Augsburger
Bilder.*

In 1800 the facings were as follows (all buttons white):

	a (collar, cuffs and lapels)	b (piping)
Leib-regiment	a black	b yellow
Jutland	a green	b none
Fünen	a light blue	b yellow

Hussars

Black Mirliton (winged cap) with white trim and plume, light blue dolman with crimson collar and cuffs, crimson pelisse with black fur, white lace and buttons, white and crimson sash, buff leather breeches and hussar boots.

Over the breeches were worn crimson 'Scharawaden' (thigh stockings) decorated white. Brown belts, crimson saddle furniture and sabretasche, the latter edged white and bearing 'C7' in white. Curved sabres in steel sheaths, carbine and pistols.

Mounted Feldjäger

As for foot Jägers but with yellow skirt turnbacks.

Bosniaks

Oriental costume—red fez with white turban, long, light blue coat and wide breeches both trimmed red, hussar boots, lances, curved sabres, pistols and carbines, light blue saddle furniture trimmed red.

In 1808 the Bosniaks were converted to lancers with red-topped czapka, light blue kurtka with red facings and white buttons.

Norwegian Regiments

The Norwegian regiments of the Danish army were as follows:

Infantry

Söndenfjaeldske, Nordenfjaeldske (both full time regiments) 1st and 2nd Akershusske, Oplandske, Telemarkske, Vesterlenske, Bergenhusske, 1st and 2nd Trondhjemske (all 'national' or volunteer regiments), the Norske Jägerkorps, Nordenfjaeldske ski battalion, the Leirdalske light infantry company and the Rörosske volunteer mountain corps.

Cavalry

Four dragoon regiments – Akershusske, Smaalenske, Oplandske and Trondhjemske.

Artillery

One brigade.

France

Republic from 1792 – 1804 thence Empire

(Cockade blue within white within red)

Rank Badges

Generals

Large cocked hat with cut white feather edging, gold lace edging, loop and button, blue within white within red cockade, gold hat tassels in the corners. Dark blue double-breasted coat with red collar and cuffs for parades, blue for daily wear, gold buttons, gold embroidery around collar, cuffs and horizontal pocket flaps, single for Generals de Brigade, double for Generals de Division; gold epaulettes with heavy bullion fringes bearing two five-pointed stars for a General de Brigade, three for a General de Division, crossed batons within a ring of silver stars for a Marshal of France. White waistcoat and breeches, high black boots, buckle-on steel spurs. Badge of office was a wide silk waist sash striped with gold and having gold tassels tied on the left side. Colouring was according to rank: Marshal—white, General de Division—red, General de Brigade—light blue.

Commissioned Officers

Colonel—bicorn; two gold/silver epaulettes with heavy bullion fringes, gold portepee. Major—shako with gold/silver top band, side chevrons and cords, two epaulettes in gold/silver with fringes in the reversed colours; gold portepee. Chef de Bataillon—as for colonel but with a shako as for major and only the left epaulette is fringed. Captain—as above but with thin epaulette fringes. Adjutant-major—as for captain but the right epaulette is fringed. Lieutenant—as for captain but with single red line along epaulette strap. Sub-lieutenant—as for lieutenant but with two red lines along the epaulette straps. Adjutant—as for sub-lieutenant but with two white/yellow lines across the epaulette strap and the epaulette fringes mixed with red.

Officers of hussars and Chasseurs à Cheval did not wear epaulettes but their ranks were indicated by numbers of gold/silver chevrons above the pointed cuffs and around the elaborate thigh knots on the Hungarian breeches.

Except where otherwise stated the belts and the 'small clothes' (waistcoats, trousers) were white, gaiters were white in summer, black in winter.

NCOs

Maréchal des logis chef—red and gold/silver (the button colour) mixed shako cords and epaulette fringes; two gold/silver diagonal bars* on the lower sleeves on red backing. Maréchal des logis—as above but only one gold/silver bar* on lower sleeves. Fourrier—one gold bar* on the upper left arm; two red bars* on orange backing on the lower sleeves. Corporal—two red bars* on orange backing on the lower sleeves.

Years of service were indicated by red chevrons, point up, on the left upper arm.

*In units with Polish (pointed) cuffs these bars were replaced by chevrons, point up.

Guard Infantry

In 1791 a 'Garde Constitutionelle' was raised which had white edging on their bicorns, dark blue coats with red lapels, cuffs and turnbacks. In 1792 this was renamed the 'Garde de la Convention' and in 1799 the Consular Guard was raised to guard the headquarters of the Consuls; it was from this latter formation that the famous Imperial Guard was later raised. Grenadiers of the Consular Guard wore black bearskins with brass plate, yellow cords, red plume, red top patch with white cross, cockade, dark blue coat with similar collar, square cut white lapels, red cuffs with trident shaped white cuff flaps (French cuffs), long skirts with red turnbacks with yellow grenade badges and a copper grenade badge on the lid of the black cartridge pouch. Yellow buttons, red epaulettes.

The Imperial Guard (1804–15)
All guard units wore the imperial eagle on their buttons.

1st and 2nd Foot Regiments
As for Grenadiers of the Consular Guard but with white cords to the bearskin. The bearskin plate bore the imperial eagle between two flaming grenades. The top of the bearskin was red with a white woollen grenade. Red epaulettes.

3rd Foot Regiment (raised in 1810 from the disbanded Dutch army)
Bearskin with no front plate; white cords; red plume and top patch with white cross; white coats, crimson collar, lapels, cuffs and turnbacks, vertical pockets with crimson piped flaps, white cuff flaps, yellow grenades in the turnback corners, yellow buttons, red epaulettes.

Chasseurs
As for 1st and 2nd Grenadiers except: no bearskin plate, red over green plume, lapel bottoms pointed; red Polish cuffs piped white; turnback badges a yellow grenade and a yellow hunting horn, green epaulettes with red fringes.

Fusilier Grenadiers (1806–14)
As for 1st and 2nd Grenadiers except: white epaulettes with two red lines along the straps. Shako with white cords and side struts, red plume, brass imperial eagle badge and chinscales.

Fusilier-Chasseurs (1806–14)
As for Chasseurs except: shako with white cords and red over green plume.

Tirailleur Grenadiers (1809–14)
Shako with white side struts, red cords and red over white plume; short-skirted blue tunic, red collar piped blue; pointed blue lapels, red Polish cuffs,

red shoulder straps and red turnbacks (bearing a white eagle) all edged white, white piping to vertical pocket flaps.

Tirailleur Chasseurs (1809)
As for Tirailleur Grenadiers except: white cords and green ball pompon to shako, green shoulder straps edged red, green eagles on the turnbacks.

Voltigeur-Chasseurs (1810–14)
As for Fusilier-Chasseurs except: white piping to lapels, yellow collar, white hunting horns in the turnback corners, yellow buttons, green epaulettes with yellow crescents.

Flanquer Grenadiers (1812–14)
Shako with white side struts, red cords, and red over yellow ball pompon, green Spencer, green collar, shoulder straps and lapels, red cuffs all edged yellow, yellow piping to vertical pocket flaps, white eagles in the red turnbacks, yellow buttons, no sabres.

Flanquer Chasseurs (1812–14)
As for Flanquer Grenadiers except: white cords and yellow over green pear-shaped pompon to shako, green cuffs, white hunting horns in the turnback corners.

Recruit Grenadiers (1809–10)
Shako with white side struts, red cords and plume, short blue tunic, blue collar, lapels and shoulder straps all edged red, red cuffs, white cuff flaps, red pocket flap piping, white turnbacks with red eagles, yellow buttons.

Recruit Chasseurs (1809–10)
As for the Recruit Grenadiers except: white cords and green, pear-shaped pompon to shako, red collar, green shoulder straps edged red, red Polish cuffs edged white, blue turnbacks with green hunting horns.

National Guard (1810–13)
Shako with red cords, ball pompon and tuft, short blue tunic with pointed white lapels and turnbacks edged red (blue eagles in the latter) red collar and Polish cuffs edged white, yellow buttons.

Pupilles de la Garde (1811–14)
As for Flanquer Grenadiers except: green cords and yellow ball pompon to shako, green cuffs and turnbacks (the latter with yellow eagles), lateral pocket flaps; no sabres.

Veterans of the Guard (1804–14)
Bicorn with red pompon, red lapels, blue cuff flaps and lateral pocket flaps otherwise as for the 1st and 2nd Grenadiers.

Plate 13   France: Imperial Guard (and Line Cavalry) c 1805
(l to r)   Officer of Mamelukes, elite gendarme, Kürassier, dragoon, Mameluke. The
Mameluke officer has white turban, crimson and gold waistcoat; bandolier and sash,
green and gold shirt, red breeches, yellow boots, His trooper (far right) has a blue
fez, yellow turban, red shirt and breeches, dark green and gold waistcoat, dark blue
sash and dark blue saddle cloth edged yellow, buff belts, black boots. *Augsburger*
Bilder.

Plate 14   France: Cavalry of the Imperial Guard
(*l to r*) Foreground – Corporal, Chasseurs à Cheval (Napoleon liked to have his portrait painted wearing the uniform of this regiment), elite gendarme (mounted), Grenadier à Cheval (rear view), (note aiguillette on left shoulder and white grenades in turnbacks), trooper, Empress Dragoons. In the left background is a mounted figure in red coat faced dark green, probably a trumpeter of the Empress Dragoons. *Augsburger Bilder.*

Marines of the Guard

Shako with orange binding top and bottom, orange cords, red plume, brass eagle and anchor plate, dark blue dolman with blue collar and red Polish cuffs, yellow buttons and brass scale epaulettes, orange lacing as for hussars;

116

Plate 15   France: Imperial Guard
(*l to r*) Unidentified infantryman in shako with brass rhombic plate; sappeur, grenadiers, dismounted elite gendarme (rear view), (note buff belts edged white), Port-Aigle (obscured), Chasseur à Pied with dark green epaulettes, grenadier officer in summer parade dress (the yellow cuff flaps shown here are in error), tambour-major and grenadier drummer. *Augsburger Bilder.*

dark blue, wide-legged trousers with orange side stripes and Hungarian thigh knots, black belts.

The Guard wore short pigtails long after they had been abolished for Line units.

Line Infantry

At the outbreak of the Revolution most of the regiments wore white coats, small clothes and bicorns; pigtails were obligatory; grenadiers wore bearskin bonnets. In 1789 the National Guard had been raised with the following uniform: bicorn with cockade (and red, dropping plume for grenadiers) long-skirted blue coat with white lapels, cuff flaps and turnbacks, red collar and cuffs. Blue shoulder straps for fusiliers, red epaulettes for grenadiers. Belts and small clothes were white, packs were made of calfskin, ammunition pouches were black and bore a grenade badge for grenadiers. Uniformity of dress was impossible to enforce in those chaotic days and old items of clothing were worn long after the theoretical introduction of new patterns. Thus bearskin bonnets and the old Chasseur helmet with black fur crest and leopard skin turban were frequently seen mixed in with the authorised items of dress.

In 1793 the National Guard uniform was issued to the line infantry as a whole at the time of the formation of Half Brigades but of course the old uniforms continued to be worn out over a number of years after this and the changeover was gradual and irregular. Each Half Brigade consisted of one battalion of line infantry and two of volunteers or National Guard. In 1803 this organisation was abandoned and regiments were formed again.

The only major uniform change up until 1807 was that the grenadiers now wore much larger bearskin bonnets than before. These bonnets had a copper front plate bearing a grenade or in some regiments just a copper grenade. The shako was introduced in 1804 to replace the bicorn but it was some years before all men had them; for instance most units wore the bicorn during the 1806 campaign in Prussia. The pigtail was officially abolished in 1805 but was also to be seen years afterwards.

In 1806 Napoleon ordered white tunics to be issued to replace the blue but only a few regiments actually received the new items before the idea was abandoned in October 1807 and blue was reconfirmed as the French infantry's colour and all pocket flaps were ordered to be vertical.

In 1805 each infantry battalion was augmented by a further elite company —the Voltigeurs. A battalion now consisted of one grenadier, four fusilier and one Voltigeur companies. The function of the Voltigeurs was to form the cloud of skirmishers which protected the assault columns (always headed by the grenadiers). The distinguishing badges of the Voltigeurs were a yellow and green or yellow and red plume, yellow or green ball pompon, green cords and green epaulettes with yellow half moons. Like the grenadiers they often carried sabres (with green sabre knots); their turnback badges were green hunting horns and on the pouch lid they wore a brass hunting horn.

The line infantry shako bore a cockade at the top front centre and below this was the plate either a rhombus bearing the eagle over the regimental number or an eagle over a semi-circular plate again pierced with the regimental number. Fusilier companies were distinguished by lenticular pompons in the following colours: 1st Company—green; 2nd—sky blue; 3rd—orange; 4th—violet. Their brass chinscale bosses were decorated with a five-pointed star (grenade for grenadiers, hunting horn for Voltigeurs) and their turnback badges were either five-pointed stars or the crowned 'N' in dark blue cloth. Fusiliers carried no sabres and their bayonet scabbards were held in frogs attached to the ammunition pouch bandolier.

Later in the period the fusiliers' lenticular pompons had white centres bearing the company number in black. In 1812 the cut of the coat altered in that the lapels were now hooked together to waist level. The grenadiers lost their bearskins in 1808 and received shakos, taller than those of the fusiliers and with red top and bottom bands and side struts, red pompon, red cords and plume for parades. Voltigeurs' shakos had yellow borders and side struts.

According to regulations, drummers had gold edging to collars, cuffs and lapels and plain red swallows' nests but as each regimental commander was allowed to dress the 'Tête de Colonne' (musicians and pioneers) as he wished, there was a great variety of dress to be seen.

A decree of 19 January 1812 sought to regulate matters and introduced for musicians the dark green, single-breasted Spencer with red collar and cuffs. All parts were edged with a dark green lace having yellow discs along its length bearing alternately the imperial eagle and the crowned 'N' in dark green. On each sleeve were seven chevrons (point up) of this lace.

Regiments were distinguished only by their number on the shako plate and on their buttons; each regiment had from one to six battalions.

Light Infantry

In 1791 there were fourteen light infantry battalions organised as for the line infantry except that the elite companies here were called 'Carabiniers'. The centre companies were called 'Chasseurs' and originally wore the bicorn with green plume. The long-tailed coat was dark blue and pointed dark blue lapels, dark blue Polish cuffs and turnbacks all piped white; the collar was red, the epaulettes green with red half moon, buttons white with the regimental number. Small clothes were dark blue, the waistcoat edged white, the trousers had white side piping. Short black gaiters with hussar tops trimmed white or red and white belts completed the uniform.

Carabiniers had bearskin bonnets with red, drooping plumes, red cords and top patch bearing a white cross, red epaulettes and sabre knots. They wore a brass grenade on the pouch and red grenades in the turnbacks. In 1799 the light infantry received the shako with rhombic front plate, cockade and plume to the left-hand side and cords (white for Chasseurs, red for Carabiniers). In 1804 Voltigeur companies were raised and they were distinguished by yellow over green plumes, green cords and pompon, yellow collars with white (or red) edging, green epaulettes with yellow half moons, white (or yellow) hunting horn turnback badges, green sabre knots.

In 1808 the Carabiniers lost their bearskins and received shakos with red plume and pompon and white cords. The coat was now closed to the waist and the lapels thus had squared bottoms.

Guard Cavalry

Horse Grenadiers

In the cavalry of the Guards of the Directory there was a troop of horse grenadiers with bearskin bonnets, yellow cords and chinscales, red plume and top patch with white grenade; the long blue coat had a red collar, white lapels and turnbacks both edged red. Red trefoil epaulettes edged white, yellow buttons, white waistcoats, buff breeches, heavy cavalry boots, white belts and gauntlets. The Directorial Guard then became the Consular Guard and, in its turn, the Imperial Guard and this unit developed into the Horse Grenadiers. The bearskin remained as before, without front plate; the collar changed to blue, lapels were white, turnbacks red with yellow

Plate 16   France: Sappeur, Line Infantry 1807
This figure was painted from life by C. Suhr in Hamburg and shows the red cords, plume, epaulettes, collar, lapels, service stripes and sappeurs badges. From *Die Uniform aller in Hamburg zwischen 1806–1813 gewesenen Truppen.*

grenades; yellow, fringeless epaulettes, yellow aiguillette on right shoulder, yellow buttons, white small clothes; brass sheath and hilt to sword. Trumpeters had white bearskins, sky blue coats, red lapels, gold edgings to facings, gold trumpet, gold cords, sky blue trumpet banner embroidered gold with a crowned eagle on one side and the crowned 'N' on the other. Dark blue saddle furniture edged yellow, black harness.

Chasseurs à Cheval
Brown fur colpack with red bag, yellow cords and red over green plume, green dolman with green collar, red cuffs, yellow lace and buttons, buff breeches, red pelisse with black fur and yellow lace and buttons, red and green barrel sash, black sabretasche with gold crowned imperial eagle, white belts, yellow trimmed hussar boots. Dark green saddle furniture trimmed yellow, yellow imperial eagle in the rear shabraque corners, black Hungarian harness with brass fittings.

Trumpeters wore white colpacks with red over sky blue plumes, sky blue dolman with red collar and cuffs edged yellow, gold lace, buttons and Hungarian thigh knots. Trumpet banners as for Grenadiers à Cheval.

Chevau-Légers Lanciers
1st (Polish) Regiment Polish costume was introduced when this regiment was raised in 1807 as a Chevau Légers regiment; in 1809 the front rank were equipped with lances (the rear with carbines) and their title was changed accordingly. The uniform consisted of the czapka with crimson top piped white, white cords and plume, white cockade bearing the white Maltese cross, brass sunburst plate with silver centre bearing a brass crowned 'N', brass chinscales. Slate blue kurtka with crimson collar, lapels and Polish cuffs all edged white, crimson turnbacks and piping to seams on sleeves and rear; white buttons, epaulettes and aiguillette (left shoulder for those with lances, right for others); slate blue breeches with double crimson side stripes, white belts and gauntlets. Slate blue saddle furniture edged crimson and piped white, white corner emblems (eagle and crowned 'N'). Black Hungarian harness with brass fittings, brass hilted sabre in steel sheath, brown lance with crimson over white pennants.

Trumpeters—as above except: white czapka top, red plume, crimson and white cords, white kurtka, crimson and white epaulettes and aiguillette, crimson breeches and saddle furniture, brass trumpet, gold cords, crimson trumpet banner with silver devices as for Grenadiers à Cheval. Grey horses.

2nd (Dutch) Regiment Raised in 1810 from Dutch units; uniform as for 1st Regiment except: red czapka top, kurtka and breeches, dark blue facings and saddle furniture, yellow buttons and lace.

Trumpters—white czapka top and kurtka, red plume and facings, red and gold cords to brass trumpet, red banner with gold devices as before.

3rd (Lithuanian) Regiment Raised in 1812 and largely destroyed that same year. Uniform as for 1st Regiment but with gold buttons and lace.

Dragoons of the Guard (Dragons de l'Imperatrice from 1810)
Brass helmet with leopard skin turban, brass combe, black horsehair crest, red plume, tunic as for Grenadiers à Cheval but dark green with white lapels, red cuffs and turnbacks, yellow buttons, contre-epaulette and aiguillette (right

shoulder). White belts, breeches and gauntlets, heavy cavalry boots. Dark green, heavy cavalry saddle furniture edged yellow (crown in rear corners), black harness with brass fittings.

Trumpeters—as above except: sky blue plume and tuft to black crest, white tunic faced sky blue and trimmed gold; brass trumpet, sky blue and gold cords, sky blue saddle furniture edged gold, sky blue trumpet banner with gold eagle and crowned 'N' devices. Grey horses.

Mamelukes
This unit was taken into imperial service after Napoleon's Egyptian campaign in 1800 and there are conflicting accounts of their elaborate uniforms. Red 'fez', white turban and horsehair plume, brass crescent front plate. Light blue waistcoat edged red, dark green shirt, red sash, baggy red breeches, black belts. Ivory hilted sabre in black sheath with brass fittings. Turkish saddle with black harness. Dark green shabraque edged red, piped white.

Kettledrummer—as above except: white feather plumes and gold decoration to fez and turban, red waistcoat and light blue shirt with gold braid and edging, light blue waist sash, white breeches, gold decoration to shabraque. Dark green drum banners with gold, crowned imperial eagles and fringes. Grey horse with red, ceremonial Turkish harness.

Lithuanian Tartars of the Guard (raised 1812)
Black lambskin shako with yellow turban, dark green bag trimmed yellow, brass edged peak, brass front badge consisting of four, six-pointed stars and a crescent lying on its back. Crimson waistcoat edged yellow, dark green shirt and baggy breeches with double crimson side stripes; white gauntlets.

Gendarmerie d 'Elite
Uniform as for Grenadiers à Cheval except: white plume and cords, black peak edged white, white chinscales, red lapels, cuff flaps, white buttons, contre-epaulettes and aiguillette (left shoulder) and grenade badges on turn-backs, yellow small clothes and gauntlets, yellow belts edged white. Dark blue, heavy cavalry saddle furniture edged white.

Trumpeter—as above except: red plume, red coat with dark blue facings edged white, red outer trim to saddle furniture. Brass trumpet, red banner with silver cords and devices as before. Grey horses.

Foot Artillery of the Guard
In 1791 the uniform was of infantry cut with bicorn, red pompon, cockade. Dark blue coat with dark blue collar and lapels edged red, red cuffs, cuff flaps and epaulettes and turnbacks with blue grenades; yellow buttons.

In 1792 the cuff flaps changed to blue with red edging. Small clothes were dark blue, belts white. The bicorn was rapidly replaced by a peaked bearskin with brass edging to peak, brass chinscales, red top patch with yellow grenade, red cords and plume.

Horse Artillery of the Guard
Brown fur colpack with red cords, bag and plume, dark blue dolman with red lace and trim and yellow buttons, blue pelisse with red lace and black fur, red and yellow barrel sash, blue Hungarian breeches with red side stripe and thigh knots, hussar boots with red trim and tassel; white belts. Blue sabretasche edged red with yellow, crowned imperial eagle on crossed cannon barrels. Officers had gold braid and white pelisse fur.

Trumpeters—as for gunners except: white busby with sky blue bag, sky blue plume with white tip; sky blue dolman, pelisse and breeches, red and gold lace, black fur. Sky blue sabretasche with gold edging, badge as before.

Artillery Train of the Guard

This corps was placed on a military basis in 1807. Shako with white plate and chinscales, red plume and cords; grey single-breasted coat and trousers, light blue facings piped red, red epaulettes, grey waistcoat laced red, grey breeches with red Hungarian knots. Artillery drivers (of gun team) wore train uniform.

Artillery Park of the Guard (1807–15)

As for artillery train but with no red piping to facings.

Engineers of the Guard

Steel helmet with brass eagle plate, combe, peak and neck shield trim, brass chinscales, black fur sausage crest, red pompon and plume above left hand chinstrap boss; dark blue coat, black collar, cuffs, cuff flaps and lapels all piped red; red epaulettes, red turnbacks with dark blue grenades, yellow buttons, dark blue small clothes, white belts.

Line Cavalry

Cuirassiers

In 1791 the existing cuirassier regiment of the French army (Cuirassiers du Roy) were given the number 8 in the heavy cavalry; their uniform was a large bicorn with cockade and white edging, blue coat with yellow collar, cuffs and turnbacks, a single row of white buttons, buff breeches and belts, heavy cavalry boots.

The cuirass was of polished steel with brass shoulder scales and a red, white-edged 'cuff' around the rim. In 1802 the 5th, 6th and 7th Heavy Cavalry Regiments also received cuirasses and in 1804 there were twelve regiments. It was in this year that the bicorn was replaced by the steel helmet with black fur turban, brass combe, chinscales and peak edging, black horsehair aigrette and crest and red plume.

In 1812 the coat skirts were shortened and in the turnback corners were white grenades; red epaulettes completed the uniform.

The regimental facings were as follows:

	a (collar, turnbacks and pocket flap edging)	b (cuffs and cuff flap trim)	c (cuff flaps)
1st Regiment	a red	b red	c red
2nd Regiment	a red	b red	c blue
3rd Regiment	a red	b blue	c red
4th Regiment	a orange	b orange	c orange
5th Regiment	a orange	b orange	c blue
6th Regiment	a orange	b blue	c orange
7th Regiment	a yellow	b yellow	c yellow
8th Regiment	a yellow	b yellow	c blue
9th Regiment	a yellow	b blue	c yellow
10th Regiment	a pink	b pink	c pink
11th Regiment	a pink	b pink	c blue

Plate 17   France: Foreign Troops, The Portuguese Legion 1809–1813
(l to r) Trooper, Chasseurs à Cheval (mounted), (dark brown uniform faced red, piped white, red shabrack edged white, dark brown portmanteau edged white, white sheepskin), grenadier, infantry regiment (rear view), (uniform as above, red cords, plume and epaulettes, white piping to rear), fusilier private (uniform as above with dark brown lapels piped white, white cap cords; this man is probably wearing the light fatigue cap), Voltigeur, infantry regiment (uniform as before but with red lapels, brass horn badge to cap), corporal of Voltigeurs (seated), (green cords, plume and epaulettes with yellow half moons), officer of Chasseurs à Cheval (elite company), (red pompon and turnbacks, red bandolier edged silver, silver epaulettes), infantry officer (silver epaulettes, dark brown lapels piped red, red waist sash, red cuffs and cuff flaps), trooper, Chasseurs à Cheval (colours as for first figure). *Augsburger Bilder.*

	a	b	c
12th Regiment	a pink	b blue	c pink
13th Regiment	a lilac	b lilac	c lilac
14th Regiment	a lilac	b lilac	c blue

Dark blue saddle furniture with white edging and grenades.

Trumpeters—imperial livery (dark green) with regimental facings, no cuirasses, white aigrette and crest, grey horses.

Dragoons

Prior to the Revolution the French dragoons had worn a brass helmet (without peak) with brown fur turban, brass combe and black aigrette and horsehair crest. In the 1790s this helmet had a peak and a red plume added to the left-hand side.

The coat was dark green with similar collar, white lapels and buttons, dark green shoulder straps edged in the facing colour. The elite companies wore red epaulettes and brown fur busbies with red plumes and cords. By 1812 there were thirty regiments of dragoons and in this year the cut of the lapels changed from being cut out in an inverted 'V' at the front to being straight across the waist (the Spencer style). Small clothes were white as were belts and gauntlets.

Trumpeters—as above except: white aigrette and crest, either the new imperial livery or the old reversed colours.

Regiments were grouped in sixes for facing colours, ie the Regiments 1–6 had red facings; 7–12 crimson; 13–18 pink; 19–24 yellow and 25–30 light orange. Lapels and turnbacks were in the facing colour for all regiments and the other distinguishing items were as follows:

	a (collar)	b (cuffs)	c (cuff flaps)
1st* and 4th† Regiments	a red	b red	c red
2nd* and 5th†	a green	b red	c green
3rd* and 6th†	a red	b green	c red
7th* and 10th†	a crimson	b crimson	c crimson
8th* and 11th†	a green	b crimson	c green
9th* and 12th†	a crimson	b green	c crimson
13th* and 16th†	a pink	b pink	c pink
14th* and 17th†	a green	b pink	c green
15th* and 18th†	a pink	b green	c pink
19th* and 22nd†	a yellow	b yellow	c yellow
20th* and 23rd†	a green	b yellow	c green
21st* and 24th†	a yellow	b green	c yellow
25th* and 28th†	a light orange	b light orange	c light orange
26th* and 29th†	a green	b light orange	c green
27th* and 30th†	a light orange	b green	c light orange

* lateral pocket flaps   † vertical pocket flaps

Chasseurs à Cheval

At the time of the Revolution there were six regiments of this arm dressed in black helmets with bearskin crests, turbans and peaks (very similar to the British light dragoon helmet of the period), short green coat with white hussar frogging on the chest; collar and pointed cuffs as well as the white-laced waistcoat were in the regimental facing colour; white buttons, green breeches with Hungarian thigh knots and side stripe, hussar boots with white trim and tassel, white gauntlets and belts.

Plate 18 *France: Foreign Regiments 1810–1813*
(*l to r*) 13e Chasseurs à Cheval – originally the cavalry of the Belgian-manned 'Legion Franche Etranger' of 1793, orange facings, 21e Dragoons – originally the Piemontese Dragoons, absorbed into the French army in August 1801, yellow facings. After Fieffe *Die Geschichte der Fremdtruppen im Dienste Frankreichs.*

126

Regimental facings were: 1st Regiment—red; 2nd—pink; 3rd—yellow; 4th—lemon yellow; 5th—orange; 6th—white.

On the jacket shoulders were white contre-epaulettes. The hair was worn in three plaits, one to the rear, the others in front of the ears.

The helmet was soon replaced by the 'Mirliton' or winged cap in black with white trim, wing lined in the facing colour, white cords and plume at left top side. The coat became a dolman and the barrel sash was also introduced. The pelisse was not worn but sabretasches were carried until 1805. In this year the shako with white rhombic plate bearing the eagle over the regimental number, cockade and company pompon. Elite companies wore the colpack with red bag and plume and red epaulettes. The hussar costume was also now replaced by a dark green 'Surtout' with similar shoulder straps and lapels edged in the facing colour, pointed cuffs and turn-backs also in the facing colour. In 1812 the Spencer replaced the Surtout, green button overalls were often worn instead of the Hungarian breeches.

In 1812 the regimental facings (on cuffs and piping) were as follows:

1st*, 2nd† and 3rd* Regiments	scarlet
4th*, 5th† and 6th*	yellow
7th*, 8th† and 9th*	pink
10th*, 11th† and 12th*	crimson
13th*, 14th† and 15th*	orange
16th*, 17th† and 18th*	sky blue
19th*, 20th† and 21st*	light orange
22nd*, 23rd† and 24th*	dark orange
25th*, 26th† and 27th*	madder red
28th*, 29th† and 30th*	pale purple
31st*	buff

* collar in the facing colour piped green   † green collar piped in the facing colour

The 5th, 8th and 27th Regiments had buff leather work, the others white. Saddle furniture was dark green trimmed in the facing colour; black Hungarian harness with brass fittings.

Trumpeters wore reversed colours, colpacks and rode greys.

Chevau Légers Lanciers 1807–15

The regiments 1–6 were raised in France and their uniform was a brass helmet with brown fur turban, brass edged peak, brass chinscales and combe, black 'sausage' crest. Dark green Spencer with Polish cuffs; facings shown on collar, cuffs, turnbacks and piping. All buttons were yellow. In the turn-back corners was a green, crowned 'N'. Elite companies had colpacks with red bag, cords and plume, red epaulettes. Only the front rank carried lances and these had red over white pennants. Facings were as follows: 1st Regiment —scarlet; 2nd—light orange; 3rd—pink; 4th—crimson; 5th—sky blue; 6th—madder red.

Breeches were green with side stripes in the facing colours; white belts, black pouches with brass crowned 'N' (flaming grenade for elite companies). Hussar boots with yellow trim and tassel.

Trumpeters wore imperial livery. Green saddle furniture with white lace and regimental number. Black harness with brass fittings.

The Polish regiments (7th–9th) wore dark blue czapkas, kurtkas and trousers, white fringed epaulettes, white buttons and facings shown on collars, cuffs, turnbacks and piping as given below: 7th—yellow; 8th—yellow (blue collar); 9th—buff.

127

Dark blue saddle furniture edged in the facing colour, black harness with brass fittings.

Hussars

In 1791 there were six regiments of this arm and they lost their old names and were given numbers instead. Their uniform did not change greatly during the revolution. Troopers wore the mirliton with a red-tipped black tuft at the top right-hand side, officers had brown fur colpacks. The regimental details were as follows:

	a (dolman)	b (pelisse)	c (lace)	d (breeches)	e (mirliton)
1st Regiment (old name Bercheny)	a sky blue	b sky blue	c white	d light blue	e red and black
2nd (Chamboran)	a brown	b brown	c white	d sky blue	e sky blue and black
3rd (Esterhazy)	a blue-grey	b blue-grey	c red	d blue-grey	e white and black
4th (Saxe)	a green	b green	c yellow	d red	e green
5th (Colonel-Géneral)	a blue	b red	c yellow	d blue	e black
6th (Lauzan)	a blue	b white	c blue	d blue	e red and black

The 4th Regiment (Saxe) then emigrated and the 5th and 6th regiments became the 4th and 5th respectively. In the last years of the eighteenth century many volunteer hussar regiments were raised and later disbanded, the shako was introduced in about 1800 and the three-plaited hair style was retained. From 1803–12 the regimental distinctions were as follows:

	a (dolman)	b (collar)	c (cuffs)	d (pelisse)	e (lace)	f (breeches)
1st Regiment	a sky blue	b sky blue	c red	d sky blue	e white	f sky blue
2nd Regiment	a brown	b brown	c sky blue	d brown	e white	f sky blue
3rd Regiment	a grey	b grey	c red	d grey	e red	f grey
4th Regiment	a royal blue	b royal blue	c red	d red	e yellow	f royal blue
5th Regiment	a sky blue	b sky blue	c white	d white	e yellow	f sky blue
6th Regiment	a red	b red	c red	d royal blue	e yellow	f royal blue
7th Regiment	a green	b red	c red	d green	e yellow	f red
8th Regiment	a green	b red	c red	d green	e white	f red
9th Regiment	a red	b sky blue	c sky blue	d sky blue	e yellow	f sky blue
10th Regiment	a sky blue	b red	c red	d sky blue	e white	f sky blue
11th Regiment	a royal blue	b red	c red	d royal blue	e yellow	f royal blue

The fur trim on all pelisses was black except for the 11th Regiment which was white; the barrel sashes were crimson and white or yellow according to the lace and button colour. Up to 1804 the sabretasche badge was an axe in a bundle of staves, under a red cap and flanked by the letters 'R' and 'F' in green wreaths. In 1804 this changed to the crowned imperial eagle and later the pattern changed again to black leather bearing the regimental number in brass. The Hungarian breeches were often covered with button overalls either in grey or in the breeches colour. Elite companies wore colpacks with red bag and plume. All regiments wore hussar boots with trim and tassel in the regimental lace colour.

In 1813 the 9th Regiment was renumbered 12th and retained its old uniform but with white lace; the newly raised 13th Regiment was dressed as for the 2nd Regiment but with a light blue dolman collar and a cylindrical red shako.

All regiments wore black Hungarian harness with brass fittings and the saddle furniture was generally a white sheepskin trimmed in the dolman colour.

Trumpeters wore white colpacks and reversed colours and rode greys.

Gardes d'Honneur (1813–14)
There were four of these regiments with the following uniform: red shako with white eagle plate and top band, green dolman and pelisse with white lace and buttons, red collar and cuffs to dolman, crimson and white barrel sash, red Hungarian breeches with white knots and side stripes, black sabretasche with white eagle. White sheepskin saddle covers with green edging. The regiments were distinguished by the coloured tips to the green shako plumes: 1st—red, 2nd—blue, 3rd—yellow, 4th—white. Black Hungarian harness with brass fittings.

Foot Artillery
As for foot artillery of the guard but with shako having red plume and cords, yellow front plate and chinscales.

Horse Artillery
As for horse artillery of the guard; dark blue hussar uniform with red lace; initially (1792) with the small, black, crested Chasseur helmet, later with felt caps and then shakos with red cords and plume.

Artillery Train
As for the train of the guard but with grey shoulder straps edged red.

Baggage Train
As for artillery train but light grey facings edged dark blue; Polish cuffs.

Bridging Train
As for artillery train but with black facings edged red.

Engineers
In 1793 a corps of twelve battalions of sappers and six companies of miners was raised. The uniform was a bicorn, dark blue, single-breasted coat, yellow buttons, black collar, lapels, cuffs and cuff flaps all edged red, red turnbacks and epaulettes.

Gendarmerie 1791–1814
Large bicorn with white edging and national cockade, blue coat with red facings and white buttons, yellow belts edged white, buff small clothes. Mounted gendarmes had buff gauntlets and heavy cavalry boots.

Foreign Troops in French Service

Coptic Legion
While in Egypt in 1799, Napoleon formed the Coptic Legion; uniform was a bicorn with French cockade, company pompon, light green infantry coat with light green lapels and Polish cuffs, yellow collar and piping to lapels and cuffs, white buttons and small clothes, short grey gaiters, black belts. Grenadiers had drooping red plumes, red epaulettes.

Dromedary Riders
Also at this time a corps of Dromedary Riders was raised in Egypt: shako with yellow rhombic plate, white cords, cockade and plume to top left side, light blue dolman and breeches with white buttons and lace, red, long-skirted, short-sleeved tunic edged in black fur; white Arab burnous, black sabretasches with brass badge of axe and staves, white breeches, hussar boots and sabre.

Foreign Regiments in French Service

1er Régiment (originally 'La Tour d'Auvergne)
Shako with brass eagle plate and chinscales, cockade and company pompon; dark green tunic, breeches, lapels*, cuffs* and waistcoat; red collar*, French cuff flaps* and turnbacks*; white belts, short black gaiters. White buttons with the peripheral legend 'Régiment Etrangér'; in the centre the figure '1'.

2e Régiment (originally the 'Régiment Isenburg')
As for 1er Régiment but sky blue coat, breeches, lapels†, waistcoat and cuffs†; yellow collar, French cuff flaps and piping; the centre of the white buttons bore a '2'.

3e Régiment (originally the 'Irish Legion')
As for 1er Régiment but yellow collar, lapels, cuffs and piping, green French cuff flaps†, red turnbacks, white waistcoat and breeches. Yellow buttons with '3' in the centre.

4e Régiment (originally the 'Régiment Preusse')
As for 1er Régiment but red turnbacks and piping; yellow buttons with central '4'.

The Croatian Regiments 1809–13 (The old 1st–4th, 10th and 11th Austrian Grenz-Infanterie-Regimenter)
Initially Austrian uniform with French cockade and rank and company badges; later French shako with cockade, brass rhombic plate and chinscales, company pompon; dark blue, single-breasted coat and shoulder straps*; facings shown on collar, Polish cuffs and turnbacks; long, plain, light blue Hungarian breeches.
    The facings were as follows: 1er Régiment (the old Liccaner)—red; 2e (Ottochaner)—crimson; 3e (Oguliner)—light yellow; 4e (Szluiner)—dark brown; 5e (1st Banalisten)—light blue; 6e (2nd Banalisten)—dark green.
    In 1812 these six regiments were reduced to three by pairing the 1er and 2e, 3e and 4e, 5e and 6e and were given white rhombic shako plates bearing a hunting horn (or eagle plates); French light infantry uniform in dark green with yellow collars (the 'new' 3e Régiment had light blue piping to their collars); dark green lapels piped yellow, yellow Polish cuffs, turnbacks and trim to hussar-style black gaiters; dark green breeches piped yellow; white belts and waistcoats.

Régiment d'Illyrie
Shako with white rhombic plate and chinscales, cockade, company plume and pompon; dark blue, French light infantry-style coat with lapels, Polish cuffs, turnbacks, breeches and shoulder straps all piped white;

*piped white   †piped yellow

130

red collar and swallows' nests (the latter piped white); white buttons bearing in the centre: 'Régiment d'Illyrie' and around the periphery 'Empire Française'.

The Portuguese Legion 1808–14 (three infantry regiments, two cavalry regiments)

Infantry Portuguese shako with raised front plate, brass front band pierced with the regimental number (above this a brass grenade or hunting horn for elite companies), brass chinscales, company cords and plumes. Dark brown coat, red collar, lapels, turnbacks, cuffs and Brandenburg cuff flaps; red and green epaulettes for elite companies, brown shoulder straps piped red for fusiliers. Dark brown breeches with short, white gaiters or white trousers with wide red side stripe; white belts. Turnback badges were grenades or hunting horns for elite companies.

Cavalry Black leather helmet with black combe and sausage crest, black fur turban, oval, brass front plate, chinscales and side struts (elite companies wore black fur colpacks with red pompons). Dark brown, short-skirted tunics with red collar, red piping to dark brown lapels and shoulder straps, red Polish cuffs and turnbacks, white (or brown) breeches, waistcoats and belts, plain hussar boots. Red saddle furniture edged white.

The Swiss Regiments 1806–14 (French uniform)

Shako with brass eagle plate and chinscales, cockade and company pompon (bearskin with brass eagle plate and chinscales, white cords and red plume for grenadiers), red, long-skirted coats with regimental facings shown on collar, lapels and cuffs (all of which were piped with regimental colour as were the red collar and the red shoulder straps of the fusilier companies), white turnbacks, waistcoat, breeches and belts; yellow buttons, black gaiters.

	a (facings)	b (buttons)
1er Régiment	a yellow	b sky blue
2e Régiment	a royal blue	b yellow
3e Régiment	a black	b white
4e Régiment	a sky blue	b black

Bataillon de Neuchâtel 1807–13 (French uniform)

Shako with brass rhombic plate bearing an eagle, cockade and company pompon white chinscales; deep yellow tunic with scarlet collar, cuffs, French cuff flaps, lapels and turnbacks (yellow shoulder straps edged red for fusiliers), white buttons with central inscription 'Bataillon de Neuchâtel' and peripheral inscription 'Empire Française'. White belts and breeches, black gaiters.

Battle History

French troops were involved in every European and colonial campaign from 1792–1815 with the exception of the wars between Sweden and Russia and Turkey and Russia.

Major battles include Marengo—1800, Hohenlinden—1800, Austerlitz—1805, Jena and Auerstädt—1806, Friedland and Preussisch-Eylau—1807, Abensberg, Linz, Aspern-Essling, Wagram, Znaim—1809, Smolensk,

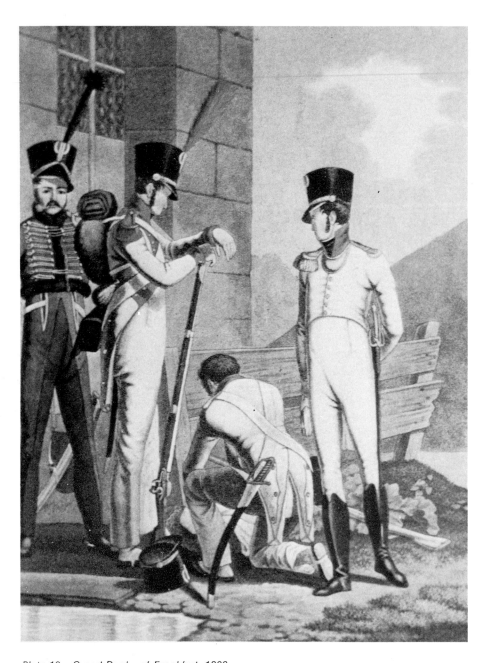

Plate 19   Grand Duchy of Frankfurt: 1808
(*l to r*) Hussars (a police formation), (dark blue with yellow buttons and lace), grenadier private (red plume, facings and epaulettes, white buttons), fusilier private (kneeling), (as above but white shoulder straps edged red), fusilier officer (as private, gold gorget). *Augsburger Bilder.*

Borodino, Malo-Jaroslawetz, Beresina—1812, Dresden, Kulm, Dennewitz, Katzbach, Leipzig, Hanau—1813, Troyes, Arcis sur Aube, Paris—1814, Ligny, Quatre-Bras and Waterloo in 1815. In Spain 1808–15 there was Baylen, Bussaco, Talavera, Salamanca, Albuera, Vittoria, Pyrenees. They were also heavily engaged in the West Indies and in India.

GRAND DUCHY OF

Frankfurt

(Cockade initially black, later red within white)

Frankfurt joined the Confederation of the Rhine on 18 July 1806 and had to provide an infantry regiment. Uniform was a bicorn for fusiliers, a white coat of Austrian infantry pattern with red collar, cuffs and turnbacks, white buttons; white belts and breeches, black gaiters. Grenadiers had bearskin bonnets with a white plate bearing a wheel badge, red cords and plume, red top patch with white cross, red epaulettes and sabre knot. Light companies had a green shako trimmed black, black plume, cockade and red and white cords. Green tunic and breeches, white buttons, red piping to green collar, cuffs, cuff flaps, shoulder straps and lapels; yellow waistcoat, black belts and gaiters.

Between 1808 and 1809 it seems that French light infantry-style uniforms in dark blue with red lapels, pointed cuffs and turnbacks, white piping and buttons and dark blue breeches were introduced. The French shako had French company and rank distinctions, red within white cockade over a white shield bearing a crowned wheel.

Drummers had white lace with a red zig-zag to collar, lapels, cuffs, turnbacks, trouser side seams and Hungarian thigh knots. In 1814 the 1st and 2nd Infantry Battalions became the 14th Bavarian Line Infantry Regiment.

Battle History

1806—Prussia (saw no action); 1809–13—Spain in 3rd Brigade, Leval's Division IV Corps. The Frankfurt battalion in Spain went over to the English in December 1813. 1812—Russia as part of 1st Brigade, 'Division Princiére'; 1813—besieged in Danzig.

KINGDOM OF

Great Britain

(Cockade Black)

In 1791 the red coat was already the traditional habit of the British army although certain cavalry regiments and the artillery wore dark blue. Later in the period the new rifle regiments wore dark green.

133

Plate 20   Great Britain: 1792
Sergeant of Grenadiers, 3rd Foot Guards (brass cap plate, gold cords, red tunic, dark blue facings, yellow lace buttons and tassels to shoulder straps and wings, crimson waist sash). After E. Dayes, *Military Figures* 1792. (*Courtesy National Army Museum*).

Rank Badges

Generals

Bicorns, double-breasted scarlet coats with dark blue collar lapels and Swedish cuffs, white turnbacks, gold buttons and lace embroidery to collars, cuffs and lapels. Rank was indicated by gold epaulettes and gold chevrons, point down, on the forearms, each chevron having a button on its point. Around the waist was a gold and crimson sash and a gold sword knot was worn on the hilt of the sword or sabre. White breeches and high boots with spurs completed the costume. A gold gorget was worn by dismounted officers.

Field officers

Officers of junior rank (colonel and below) had no chevrons on the sleeves and their waist sashes were plain crimson silk. Swords were carried on white leather baldrics over the right shoulder to the left hip and these had a regimental buckle plate on the chest. Officers of cavalry and of grenadier and light companies were initially the only ones to wear epaulettes (these in the button colour) but these were extended to all officers after 1791. Officers carried canes with gold or silver knobs and cords. In 1800 the officers of the Household (Guards) cavalry already had a well developed system of rank badges. Field officers wore two gold epaulettes with badges on the fields as follows: Colonel—a crown over a four-pointed star; Lieutenant-colonel—a crown; Major—a star.

Junior officers

Only one epaulette with badges as follows: Captains—two stars; Lieutenants —one; Second lieutenants (cornets)—none.

NCOs

Sergeant-majors wore officer-style coats, sergeants' and other ranks' coats were single-breasted and had shorter coat tails. The senior NCOs carried spontoons and sergeants wore crimson waist sashes with a central stripe in the regimental facing colour. Chevrons in white tape on the upper sleeves were introduced in 1801 and initially some regiments wore them point up, others point down. By 1803 they all seem to have been point down: Sergeant-major—four under a crown, Sergeant—three; colour sergeant—three under a flag and crossed swords badge; corporal—two; lance corporal—one.

Guards Infantry 1792

There were three regiments of foot guards, 1st (later Grenadiers) with its buttons and laces worn singly, 2nd (or Coldstream) buttons and laces in pairs, and 3rd (or Scots) buttons and laces in threes. Their shoulders were decorated with dark blue wings (their facing colour) edged and decorated with white tape.

Guards Cavalry: Life Guards (1st and 2nd Regiments)

Heavy cavalry uniform with red coat, dark blue facings and yellow buttons with gold lace on collar, forearms (chevrons) and lapels. Gold bicorn edging. The 2nd Regiment had red collar patches.

Royal Horse Guards (The Oxford Blues)

As above but dark blue coats faced red. In 1812, when the new helmets were issued the Life Guards had a large red over black sausage crest, the Royal Horse Guards had blue over red crests. Buff breeches.

Line Infantry 1792

Almost every regiment in the British army expressed its identity with commemorative badges on shako plates, belt plates, buttons or in some other peculiarity of dress but it lies far outside the scope of this book to mention them.

Centre companies wore bicorns and had simple shoulder straps with white worsted tufts at the outer ends. In their shakos they wore white over red tufts (officers had feather plumes). Grenadiers had all white plumes and, in addition to the shoulder straps, had red wings decorated and edged with white lace and fringed in white worsted tufts.

The light companies had green shako tufts and wings as for grenadiers. Some regiments seem to have worn grenades and hunting horns in the corners of the white turnbacks. In the 1790s many light companies wore small leather helmets of individual design with various front plates, crests and other decoration. Belts were white and worn crossed on the chest; equipment was a canvas pack (often painted in the regimental facing colour and bearing a badge or title) and black cartridge pouch, white haversack and round blue wooden canteen (also painted with regimental and company designation). White breeches and below knee black gaiters with black buttons completed the costume but were replaced by grey trousers in 1810.

In 1800 the 'stovepipe' shako replaced the bicorn for other ranks. On the front was a brass plate with regimental badge and designation and the reversed royal cypher 'GR'. At the top front was a regimental button holding the black cockade and over this the company plume.

In 1808 the pigtail was abolished but the 23rd Foot appear not to have received the order and still today wear a 'flash' of black ribbon on the back of their tunic collars to commemorate the fact that they wore pigtails years after everyone else.

Fusilier regiments wore black fur caps with red cloth backing (usually bearing the white, springing horse of Hanover), brass front plates, peaks and with a plume to the left side. White cords ran from plume base across the front and two tassels hung to the right side. These cords were gold for officers.

Light infantry regiments wore bugle horn shako badges under their regimental number. In 1812 the famous 'Belgic Cap' shako with its high, rounded front plate was introduced for all ranks from colonel down, the plume and cockade were on the top left side, cords crossed the front with two tassels on the right and a brass front plate decorated the front.

Drummers wore reversed colours and had lace decoration to facings and to sleeve seams and back seams of the jacket. Their sleeves were covered with five lace chevrons, point up; drums were brass, the hoops being usually in the facing colour.

Highland regiments can only be briefly covered here. They usually had the bonnet with red, white and black diced headband and black ostrich feather top with plume and cockade on the left and the kilt with red and white diced hose. Military tartans of this era were all derivatives of the Black Watch (the Military Sett) with white, yellow or red lines added for regimental distinction. Officers who were mounted wore trews (trousers made of tartan). Highland officers wore their crimson silk sashes over the left shoulder and hanging to the right hip. On campaign the expensive feather bonnets were often replaced by a normal shako with the three-line deep red, white and black dicing around the lower crown and the kilt was replaced by grey trousers.

TABLE OF BRITISH LINE INFANTRY IN 1815 (After the Army List 1815) Each regiment usually had only one battalion. All men's lace white with worms as shown (*bastion-end lace, unmarked—square ended). All buttons white for soldiers.

	a (facings)	b (men's lace) (1 = singly, 2 = in pairs)	c (officers' lace)
1st or Royal Scots	a dark blue	b2 blue diamond pattern	c gold
2nd or Queens	a dark blue	b1 a blue stripe	c silver
3rd or East Kent (Buffs)	a buff	b2 red, black and yellow stripes	c silver (buff breeches)
4th or King's Own	a dark blue	b1 a blue stripe*	c gold
5th or Northumberland	a gosling green	b1 two red stripes*	c silver
6th or 1st Warwickshire	a deep yellow	b2 red and yellow stripes	c silver
7th or Royal Fusileers	a dark blue	b1 a blue stripe	c gold
8th or King's	a dark blue	b1 blue and yellow stripes	c gold
9th or East Norfolk	a bright yellow	b2 two black stripes	c silver
10th or North Lincolnshire	a bright yellow	b1 a blue stripe	c silver
11th or North Devonshire	a dark green	b2 two red and two green stripes*	c gold
12th or East Suffolk	a dull yellow (white in 1815)	b2 black, yellow and red stripes*	c gold
13th or 1st Somersetshire	a yellow	b2 a yellow stripe*	c silver
14th or Buckinghamshire	a buff	b2 a yellow stripe and a red and blue stripe	c silver
15th or Yorkshire East Riding	a yellow	b2 a red stripe and a black and yellow stripe	c silver (buff breeches)
16th or Bedfordshire	a yellow	b2 a red stripe	c silver
17th or Leicestershire	a white	b2 a thin yellow stripe between two wide blue ones	c silver
18th or Royal Irish	a dark blue	b2 a narrow blue stripe	c gold
19th or 1st Yorkshire North Riding	a dark green	b2 a red stripe, a green stripe and a mixed red and green stripe	c gold
20th or East Devonshire	a dull yellow	b2 a black stripe and a red stripe	c silver
21st or North British Fusileers	a dark blue	b2 a narrow blue stripe	c gold
22nd or Cheshire	a buff	b2 a red stripe and a blue stripe*	c gold (buff breeches)
23rd or Royal Welch Fusileers	a dark blue	b1 red, blue and yellow stripes*	c gold
24th or Warwickshire	a dark green	b2 a wide green and a narrow red stripe	c silver
25th or King's Own Borderers	a dark blue	b1 blue, yellow and red stripes*	c gold

Regiment	a (facing)	b (lace)	c (metal)
26th or Cameronians	*a* pale yellow	*b2* narrow yellow, blue and yellow stripes	*c* silver
27th or Inniskilling	*a* buff	*b1* a narrow blue and narrow red stripe	*c* gold (buff breeches)
28th or North Gloucestershire	*a* bright yellow	*b2* narrow black, yellow and black stripes	*c* silver
29th or Worcestershire	*a* yellow	*b2* blue, yellow and blue lozenges	*c* silver
30th or Cambridgeshire	*a* dull yellow	*b1* a wide blue stripe*	*c* silver
31st or Huntingdonshire	*a* brown (buff in 1815)	*b1* a wide blue and yellow stripe and a narrow red stripe	*c* silver
32nd or Cornwall	*a* white	*b2* black chevrons and a narrow black stripe	*c* gold
33rd or 1st Yorkshire, West Riding	*a* red	*b2* a narrow red stripe*	*c* silver
34th or Cumberland	*a* bright yellow	*b2* a wide blue and yellow stripe and a narrow red stripe	*c* silver
35th or Sussex	*a* white (orange in 1815)	*b2* a narrow yellow stripe	*c* silver
36th or Herefordshire	*a* gosling green	*b2* a narrow red and a narrow green stripe	*c* gold
37th or North Hampshire	*a* bright yellow	*b2* a wide red and a wide yellow stripe	*c* silver
38th or 1st Staffordshire	*a* bright yellow	*b1* narrow red, yellow and red stripes*	*c* silver
39th or Dorsetshire	*a* pea green	*b2* a narrow black and a narrow red stripe	*c* gold
40th or 2nd Somersetshire	*a* buff	*b2* a narrow black and a narrow red stripe	*c* gold (buff breeches)
41st	*a* blue (red in 1815)	*b1* a black and white cord and a button*	*c* silver
42nd or Royal Highland Regiment	*a* dark blue	*b1* a narrow red stripe*	*c* gold (kilt in military sett
43rd or Monmouthshire Light Infantry	*a* white	*b2* a narrow red and a narrow black stripe	*c* silver
44th or East Essex	*a* yellow	*b1* narrow black, yellow and blue stripes	*c* silver
45th or 1st Nottinghamshire	*a* dark green	*b2* green laurel leaves*	*c* silver
46th or South Devonshire	*a* pale yellow	*b2* narrow red and purple stripes	*c* silver
47th or Lancashire	*a* white	*b2* narrow black, red and black stripes	*c* silver
48th or Northamptonshire	*a* buff	*b2* narrow red and black stripes	*c* gold (buff breeches)
49th or Hertfordshire	*a* dark green	*b1* narrow red, green and red stripes*	*c* gold
50th or West Kent	*a* black	*b2* a narrow red stripe	*c* silver
51st or 2nd Yorkshire, West Riding Light Infantry	*a* grass green	*b2* a wide green stripe	*c* gold
52nd or Oxfordshire Light Infantry	*a* buff	*b2* red chevrons and a narrow yellow stripe	*c* silver
53rd or Shropshire	*a* red	*b2* a narrow red stripe	*c* gold
54th or West Norfolk	*a* dark green	*b2* a narrow green stripe	*c* silver
55th or Westmoreland	*a* dark green	*b2* two narrow green stripes	*c* gold

56th or West Essex	*a* purple	*b2* a wide black stripe	*c* silver
57th or West Middlesex	*a* bright yellow (white in 1812)	*b2* a wide black stripe	*c* gold
58th or Rutland	*a* black	*b1* a wide red stripe	*c* gold
59th or 2nd Nottinghamshire	*a* white	*b1* wide red and yellow stripes*	*c* gold
60th or Royal American Regiment	*a* dark blue (red in 1815)	*b2* two narrow blue stripes	*c* silver
61st or South Gloucestershire	*a* buff	*b1* a wide blue stripe	*c* silver (buff breeches)
62nd or Wiltshire	*a* buff	*b2* a wide blue stripe and narrow yellow and blue stripes	*c* silver (buff breeches)
63rd or West Suffolk	*a* dark green	*b2* a narrow green stripe	*c* silver
64th or 2nd Staffordshire	*a* black	*b2* narrow black and red stripes	*c* gold
65th or 2nd Yorkshire North Riding	*a* white	*b2* narrow stripes, one black and red, the other black	*c* gold
66th or Berkshire	*a* gosling green	*b1* narrow purple, green and purple stripes	*c* silver
67th or South Hampshire	*a* dull yellow	*b2* a wide green stripe, narrow purple and narrow yellow stripes	*c* silver
68th or Durham Light Infantry	*a* bottle green	*b2* a wide black and narrow yellow stripe	*c* silver
69th or South Lincolnshire	*a* dark green	*b2* narrow green, red and green stripes	*c* gold
70th or Glasgow Lowland (Surrey in 1812)	*a* black	*b1* a narrow black dotted line	*c* gold
71st or Highland Light Infantry	*a* buff	*b1* light green line	*c* silver (kilt in military sett)
72nd Highlanders	*a* yellow	*b1* plain white*	*c* silver (kilt in military sett)
73rd Highlanders	*a* dark green	*b1* a narrow red line*	*c* gold
74th Highlanders	*a* white	*b1* a narrow red line	*c* gold
75th Highlanders	*a* yellow	*b2* red and yellow lines	*c* silver
76th	*a* red	*b2* one black stripe	*c* silver
77th or East Middlesex	*a* yellow	*b1* red and yellow lines	*c* silver
78th Highlanders or Rosshire Buffs	*a* buff	*b1* a green line*	*c* gold (kilt in military sett)
79th or Cameron Highlanders	*a* dark green	*b2* red lines flanking a yellow line	*c* gold
80th or Staffordshire Volunteers	*a* yellow	*b2* black lines flanking a red line	*c* gold
81st	*a* buff	*b2* red and blue lines	*c* silver (buff breeches)
82nd or Prince of Wales' Volunteers	*a* yellow	*b2* a black line*	*c* silver
83rd	*a* yellow	*b2* red and green lines	*c* gold
84th or York and Lancaster	*a* yellow	*b2* a black line flanked by yellow and red lines	*c* silver
85th or Bucks Volunteers Light Infantry	*a* yellow	*b2* a red, crenellated line between green lines	*c* silver

Unit	a	b	c
86th or Royal County Down	*a* dark blue	*b2* black edges, red lines	*c* silver
87th Prince of Wales' Own Irish	*a* dark green	*b2* a red line	*c* gold
88th or Connaught Rangers	*a* yellow	*b2* black, red and yellow lines	*c* silver
89th	*a* black	*b2* a red line	*c* gold
90th or Perthshire Volunteers	*a* buff	*b2* black and yellow lines	*c* gold (buff breeches)
91st	*a* yellow	*b2* two black dotted lines	*c* silver
92nd (later the Gordon Highlanders)	*a* yellow	*b2* a blue line	*c* silver (kilt in military sett)
93th (later the Sutherland Highlanders)	*a* yellow	*b2* a yellow line*	*c* silver (kilt in military sett)
94th	*a* dark green	*b2* a red line	*c* gold
95th Riflemen	*a* black	*b* none	*c* silver
96th	*a* buff	*b2* black, yellow and red lines	*c* silver
97th or Queen's Own	*a* dark blue	*b2* black and red lines	*c* silver
98th	*a* buff	*b1* red and green lines	*c* silver (buff breeches)
99th or Prince of Wales' Tipperary	*a* pale yellow	*b1* a yellow stripe	*c* silver
100th or HRH The Prince Regent's County of Dublin	*a* deep yellow	*b1* black edges, red lines	*c* silver
101st or Duke of York's Irish	*a* white	*b2* a green line	*c* silver
102nd	*a* yellow	*b2* a scarlet stripe	*c* silver
103rd	*a* white	*b1* red and light blue lines	*c* silver (buff breeches)
104th	*a* buff	*b2* black, yellow and red lines	*c* silver
Garrison Battalions (six)	*a* dark blue	*b2* a red and a dark blue line	*c* gold
Veteran Battalions (thirteen)	*a* dark blue	*b2* a dark blue line	*c* gold

Foreign Corps in British Service 1812

Unit	a	b	c
Royal York Rangers (dark green dolman and breeches, silver ball buttons)	*a* red	*b* none	*c* gold
Royal West Indian Rangers	*a* red	*b1* a black stripe	*c* gold
Cape Regiment (dark green dolman and breeches, silver ball buttons)	*a* black	*b* none	*c* silver
Bourbon Regiment (dark green dolman and breeches, silver ball buttons)	*a* black	*b* none	*c* silver
Royal Corsican Rangers (dark green dolman, dark blue breeches, black belts)	*a* red	*b* none	*c* silver

Greek Light Infantry (1810–16)—national costume with white trousers and 'Evzone' skirt, red stockings, jacket and waistcoat, red skull cap

Unit	a	b	c
1st Regiment	*a* yellow	*b* yellow	*c* gold
2nd Regiment	*a* dark green	*b* yellow	*c* gold

Plate 21   Great Britain: Trooper 2nd or Royal North British Dragoons 1815
This regiment was also known as the Scots Greys from the colour of their horses. The 'fusileer' cap can clearly be seen with the white horse of Hanover on a red ground on its top patch; the brass front plate bore the royal arms. Red coat, dark blue facings, yellow lace. The shape of cuff shown (Polish or pointed) seems not to have been worn by all dragoon regiments. After *Costumes of the Army of the British Empire according to the Last Regulations 1814.* (*Courtesy National Army Museum*).

Plate 22   Great Britain: Riflemen 1814
(*left*) 60th (Royal American) Regiment, 5th Battalion (green tuft and cords, silver bugle badge, dark green tunic, red facings, white buttons, dark blue breeches with red side piping), (*right*) private, 95th Regiment (Riflemen), (dark green tuft, cords, coat and trousers, black facings, white piping and buttons); both men are using the Baker Rifle. From *Costumes of the Army of the British Empire . . . 1814.* (*Courtesy National Army Museum.*)

141

Plate 23   Great Britain: Royal Artillery, Mounted Rocket Corps 1814
The uniform shows the Tarleton helmet with dark blue turban, brass fittings and bearskin crest and the hussar dolman in dark blue with red facings and yellow buttons and lace, grey overalls with red side stripe. The dark blue portmanteau is edged yellow and the yellow initials on the end (here obscured) are:

A

R R

C

Royal Artillery Rocket Corps – and the dark blue shabraque is edged yellow with the crowned yellow cypher GPR in the corners – this should surely be the reversed royal cypher 'GR'. The man carries rocket staves on his saddlery, which is black with steel fittings. From *Costumes of the Army of the British Empire . . . 1814. (Courtesy National Army Museum)*

Foot Artillery

As for the infantry but dark blue coat, red facings, yellow (bastion ended) lace and yellow buttons. Drivers wore black leather caps with 'C D R A' in yellow on the front (Corps of Drivers, Royal Artillery), waist-length dark blue jackets of dolman style with red collar and Swedish cuffs and three rows of buttons on the chest; white breeches and black 'butcher' boots. Belts were white.

Plate 24   Great Britain: Grenadier Drummer and Musketeer, Coldstream Guards 1792
The lacing of the drummer's tunic is complex and the chevrons on the sleeves point down at this time; the cap has the royal arms as a front plate with white plume and cords. Note that the wings of the blank company of this unit are in the facing colour (dark blue) and that the buttons are arranged in pairs – a custom still observed today and which indicates the seniority of the regiment – 2nd. The musketeer wears standard infantry uniform with white lace edging added to lapels and cuffs. *(Courtesy National Army Museum)*

Horse Artillery
As for the light dragoons; black fur crested 'Tarleton' helmet with white over red plume on the left side, dark blue turban and brass chinscales and peak edging, dark blue dolman with red collar and pointed cuffs, yellow lace and buttons, white breeches and hussar boots or grey overalls.
Engineers   *a* purple   *b* none   *c* gold (red coat)
Sappers   *a* dark blue   *b1* yellow   *c* gold (red coat)
Royal Foreign Artillery   *a* red   *b1* yellow   *c* gold (dark blue coat)

Waggon Train
In 1803 they were as for horse artillery but white lace and buttons. In 1811 other ranks wore the stovepipe shako with crowned royal cypher badge, red tunic with dark blue collar and Polish cuffs piped white, white buttons, grey breeches and boots; black belts. By 1815 they had light dragoon shakos with white top band, loop, button and chinscales, red tunic faced dark blue with white lace and three rows each of eight buttons on the chest; grey overalls with tan leather strappings.

Plate 25 Great Britain: Drum-major, Pioneer and Drummers of the Line Infantry 1814

The green facings and the arrangement and pattern of the lace indicate that the regiment is the 66th or Berkshire Regiment of Foot. The emblem on the pioneer's bearskin cap is unclear — perhaps a crossed axe and shovel. The diminutive drummer and fife-player emphasise the custom of recruiting quite young boys for the regimental bands. (*Courtesy National Army Museum*)

Cavalry

Heavy Cavalry (Dragoon Guards and Dragoons)
Bicorn with large white over red plume, regimental loop and button, red, single-breasted tunics with facings on collar turnbacks and Swedish cuffs,

144

Plate 26   Great Britain: Grenadiers of the 42nd and 92nd Highlanders 1814
The grenadier wings in this illustration are shown in the facing colour for line regiments; only the guards had this privilege – line units' wings were red. The kilt of the corporal of the 42nd Foot (Black Watch) has a red line in the sett to indicate grenadier status; the private of the 92nd (Gordon Highlanders) has yellow facings and a plain (black and dark green) kilt. (*Courtesy National Army Museum*)

regimental lace across chest and on officers' collars. White belts and gauntlets, white breeches and high boots (on campaign these were often replaced by grey button overalls over short boots).

In 1811 the bicorn was replaced by a low-crowned black leather helmet with brass combe, falling, black horse hair crest, brass front plate with crowned royal cypher (GR) and regimental designation and brass chinscales. On the left side was a white over red plume. It was about this time that black sabretasches were introduced and the tunic style was altered. It now hooked together down the front and two broad bands of yellow or white lace (gold or silver for officers) each with a narrow centre stripe in the facing colour ran up the front of coat and around the short skirt turnbacks. The cuffs were also edged in this lace and the shoulder straps were in the facing colour and edged yellow. Around the waist was worn a yellow sash with twin, narrow blue stripes. This sash was gold and crimson for officers. The North British Dragoons (Royal Scots Greys) wore fusilier caps with brass front plates, white cords and red backing with the white horse of Hanover.

The individual regiments were as follows in 1815:

Plate 27 Great Britain: Corporal 10th (Prince of Wales' Own) Royal Hussars, Review Order 1814
The fur busby shown was unpopular with the hussars when introduced in 1812 as it soaked up rain and became very heavy. The bag was red, facing colour buff, buttons and lace yellow, dolman and pelisse dark blue, sash red and yellow, shabraque (which should have been dark blue according to some sources) is shown here red with buff vandyking and yellow lace and cyphers. Over his cuffs this NCO wears a chevron (rank badge) surmounted by what appears to be the Prince of Wales' plumes. (*Courtesy National Army Museum*)

Dragoon Guards (the collar with small red patches at the front ends)

	a (facings)	b (lace)
1st (King's)	a dark blue	b gold
2nd (Queen's)	a black	b silver
3rd (Prince of Wales')	a white	b gold
4th (Royal Irish)	a dark blue	b silver
5th (Princess Charlotte of Wales')	a dark green	b gold
6th (Carabineers)	a white	b silver
7th (Princess Royal's)	a black	b gold

Dragoons (the coat lace ran up the front of the collar)

	a (facings)	b (lace)
1st (Royal)	a dark blue	b gold
2nd (North British)	a dark blue	b gold
3rd (King's Own)	a dark blue	b gold
4th (Queen's Own)	a dark green	b silver
5th (Royal Irish) disbanded 1798	a dark blue	b silver
6th (Inniskilling)	a yellow	b silver

The yellow lace edging to jacket front, cuffs and turnbacks had a central stripe in the facing colour, the yellow waist sash two such stripes.

146

Light Cavalry

Several regiments of dragoons had been converted to light dragoons in 1763 and they all adopted crested leather helmets as had been worn by the light companies of dragoon regiments. In 1784 their coats changed from red to dark blue and they adopted the black crested Tarleton helmet with front peak, coloured turban, plume to left side (white over red) and regimental badge on the right side. They wore very short-skirted jackets with Polish cuffs and lacings and buttons on the chest, lace to collar, cuffs and rear seams, just like hussar dolmans. Regimental facings were shown on collar, cuffs and turnbacks and the turban was frequently also in the facing colour. Sabre and pouch were carried on crossed, buff bandoliers until about 1807 when the sabre belt was worn around the waist. By 1809 the jacket had become a true dolman with no skirts and sabretasches had been introduced; plain black leather for the men, dark blue with edging and crowned royal cypher in the regimental lace for officers.

In 1812 the light dragoons (Regiments 8, 9, 11–14, 16, 17, 19–25) were reuniformed with bell topped shakos having a black within white frontal cockade, regimental loop and button, white over red plume and top band and chinscales in the button colour. Instead of the dolman they now wore a short-skirted, double-breasted dark blue tunic with facings shown on collar, lapels, Polish cuffs, turnbacks and pocket piping. Epaulettes in the button colour were worn and around the waist was a dark blue sash with two wide stripes in the facing colour. Legwear, as before, was white breeches in hussar boots or grey button overalls with twin side stripes in the facing colour. Belts were white, sabre and sabretasche as before. Shabracks were dark blue edged in the facing colour and decorated with the crowned cypher 'GR' and the regimental designation.

Regiments, 7, 10, 15 and 18 were converted in 1812 to hussars with brown fur busbies, red bag (blue for the 18th), silver cords and white over red plume at the front. Dolman, lace, facings and buttons as before, a dark blue pelisse was added and the barrel sash was red and yellow for men of the 10th and 15th, blue and white for men of the 7th and 18th, crimson and gold for officers. Individual regimental details were as follows in 1800, colours in brackets are those worn in 1812.

Light Dragoons (continuing numerically from Dragoons above)

	a (facings)	b (lace)	c (turban)	d (buttons)
7th (Queen's Own)*	a white	b silver	c white	d silver
8th (King's Royal Irish)	a red	b gold	c red	d gold (sash white)
9th	a buff (crimson)	b gold	c red	d silver (gold; sash yellow)
10th (Prince of Wales' Own Royal)*	a scarlet	b silver	c scarlet	d silver
11th	a buff	b silver	c buff	d silver
12th (Prince of Wales')	a yellow	b silver	c yellow	d silver
13th	a buff	b gold	c buff	d gold
14th (Duchess of York's Own)	a orange	b silver	c orange	d silver
15th (King's)*	a scarlet	b silver	c scarlet	d silver
16th (Queen's)	a scarlet (white lapels)	b silver	c scarlet	d silver
17th	a white	b silver	c white	d silver
18th*	a white	b silver	c white	d silver
19th	a yellow	b gold	c yellow	d silver (gold)

20th	*a* yellow (orange)	*b* silver (gold)	*c* yellow (orange)	*d* silver (gold)
21st	*a* black (pink in 1815)	*b* silver (gold in 1815)	*c* black (pink in 1815)	*d* silver (gold in 1815)
22nd (French grey uniforms in 1800)	*a* white	*b* gold	*c* yellow	*d* silver
23rd	*a* yellow (crimson)	*b* silver	*c* yellow (crimson)	*d* silver
24th	*a* yellow (light grey)	*b* gold	*c* yellow (light grey)	*d* gold
25th (French grey uniforms in 1800)	*a* red (light grey)	*b* silver	*c* red (light grey)	*d* silver
26th†	*a* green (changed to blue in 1796)	*b* silver	*c* green (changed to blue in 1796)	*d* silver
27th†	*a* white	*b* silver	*c* white	*d* silver
28th†	*a* yellow	*b* white	*c* yellow	*d* white
29th†	*a* buff	*b* silver	*c* buff	*d* silver

The 30th (Prince of Wales'), 31st, 32nd and 33rd (Ulster) Light Dragoons were all raised in 1794 and disbanded in 1796, never having seen service.

* Converted to hussars in 1812   † disbanded by 1812

Hanover

Electorate until 1803; part of Westfalia 1806 – 13; 1815 kingdom

(Cockade black until 1803 thence black within yellow within white)

Rank Badges

Generals

Bicorn with gold lace edging, yellow and silver tassels, black silk cockade and loop, scarlet coat with white turnbacks and small clothes, dark blue collar, cuffs and lapels, gold buttons and epaulettes, gold embroidery to facings.

Aides de Camp

As above but no gold embroidery to facings, gold buttonholes 'in the English style' to cuffs and pocket flaps.

Infantry

Officers wore yellow and silver waist sashes and sword knots and one epaulette in the button colour on the right shoulder. Grenadier officers wore grenadier caps with red cloth front plates and backing, the small label on the front and the headband were in the regimental facing colour. This front label bore the springing white horse and a motto (the Guard had the royal crest). Around the headband were embroidered trophies of arms with a grenade at the rear. Grenadier NCO's caps were edged in gold or silver in the button colour, privates with yellow or white lace. Officers and all ranks of the guard had yellow pouch lids, others black.

Uniforms in 1787 consisted of a bicorn, red coats, white turnbacks and small clothes, regimental facings shown on cuffs, collars and lapels; white buttons bearing the regimental number. White small clothes and belts, black stocks and gaiters with black leather buttons. Officers' and NCOs' hats were edged silver, privates white.

The guard had gold edging to hat and facings for all ranks. Musketeer NCOs carried spontoons, grenadier NCOs short muskets. There were one grenadier and eight musketeer companies per battalion.

	a (cuffs and lapels)	b (shoulder straps)
1st Infantry Regiment	a dark green	b green
2nd	a dark blue	b red
3rd	a black	b white
4th	a light blue	b blue
5th	a lemon yellow	b red
6th	a light green	b green
7th	a light green	b red
8th	a white	b red
9th (disbanded 1798)	a white	b white
10th	a dark green	b white
11th	a black	b red
12th (disbanded 1798)	a lemon yellow	b yellow
13th	a light blue	b red
14th	a green	b yellow

In 1798 each regiment had two battalions each of one grenadier and three musketeer companies.

Artillery
Bicorn, light blue coat, red facings and turnbacks and red waistcoat all trimmed gold, white breeches, black gaiters, light blue shoulder strap.

Engineers
As for artillery but dark blue coat, gold epaulettes.

Cavalry
Cavalry NCOs were distinguished by gold/silver lace edging to collar, cuffs and lapels for corporals, sergeants and above had double cuff edgings and a single edging to the pocket flaps. NCOs of dragoon regiments also had lace buttonholes on lapels (7), cuffs (2) and collar (2).

Leib-Garde-Regiment
Large bicorn edged gold, yellow and silver tassels, black silk cockade and loop; scarlet coat (all other cavalry regiments wore dark blue), dark blue edged gold lapels, cuffs and collar, gold buttons and lace; gold epaulettes, red greatcoats, white small clothes and belts, black stocks.

For the line cavalry (dark blue coats and greatcoats) the men's hat tassels were in the facing colour. In 1798 each regiment consisted only of two squadrons.

149

	a (lapels, cuffs and collar)	*b (buttons and lace)*
1st or Leib-Regiment	*a* red	*b* gold
2nd Cavallerie-Regiment	*a* white	*b* gold
3rd	*a* lemon yellow	*b* silver
4th	*a* white	*b* silver
5th (Dragoons)	*a* white	*b* silver
6th (Dragoons)	*a* lemon yellow	*b* silver
7th (Dragoons)	*a* lemon yellow	*b* gold
8th (Dragoons)	*a* white	*b* gold
9th (Königin Leichte Dragoner) British light dragoon pattern helmet	*a* red	*b* gold
10th (Leichte Dragoner)	*a* red	*b* silver

Cavalry regiments were armed with carbines, pistols and sabres, dragoons had muskets, pistols and sabres. NCOs had only pistols and sabres. The wooden sabre sheaths were fitted with brass.

The light infantry were armed with smooth bore muskets, NCOs and all Jägers had rifles, buglers replaced drummers.

In 1801 Hanover was invaded by Prussia and the regiments of the army were forced to be reduced to cadre strengths. Russian and British political pressure brought about the evacuation of the Prussian army but in 1803 the French Marshal Mortier with 13,000 men entered the electorate and was permitted by political indecision on the Hanoverian part to manoeuvre their (the Hanoverian) 9,000 strong army into a tactically impossible situation which led to the signature of the Convention of Artlenburg (5 July 1803) under which the Hanoverian army was disbanded.

As a result of this, the British king, George III, resolved to raise a Hanoverian army in exile and this was given the title 'The King's German Legion'. Recruitment began in 1803 and soon there were eight line infantry battalions, two light battalions, two heavy dragoon regiments, three light dragoon regiments, artillery (two horse and four foot batteries) and engineers. The Legion was disbanded in 1816.

Uniforms, rank badges and inter-company distinctions were completely British, unit designations were shown on baldric plates, cap plates, buttons and on infantry officers' turnback badges.

Line Infantry 1803
Stovepipe shako with brass plate, black cockade, regimental button and short tuft (white over red for centre companies, white for grenadiers), red, single-breasted, short-skirted tunic with dark blue collar, shoulder straps and round cuffs, brass buttons, white lace bars to chest, cuffs and pocket flaps; white skirt turnbacks, white edging to collar and shoulder straps. White belts and breeches, black gaiters. Centre companies wore white worsted tufts to the ends of their shoulder straps, flank companies had red wings, trimmed white and edged in white worsted fringing; the light companies had green plumes.

In 1812 the high fronted 'Belgic' shako was adopted with crowned brass front plate bearing the reversed cypher 'GR' over the unit designation and number. Grey trousers replaced the white knee breeches. Canvas packs of British issue and round wooden water bottles were used. The pigtail was worn until 1808.

Drummers had blue and white lace edging to all facings and in place of the usual white lace on the chest, they wore red wings edged in this lace and had six such lace chevrons, point up on each sleeve.

1st Light Battalion

Conical shako as above with black cords and tuft, white stringed bugle horn badge, dark green coat, black facings, white buttons, black belts, grey trousers. Part of the men were issued with the Baker rifle.

2nd Light Battalion

As for 1st except dark green pompon and shako cords, dark green dolman with black facings and shoulder rolls, white buttons. Officers of this battalion wore a Mirliton or winged hussar cap.

Foot Artillery

As for British equivalents; dark blue coats faced red, yellow lace and buttons.

Horse Artillery

As for British horse artillery; low-crowned, light dragoon Kasket with black fur crest, dark blue turban, brass chinscales and fittings, white over red plume, dark blue dolman, red facings, yellow lace and buttons, white breeches and hussar boots or grey overalls.

Cavalry

1st Heavy Dragoons 1803–13

As for British counterparts; large bicorn with cockade loop, button and white over red plume, red, single-breasted tunic, dark blue collar, cuffs and turnbacks, yellow buttons and lace, white belts and breeches, heavy cuffed boots.

2nd Heavy Dragoons 1803–13

As above but black facings. In 1813 these regiments were converted to light dragoons with the following uniforms.

1st Light Dragoons 1813–16

Shako with slightly belled out top, white top band and chinscales, cockade, loop, plume and buttons as before. Dark blue tunic with red collar, lapels, pointed cuffs, turnbacks and piping to rear of coat; yellow buttons and epaulettes. Dark blue and red striped waist sash, white belts, grey overalls with red side stripes, black sabretasches. Curved, brass hilted sabres in steel sheaths.

2nd Light Dragoons 1813–16

As above but white buttons and epaulettes.

1st Light Dragoons 1803-13

British light dragoon costume, ie fur-crested, low-crowned black leather helmet with peak, dark blue turban, white metal fittings and white over red plume on the left side, regimental badge on the right. Dark blue tunic with red collar, pointed cuffs, lapels and short turnbacks all edged white, white belts, buttons and breeches, hussar style short boots.

151

2nd Light Dragoons 1803-13
As above but white facings.

3rd Light Dragoons 1803–13
As above but yellow facings. In 1812 these three regiments were converted to hussars and wore dark blue dolmans and pelisses, yellow buttons and lace, red and yellow barrel sashes, grey overalls with yellow side stripes and regimental facings as before. The 1st Regiment wore fur colpacks, the 2nd and 3rd peaked versions of the same item (shakos were also worn); plumes were white over red and red bags decorated the right side of the colpack.

The King's German Legion was disbanded in 1816 and its men were used to form the new Hanoverian army. The uniforms of this newly raised army were on the British pattern but with silver and yellow waist sashes and sword knots for officers.

THE

Hanseatic Cities

HAMBURG, BREMAN and LUBECK

(Cockade white with an upright red cross)

Until 1810 these city states maintained only very limited militia formations for internal security duties. In that year they were absorbed into Metropolitan France and forced to provide contingents for the 127ᵉ, 128ᵉ and 129ᵉ de Ligne (the latter together with the Duchy of Oldenburg). From 1810–14 they wore French infantry uniform (see section on French Line Infantry p 118).

Even today Hamburg and Bremen are still independent city states within Federal Germany.

Battle History

1812—Russia; December 1812–April 1814—blockade of Hamburg by the allies.

GRAND DUCHY OF

Hessen-Darmstadt

(Cockade black until 1807 then red within white)

In the latter half of the eighteenth century Hessen-Darmstadt uniforms were closely modelled on those of Prussia with the same system of rank badges and company distinctions.

Infantry

Only officers wore the black cockade and they had white and red plumes. Musketeers—white edged bicorn with regimental button, loop, company pompon and red and white hat cords. Dark blue coats with facings shown on collar, lapels, cuffs. Turnbacks were red with a small tab at the junction in the facing colour. Lapels, pocket flaps and cuff flaps were decorated with white lace, buttons, small clothes and belts were white, long gaiters were black. The infantry was organised into three brigades each of three battalions. The 3rd Battalion of each brigade was a Füsilier Battalion and wore dark green coats. The facings for each brigade were: Leib-Brigade—red; Brigade Landgraf—light blue; Brigade Erbprinz—yellow.

In July 1806 Hessen-Darmstadt (which had been a 'Landgrafschaft' county) was elevated to a 'Grand Duchy' and joined the Confederation of the Rhine, changing its cockade to red and white. French rank badges and company distinctions, French equipment, weapons, drill and tactics were adopted. The pigtail was abolished in 1806.

Officers wore bicorns with red plumes with black tips to distinguish them from the Prussians. The uniform remained dark blue but was modernised in style; French shakos were introduced in 1809 with white metal front shields bearing the rampant Hessian lion, above this the cockade under a white loop and button, above this a company pompon surmounted by a red tuft. Company pompon colours were: 1st—white; 2nd—black; 3rd—blue; 4th—red; 5th—yellow; 6th—black over white; 7th—blue over white; 8th—red over white. Black plumes for parades, white metal chinstrap bosses, black leather chinstrap edged in the facing colour. The Füsilier-Bataillone were disbanded and the infantry was now organised in regiments each of two battalions each of four fusilier companies: Leib-garde-regiment—red; Leib-regiment—light blue; Regiment Erbprinz—yellow. On the shoulders were dark blue, fringeless epaulettes edged in the facing colour. In 1809 this latter regiment was organised and badged on French lines (two battalions each of one grenadier, one Voltigeur and four fusilier companies). It was in Spain and thus away from its headquarters and had to comply with French orders.

In 1812 a Provisional Light Infantry Regiment was raised; it wore uniform as the Leib-garde-regiment with scarlet facings and white buttons, white hunting horn badges in the turnback corners. Officers wore curved sabres and cartouches on black bàndoliers crossed on the chest, other ranks' leatherwork was black. This regiment later became the Garde-Füsilier-Regiment. By 1812 the shakos had white chinscales.

The Regiment Prinz Emil was raised in 1813 and had uniform as above but with pink facings. In 1814 the contre-epaulettes were discarded and replaced by dark blue shoulder straps edged in the facing colour.

Foot Artillery

Bicorn (with wide, scalloped gold border for officers) dark blue coat of infantry style, dark blue cuff flaps, black collar, lapels and cuffs, red turnbacks, yellow buttons, white small clothes, black gaiters. In 1803 buttons changed to white and the white lace buttonhole decoration was added. In 1807 the shako with red pompon replaced the bicorn and the black facings were piped red; dark blue breeches.

153

Plate 28 Grand Duchy of Hessen-Darmstadt: 1809
(l to r) Trooper, Chevau Légers (brass helmet fittings, dark green coat and breeches, black lapels, cuffs, cuff flaps and front patches to collar, red collar, shoulder straps and piping, white buttons and lace), musketeer private, Brigade Landgraf (light blue facings, white lace and buttons). The absence of the white shield bearing the Hessian lion on the infantry shako is unexplained, musketeer private, Leib-Brigade (red facings, white over red plume, white lace and buttons), fusilier officer, Lieb-Brigade (dark green coat, red facings, gold epaulettes), fusilier private, Brigade Landgraf. *Augsburger Bilder.*

Cavalry

A Chevau Légers regiment was raised in 1790; its uniform was British style: light dragoon helmet in black leather, trimmed in brass with brass front cypher ('LLX'—Landgraf Ludwig X), black crest. Dark green coat with red collar, having black patches at the front, red turnbacks, black lapels and round cuffs, white buttons and buttonholes; buff small clothes, short hussar boots. On each cuff one button in the centre of a white 'V' of lace, above each cuff two such buttons and 'V's. Green shabraques, black vandyke edging, white piping and cypher in rear corner. Buff bandoliers, black harness with brass fittings. In 1809 the tunic cut was modernised, belts became black, breeches dark green with red side piping and the helmet was more the Bavarian Raupenhelm style with white metal fittings, crowned cypher 'L', black crest and plume. Curved sabre in steel sheath with brass hilt.

There was also a troop of mounted life guards in bicorns, buff tunics edged in red and white lace, red waist sash, facings and turnbacks, white breeches, high cuffed boots and heavy cavalry swords.

Battle History

1806—✂ Jena with the French; 1807—siege of Graudenz; 1808–12—Spain;

1809—with 1st Division, IV Corps of Grande Armée—⚔ Wagram; 1812—Russia in 4th Division, I Corps; in 30th Light Cavalry Brigade, IX Corps and in 30th Division, XI Corps; 1813—Saxony with the French until after Leipzig, thence with the allies.

ELECTORATE OF

Hessen-Kassel

1792 – 1815

(Cockade red within white)

The state was a county until 1803 when it was elevated to an electorate, in 1806 Napoleon abolished it but it was re-established in 1813, again as an electorate even though the Holy Roman Empire (whose Emperor the elector elected) had vanished in 1805.

Until 1806 all uniform and rank details were very similar to Prussia with the exception of the sash, sword knot and cockade colours. Grenadiers wore Prussian-style mitre caps, the musketeers small bicorns with white edging. Coats were dark blue, small clothes and belts white.

Infantry 1792–1806

	a (facings)	b (buttons)	c (soldiers' lace)	d (officers' lace)
Regiment Garde	a red	b white	c white	d silver
Garde-Grenadier-Regiment	a red	b white	c white	d silver
Erbprinz (1803—Kurprinz, 1805—Wurmb)	a pink	b white	c none	d none
Prinz Karl (1805—Landgraf Karl)	a red with yellow edging	b yellow	c none	d gold
Leib-Regiment (1803—Kurfürst)	a yellow	b white	c white	d silver
Kospoth (1801—Biesenrodt, 1805—Kurprinz)	a black	b yellow	c none	d none
Lossberg (1799—Linsingen, 1805—Biesenrodt)	a orange	b white	c none	d none
Hëymel (1789—Ditfurth then Hanstein; disbanded 1795)	a orange	b yellow	c none	d gold
Feldjäger (1793–Jäger-Bataillon) (dark green coat and breeches)	a crimson	b white	c none	d none

In 1795 each regiment had one grenadier battalion and two musketeer battalions each of four companies.

Artillery
Infantry uniform, dark blue coat, crimson facings, yellow buttons, gold lace for officers.

Cavalry 1792

Garde du Corps—as for the Prussian equivalent but with Hessian cockade. Gensdarmes—bicorns, buff tunics, red facings, white belts and breeches. Carabiniers-Regiment—bicorns, white tunics, light blue facings; lace white with a light blue central stripe. Leib-Dragoner-Regiment—bicorn, light blue coat, red facings, yellow buttons (gold lace for officers), white belts and breeches, high boots. Prinz Friedrich Dragoner—as above but yellow facings, white buttons (silver lace for officers). Husaren-Regiment—colpack with white plume, white dolman and pelisse, light blue facings, yellow lace and buttons, black fur.

The army was disbanded in 1806 and some men later joined the regiments of the Kingdom of Westfalia.

In 1813 the Elector re-raised the army and dressed it entirely in contemporary Prussian style with the exception that he insisted that all ranks wear white powdered pigtails which had been discarded by all other armies years before.

The Kur-Hessian Corps 1809

The dispossessed Kurfürst of Hessen-Kassel raised a Frei-Korps in Bohemia in 1809 to fight Napoleon. Austria provided money and equipment. The corps took part in several actions before being disbanded after the battle of Wagram.

Data on the uniforms worn is sparse but the following has been established.

Grenadier Battalion
Austrian bearskin with white frontal grenade and edging to peak, red bag with white trim and tassel, red and white cords, white over red plume, red within white cockade. Dark blue coat with red collar, straight lapels, Swedish cuffs and turnbacks, white buttons, belts and small clothes, high black gaiters. Moustaches, short pigtails to the bottom of the collar.

Line Infantry Battalion
Austrian shako with red within white cockade, white button and loop up to red within white pompon, red and white cords, white plume with red tip and base, black chinstrap. Leaf green, single-breasted coat, red collar, Swedish cuffs and turnbacks, white buttons; leaf green breeches, black belts and boots. Officers had drooping white feather plumes, silver contre-epaulette and aiguillette to right shoulder, leaf green breeches with silver thigh knots and side stripes, silver trim and tassels to hussar boots; sabres in steel sheaths with silver and red straps and tassels, silver waist belt and clasp.

Dragoon Squadron
Austrian cavalry helmet with red over white crest, brass fittings, crowned 'WK' (Wilhelm, Kurfürst) on the front plate, brass chinscales. Light blue, double-breasted tunic of Prussian cut, red collar, Swedish cuffs and edging to light blue turnbacks, white buttons and belts. Buff gauntlets, grey button overalls. Austrian Kürassier pattern sword in steel sheath. White sheepskin saddle cloth edged red, light blue holster covers edged red, black harness.

Hussar Squadron

Black Austrian shako with white over red plume, red within white pompon and cockade, red and white cords, white loop and button. Yellow dolman faced light blue with white buttons and lace, light blue pelisse with black fur, red and white sash, black belts, grey button overalls, light blue sabretasche with white edging and crowned 'WK' cypher. Black sheepskin saddle cloth edged light blue, black harness with steel fittings. Moustaches were worn and hair was in three plaits (the pigtail and one in front of each ear).

Infantry 1813

The 1813 uniform was as follows: Prussian-style, leather-reinforced shako with red within white pompon, white chinscales and cords; dark blue, double-breasted Prussian tunics (with similar cuff flaps for the line); facings shown on collar, shoulder straps and cuffs, turnbacks red. White breeches and belts, black, short gaiters.

The individual regimental distinctions were as follows:
1 Leib-Grenadier-Garde—bearskin with white metal plate bearing 'WK' under an electoral cap, white cords, white plume with red tip. Red collar, shoulder straps and Swedish cuffs, white buttons and guards lace.
2 Garde-Grenadier-Regiment—shako with white grenade badge, otherwise as above.
3 Kurfürst—yellow facings, white buttons; Kurprinz—white and yellow; Landgraf Karl—red and yellow; Solms-Braufels—crimson and white.
4. Jäger-Bataillon—shako as for the line, dark green coats, crimson facings, white buttons, black belts, grey breeches.

Landwehr infantry were also raised and wore Prussian Landwehr-style uniforms. The facings were: 1st Regiment—crimson; 2nd—black; 3rd—red; all buttons white. All wore shakos in black covers with white Teutonic crosses on the front.

Foot Artillery

Shakos with brass grenade badge, same badge on the pouch; dark blue tunic, crimson facings, red turnbacks, yellow buttons and yellow guards lace to collar; white breeches, black belts, black gaiters.

Horse Artillery

As above but dark green plumes, dark blue overalls with crimson side stripe, dark blue turnbacks with crimson edging and red piping, white belts.

Cavalry 1813

Garde du corps

As in Prussia but with Bavarian Raupenhelm with white metal fittings and plate bearing 'WK'.

Garde-Husaren

Brown fur colpack with red bag and white plume and cords, dark blue dolman and pelisse, red collar and cuffs and sabretasches with white edging and crowned cypher 'WK', white lace and buttons, white fur, buff leather breeches in hussar boots, white belts.

Leib-Dragoner-Regiment
Infantry shako. Prussian-style, light blue tunic, red facings, yellow buttons; buff leather breeches and hussar boots or grey overalls with red side piping.

Husaren-Regiment
Shakos, otherwise as for the Garde-Husaren but with black bandolier.

Battle History

1792–5—the Rhine; 1798—the Rhine; 1814—France.

THE

Italian Republics

AND THE KINGDOM OF

Italy

1796 – 1814

(Cockade green within red within white)

In 1805 the kingdom of Italy was formed from the Cispandane and Cisalpine Republics and other north Italian territories. The period 1792–6 saw these states as part of the Austrian Empire. Rank badges and inter-company distinctions as in France.

Lombard Legion 1796–7
Corsican hat with left brim upturned and bearing a yellow loop and button; cockade and white over red over green plume; square brass front plate inscribed 'Viva la Liberta'. Dark green single-breasted tunic, red collar, shoulder straps, pointed cuffs and turnbacks, white buttons with peripheral inscription 'Legione Lombarda, Liberta, Eguaglianza'. Dark green breeches with red side stripe, short black gaiters, white belts.

The Cisalpine Legion 1796–7
As above except: bicorn with yellow loop and button; peripheral button inscription: 'Legione Italiana, Liberta, Eguaglianza'.

Artillery
As above (for each legion) but with black facings.

Cisalpine Hussars 1796–7
Black shako with white top band and cords; cockade and plume as above at top front, white lozenge front plate and chinscales. Dark green dolman, white buttons and lace; red and white sash. Dark green breeches with white lace decoration, white trim to hussar boots, white belts, dark green saddle furniture edged white, black harness with steel fittings.

Plate 29   Italy: Line Horse Artillery 1808
Red tufts and cords, brass badge, dark green tunics and waistcoats, white buttons, red piping, red cuff flaps and turnback grenades. (*Reproduced by Gracious Permission of Her Majesty the Queen.*)

Plate 30 Italy: Gardes d'Honneur 1806–1815
Dark green coat, pink facings (Milanese company), silver lace and buttons, dark
green horse furniture trimmed silver. (*Reproduced by Gracious Permission of Her
Majesty the Queen.*)

Cispadanane Chasseurs à Cheval 1796–7
As for Cisalpine Hussars except: black Mirliton with yellow flame and white
trim.

The Polish Legions

Infantry
Czapka with dark blue top piped white; white cords and headband;
initially the French cockade, yellow chinscales, white over red pompon.
Dark blue kurtka, crimson collar, lapels, Polish cuffs and turnbacks,

160

crimson piping to dark blue shoulder straps, white buttons. Dark blue breeches with crimson side stripe, white waistcoat and belts, short black gaiters with white trim and tassel.

Cavalry
As for the infantry but with crimson facings for one regiment, yellow for the other (squadron identity was expressed by the arrangement of the red, white and blue colours of the plume); hussar boots with trim and tassel in the facing colour. Dark blue saddle furniture edged white, white sheepskin saddle cloth edged red, black harness with steel fittings.

In 1800 a grenadier battalion was raised in the Polish Legion infantry; it was dressed as for the other battalions but with drooping red hair plume, red epaulettes, black belts, red sabre knot and gaiter trim and red and blue waist sash. Also in this year the Cispadane Legion was augmented by a battalion of Carabiniers in light infantry shako, white cuff flaps, red plume sabre knot and epaulettes, otherwise as for the other infantry units.

In 1803 the Cisalpine Republic (as these two states had now become) raised a presidential guard consisting of a battalion, each of Grenadiers and Chasseurs à Pied (eight companies in all), a squadron each of Grenadiers à Cheval and Chasseurs à Cheval, a company of horse artillery and a company of artillery train. These units were uniformed exactly as for the French Consular Guard but with dark green coats instead of dark blue. In 1805 (when Italy became a kingdom) this guard was expanded to two battalions each of grenadiers and Chasseurs à Pied and twelve companies of Vèlites (grenadiers and chasseurs). The cavalry was increased by a regiment each of Gardes d'Honneur and Dragoons, a company of foot artillery and a corps of Gendarmerie d'Elite were also raised.

Royal Italian Guard

Grenadiers
As for Imperial Guard except: Italian cockade, dark green coats, white buttons and white front plate to bearskin bearing a grenade flanked by 'R' and 'I'. The Italian eagle was similar to the French version but had a five-pointed star on its chest enclosing the letter 'N' under the Iron Crown of Lombardy.

Chasseurs
As above except red collar with cuffs, white piping to collar, lapels, turn-backs and pockets, shako with white top band, cords, loop and button, brass eagle front plate, green plume, cockade.

Vèlite Grenadiers
As for grenadiers except: yellow front plate to bearskin, white coat with green collar, lapels, cuffs, French cuff flaps, turnbacks and pocket flap piping, white piping to collar, lapels and cuff flaps, red epaulettes, yellow buttons.

Vèlite Chasseurs (Carabiniers)
Bearskin bonnet with red and green plume, yellow plate, white coat with facings as for Vèlite Grenadiers.

Conscripts of the Guard
As for Chasseurs.

Gardes d'Honneur

Brass helmet as for French Carabiniers but with the combe in the form of an eagle, steel turban with crowned 'N' badge, black peak and neck shield edged in steel, black crest, white plume, yellow chinscales. Dark green, dragoon style coat, facings in company colour on collar, lapels, round cuffs, turnbacks and pocket piping; collar and cuffs were each decorated with two white lace loops; brass scale epaulettes with backing in the facing colour, yellow aiguillette on the right shoulder; white waistcoat, breeches and belts, high cuffed boots. Dark green saddle furniture edged white with white iron crown in rear corner, black harness with brass fittings.

Company titles and facings were: 1st 'Milan'—pink; 2nd 'Bologna'—yellow; 3rd 'Brescia'—buff; 4th 'Romagna'—scarlet; 5th 'Venezia'—orange.

Dragoons of the Guard

As for the Empress Dragoons of the Imperial Guard but with white lace and buttons.

Foot Artillery of the Guard

Black bearskin with no front plate, red top patch with white cross, red cords and plume; cockade. Dark green coat, black collar and lapels piped red, red cuffs and French cuff flaps, red epaulettes and turnbacks with green grenade badges, white belts, green breeches and waistcoat, black boots.

Horse Artillery of the Guard

As for horse artillery of the Imperial Guard.

Train of Artillery of the Guard

Black czapka with brass badge of crossed cannon barrels under the iron crown on the upper left side, brass chinscales, red plume and pompon, cockade. Grey coat, dark green collar, Polish cuffs and turnbacks, the latter with white grenade badges, white buttons; dark green epaulettes and five dark green lace bars across the chest, buff breeches, white belts, high boots.

Gendarmerie d'Elite

As for French Gendarmerie d'Elite but with Italian cockade.

Italian Line Infantry

Prior to 1807 they wore the bicorn, regimental button and loop, Italian cockade and company pompon. In 1807 this was replaced by the French infantry shako with lozenge plate in the button colour. Coats were dark green until late 1806 thence white with facings as below:

	a (collar)	b (lapels and shoulder straps)	c (cuffs)	d (cuff flaps)	e (turn-backs)	f (buttons)
1st Regiment	a green	b red	c red	d green	e red	f yellow
2nd	a white†	b red*	c white†	d red*	e white†	f yellow

162

3rd	*a* red*	*b* red*	*c* red*	*d* red*	*e* red*	*f* yellow
4th	*a* red*	*b* white‡	*c* white‡	*d* green*	*e* white‡	*f* white
5th	*a* red*	*b* green*	*c* green*	*d* red*	*e* white†	*f* white
6th	*a* white†	*b* green*	*c* white†	*d* green*	*e* white†	*f* yellow
7th	*a* green	*b* white‡	*c* red*	*d* none	*e* white‡	*f* white

(This regiment had pointed cuffs)

*=piped white; †=piped green; ‡=piped red

Istrian Chasseurs

1806 French light infantry uniform in dark green with light blue facings and white buttons.

Dalmatian Infantry Regiment

As for light infantry with red facings and yellow buttons. The brass lozenge shako plate bore 'RDI' under the iron crown.

Foot Artillery

Peakless shako with red cords and plumes, brass badge of crossed gun barrels. Dark green coat and waistcoat, dark green collar, lapels, cuffs, shoulder straps and turnbacks piped red (red grenades in the turnbacks), red cuff flaps, dark green breeches, black gaiters, white belts.

Horse Artillery

Black czapka, red plume brass chinscales, cockade, dark green dolman, red collar, pointed cuffs and lace, yellow buttons; dark green breeches with red trim to hussar boots, white belts.

Artillery Train

As for foot artillery but single-breasted coats.

Engineers

As for foot artillery but French shakos, red epaulettes and black pointed cuffs piped red.

Line Cavalry

Dragoons

French uniform, the helmet with black fur turban and green plume on the left; dark green coats and shoulder straps, white buttons, belts and small clothes. Facings: 1st Regiment ('Dragoni Regina')—pink; 2nd ('Dragoni Napoleoni)—crimson (green collar and red facings in 1812).

Chasseurs à Cheval

Shako bearing only the cockade, loop and button at the top front, white chinscales, dark green plume with tip in the regimental colour. Dark green, single-breasted tunics and breeches, white buttons and lace bars across the chest, collar, pointed cuffs and turnbacks in the following colours: 1st Regiment—yellow; 2nd—red; 3rd—red (this regiment wore black fur colpacks with cockade and red plume at the top front); 4th—violet. The breeches had white Hungarian lace to sides and thighs. Dark green saddle furniture edged in the regimental colour, black harness with brass fittings.

In 1814 the army ceased to exist.

Battle History

1796–8 and 1800—campaigns in Italy against Austria; 1805 and 1809—against Austria; 1806—against Prussia; 1808–13—against Spain and Portugal; 1812—in Russia as 14th and 15th Divisions, IV Corps; 1813—in Saxony against the allies.

GRAND DUCHY OF

Kleve-Berg

1806 – 13

(Cockade red within white)

Badges of rank and inter-company distinctions as for the French army.
There were no guards units as such although the 1st Lancers were attached to the Imperial Guard for a long time in France and Spain.

Line Infantry

The Bavarian Infantry Regiment 'Kinkel' formed the basis of this corps together with some troops from Nassau-Oranien.

1st Regiment (raised 24 April 1806)
Initially their old Bavarian uniforms but by 1807 the French pattern replaced this. Shako with either the brass lozenge plate with the eagle or an oval brass plate bearing the crowned rampant lion of Berg or the crowned initial 'J' (Joachim Murat, Grand Duke of Berg until 1808). Company trim as in the French army. White coat with light blue lapels, collar, round cuffs (later augmented by white trident cuff flaps edged light blue) and turnbacks, white belts and breeches; yellow buttons, short black gaiters with light blue hussar trim. Oval brass pouch plate with crowned 'J' (later the rampant lion). French equipment.

2nd Regiment (raised 29 August 1808)
As above but with light blue Polish cuffs.

3rd Regiment (raised October 1808)
As for the 1st Regiment but with light blue trident cuff flaps.

4th Regiment (raised 9 August 1811)
As for 1st Regiment but with plain, round light blue cuffs.

1st Chevau Légers (raised 1807)
Polish costume in white with pink facings and white buttons. In 1809

164

they were converted to Chasseurs à Cheval with pink shako, dark green uniform, pink facings and white buttons. In 1810 they were remustered as Chevau Légers Lanciers in Polish costume again, dark green, pink facings, white buttons, crimson over white lance pennants.

2nd Regiment (raised 1 April 1812)
Uniform as for the 1st Regiment.
    Trumpeters wore brown fur colpacks, red plumes and cords, pink bag, reversed colours.

Foot Artillery
Shako with red plume and cords, yellow shield plate and chinscales, dark blue coat and breeches, red collar, shoulder straps, cuffs, turnbacks and edging to dark blue lapels and squared dark blue cuff flaps. Yellow buttons, white belts, red sabre knots, black gaiters.

Horse Artillery
As for foot artillery but dark blue Hungarian breeches with red thigh knots and side stripes, red trimmed hussar boots.

Train
Shako with oval brass lion plate, light blue pompon, grey coat, light blue collar, lapels, turnbacks and pointed cuffs, grey shoulder straps piped light blue, yellow buttons. Grey overalls, black bandolier, red sabre knot.

Gendarmerie
As in France but with Berg cockade.

Battle History

1808–13—Chevau Légers and 1st and 2nd Infantry Regiments in Spain as part of the Imperial Guard and the German Division respectively; 1809—Aspern and Wagram as part of the Reserve; 1812—Russia as part of 26th Division, IX Corps (destroyed at the Beresina crossing); 1813—in Saxony.
    In 1815 the cavalry became the 11th Prussian hussars and the infantry became the 28th and 29th Prussian infantry regiments.

PRINCIPALITY OF

Lippe-Detmold,

AND THE COUNTY OF

Schaumburg-Lippe

(Cockade red and yellow)

Until joining the Confederation of the Rhine on 18 April 1807 these states had no standing troops. Together they were required to provide a 650-strong contingent which wore the following uniform: bicorn with green plume, white coat, buttons, breeches and belts, dark green collar and cuffs; French badges of rank and inter-company distinctions. By 1812 the French shako had replaced the bicorn; it had a white rhombic plate bearing a crowned, eight-pointed star, cockade, company pompon, cords and plume, white chinscales. The coat was now closed to the waist and had white lapels, shoulder straps (fusiliers) and cuff flaps all piped green, dark green collar, cuffs and turnbacks, French equipment, short black gaiters. Drummers were distinguished by a dark green bar across the top of the sleeve, brass drum, green and white striped hoops. Pioniers wore brown bearskins, buff aprons and gauntlets, grenadier's badges and full beards.

Battle History

1807—siege of Glogau against Prussia; 1809—Tyrol; 1809–11 Spain; 1812—Russia as part of 2nd Brigade, 'Division Princiére'; 1813—besieged in Danzig. The states left the Confederation of the Rhine in November and December 1813 respectively.

GRAND DUCHY OF

Mecklenburg-Schwerin,

AND

Mecklenburg-Strelitz

(Cockade yellow within blue within red)

Musketeer Battalion
Uniform very similar in style to the contemporary Prussian model: small bicorn with white edging, loop, buttons and tassels, red over white pompon, dark blue tunic with red lapels, round cuffs, collar and turnbacks, white belts, buttons and small clothes, black gaiters to above the knee. Badges of rank were on the Prussian model (officers—gold, red and blue waist sashes and sword knots, canes; NCOs—silver collar and cuff edging, red, yellow and blue mixed sabre tassels, canes and spontoons).

7th Regiment of the Confederation
Schwerin joined the Confederation of the Rhine on 24 April 1808 and Strelitz on 18 February that year; together they provided the two-battalion '7th Regiment of the Confederation'. While retaining strong Prussian style in the uniform, badges of rank and inter-company distinctions, organisation, tactics and weaponry were all fashioned on the French model. Shako with brass chinscales and front badge reversed 'FF' (Friedrich Franz), company pompon, cords and plume; dark blue, double-breasted coat with two close rows of white buttons on the closed lapels, red collar, round cuffs and turnbacks, grey breeches, short black gaiters, white belts. NCOs had blue tips to plumes and pompons, red, white and blue mixed shako cords. Drummers wore red plumes and cords, brass drum, red, yellow and blue striped hoops. Pioneers had brown bearskin caps, red cords, plumes and

epaulettes, white apron; crossed axes badge on pouch; beards were worn.

Junior officers had silver pompon and shako trim, gold sunburst plate with ducal crest, black plume. Senior officers had gold pompon and white plumes. All officers wore sashes and sabre knots as before, silver epaulettes, sabres on white bandoliers.

Garde-Grenadier-Bataillon
Bearskin bonnets, white cords, red plume on the left, red top patch with white cross, dark blue coat as for the 7th Confederation Regiment but with dark blue cuff flaps bearing three white buttons and buttonhole laces and two such laces on each side of the collar; the men wore red epaulettes.

Foot Artillery Battery
As for fusiliers but with black plumes and facings. For the 1812 campaign Mecklenburg-Strelitz raised an infantry regiment and artillery battery while Mecklenburg-Schwerin provided an infantry battalion (3rd Battalion, 7th Confederation Regiment).

Mecklenburg-Schwerin Infantry Battalion
Uniform as for the Strelitz regiment except: yellow buttons, officers had dark blue plumes with a red base, gold oak leaf top band to shako, gold front plate of Mecklenburg crest with supporters, gold epaulettes, gold oval buckle to waist sash, sabre on waist belt slings, grey breeches.

Mecklenburg left the Confederation of the Rhine on 14 March 1813. In 1813 Mecklenburg-Strelitz raised a regiment of hussars which captured the eagle of the Marines of the Imperial Guard during the three-day Battle of Leipzig (16–18 October 1813).

Their uniform was a shako with cockade, brass 'Wendish' cross, yellow cords and chinscales; black dolman and pelisse, yellow lace and buttons, white fur, light blue Hungarian breeches laced yellow, black and yellow barrel sash, black belts and black sabretasche with crowned brass 'C', brass hilted sabre in steel sheath. Saddle furniture was a black sheepskin edged light blue, black Hungarian harness with brass fittings.

Battle History

1809—garrison duty in Prussia; 1812—Russia as part of the 3rd Division, I Corps and 5th Division I Corps; 1813—Saxony with the allies; ✗ Leipzig.

KINGDOM OF

Naples

1806 – 14

(Cockade crimson within white)

This state was created by Napoleon for his brother Joseph and later given to Joachim Murat in 1806 from the mainland portion of the Kingdom of the Two Sicilies (see p 237).

All rank badges and inter-company distinctions as in the French army.

Guard Infantry

Vèlites (two regiments)
Bearskin with no front plate, green cords and plume (with red tip for 1st Regiment), carmine top patch with gold grenade. White coats, belts, breeches, carmine collar, Polish cuffs, lapels and turnbacks all piped white, yellow buttons, gold lace loops to collar (2), lapels (7) and cuffs (3). Officers had white plumes, gold cords, epaulettes, gorget, sword knot and trim to hussar-pattern boots. Drummers had carmine and white lace edging to facings and to carmine swallows' nests and seven such lace chevrons, point up, on each sleeve with similar lace down the sleeve seams. Brass drum, carmine and white dogtoothed hoops.

Grenadiers (one regiment)
As for Vèlites except: red cords and plume, dark blue coat with light crimson collar, lapels, cuffs, French cuff flaps and turnbacks (all but the latter piped white), yellow buttons and tasselled buttonholes to collar (2), cuff (2) and lapel (7). Red epaulettes and sabre knot, white breeches and belts, black gaiters. Drummers wore reversed colours.

Voltigeurs
As for Vèlites but buff shakos with green cords and pompon, buff collars.

Marines
Shako with crowned brass plate in shield shape (some sources give a bearskin with red cords and plume), cockade, red pompon and cords, brass chinscales, dark blue coat and breeches, red collar, cuffs, lapels and turnbacks, red epaulettes with white half moons, yellow buttons, buff belts edged white.

Guard Artillery
As for that of the Imperial Guard but with pale purple facings.

Line Infantry

French shako with brass, crowned shield-shaped plate bearing 'JN', pompon and cockade but no cords; white coat, shoulder straps, belts and breeches, short black gaiters; yellow buttons. Facings shown on collar, cuffs, lapels, turnbacks, scalloped cuff flaps and piping. 1st Regiment—sky blue; 2nd— light red; 3rd—black; 4th—pale purple; 5th—dark green; 6th—orange; 7th—yellow; 8th—pink; 9th light blue; 10th*—dark blue; 11th*—pale purple; 12*—green; (*raised 1814). The 7th Regiment was composed of Negroes. Drummers—red, white and blue (later carmine and white) lace to facings, carmine swallows' nests (initially in the facing colour), sleeves and seams, brass drums with carmine and white hoops. Pioneers—grenadier distinctions, red crossed axes under a flaming grenade on both upper arms, white aprons, full beards.

Light Infantry

(Two regiments plus the Royal Corsican Regiment until 1813, then the Royal Corsican became the 1st, the two existing regiments became the 2nd and 3rd and a new 4th was raised.)

Uniform as for the line infantry except: white metal shako plate and buttons, mid-blue coat and trousers of French light infantry cut, facings shown on cuff flaps and piping to blue lapels and cuffs (all collars yellow), yellow over green, carrot-shaped pompon, white hunting horn badges on the blue turnbacks; green epaulettes with yellow half moons, green sabre straps. Carabiniers wore bearskin caps with red cords, plume and top patch having a white grenade, red epaulettes and sabre strap, collars in the facing colour.

Facings in 1813: 1st Regiment black; 2nd yellow; 3rd red; 4th orange.

Foot Artillery of the Guard
Shako with light crimson plume, pompon and cords, yellow plate, chinscales, loop and button; cockade. Dark blue coat, waistcoat and breeches, light crimson facings, yellow buttons, black gaiters, white belts; guards' lace loops to collars.

Horse Artillery of the Guard
Brown fur colpack with light crimson pompon, plume bag and tassel, yellow trim to bag; dark blue coat, lapels and pointed cuffs, light crimson collar, turnbacks, epaulette, aiguillete on right shoulder and piping to lapels and cuffs; yellow buttons, white belts. Dark blue breeches with light crimson lace, dark blue waistcoat with light crimson lace and yellow buttons. Hussar boots with light crimson trim and tassel, black sabretasche with gold edging and crowned 'JN' cypher.

Train of Artillery of the Guard
As for the foot artillery of the guard except: light blue tunic and breeches, white buttons.

Foot Artillery of the Line
Infantry uniform in dark blue with red facings and yellow buttons, as in France but with 'JN' cyphers.

Horse Artillery of the Line
As for French horse artillery but with Neopolitan cockade and 'JN' cyphers.

Artillery Train
As for that of the guard but with black facings and red epaulettes.

Cavalry of the Guard

Gardes d'Honneur (later converted to Gardes du Corps)
Black colpack with red bag and yellow trim, tassel and cords, white dolman
faced red, yellow lace and buttons, crimson and yellow sash, red pelisse
with black fur, light green breeches with yellow lacing, yellow trim to
hussar boots; green shabraque edged red and piped yellow.

Gardes du Corps (the converted Gardes d'Honneur)
Bicorn with cockade, white button, loop and plume; red, single-breasted tunic,
yellow collar, cuffs and turnbacks, red cuff flaps and yellow piping to vertical
pocket flaps. White buttons, epaulettes and aiguillette on right shoulder,
white breeches, heavy cavalry boots, white belts, black harness and brass
fittings. Blue saddle furniture with white edging and red piping, square blue
portmanteau. In the rear shabraque corners the crowned white cypher 'JN'.

Vèlites à Cheval
Shako with gold top band, chinscales and sunburst plate bearing crowned
'JN', gold cords, white plume; dark blue kurtka with yellow facings and
buttons; dark blue breeches with double yellow side stripes, dark blue saddle
furniture edged yellow and with yellow cypher. Officers—as above but gold
epaulettes and aiguillette, gold bandolier edged dark blue. Trumpeters—
reversed colours and lace as for Guardia d'Onore.

Hussars of the Guard (raised from the disbanded Vèlites à Cheval in 1814)
Black shako with brass fittings, white top band and cords; sky blue dolman
with crimson facings, white buttons and lace; crimson pelisse with black fur,
crimson and white sash, sky blue breeches with white lacing. Sky blue
saddle furniture edged white with the crowned white cypher 'JN' in the rear
corner. White belts, black harness with brass fittings.
   Trumpeters had uniform as above except crimson dolman, faced sky blue,
sky blue pelisse, white fur, crimson breeches.

Line Cavalry

1st Chevau-Légers (3rd Chevau Légers from March 1813)
French shako with semi-circular, white, sun ray plate with brass centre bearing
the crowned 'JN', white top band, cockade and crimson within white pompon.
Light blue, double-breasted tunic, light blue collar, lapels, shoulder straps
and pointed cuffs all edged crimson, crimson turnbacks with white hunting
horn badges, white buttons. Light blue breeches with double crimson side
stripes, hussar boots with white trim and tassel; white belts, light blue
saddle furniture edged crimson with white, crowned 'JN' in the rear corner
and the regimental number in white on the round ends of the portmanteau.
Trumpeters wore reversed colours, facings edged in crimson and white lace,
the elite company had black fur colpacks with red pompon, plume, cords,
epaulettes and sabre straps.

Chasseurs à Cheval (two regiments raised in 1806; in March 1813 they were converted to the 1st and 2nd Chevau Légers)
Shako with brass lozenge plate bearing '1' or '2', brass chinscales white top band, cords, loop and button; cockade. Dark green plume with red tip. Dark green tunic with red turnbacks and red piping to dark green collar, lapels, pointed cuffs and shoulder straps; white buttons and white hunting horns in the turnbacks. Red breeches with twin dark green side stripes, hussar boots trimmed white. Dark green saddle furniture edged red with white crowned 'JN' (and regimental number on the round ends of the portmanteau). White belts, black harness with brass fittings. Trumpeters wore red tunics with dark green collar, cuffs, lapels and turnbacks, red shoulder straps edged green, crimson and white lace edging to collar and cuffs; dark green breeches striped red.

In March 1813 all three line cavalry regiments received black lances with crimson over white pennants. In May 1814 the green uniforms were ordered to be replaced by sky blue and the 2nd Regiments' facings changed to crimson.

Gendarmerie
As in France but with light crimson facings.

Battle History

1809—against Austria; 1809–14—against Spain; 1812—against Russia as 33rd Division of XI Corps; 1813—Saxony against the allies.

DUCHY OF

Nassau

1792 – 1815

(Cockade black)

This state was formed of the principalities of Nassau-Usingen and Nassau-Weilburg and contracted with various other tiny German states to raise troops to satisfy their contributions due under the terms of the Confederation of the Rhine (which Nassau joined on 12 July 1806) in return for financial settlements. They raised two infantry regiments (the 2nd and 3rd of the Confederation) and a regiment of Chasseurs à Cheval.

In 1792 Nassau provided an infantry regiment for the 'Oberrheinischen Kreis' of the Holy Roman Empire. It wore bicorns, blue coats faced white, white belts, buttons and small clothes and black gaiters.

In 1803 the 'Leib-Bataillon von Todenwarth' was raised, it wore the Bavarian Raupenhelm with black woollen crest and black plume (red for grenadiers), brass grenade badge, front band and reinforcing struts to the sides. The single-breasted tunic was dark green with red collar, Swedish cuffs, shoulder straps and turnbacks, yellow edging to collar and cuffs, yellow lace loops to collar (2) and cuffs (one on and one above); white waistcoats and breeches, buff leatherwork, black gaiters.

In 1808 this unit became the 1st Nassau Infantry Regiment (2nd Confederation) and a 2nd (3rd Confederation) was also raised; each regiment had two battalions. All badges of rank and inter-company distinction were now after the French model. They wore French shakos (the grenadier companies initially wore the old Raupenhelm with red plumes on the left). The 3rd Battalion was partially armed with rifles and wore black belts and bicorns until late in 1806. Dark green, single-breasted tunics, dark green turnbacks, black collar and Swedish cuffs, yellow buttons and orange lace edging and loops to collar and cuffs as before; white waistcoats, buff leatherwork, grey breeches with black Hungarian thigh lacing (yellow for the 3rd Battalion), short black gaiters (boots for the 3rd Battalion). Officers wore gold epaulettes, gorgets and sword knots, buff baldrics with oval gilt plate bearing the Nassau lion.

In 1810 the Raupenhelm of the grenadiers were replaced by brown fur colpacks with red pompon, plume and cords, red bag and the collar and cuff lace loops were discarded and replaced by a simple yellow piping. Drummers wore black swallows' nests laced and edged yellow and six yellow chevrons, point up on each sleeve. Drums were brass with red and blue dogs' tooth hoops.

The 1st Regiment was disarmed and interned by the French in Spain on 22 December 1813, the 2nd Regiment had defected to the British there in October 1813.

Two new regiments were raised in 1814; the uniform was as before with a slightly bell-topped shako with brass front plate of an oval shield bearing the regimental number amid trophies of arms, brass chinscales, company pompon. Dark green tunic faced black, piped yellow, yellow buttons. Green trousers with wide yellow side stripe.

Fusiliers had black shoulder straps edged yellow, elite companies also had large yellow 'wings'. Grenadiers wore the colpack as before, Voltigeurs had a brass hunting horn badge enclosing the regimental number, yellow cords, black cockade, green pompon, green plume with yellow tip. The Regiment Nassau-Oranien apparently wore the same uniform in 1815.

Chasseurs à Cheval
Bavarian Raupenhelm with black crest, white metal fittings and oval front plate bearing 'FA', all green dolman and breeches with white buttons and lace, black belts and sabretasche with white metal crowned 'FA' badge. Dark green saddle furniture edged white, black harness with white fittings. The Raupenhelm were later replaced by brown fur colpacks with red bags. The Chasseurs à Cheval were disarmed and interned by the French in Spain on 25 November 1813.

Battle History

1807—Berlin; 1809 (1st Regiment)—Tyrol as part of VIII Corps; 1809–13—Spain; 1814—France; 1815—Quatre-Bras and Waterloo.

Netherlands

1795 – 1815
Batavian Republic 1795 – 1806;
kingdom of Holland 1806 – 10; Part of Metropolitan France 1810 – 14;
kingdom of the Netherlands from 1814.

Until 1814 all rank badges and inter-company devices were generally as in France, from 1814 and 1815 officers wore orange waist sashes but otherwise the old system of epaulettes, sword knots and chevrons on the lower sleeves for NCOs seems to have been retained.

Infantry

Batavian Republic 1795 (black cockade)
The uniforms had a strong revolutionary French flavour: bicorns with black cockade, regimental loop and button, dark blue, long tailed coats with collars, lapels and cuffs, turnbacks and piping varying for each Half Brigade of three battalions. Waistcoats, breeches, belts and buttons were white, the long gaiters black. French rank badges and inter-company distinctions were used.

	a (collar, lapels, cuffs and cuff flaps)	b (turnbacks)	c (piping)
1st Half Brigade	a red	b red	c white
2nd	a crimson	b white	c white
3rd	a white	b white	c white
4th (red collar, piped white)	a white	b red	c red
5th	a yellow	b yellow	c white
6th	a light-blue	b white	c white
7th	a yellow	b yellow	c white

The foreign regiments in Batavian service were similarly dressed: Regiment Waldeck a, b and c—yellow. Regiment Sachsen-Gotha a, b and c—red. Officers wore red, white and blue waist sashes and had silver sword knots.

In 1803 facings changed and each battalion had its own system of colour coding.

Kingdom of Holland 1806
In 1806 Napoleon raised the Batavian Republic to the status of a kingdom, putting his brother, Louis, on its throne. The infantry was reorganised into nine regiments and clad in white uniforms with shakos for fusiliers, bearskin bonnets for grenadiers. The front of the shako was decorated with the regimental number in brass, on the left side was a brass loop and button, and on top of this a pompon in the facing colour; cords were in the company

173

Plate 31   The Netherlands: Infantry 1806–1810
(*l to r*) Grenadier of the Royal Guard (red plume, crimson facings, yellow lace and buttons), fusilier, 8th Infantry Regiment (light violet facings, yellow '8' on shako and yellow buttons), grenadier of the Royal Guard. *Augsburger Bilder.*

colour. The coat, breeches and belts were white, buttons yellow. Short black gaiters coming to a point at the front were worn. Facings were shown on the collar, plain round cuffs, lapels and turnbacks: 1st Regiment (Guards)—bearskin bonnet with red plume and top patch with white grenade badge, white cords, crimson facings with tasselled yellow buttonholes to collar and lapels; long black gaiters, red epaulettes; 2nd Regiment (Line)—light blue; 3rd—red; 4th—pink; 5th—dark green; 6th—grass green; 7th—yellow; 8th—light violet; 9th—black.

Officers wore gold gorgets and had gold sword knots but had no waist sashes. Their coat tails were long and they wore boots.

Metropolitan France 1810
In 1810 Napoleon absorbed the Kingdom of Holland into Metropolitan France and the army was also taken over and given French titles and numbers. The old Dutch Guard infantry (1st Regiment) became the 2nd (then 3rd) Grenadiers of the Imperial Guard; the line were given French uniforms and new numbers as follows (for further details see the French section p 112) 123ᵉ, 124ᵉ, 125ᵉ, 126ᵉ. In 1812 the 131ᵉ Ligne was raised from the Walcheren Regiment (formerly the Legion of the Islands).

174

Plate 32   The Netherlands: Artillery 1806–1810
(l to r) Foot artilleryman on cannon (dark blue uniform, red facings, cord and pompon, yellow buttons), horse artillery (as above but dark blue dolman with red lace and yellow buttons), foot artillery of the guard (as for foot artillery but yellow edging to bicorn, yellow laces to collar and lapels). *Augsburger Bilder.*

Kingdom of the Netherlands 1814

When in 1814 Belgian provinces fell under Austrian control, a Belgian Legion was raised. The infantry wore Austrian uniforms, white, with regimental facings shown on collar, Polish cuffs, turnbacks and piping to front of jacket and to shoulder straps. The shako bore 'LB', buttons were yellow. It seems that French badges of rank were worn and officers wore gold gorgets. The 1st regiment had green facings, the 2nd yellow, 3rd light blue and 4th red.

The Belgian Legion was absorbed into the Dutch-Belgian army in 1815. The 1815 uniforms consisted for the Dutch infantry units of the Austrian shako with front and rear peaks and slightly extended top, white plume, orange cockade, loop and button over a crowned brass plate bearing 'W', black chinstrap; dark blue, single-breasted tunic with red turnbacks and facings shown on collar, cuffs and piping to front, to shoulder straps and to French cuff flaps which were dark blue. Buttons were brass, belts were white; trousers white or grey. French equipment was worn, and rank badges were French except that chevrons (point up) were used instead of bars on the lower sleeve. Flank companies were distinguished by dark blue shoulder rolls piped white and by plumes—a red tip for grenadiers, green for light companies.

Drummers had swallows' nests in the facing colour edged and decorated with yellow lace and having a white and yellow fringe. The drums were brass with blue, white and red triangles on the hoops.

175

Officers wore orange waist sashes, long coat tails, gold epaulettes and sword knots, large white feather plumes.

Belgian units were dressed as above but with the 'Belgic cap' shako as worn by the British army, white cords, brass front plate, orange cockade on top left side.

Facings were: 1st* and 9th Battalions—orange; 2nd* and 10th—yellow; 3rd and 11th—white; 4th* and 12th—red; 5th and 13th—crimson; 6th and 14th—light green; 7th* and 15th—light blue; 8th and 16th—pink. (*Belgian unit; unmarked units were Dutch). It is likely that by June 1815 all regiments wore white facings.)

Jägers 1795

As for the line except dark green coats, waistcoats and breeches, dark green feather plumes and pompons to bicorns, black belts, dark green epaulettes and turnbacks. Facings were shown on collars, cuffs and Brandenburg cuff flaps and piping to waistcoat and turnbacks. 1st Battalion—red, yellow buttons; 2nd—black (lapels also black), buttons white; 3rd—black (dark green lapels), buttons yellow; 4th—crimson, white buttons. In the turnbacks were hunting horns in the facing colour.

In 1806 they retained their dark green colouring for coat, shoulder straps, lapels, waistcoat, breeches, pompon and cords. All buttons brass.

1st Battalion (Jägers of the Guard) uniform as for the Grenadiers of the Guard but with green and yellow plumes and epaulettes. 2nd Battalion—collar, pointed cuffs, turnbacks and piping—light blue. 3rd Battalion—yellow. In 1810 they became the 33e Léger.

The Regiment 'Oranien-Nassau' was taken into Dutch service on 8 November 1814 and wore Nassau army uniform (facings unknown). On 3 January 1816 this unit was combined with the 1st Regiment of Nassau to form the 35th Prussian Fusiliers. On 15 June 1815 they are reported as carrying 'French muskets with only ten rounds per man' (letter from General von Kruse, Wiesbaden, 7 January 1836).

Jägers 1815

As for line infantry except dark green plume, shako badge with a brass hunting horn under the battalion number; coats dark green, facings yellow, black belts. Hornists—red plume and cords, yellow swallows' nests, brass horn on black strap. Flank company plumes green tipped red for Carabiniers, green tipped yellow for Chasseurs.

Cavalry

Batavian Republic 1795

1st Heavy Cavalry Regiment—large bicorn with white plume, cockade loop, button and white tassels, white, long-tailed coat with black collar, epaulettes, lapels, round cuffs and turnbacks, white buttons, belts and small clothes, high black boots, brass hilted swords in brown leather sheaths. Crimson turnbacks, crimson saddle furniture edged white. 2nd Heavy Cavalry Regiment—as above but faced light blue; yellow saddle furniture edged white. Dragoons—dark blue coats, pink facings white buttons and epaulettes, otherwise as above. Hussars—shakos, blue dolman and breeches, red collar and cuffs, yellow buttons and lace.

In 1804 the 1st and 2nd Heavy Cavalry were converted to two regiments of light dragoons with English style Tarleton helmets having a black fur crest, a red turban and white plume. They had short white coats with facings on collar, lapels, cuffs and turnbacks, black for the 1st Regiment, light blue for the 2nd. In 1804 these crested helmets were replaced by French dragoon-pattern helmets in brass and in 1805 their coats changed to dark blue with pink facings. They wore white laces on collars (2), cuffs (2) and lapels (8). In 1805 the 2nd Cavalry Regiment was disbanded; the 1st became the 2nd Light Dragoons and the old Dragoons became the 1st Light Dragoons.

Kingdom of Holland 1806

A regiment of Guards cavalry was raised; it wore the same uniform as the Grenadiers of the Guard (bearskins with white cords, red plume and top patch, white grenade, white coat faced crimson with yellow buttons and tasselled lace, yellow shoulder scales, white breeches and high boots).

A regiment of Hussars of the Guard was also raised; it had shakos, red dolman and breeches, yellow buttons and lace, white pelisse with black fur trim and white belts.

The two regiments of line hussars wore similar uniforms with the regimental number on the front of the shako, above this the cockade, loop and button and a black plume. One regiment wore dark blue dolman, pelisse and breeches with red collar and cuffs, yellow buttons and lace and black fur, the other light blue.

The Kürassier Regiment of 1807 was created by converting the 2nd Light Dragoons; it had a brass helmet with combe, drooping black horsehair aigrette and crest, red plume, brown fur turban; brass chinscales, black peak. White tunic with light blue collar lapels, round cuffs and turnbacks, red epaulettes, buff belts, white small clothes, high cuffed boots. Apparently no Kürass was worn. In 1810 the Kürassiers became the 14ᵉ French Cuirassiers; the Hussars become the 11ᵉ French Hussars.

Kingdom of the Netherlands 1814

The Chevau Légers of the Belgian Legion in 1814 wore Austrian helmets with white metal front plate (bearing 'LB'), combe and fittings, yellow crest; dark green, single-breasted tunic and trousers with yellow collar, Polish cuffs, turnbacks and front piping, white belts and buttons, yellow trouser stripe, plain hussar boots. The cavalry of 1815 was numbered throughout regardless of arm.

The Carabiniers wore steel helmets with brass lion's head over the peak, brass combe, chinscales and edging, black sausage crest and white plume on left side, dark blue coats with red turnbacks and white buttons, white belts and breeches; black harness and sheepskin saddle covers, dark blue saddle furniture edged white and piped red with white grenade badges.

Regimental distinctions were: 1st Regiment—blue collar piped red, dark blue lapels; 2nd—blue collar piped red, red lapels (Belgian regiment); 3rd—yellow facings.

The Light Dragoons wore shakos with black plume, cockade loop and button over white, crowned front plate bearing 'W', white chinscales. Nine rows of white hussar type lace and three rows of white buttons on the chest; collar, cuffs and seams piped white; grey overalls with white side stripe; white belts. Black harness with brass fittings, sheepskin saddle covers (black and white it seems). Saddle furniture in the coat colour edged yellow (4th) or white (5th Regiment). Distinctions were: 4th Regiment dark blue coat, red facings and turnbacks; 5th dark green coat and shako, yellow facings and turnbacks (a Belgian unit). This unit was raised from the cavalry of the Belgian Legion.

Hussars
Traditional hussar costume, black French style shakos with yellow top band, brass chinscales and crowned 'W' badge, yellow and black cords, black plume. The 6th Hussars had light blue dolman, pelisse, breeches and saddle furniture; red collars, cuffs and sabretasches (with white edging and crowned 'W'), red and white sash, white buttons and lace and black fur. The 8th Hussars (the 7th was a colonial regiment) was uniformed all in light blue with black and yellow lace, yellow buttons, dark blue pelisse (a Belgian unit). Trumpeters wore reversed colours.

Foot Artillery 1795
Uniform of infantry style but dark blue with red facings and yellow buttons; dark blue waistcoat and breeches. In 1806 again infantry style; dark blue coat and breeches, dark blue lapels and cuff flaps, red shako cords, collar, cuffs and piping. The shako pompon (at the top left side) was red for the 1st Battalion, white for the 2nd, blue for the 3rd and yellow for the 4th. The shako badge was a brass crown over crossed cannon barrels. White belts, black gaiters. In 1810 the artillery became the 9e French foot artillery regiment. In 1814–15 they had the Austrian shako with black plume, with red tip, red cords, brass crowned plate bearing 'W', cockade loop and buttons; dark blue, single-breasted tunic with dark blue French cuff flaps, black collar and cuffs piped red, red piping to cuff flaps, shoulder straps and front of tunic, red turnbacks. Grey trousers, white belts.

Foot Artillery of the Belgian Legion 1814
The artillery of the Belgian Legion in 1814 wore French shakos with black plume, red pompon, cords and trim; dark blue French artillery coat and breeches with dark blue facings piped red, red epaulettes, thigh knots and side stripes; red waistcoat laced dark blue, yellow buttons, white belt.

Horse Artillery 1795–1814
Dragoon hats, dark blue coat and lapels, red collar and cuffs, yellow leather trousers and high cuffed boots. In 1806 they received hussar style uniforms: shako with red top band, cords and plume, dark blue dolman, pelisse and breeches, red lacing, yellow buttons and black belts. In 1810 they became the 7e French Horse Artillery Regiment. In 1814 they wore the Austrian shako with crowned crossed gun barrels in brass, black plume, red cords; cockade loop and button, dark blue, single-breasted tunics and cuff flaps, black collar and cuffs piped red, yellow buttons; grey overalls with red side stripe. The jacket had dark blue shoulder rolls piped red.

Horse Artillery 1815
Austrian shako with black plume, brass front badge of crowned, crossed cannon barrels, red cords; tunic as for foot artillery but with red shoulder

rolls piped yellow; black grenade badges in red turnbacks, grey breeches with red side stripe or grey button overalls with red side stripe and black booting.

Artillery Train

As for the foot or horse artillery but grey coat and trousers, black collar and cuffs piped red, white buttons. Horse artillery shako but white, crowned crossed gun barrel badge and no cords; grey tunic with black collar, cuffs and cuff flaps piped red; red turnbacks, white buttons, black belts, grey button overalls with red side stripe. In 1810 they became the 14e French artillery train battalion.

Engineers

As for foot artillery but with white buttons; 1810–13 French uniform; 1814 shako with black feather plume, orange pompon and cockade, loop and button, gold crowned 'W' badge, dark blue single-breasted tunic with light blue collar and Swedish cuffs, red front piping and turnbacks, white trousers and belts.

Engineers 1815

Infantry shako (Dutch model), black plume, brass badge, dark blue tunic with red turnbacks, light blue collar and Swedish cuffs, red front piping, brass buttons, white or grey trousers. Dark blue shoulder rolls piped light blue, white belts.

DUCHY OF

Oldenburg

From 1775 there had been a company of infantry in this state; it was dressed entirely in Prussian style, small bicorn edged white with red over blue pompon, dark blue coat with red collar, lapels, Swedish cuffs and turnbacks, white buttons, belts and small clothes. Below each lapel, above each cuff and at the rear of the waist were pairs of white laces with blue and red worms and tassels. Long black gaiters extended to over the knee; badges of rank were Prussian. In October 1808 Oldenburg was forced to join the Confederation of the Rhine and to provide a battalion of infantry consisting of one company each of grenadiers and Voltigeurs and four of fusiliers. The coat was dark blue, double-breasted, Prussian-style with two parallel rows of eight white buttons on the chest, red collar, Swedish cuffs, piping and turnbacks, white shoulder straps piped white, grey breeches and short, black gaiters. Headgear was a bearskin with white cords and red top patch for grenadiers, Voltigeurs and fusiliers wore Corsican hats with the left-hand brim upturned and extended to above the crown, button, loop and white plume for fusiliers, green for Voltigeurs. Belts were white.

In May 1810 Oldenburg was annexed into Metropolitan France and the troops became part of the 129ᵉ de Ligne (for uniform details see French line infantry p 118). In November 1813 Oldenburg was again free of occupation and raised two battalions of infantry for the Allies.

They wore French style shakos with crowned brass shields (silver for officers) bearing a 'P', white cords and chinscales, black plume. Prussian-style dark blue tunic faced red with white buttons and French cuffs. Belts were white, trousers dark blue in winter, white in summer and worn over the short black gaiters. Shoulder straps were white and French rank badges were retained until 1818.

Drummers wore red swallows' nests edged in white tape with a red worm and had four chevrons, point down of the same lace on each sleeve. Brass drum, red and blue hoops.

Battle History

1812—Russia as part of 10th Division, III Corps; 1813—part of Danzig garrison.

THE

Ottoman Empire

The information given below on the Janissaries is taken from Book 1 of a series of 22 books written by Colonel d'etat-major Ahmed Djevad Bey *Etat Militair Ottoman depuis la fondation de l'Empire Ottoman Jusqu'à nos Jours*, Constantinople 27 Rebi-ul-Ewel 1299 (4/16 Fevrier 1882), reference 355.318(56) in the MOD Library.

The Janissaries

Prior to the suppression of the Janissaries in 1826, the Ottoman land forces were composed of two types of soldiers; those receiving pay and those serving without pay. This distinction existed in the infantry and cavalry. The infantry consisted of the Capou-Koulis (who were 'Eulufelis' or paid soldiers) and those without pay called 'Musselem'. In the cavalry too, the Capou-Koulis received pay whereas the 'Timars' or the 'Ziamets' received none. The paid section of the armed forces were the regular army, the unpaid the irregulars but this division is blurred and the Empire owes its size and glory partly to these irregulars.

The various corps of paid troops were called 'Odjaks' and their commanders were called 'Odjak-Aghalari' or 'Aghayian-i-Biroun' (Aghas External) to distinguish them from the 'Aghayian-i-Enderoum' (Aghas Interior) who were specialist officers attached to the imperial household.

The corps of the Capou-Koulis were originally slaves and formed part of the one-fifth of the war booty which traditionally went to the Sultan. They consisted of:

Plate 33   Ottoman Empire: Infantry
(*l to r*) Officer of Janissaries (white hat with gold band and plume holder, red tunic, gold and green sleeves, yellow boots), two infantrymen (irregulars), Janissary (white hat with brass band and plume holder, blue tunic, white breeches). *Augsburger Bilder.*

1   The Janissaries.
2   The Adjani-Oghlanlar (novices).
3   The Toptchi's (gunners).
4   The Djebedjis (armourers).
5   The Top-Arabadjis (conductors of the artillery).
6   The Khoumbaradjis (bombardiers).
7   The Sakkas (water carriers).

The Ottoman army was never regular in character; it was composed of Moslem volunteers who rallied to the Sultan in time of war and who returned to their usual occupations as soon as peace was established. Apart from the infantry there were the mounted volunteers, the 'Akindjis'. The army had no uniform, each man wore a costume of his own choosing but they co-ordinated well as a body on the battlefield. The cavalry charged 'en muraille' (as a wall), a phrase still used today to describe this tactical form.

When a war was planned, the town criers would advertise the fact that those desirous of serving under the Sultan should assemble at appointed places on pre-determined days. Apart from this volunteer levée, the Sultans maintained a core of officers and soldiers on a regular basis and these formed the backbone of the field army. In the reign of Orkhan Khan the first paid soldiers were engaged; these soldiers were called 'Yaya' or 'Peyade' (infantry-

Figure 30   Turkish Janissary Ortah Badges

a 1st Ortah: yellow camel, red and white banners
b 3rd: red flag, white scimitar
c 44th: white flag and rose
d 48th: white flag, red symbol
e 82nd: red gun and bow
f 15th: red dog
g 16th: white flags, yellow cannon barrels
h 31st: red anchor
i 79th: white elephant, red cloth
j 50th: red hawk
k 18th: yellow cannon barrels
l 24th: red hand
m 71st: white dog
n 94th: yellow, white and red flag
o 2nd: white tent with red and black stripes, yellow flags

men) and their officers were graded as 'On-bachi' (corporal); 'Yus-bachi' (captain) and 'Bin-bachi' (major). The army was also organised; the numbers of paid soldiers steadily increased and each soldier was paid one 'aktche' (a Turkish coin) per day.

Due to popular discontent with the conditions of army service (low pay etc) the Sultan Murad's (?–1451) advisers recommended a scheme presented by Tchandarli Kara-Khalil, who was concerned with the problems of maintaining Turkish power in the newly conquered Thracian provinces, that 1,000 young Christian men who had accepted Turkish suzereinty should be recruited into armed service. They were to receive rations and pay in peace as well as in war. The scheme was accepted and a 'Devchurme' or levée was organised. These Christians were to be clothed in Turkish fashion and were to be housed in barracks in the capital and paid and fed daily. The pay was one 'aktche' per day but this was not a fixed rate and could be augmented according to the valour of the individual soldier. This augmentation was called the 'Terraki'.

This body of Christian troops was called the 'Yeni-Tcheri' and the name was arrived at as follows. Sultan Orkan Ghazi asked the holy man Hadji Bektach to decide upon the name of this new corps. The holy man placed his hands on the head of one of the new soldiers (the large sleeve of his habit covered the soldier's head) and said: 'These new soldiers shall be called "Yeni-Tcheri"—God sees that their faces are white, their arms strong and massive, their sabres sharp, their arrows deadly and this combination victorious'. As a souvenir of this event the Janissaries wore a pointed hat modelled on the sleeve of the saint's robe and called a 'Beurk' and made mainly of felt. The commander of the Janissaries had the title 'Aghayian-i-Bektachian'; the holy man was considered to be their patron saint. This 'standing army' was established in 1326 and may be considered the first of its type, long before that of Charles VII in 1449.

During the expansionist reign of Hudarendighiar Ghazi Sultan Mouhrad I the ranks of the Janissaries were swelled with many new recruits who were termed the 'Adjani-Oghlans' or novices.

The Various Divisions of the Janissaries

The whole corps was known as an 'Odjak' and was divided into 'Ortas' and 'Odas'. An 'Orta' was an indefinite and varying organisation; the 'Oda' was a local lodge. Certain historians have used 'Orta' to equate to 'regiment' and 'Oda' to 'company'; but an 'Orta' in modern military parlance is a 'tactical unit'. During history, an 'Orta' has consisted of 100, 400 or 500 men. In the reign of Sultan Suleiman the Lawgiver, the Janissaries had an effective strength of 12,000; in the following years this grew to 50,000 and in the reign of Sultan Selim Khan III an 'Orta' reached the strength of 2,000–3,000 men. When on campaign, each Orta set up its own large, round tent, embroidered with its own badge. In all there were 196 'Ortas' in the Janissaries divided into three classes: the 'Djemaats' (101 Ortas); the 'Benluks' (61 Ortas), the 'Sekbans' (34 Ortas). Members of the Djemaats were called 'Yaya-Beyler'; those of the Beuluks 'Benlukliter' and those of the Sekbans 'Seimenler'.

The Special and Collective Names of the 'Ortas'

Certain of the Ortas were awarded special titles some of which are reproduced here. The 1st, 2nd, 3rd and 4th Ortas of the infantry (Yaya) were called 'Devedjis' (chameliers-camel drivers) and their commanders were senior to other Orta commanders. When in fortresses or garrison they were in charge of the administration. According to Hammer they wore a Heron plume with aigrette and diamonds, yellow leather boots and had silver embroidered harness.

The 5th Orta of the Beulukilers was called the 'Bach-Tchaoudh-Ortassi' and its commander the 'Bach Tchaouch' (chief of the messengers). In war he wore a bonnet without a horsetail and marched in front of the Agha of the Janissaries carrying the mech'ala (a torch of resinous wood).

The 14th, 49th, 65th and 67th Djemaats were called 'Hassakis' (privileged) and Hammer tells us that members of these Ortas were addressed by the honorific title of 'Agha'. Their 'Tchorbadjis' (commanders) wore yellow leather boots and achieved the ranks of 'Samsoundji-bachi' (chief guardian of the mastiffs), 'Tournadji-bachi' (chief guardian of the grues—cranes or geese) and Zaghardji-bachi (chief guardian of the bloodhounds) or of the Sultan's hunting dogs).

The 16th and 18th Ortas marched with the artillery and carried on their standard the emblem of cannons. The 35th Orta was called 'Sekban-Avdjilari' (chasseurs). The 64th Orta (Djemaat) was called 'Zaghardji' and the commander was called 'Zaghardji-bachi' (guardian of the bloodhounds)—34 soldiers of this Orta accompanied the Sultan on his hunts to control the dogs. The 63rd Orta was entitled 'Tournadjis' (guardians of the cranes or geese) and Ortas 64, 68 and 71 were Chasseurs.

The 17th Orta (Djemaat) was called 'Samnoundji' (?) and these men cared for the bear hunting hounds. Ortas 60–3 were called 'Solak' (archers) and the archers of the Sultan's garde du Corps were drawn from these units. The Solaks had a bonnet with a horsetail and on ceremonial duty they wore a long white tunic and a white kaftan with four sleeves. The two 'spare' sleeves were tucked into their belts and they had a quiver to hold their arrows.

The 55th Orta (Djemaat) was called 'Talim-Hanedjilar' (instructors) and were charged with weapon training for the Janissaries including firearms. The chief of this Orta is distinguished by the arrows, the longbow and the hat, 'Mudjveze', that he wears the Mudjveze is the type of hat which Pashas wear in everyday costume. The men of this Orta wore cylindrical turbans. The 84th Orta (Djemaat) was called the 'd'Imam-Ortassi'.

Two of the Beulukliler Ortas were directly under command of high officials; one under the 'Kehaya-yeri' (lieutenant to the Agha of the Janissaries) and the other under the 'Mouhzir Agha' ('hussier' or sergeant assistant). The 56th Orta provided halberdiers (Harbadjis) for guard duty for the Agha of the Janissaries.

The 99th Orta was a military band. A drum and a horsetail—both signs of distinction—were awarded to the 'Woiwodes' in Wallachia and Moldavia and to the Khans of the Crimea.

The Ortas of the Yaya-Beylers or the Djemaats were charged with guarding strategic points on the frontiers. Their officers held the keys to these fortresses and were privileged to remain on horseback before the Agha of the Janissaries. As a sign of this distinction they wore red boots.

The Beuluklilers had the privilege of providing the personal guards for the Sultan and for the Sandjak-Cherif (flag of the Prophet) but their Tchorbadjis (commanders) were not mounted and wore red leather leggings sewn to their trousers.

The 'Kehaya-yer' and the 'Mouhzir Agha' (sergeant assistant) each commanded an Orta of the Beuluklis which were entitled 'Kehayayerliler' and 'Mouhzirler' but as these two officers had special duties within the 'Odjak' of Janissaries as well as their normal duties, they wore yellow leather leggings and were mounted on horseback.

Officers of the Ortas of the Sekbans wore boots or leggings of red leather (except those of the 31st Orta).

Apart from the three divisions of Janissaries (Djemaat, Beuluk and Sekban) there was another class of soldiers called the 'Coroudjis' (guards of the forests) who patrolled the forests and guarded the water supply system.

Old or invalided Janissaries were removed from active service and given an adequate pension (Eulufe) and were known as 'Outourakli' or pensions. Orphans of Janissaries were also taken care of by the Odjak in recognition of their fathers' services. They received rations and a pension and were called 'Fodola-Haran' or pensioners.

Poland

1792 – 1815

(Cockade white)

Kingdom 1792–5, dismembered 1795 between Prussia, Russia and Austria, partially reformed in January 1807 by Napoleon as 'Grand Duchy of Warsaw' until 1813 when Prussia and Russia re-established their control and only the Duchy of Krakow remained independent.

Position prior to 1795

Infantry

The Polish army was disbanded in 1795; prior to that its infantry had worn the following uniforms: black felt 'top hat' with front peak and narrow side and rear brim; white front plate bearing the Polish eagle, this backed by a black leather plate in an apex, the top edge of which was edged in black bristles. From the rear lower brim a black hair plume bent forward over the hat and touched the top of the black front plate. Dark blue tunic very much in the style of the Russian army uniform was introduced in 1789 with facings shown on collar, Swedish cuffs, lapels and the small turnbacks at the front of the skirts. Dark blue overalls with wide stripe in the facing colour, white belts. Regimental distinctions as follows:

	a (facings)	b (buttons)
Stanislas Potocki	a light blue	b yellow
Ozarowski	a orange	b white
Wodzicki	a orange	b yellow
Grossfeldherr	a green	b yellow
Unterfeldherr	a buff	b white
Füsiliers	a black	b yellow
Lanowy	a parrot green	b white
Czapski	a green	b white
Racryski	a pink	b white
Dziasynski	a pink	b yellow
Ilinski	a buff	b yellow
Malezewski	a parrot green	b yellow
Ordination Ostro	a black	b yellow
Königin Hedwig	a light yellow	b white

Officers wore the traditional square-topped Polish 'Konfederatka', silver and crimson waist sashes and sword knots.

Artillery

Bicorn with white plume, dark green tunic of infantry cut with black facings and trousers, yellow buttons. Officers' Konfederatkas were black.

185

Pontoniers

As for artillery but white facings and brown belts.

Cavalry

As for the infantry but all ranks wore the Konfederatka; examples of regimental distinctions were:

Ulanen 'König' a (facings)—crimson b (buttons)—yellow

Nationalgarde a—bright red b—yellow.

Position after 1795

After the partition of Poland in 1795 many Poles sought refuge in France and later took service with the infant republic of Lombardy under their leader, Dombrowski. They wore their old uniform with French cockade. By 1798 the legion was reorganised into two each of three battalions of ten companies and a company of artillery. In 1798 the 2nd Legion was captured at the fall of Mantua and disbanded, the 1st Legion was reformed into the 'Legion Italique' in February 1800, and another Polish formation the 'Danube Legion' was also raised in France that year, and fought at the battle of Hohenlinden on 3 December 1800. It had four infantry battalions, four cavalry squadrons and an artillery battery.

The Legion Italique had seven infantry battalions. Both legions were disbanded on 21 December 1801 and converted into three foreign 'demi-brigades' the 1er and 2e being the old 'Legion Italique', the 3e being the Danube Legion. The 2e and 3e were later renumbered 114e and 113e respectively. Both were sent to San Domingo in the French West Indies and were either killed by disease or captured by the British. The 1er Demi-Brigade Etrangér was incorporated into the 1st Division of the army of the Cisalpine Republic.

After creating the Grand Duchy of Warsaw (under nominal control of the king of Saxony and a member of the Confederation of the Rhine) Napoleon ordered the raising of an army as quickly as possible and sent the old 'Legion Italique' from Italy to join it with three battalions of infantry and a regiment of lancers. A new Polish formation in French service also appeared: the 'Legion du Nord' which in August 1807 became the 5th Infantry Regiment of the Duchy while the 'Legion Italique' became the Legion of the Vistula in French service with three infantry regiments and a lancer regiment (later the 7th (French) Lancers). A regiment of Polish volunteer lancers became the famous 1st Chevau Léger Lanciers of the Imperial Guard and two more regiments of cavalry of the Vistula Legion became the 8th and 9th (French) Lancers. In 1812 the Lithuanians provided the 3rd Chevau Léger Lanciers and the Tartars of the Imperial Guard (see Foreign Troops in French Service p 129).

Line Infantry

Each regiment of three battalions of six companies—one grenadier, one Voltigeur and four fusilier; all badges of rank and inter-company distinctions as in the French army but Polish generals had crimson facings decorated with a special zig-zag silver lace.

In 1807 all wore a black czapka with brass sun-burst plate, dark blue kurtka with buttons bearing the regimental number, dark blue trousers over the gaiters, white belts. Facings were shown on collars, cuffs and lapels as follows:

1st Division a (lapels)—yellow b (collars)—red c (cuffs)—red d (buttons)—yellow
2nd a, b and c—crimson d—white (white cap plates)
3rd a, b and c—white d—yellow

In 1810 certain uniform details were changed: grenadiers wore peaked bearskins with red top with white cross, brass chinscales and front plates bearing the regimental number under the Polish eagle and between flaming grenades, red cords and plumes (red and silver cords for NCOs, silver for officers). Other grenadier distinctions as in France. Fusiliers—czapka with white Polish eagle over a yellow front band bearing the regimental number, white cockade above the eagle and on top of this a black pompon, white cords for parades. Voltigeurs—czapka or shako with eagle plate and band as before, green or yellow plume, epaulettes green and yellow (red and yellow for musicians). Elite companies wore moustaches, white belts, black pouch with regimental number in brass for fusiliers, number in a hunting horn for Voltigeurs, number on a grenade for grenadiers. Pioniers wore grenadier appointments, full beards, white aprons, red cloth badges on the upper sleeves of crossed axes and a grenade. Drummers wore a great variety of dress at the whim of the regimental commander. The kurtka was now dark blue for all regiments (except the 13th who wore white with sky blue facings edged yellow and white buttons) with dark blue collar edged red, red cuffs, white plastron (lapels) and turnbacks edged red, white cuff flaps and yellow buttons. Trousers were white.

The 4th, 7th and 9th Regiments served with the French army in Spain at least partially dressed in French uniforms; the 18th–21st Regiments were raised in Lithuania in 1812 as were the Chasseurs à Pied Lithuanians.

Foot Artillery
Shako with yellow metal front band bearing a grenade over crossed cannon barrels all under a white eagle, white cockade, red pompon plume and cords; dark green kurtka with black collar, cuffs, lapels and turnbacks piped red; yellow buttons, white belts and trousers.

Horse Artillery
As for foot artillery but colpack with red pompon and cords, brass scale epaulettes with red half moons and fringes, red aiguillette; single-breasted tunic with yellow grenade collar badges, yellow grenades in turnbacks, pointed cuffs, dark green breeches striped red, hussar boots, white belts. Trumpeters wore white colpacks with dark green bag, red cords, dark green over red plume, brass grenade badge and chinscales, single-breasted white jacket faced black, piped red, red epaulettes, waistcoat and breeches laced yellow, yellow trimmed hussar boots, red trumpet cords. Saddle furniture was a dark green shabrack with black edging piped red, yellow grenade over crossed cannon barrels badge in the pointed rear corner; black Hungarian harness with brass fittings.

Artillery Train
Dark blue czapka with white cockade and eagle plate, brass chinscales, red pompon and cords, dark blue, single-breasted tunic with yellow collar and Swedish cuffs, yellow piping to front of coat and to dark blue shoulder straps and turnbacks, white buttons. On the upper left arm an oval brass plate bearing the white eagle and the division and vehicle number. White belts, dark blue overalls with yellow side stripe.

Plate 34   Officers of Various European Armies c 1800
(*l to r*)   Walloon dragoons (Batavian Republic), (dark blue coat, pink facings, silver epaulettes and buttons, orange cockade and sash), Prussian Kürassiers (regiment Leib-Karibiniers), (gala uniform – white coat, light blue facings, silver buttons and lace, black and silver sash and sword knot), Portuguese infantry officer (Regiment Gena Major), red within blue cockade, dark blue coat, yellow facings, silver buttons and epaulettes, dark blue breeches, crimson sash), Danish lieutenant-general (gold hat brooch and tassels, scarlet coat faced light blue, gold lace and buttons, gold and red sabre knot, yellow breeches). From *Uniformzeichnung der vorzüglichsten Europaischen Truppen* by C. F. Mohr, Kiel 1802.

Baggage Train
As for artillery train but grey kurtka and breeches.

Engineers
As for foot artillery but gold grenades on the collar, trophies of arms on the brass buttons.

Cavalry

The various types of cavalry regiments were all mixed together and numbered sequentially.

Chasseurs à Cheval (Regiments 1, 4 and 5)
Shako with white cockade and eagle plate (elite companies wore colpacks with bag in the facing colour, red plumes and cords). Dark green single-breasted tunic with collar, cuffs and piping in the regimental facings (1st—red; 4th—crimson; 5th—orange), brass buttons, green turnbacks, dark green overalls with twin side stripes in the facing colour, or white breeches with hussar boots with black tassel. Black bandoliers (edged in gold lace for officers), black pouch with brass regimental number. Dark green shabrack edged in the facing colour, black harness with brass fittings.

Lancers (Regiments 2, 3, 6, 7, 8, 9, 11, 12, 15, 16, 17*, 18*, 19*, 20* and 21*)
Black czapka with white eagle plate, cockade, black plume; dark blue kurtka with similar turnbacks, yellow buttons bearing the regimental number, dark blue overalls with side stripes as shown; white belts.
    Elite companies wore colpacks with red plumes and cords, red epaulettes. Trumpeters wore white colpacks, red trim and various other items.
    Regimental distinctions were as follows:

	a (collar)	b (collar piping)	c (lapels)	d (lapel piping)	e (Polish cuffs)	f (cuff piping)	g (trouser stripes)
2nd Regiment	a red	b white	c dark blue	d yellow	e red	f white	g yellow
3rd	a crimson	b white	c dark blue	d white	e crimson	f white	g yellow
6th	a white	b crimson	c dark blue	d crimson	e crimson	f white	g crimson
7th	a yellow	b red	c dark blue	d red	e yellow	f red	g yellow
8th	a red	b red	c dark blue	d red	e yellow	f red	g red
9th	a red	b dark blue	c dark blue	d white	e dark blue	f white	g red
11th	a crimson	b white	c crimson	d white	e dark blue	f white	g crimson
12th	a crimson	b white	c dark blue	d white	e dark blue	f white	g crimson
15th	a crimson	b white	c crimson	d white	e crimson	f white	g crimson
16th	a crimson	b white	c dark blue	d crimson	e crimson	f white	g crimson
17th	a crimson	b white	c dark blue	d crimson	e crimson	f white	g crimson
18th	a crimson	b white	c dark blue	d crimson	e crimson	f white	g crimson
19th and 20th	a yellow	b yellow	c dark blue	d yellow	e yellow	f yellow	g yellow
21st	a orange	b orange	c dark blue	d orange	e orange	f orange	g orange

*Raised in Lithuania in 1812; it is uncertain if the 21st Regiment was ever complete. Their czapka plates bore the mounted warrior badge instead of the eagle.

Hussars (10th and 13th Regiments)
10th Regiment Light blue shako with black plume, white loop, button, cockade and large rosette, white cords and chinscales, dark blue dolman and pelisse, crimson collar, yellow lace and buttons, black fur trim, white and crimson sash, light blue breeches with yellow Hungarian decoration and trim to boots. Black belts, saddle furniture crimson edged yellow.
Elite company—black colpack with light blue bag. Trumpeters—fox fur colpack, crimson breeches.
13th Regiment—as above but with white lace and buttons. Trumpeters with crimson dolman, light blue breeches and red boots.

Kürassiers (14th Regiment—only two squadrons)
As for French Kürassiers with red facings and yellow buttons; dark blue shabrack edged yellow, white sheepskin shabrack. Trumpeters—red crest,

white plume, white tunic faced red, red epaulettes and trumpet cords, red and yellow lace bars on chest. No Kürass for trumpeters.

Krakus (light cavalry)
Crimson 'beret' with white top button and radial stripes to black astrakhan headband, white plume on left side; dark blue Litewka with crimson collar and Swedish cuffs piped white, crimson covered cartridge pouches on the chest piped in white, dark blue overalls with double crimson side stripe, black belts, brass hilted sabre in steel sheath.

Battle History 1807–15

1807—siege of Danzig; siege of Graudenz; ⚔ Friedland (14 June); 1808–11 —Spain; siege of Saragossa, ⚔ Medina de Rio Secco, ⚔ Talavera (28 July 1809), ⚔ Almonacid (11 August 1809), ⚔ Occaña (19 November 1809), ⚔ Sagunto (25 October 1811). The Vistula Legion Lancers destroyed Colborne's British infantry brigade at the ⚔ Albuferra (16 May 1811). 1812—Russia as V corps, ⚔ Smolensk (17 August), ⚔ Borodino (7 September), ⚔ Winkowo (18 October), ⚔ Medyn (25 October), ⚔ Beresina crossing. 1813—Saxony as VIII Corps and in various units in VII Corps, ⚔ Katzbach (26 August), ⚔ Dennewitz (6 September), ⚔ Leipzig (16–18 October). 1814—fragments fought on. 1815—the 3e Regiment Etranger was composed of Poles.

KINGDOM OF

Portugal

1792 – 1815

(Cockade red within blue in the shape of a rounded cross)

Rank Badges

In the first part of the period badges of rank as such were very indistinct and were restricted more to indications of membership of a certain group of ranks (generals, other officers, NCOs). In 1808 the system became much more specific.

Generals
Field Marshal—white feather edging to bicorn, dark blue coat, red lapels, collar and cuffs embroidered and edged gold, gold buttons and two heavy gold bullion epaulettes with four stars; red and silver waist sash, silver sword knot, white small clothes, boots. Lieutenant-general—as above but only a double gold embroidery edging to collar and cuffs, three epaulette stars. Major-general—as above but single embroidery edging and two stars. Brigadier-general—as above but one epaulette star.

Plate 35   Portugal: Officers of Portugese Engineers and Infantry c 1809
(*left*) Officer of engineers (blue within red cockade, dark blue coat with gold
lace, buttons and epaulettes), infantry officer, 16th Regiment (red collar and cuffs,
white turnbacks and front piping, gold buttons). Both have crimson sashes with silver
fringes. After Bradford *Sketches of Military Costume in Spain and Portugal, 1814.*

Officers
Colonel—bicorn, gold gorget, regimental uniform, two fringed bullion
epaulettes, sash and sword knot as before. Lieutenant-colonel—as for
Colonel but fringed epaulette left, contre-epaulette right. Major—fringed
epaulette right, contre-epaulette left. Captain—gold scale 'wing' epaulettes
with fringes. Lieutenant—as for captain but the right epaulette fringed.
Ensign—the left epaulette fringed. Officers carried brown canes with gold
knobs and had black tips to their plumes.

NCOs
Sergeant-major—gold scale wing epaulettes with yellow fringes, gold sabre
knot, no sash; cane with gold knob. Second sergeant and Drum major
—scale epaulettes, the right one with a yellow fringe, yellow sabre knot.
Quarter-master—scale epaulettes, the left one fringed, yellow sabre knot.
Corporal—two yellow stripes around the cuff. Lance-corporal—one yellow
cuff stripe.
   The Portuguese army had been reorganised in the 1760s by the Count of
Schaumburg-Lippe and in his honour the senior regiments bore his name.
There were no guards units.

Line Infantry

Large bicorn, dark blue coat with regimental distinctions shown on lapels, collar, cuffs, turnbacks, waistcoats, buttons and plumes, dark blue breeches, short black gaiters. Officers wore gold/silver epaulettes and hat edging, long coat skirts and hussar topped boots. Soldiers wore white/yellow epaulettes. Trousers were blue except for 1st and 2nd Armada who wore green; Colonial Moira, Almeida and 2nd Oporto—yellow; 1st Oporto—red and Valenca—white.

Regimental distinctions were as follows:

	a (collar and cuffs)	b (lapels)	c (buttons and epaulettes)	d (turn-backs)	e (waist-coats)	f (plume)
Lippe	a red	b blue*	c white	d white	e white	f white
Albuquerque	a blue, white cuffs	b white	c yellow	d white	e white	f red
Minas	a red†	b red	c white	d white	e white	f white
1st Armada (green coats)	a red†	b red	c yellow	d red	e red	f red
2nd Armada (green coats)	a red†	b red	c white	d red	e red	f white
Cascaes	a blue	b blue	c yellow	d blue	e white	f crimson
Setubal	a yellow	b blue*	c white	d yellow	e white	f red
Peniche	a white†	b blue* with white lace decoration	c yellow	d white	e white	f red
1st Elvas	a red	b red	c yellow	d blue	e blue	f white
2nd Elvas	a red†	b red*, white buttonholes	c white	d red	e white	f white
Colonial, Rio de Janeiro	a red	b none, white buttonholes	c white	d white	e white	f shakos
Serpa	a red	b yellow	c white	d red	e yellow	f red
1st Olivença	a orange	b orange with white lace	c white	d red	e white	f light blue
2nd Olivença	a orange, white cuffs	b orange*	c white	d red	e white	f red
Campo Major	a blue†	b blue*, white buttonholes	c white	d red	e red	f black
Castello de Vide	a blue, white cuffs	b blue	c yellow	d red	e white	f not known
Colonial Moira, Rio de Janeiro	a yellow	b none	c white	d yellow	e yellow	f white helmet
Lagos	a white	b white	c white	d white	e blue	f red
Faro	a red	b blue	c yellow	d blue	e white	f not known
1st Oporto	a red	b red	c white	d yellow	e yellow	f red
2nd Oporto	a blue	b yellow	c white	d red	e red	f not known
Viana	a yellow, white cuffs	b yellow	c yellow	d red	e white	f not known
Valenca	a yellow	b yellow	c white	d red	e blue	f not known
Almeida	a red	b red	c white	d red	e yellow	f none
Gena Major	a white	b red	c yellow	d white	e red	f not known
Bragança Colonial	a red	b white	c yellow	d red	e white	f not known
Bragança	a buff	b buff	c white	d white	e white	f not known

Grenadiers wore fur caps with no front plates and with long back cloths in the facing colour with elaborate decorations.

*Edged in the button colour with two such laces below.

†Cuffs edged in the button colour with similar buttonhole lace.

In 1808 the army was reorganised into three divisions containing infantry, cavalry and artillery. Apart from individual regimental facings the uniforms had turnbacks, narrow piping to collar and cuffs, and wide front piping to single-breasted jackets in the division colours. For clarity the line infantry are shown grouped in their divisional organisations.

Uniform was a shako with raised front, oval brass plate bearing the Portuguese crest above a brass front band pierced with the regimental number. Cords were mixed blue and in the divisional colour, a white plume and red within blue cockade were worn on the left side. NCOs above corporal had gold and blue cords, officers all gold. Grenadiers had a brass grenade between front band and oval plate and wore fringes in dark blue and the divisional colour to their shoulder straps or epaulettes. Dark blue single-breasted coat. Pioneers wore brass crossed axes over the front band, grenadier shoulder straps, white aprons, full beards and carried axes. Drummers had mixed blue and divisional colour lace to collar and cuff edging and across the chest. All buttons yellow, short black gaiters, trousers dark blue or white; white belts. On the pouch was the regimental number in brass.

1st or Southern Division (white piping and turnbacks)

	a (collar)	b (cuffs)
1st (Lippe's) Regiment	a blue	b white
4th (Freire's	a blue	b red
7th (Setubal)	a blue	b yellow
10th (Lisbon)	a blue	b sky blue
13th (Peniche)	a white	b white
16th (Veira Telles)	a red	b red
18th (Cascaes)	a yellow	b yellow
22nd (Serpa)	a sky blue	b sky blue

2nd or Centre Division (red piping and turnbacks)

2nd (Lagos)	a blue	b white
5th (1st Elvas)	a blue	b red
8th (Castello de Vide)	a blue	b yellow
11th (Penamacor)	a blue	b sky blue
14th (Tavira)	a white	b white
17th (2nd Elvas)	a red	b red
20th (Campo Major)	a yellow	b yellow
23rd (Almeida)	a sky blue	b sky blue

3rd or Northern Division (yellow turnbacks and piping)

3rd (1st Olivença)	a blue	b white
6th (1st Oporto)	a blue	b red
9th (Viana)	a blue	b yellow
12th (Chaves)	a blue	b sky blue
15th (2nd Olivença)	a white	b white
18th (2nd Oporto)	a red	b red
21st (Valenca)	a yellow	b yellow
24th (Bragança)	a sky blue	b sky blue

During the campaigns several regiments used the conical, British light infantry-style shako. Each regiment consisted of two battalions each of seven companies, one of them grenadiers.

Light Infantry (Caçadores)

Shortly after 1800 the Portuguese raised an experimental legion of light troops called after its commander (D'Alorna). Little is known of the uniform

193

of the infantry except that they wore conical shakos and had black facings. Each battalion had five companies, one of Atiradores (sharpshooters).

With the reorganisation of 1808 six battalions of Caçadores (rifles) were raised. They wore line infantry uniform with the following differences: green plume and cords (black plume and green shoulder strap fringes for the Atiradore company); the battalion number on the cap plate was within a hunting horn; brown coat with green piping to shoulder straps, black leatherwork, white breeches. The Atiradores were armed with rifles, the other companies with muskets; officers carried sabres on black slings. Buglers had lace in green and the divisional colour to collar, Swedish cuffs and across the chest to the eight brass buttons. Initially they had different facings for each battalion but in July 1809 all facings became black. They wore divisional colours as for the Line. Facings in 1808 were:

1st Division (white turnbacks and piping)		
	a (collar)	*b (cuffs)*
1st Battalion		
(Castello de Vide)	*a* brown	*b* sky blue
4th (Beira)	*a* sky blue	*b* sky blue
2nd Division (red)		
2nd (Moura)	*a* brown	*b* red
5th (Campo Major)	*a* red	*b* red
3rd Division (yellow)		
3rd (Tras os Montes)	*a* brown	*b* yellow
6th (Oporto)	*a* yellow	*b* yellow

In 1811 the 7th–9th battalions were raised from the Loyal Lusitanian Legion.

Artillery

Uniform as for the line infantry with red collar and cuffs, divisional piping and turnbacks, yellow buttons, red plumes, white belts, dark blue breeches, black gaiters.

Engineers (an all officer corps)

Large bicorn edged gold, white plume, gold button and loop, cockade; dark blue, double-breasted coat with similar collar and cuffs edged gold, gold buttons and epaulettes, divisional turnbacks, white breeches, gold trimmed hussar boots; gold hilted sabre in black and gold sheath on black slings.

Cavalry

In 1800 they wore light blue tunics, buff breeches, steel Kürasses, high cuffed boots, black leatherwork (some regiments had red). Headgear varied between regiments and individual distinctions were as follows:

	a (collar and cuffs)	*b (sash)*	*c (headgear)*	*d (chevrons on the cuff)*
Caés	*a* crimson with white button-holes	*b* crimson with white edging	*c* bicorn with white edging and red plume	*d* none
Alcantara	*a* pink with white loop to collar	*b* pink with white zig-zag edging	*c* black helmet with black woollen crest and white fittings	*d* three white chevrons

194

Mecklenburg	*a* light blue	*b* red with two narrow light blue stripes	*c* black helmet with red crest falling to rear	*d* three white chevrons
Elvas	*a* red	*b* red with white edging and central blue stripe	*c* bicorn with yellow edging and white plume	*d* four yellow chevrons
Evora	*a* white	*b* blue with yellow edging	*c* black helmet with brass combe and red crest	*d* none
Moira	*a* yellow	*b* as Mecklenburg	*c* bicorn	*d* none
Olivença	*a* blue	*b* crimson edged white	*c* shako with crimson plume and white cords	*d* none
Almeida	*a* light blue	*b* black with white and light blue striped edging	*c* steel helmet with red crest	*d* none
Castello Branco	*a* orange	*b* as Mecklenberg	*c* black helmet with steel combe and crimson crest	*d* three white chevrons
Miranda	*a* brick red	*b* brick red edged white	*c* black helmet with red crest	*d* none
Chaves	*a* carmine	*b* carmine	*c* bicorn with red plume	*d* none
Bragança	*a* blue	*b* as Mecklenburg	*c* black helmet with red crest	*d* none

The cavalry of the Legion D'Alorna wore a black crested helmet with black plume and brass fittings, light blue dolman with black collar and cuffs and yellow lace and buttons, white breeches with yellow Hungarian trim, hussar boots, black sabretasche and sabre sheath with brass trim, white belts; light blue shabrack edged yellow and black harness.

By 1809 the uniform had been much simplified and no Kürasses were worn; the new uniforms were very similar to those of the Legion D'Alorna. Black crested helmet with brass fittings, light blue coat with regimental and divisional facings and piping, yellow buttons and metal shoulder wings, Swedish cuffs, white belts and breeches, short hussar boots. Saddle furniture light blue edged yellow, black harness, sabres, carbines and pistols.

Facings were as follows:

1st Division (white)	*a (collar)*	*b (cuffs)*
1st (Alcantara)	*a* white	*b* white
4th (Mecklenburg)	*a* red	*b* red
7th (Caés)	*a* yellow	*b* yellow
10th (Santarem)	*a* sky blue	*b* sky blue
2nd Division (red)		
2nd Moira)	*a* white	*b* white
5th (Evora)	*a* red	*b* red
8th (Elvas)	*a* yellow	*b* yellow
11th (Almeida)	*a* sky blue	*b* sky blue
3rd Division (yellow)		
3rd (Olivença)	*a* white	*b* white
6th (Bragança)	*a* red	*b* red
9th (Chaves)	*a* yellow	*b* yellow
12th (Miranda)	*a* sky blue	*b* sky blue

Each regiment had four squadrons.

Loyal Lusitanian Legion
Raised in 1808, disbanded in 1811 after the battle of Albuferra. Conical shako with oval brass plate and front band bearing 'LLL', green cords and plume at top front over the blue within red cockade. Dark green jacket with three rows of eight white buttons, steel shoulder wings, grey breeches, black belts. It consisted of two battalions of infantry, a regiment of cavalry (green with white facings) and a battery of four 6 pdr guns (green with black facings).

Battle History

November 1807—Spain and France invaded Portugal; the Portuguese army was disbanded; May 1808—the Portuguese Legion was raised for French service (see Foreign Troops in French Service p 129); August 1808—British troops land in Portugal and the army reforms; 19 August 1808 ⚔ Roliça*; 21 August 1808 ⚔ Vimiero*; January 1809—Sir John Moore's expedition into Spain and subsequent retreat to Corunna (⚔ there 16 January, 1809*). By mid-1809 the Portuguese army was well re-established with many British officers in positions of command. 11 May 1809—⚔ Oporto*; 27–28 July 1809—⚔ Talavera de la Reina*; 27 September 1810—⚔ Bussaco*; September 1810—March 1811 Massena besieged the Anglo-Portuguese in the Lines of Torres Vedras; 4–5 May 1811—⚔ Fuentes d'Onoro; 16 May 1811—⚔ Albuferra* (Phyrric victory); 19 January 1812—storm of Ciudad Rodrigo*; 6 April 1812—storm of Badajos*; 22 July 1812—⚔ Salamanca*; 21 June 1813—⚔ Vittoria*.
*French defeat

THE KINGDOM OF

Prussia

1792 – 1815

(Cockade black until 1808, thence black within white)

Rank Badges

Generals
Prior to 1808 there were no special rank badges for officers except that generals wore white cut-feather edging to their hats. They wore dark blue coats with red collars and cuffs, embroidered gold, dark blue turnbacks and lapels edged gold, a gold aiguillette on the right shoulder, white breeches, boots. After 1808 they also wore a silver and black twisted cord on the left shoulder.

Officers
Gold gorgets, silver and black waist sashes and sword knots and carried canes and halberds and their plumes had bases in contrasting colours.

In 1808 the gorget and halberd were abolished as was the pigtail and silver and black lace was added to the shoulder straps to indicate rank: subalterns—one lace along the straps, captains—one down each side of the straps, field officers—the same but with a red piping. In 1812 Kürassier officers adopted epaulettes as in 1813 did all field officers (except hussars) and in 1814 all officers except hussars.

Subalterns had the silver and black lace along the sides of the strap, captains and field officers had it around the top of the strap as well. Field officers had silver half moons and thin fringes; junior officers no fringes and the half moons in the button colour.

NCOs

In the eighteenth century they were distinguished by a quartered black and white hat pompon and sabre knot tassel and gold or silver hat edging and edging to the facings as well as a cane and a spontoon. In 1808 gold or silver lace was worn on the cuff and on the bottom and front of the collar (top and front from 1814 when the collar was worn closed). The shako top band was gold or silver and the plume tips were in contrasting colours (ie black over white or white over black). Sabre knots continued black and white.

LINE INFANTRY NUMBERS, TITLES AND DRESS DISTINCTIONS IN 1806

	a (facings)	b (buttons)	c (other ranks' lace)	d (officers' lace)
von Kunheim	a poppy red	b white	c white	d silver
von Rüchel	a light brick red	b yellow	c buff with white tassels	d gold
von Renouard	a poppy red	b yellow	c black and white	d none
von Kalckreuth	a orange	b yellow	c white and blue	d gold
von Kleist	a pale buff	b yellow	c orange with tassels	d gold
Grenadiergarde	a scarlet	b yellow	c gold	d gold
von Owstein	a pink	b white	c none	d none
von Rüts (also Ruiz and Ruits)	a scarlet	b yellow	c blue and white	d gold
von Schenck	a scarlet	b yellow	c white, oblong	d gold
von Wedell	a lemon yellow	b white	c white and red	d silver
von Schöning	a crimson	b white	c white, crimson and blue	d silver
Prinz von Braunschweig-Oels	a light brick red	b yellow	c white	d gold
von Arnim	a white	b white	c white	d silver
von Besser	a light brick red	b yellow	c white and red zig-zag	d none
Garde	a poppy red	b white	c silver	d silver
von Diericke	a light brick red	b yellow	c white, red and black	d gold
von Treskow	a white	b yellow	c white and red	d gold
Regiment des Königs	a pink	b white	c white	d silver
Prinz von Oranien	a orange	b white	c white	d silver
Prinz Louis Ferdinand	a scarlet	b yellow	c white and blue edging	d gold
Herzog von Braunschweig	a scarlet	b white	c white and red	d silver
von Pirch	a deep red	b yellow	c white and red	d gold
von Winning	a pink	b white	c white and blue	d silver
von Zenge	a poppy red	b yellow	c white and red	d none
von Möllendorf	a scarlet	b yellow	c white and blue	d gold
Alt-Larisch	a light brick red	b yellow	c orange with tassels	d gold
von Tschammer	a poppy red	b yellow	c white wavy edging	d none
von Malschitzki	a buff	b white	c none	d gold
von Treuenfels	a crimson	b yellow	c white, crimson and blue	d none
von Borcke	a buff	b white	c white, red and blue	d silver
von Kropff	a pink	b yellow	c none	d gold
Fürst Hohenlohe	a buff	b yellow	c none	d none

Plate 36   Kingdom of Prussia: Dragoons 'von Prittwitz' No 2 1792–1806
Officer (*left*) and trooper (light blue coats, white facings, gold buttons, lace and aiguillette; the lace embroidery on the buttonholes of officers' coats differed with each regiment). After Ramm.

Plate 37   Kingdom of Prussia: Kürassier-Regiment 'von Wagenfeld No 4' 1792–1806
White tunics and breeches, black facings; the officer (*left*) has gold lace to tunic front, waistcoat in the facing colour and cuffs, the trooper's lace is white and dark blue, the sabretasche black and decorated in the regimental lace. After Ramm.

33	von Alvensleben	*a* white	*b* yellow	*c* none	*d* none
34	Prinz Ferdinand	*a* poppy red	*b* white	*c* white	*d* silver
35	Prinz Heinrich	*a* pale green	*b* white	*c* none	*d* silver
36	von Puttkammer	*a* white	*b* white	*c* none	*d* silver
37	von Tschepe	*a* crimson	*b* white	*c* none	*d* silver
38	von Pelchrzim	*a* scarlet	*b* yellow	*c* none	*d* none
39	von Zastrow	*a* white	*b* yellow	*c* white and red	*d* gold
40	von Schimonsky	*a* pink	*b* white	*c* none	*d* silver
41	von Lettow	*a* light crimson	*b* yellow	*c* yellow	*d* gold
42	von Plötz	*a* orange	*b* yellow	*c* none	*d* none
43	von Strachwitz	*a* dark orange	*b* white	*c* none	*d* silver
44	von Hagken	*a* buff	*b* yellow	*c* white and blue	*d* gold
45	von Zweiffel	*a* lemon yellow	*b* yellow	*c* white and red	*d* yellow
46	von Thiele	*a* scarlet	*b* yellow	*c* none	*d* none
47	von Grawert	*a* dark lemon yellow	*b* yellow	*c* none	*d* none
48	Kurfürst von Hessen	*a* poppy red	*b* white	*c* white with crimson tassels	*d* silver

49	von Müffling	a white	b white	c white and blue	d silver
50	von Sanitz	a light crimson	b white	c white	d silver
51	von Kauffberg	a sulphur yellow	b white	c none	d silver
52	von Rheinhardt	a scarlet	b white	c none	d silver
53	Jung-Larisch	a light yellow	b yellow	c none	d gold
54	von Natzmer	a buff	b white	c white	d silver
55	von Manstein	a crimson	b yellow	c none	d gold
56	von Tauentzien	a scarlet	b white	c none	d none
57	von Grevenitz	a light pink	b yellow	c white and pink	d gold
58	von Courbiére	a light yellow	b white	c white	d silver
59	von Wartensleben	a white	b yellow	c none	d none
60	von Chlebowski	a lemon yellow	b yellow	c none	d none

The other ranks' lace was usually limited to a pair of buttonholes under the lapels, on the cuffs and at the rear waist between the buttons there. It was worn also on the lapels by regiments 1, 6, 8, 9, 12, 14, 15, 17, 18, 21, 25 and 48. Regiments 2, 3, 5, 16, 34, 39, 47, 49, 50 and 54 had no lace on the cuff flaps. These laces were fitted with tassels in the same colour except for regiments 1, 6, 8, 9, 14, 15, 22, 24, 41 and 50 who had none. Lace edgings to lapels and cuff flaps were worn by regiments 20, 24 and 27 and only on the cuff flaps by 9 and 22. The 1st Battalion of the Garde (No 15) had lace edging to collar and lapels.

Officers' parade uniforms had embroidered lace loops on cuff flaps, pocket flaps, under the lapels and at the rear of the waist. Regiments 1, 6, 8, 12, 15, 16, 17, 18, 20, 22, 31, 35 and 48 also wore loops on the lapels; regiments 2, 9 and 27 had embroidered edging to lapels and cuffs; No 1 had embroidered buttonholes. Regiments 13, 15, 46, 47 and 56 had gold or silver aiguillettes, regiments 6, 7, 15, 33, 38, 41, 42, 47, 50, 51 and 52 had the plain Swedish cuffs.

Prussian Line Infantry 1808–15

In the chaos which followed the Prussian defeats at Jena and Auerstädt in October 1806, their demoralised army melted away or surrendered piecemeal to the French in a series of shameful capitulations.

During 1807 and 1808 new regiments were formed from what was left of the old army; any regiment which had besmirched its honour in 1806 was disbanded. The new regiments are listed below, the numbers in brackets behind the titles indicate those old regiments which contributed men to them.

No 1 (1st Ostpreussisches) (2, 11 Füsiliers)
No 2 (1st Pommersches) (8, 17, 19, 22, 31, 36, 42, 46)
No 3 (2nd Ostpreussisches) (11, 6th Füsiliers)
No 4 (3rd Ostpreussisches) (14, 51, 55 and 21st Füsiliers)
No 5 (4th Ostpreussisches) (4, 16, 35, 54, 23rd Füsiliers)
No 6 (1st Westpreussisches) (24, 25, 26, 51, 52, 53, 57 and 3rd Füsiliers)
No 7 (2nd Westpreussisches) (29, 40, 43, 54, 55, 58 and 24th Füsiliers)
No 8 (Garde zu Fuss) (15, 18)
No 9 (Leib-Infanterie Regiment) (1, 5, 13, 18, 27, 34)
No 10 (Colberg) (7, 12, 23, 30, 42, Füsilier – Bataillon Möller)
No 11 (1st Schlesisches) (28, 31, 32, 42, 46, 49, 50, 60, 11th and 15th Füsiliers and Füsilier – Bataillon Danielewitz)
No 12 (2nd Schlesisches) (33, 38, 47)

Plate 38   Kingdom of Prussia: Two Grenadiers Grenadier-Regiment 'Kaiser Alexander'
1813–1815
Brass eagle plate dark blue coat, red facings, yellow buttons, white shoulder straps
with red edgings and A. The title of this contemporary plate states: 'Grenadier u.
Füsilier' but as both figures wear eagle cap plates and black plumes, this must be an
error.

Plate 39   Kingdom of Prussia: Officer, Garde-Schützen-Bataillon 1812–1815
Silver star with black and gold centre, gold side eagles and chain, silver cords;
dark green coat, black facings, red piping, gold buttons, lace and epaulettes, the
latter with red fields and black and silver lace edging to strap; grey overalls with
double red side stripes.

Uniform

The Garde zu Fuss had a shako with white top band (silver for NCOs and
officers), white guards' star, high, wide white horsehair plume for grenadiers,
black for fusiliers. Officers' shakos had white metal eagles at each side and
white chains leading from them to the black within silver cockade, their
plumes were of drooping feathers, black or white with the base in the
reversed colour.

Dark blue tunic with two rows of eight white buttons on the chest, red
turnbacks, red collar and Swedish cuffs both decorated with white lace bars,
white shoulder straps, white breeches and belts; boots. NCOs were distinguished by silver lace (button colour) to collar or to collar and cuffs; officers'
ranks were shown by silver and black shoulder straps and they wore silver
and black waist sashes and sword knots. Their coat tails were longer than
those of the men.

Line infantry wore yellow buttons; their collars and cuffs were in various colours according to province (and had blue, oblong cuff flaps): Ostpreussen —brick red; Westpreussen—crimson; Pommern—white; Brandenburg—poppy red; Schlesien—white. Within each province the shoulder strap colour indicated seniority: 1st Regiment—white; 2nd—red; 3rd—yellow; 4th—light blue. Turnbacks were red. The shako had the frontal badges as follows: Grenadiers—a brass eagle and black plume; Musketeers—the brass royal cypher 'FWR'; Füsiliers—a large black and white cockade and black leatherwork. The Füsiliers formed the 3rd Battalion of each regiment. Musketeer and Grenadier officers carried swords. Füsilier officers had sabres in black leather sheaths. Breeches were grey with a red side piping. By 1812 the wide plume had been replaced by a tall, narrow one. In 1813 the 2nd Garde zu Fuss was raised; it dressed as for the 1st but with yellow buttons and with blue cuff flaps like the line.

In 1814 the newly raised regiments were allotted colours according to their provinces as follows: Magdeburg—light blue; Rheinland—madder red, Westfalen—light red. Shoulder strap colouring according to seniority as before. Drummers wore dark blue swallows' nests edged and decorated in the button colour and red plumes. By 1814 white cords were added to the shakos for parades and in 1815 the shako became belled out at the top.

New Formations 1810–15

On 1 July 1813 the 8th Regiment (Garde) was removed from the line numbering and thus the regiments 9–12 became the regiments 8–11 from the same date. Also that day the new 12th Regiment (Brandenburgisches) was raised as were twelve Reserve-Infanterie-Regimenter (1–12) which on 25 March 1815 became the line infantry regiments 13–24 respectively. The Normal-Infanterie-Bataillon (raised 14 May 1811) became the 2nd Garde Regiment zu Fuss on 19 June 1813 when it was joined by the 1st Bataillon Colberg Infanterie Regiment No 10 and the Füsilier Bataillon of the Leib-Infanterie-Regiment No 9.

The next increase in Prussian line infantry took place on 25 March 1815 when regiments 25–32 were raised from the units shown behind their new titles.

25th—Lütows Freikorps infantry
26th—Elbe Infanterie Regiment (formed 5 July 1813 from the Ausländer – Bataillon von Reuss)
27th—Ausländisches – Jäger – Bataillon 'von Reiche' and the infantry of Hellwig's Freikorps
28th and 29th—1st and 2nd Infantry Regiments of Berg
30th and 31st—1st and 2nd Infantry Regiments of the Russian German legion
32nd—Landwehr units

On 23 October 1815 33rd Regiment was raised from the two Swedish Pommeranian regiments 'Engelbrecht' and 'Leib-Regiment der Königin'.

On 13 December 1815 the 34th Regiment was raised from the disbanded Regiment Nassau-Oranien and men from Nassau-Saarbrücken.

Grenadier Regiments

On 14 October 1814 the Grenadier Regiment 'Kaiser Alexander No 1' was raised from the grenadier battalions of the regiments No 1, 3 and 8 (Leib-Regiment).

On 19 October 1814 the Grenadier Regiment 'Kaiser Franz' No 2 was raised from the grenadier battalions of the 2nd, 6th and 10th regiments.

In the chaotic conditions of 1813, uniformity of costume was of secondary importance to weapons, ammunition and food and thus it is difficult to generalise. Great Britain poured millions of pounds worth of artillery pieces, muskets, ammunition, vehicles, equipment and uniforms into the newly liberated states of north Germany, and the Prussian Reserve Regiments (later Nos 13–24) frequently wore conical British shakos, dark blue single-breasted tunics with white lace bars across the chest and other British decorations.

The two new Garde-Grenadier regiments raised in 1814 had red collars, cuffs and turnbacks, blue cuff flaps and shoulder straps as follows: 'Kaiser Alexander'—white with red letter 'A'; Kaiser Franz—red with yellow 'F'. Their shakos were as for the guards but with yellow, flying eagle front plate, yellow chinscales and buttons.

New Prussian Line Infantry Regiments 1815

13 (1st Westfälisches)	25 March	24 (4th Brandenburg)	25 March
14 (3rd Pommersches)	25 March	25 (1st Rheinisches)	25 March
15 (2nd Westfälisches)	25 March	26 (1st Magdeburg)	25 March
16 (3rd Westfälisches)	25 March	27 (2nd Magdeburg)	7 March
17 (4th Westfälisches)	25 March	28 (2nd Rheinisches)	25 March
18 (1st Posen)	25 March	29 (3rd Rheinisches)	25 March
19 (2nd Posen)	25 March	30 (4th Rheinisches)	25 March
20 (3rd Brandenburg)	25 March	31 (1st Thüringisches)	25 March
21 (4th Pommersches)	25 March	32 (2nd Thüringisches)	25 March
22 (1st Oberschlesisches)	25 March	33 (Ostpreussisches)	15 December
23 (2nd Oberschlesisches)	25 March	34 (Pommersches)	23 October

Prussian Fusiliers 1792–1806

Small, infantry bicorns with black edging, green plume and eagle badge in the button colour, dark green tunic of infantry cut with facings shown on collar, lapels, turnback edging and cuffs, dark green cuff flaps with three buttons, white breeches, short black gaiters, black leatherwork. By 1806 the bicorn had been replaced by a black, peaked felt shako with eagle badge and top band in the button colour.

Facings changed rapidly but in 1806 they were regulated by brigades as follows:

	a (facings)	b (buttons)
1st Ostpreussische	a light green	b yellow
2nd Ostpreussische	a light green	b white
1st Warschauer	a light blue	b white
2nd Warschauer	a light blue	b yellow
Oberschlesische	a black	b white
Niederschlesische	a black ·	b yellow
Westfälische	a crimson	b white
Magdeburgische	a crimson	b yellow

Prussian Jägers and Schützen 1808–15

In 1808 the following regiments were raised from the Feld-Jäger Regiment of the old army: 1st Jäger-Bataillon (Garde-Jäger); 2nd (Ostpreussisches); 3rd (Schlesisches Schützen Bataillon).

Infantry shako without the white top band, black within white pompon, green cords, black feather plume. The Garde-Jäger had a brass star badge, the others a black within white cockade and yellow loop and button. Officers cords were black and silver. The coat and turnbacks were dark green, collar, shoulder and Swedish cuffs red, red piping to turnbacks, yellow buttons, grey breeches, black leatherwork, boots. In 1811 the Garde-Jäger received gold lace to collar and cuffs.

The Schützen wore shakos as for the 2nd Jägers but without cords and with (from 1810) a black horsehair plume; the shako loop was of brass. Dark green tunic, turnbacks, black shoulder straps, collar and cuffs piped red, dark green cuff flaps, grey breeches, yellow buttons, black leatherwork.

In 1815 the Rheinisches Schützen-Bataillon was formed; it received red shoulder straps and the Schlesisches adopted white as the senior unit. Also in 1815 the Magdeburgisches Jäger-Bataillon was raised which received yellow shoulder straps.

On 21 June 1815 the Ostpreussisches Jäger-Bataillon assumed the number '1' when the Garde-Jäger-Bataillon lost its number.

On 19 May 1814 the Garde-Schützen-Bataillon was raised from Berthier's Neuchatel battalion.

On 21 June 1815 the Feldjäger-Bataillon was raised from the Jäger-Bataillon of the Russian German Legion; on 29 August 1815 it was retitled 3rd Jäger Bataillon and on 24 November 1815—2nd Jäger Bataillon.

On 3 October 1815 the 2nd Schützen-Bataillon (Rheinisches) was raised from men of the Saxon, Nassau and Berg light infantry regiments.

Prussian Artillery 1792–1806

Foot Artillery

Infantry style uniform, white bicorn edging, red turnbacks, dark blue collar and cuffs, yellow buttons; in 1798 black collar, Swedish cuffs and lapels, white belts and small clothes, black gaiters.

In 1808 they received infantry uniform, the shako with yellow top band and brass, three-flamed grenade under the black within white pompon, red turnbacks, red piping to black collar and cuffs, dark blue cuff flaps, shoulder straps in the brigade colour (white, red or yellow), black belts, grey breeches, black gaiters. Guards' foot artillery was the same but with yellow lace loops to collar and cuffs and on the shako the yellow guards' star.

Horse Artillery

In 1792 they wore large cavalry bicorns with white plumes, coat as for the foot artillery, buff breeches, boots, white belts. In 1802 they adopted dragoon style tunics with black collar and Swedish cuffs, edged red, black, red-piped edging to the blue coat tails; white small clothes.

In 1808 cavalry shako (leather reinforced) white plume, yellow cords and three-flamed grenade, cockade and chinscales. Dark blue double-breasted tunic, yellow buttons, black collar and Swedish cuffs piped red, black, red-piped edging to dark blue turnbacks, black belts, grey overalls. The Guard Horse Artillery wore the yellow star badge and yellow lace to collar and cuffs.

Plate 40 Kingdom of Prussia: 33rd Infanterie-Regiment 1815
This unit was originally Swedish but came to Prussia on 13 December 1815 when
Sweden ceded her part of Pomerania to Prussia. The musketier private (*left*) is from
the 2nd Battalion, brass shako loop and button, white cords, dark blue coat, red
collar, cuff flaps, turnbacks and piping to cuffs and white shoulder straps, red 33 on
shoulder straps; NCO (1st Battalion) – (*right*) – as above but with gold lace to cuff
and collar and brass commemorative band to shako bearing: 'FÜR AUSZEICHNUNG
d. VORMALIG KGL SCHWEDISCHEN LEIB-REGT KÖNIGIN'.

Pontoniers
As for foot artillery.

Engineers (an all officer and 'Kondukteure' (or senior NCO) corps)
Infantry uniform, dark blue with red collar, cuffs, lapels, turnbacks and
small clothes; wide, scalloped silver lace edging to hat, three silver laces on
each lapel.

Engineers (Pioniers)
Foot artillery uniform, black velvet facings, yellow waistcoat, boots, wide
silver hat edging. 1808 as for the foot artillery but with white buttons and
Swedish cuffs, black shoulder straps edged red.

Landwehr Infantry 1813–15
Dark blue peaked cap with white metal Teutonic cross and headband and
top piping in the collar colour; dark blue Litewka, grey, white or blue

trousers, white or black belts. Collars and buttons according to province, shoulder straps in battalion colour within each regiment: (1st—white; 2nd—red; 3rd—yellow; 4th—light blue). Provincial distinctions were:

	a (collar)	b (buttons)
Ostpreussen	a brick red	b white
Kurmark	a red	b yellow
Neumark	a red	b yellow
Westpreussen	a black	b white
Pommern	a white	b yellow
Schlesien	a yellow	b white
At the end of 1813 the following were added:		
Westfalen	a green	b white
Rheinland	a madder red	b yellow
Elbland	a light blue	b yellow

Weapons, equipment and clothing were all extremely scarce; much British equipment was gratefully used but uniformity was never achieved.

Cavalry

Prussian Kürassiers 1792–1806
Large bicorn with white plume, white tunic with facings shown on collar, Swedish cuffs and waist sash, white shoulder straps and turnbacks. (Regiment von Beeren No 2 had lemon yellow tunics.) Each regiment had its own lace which edged the front of the tunic, the turnbacks and the carbine bandolier. White breeches, gauntlets and belts, high black boots; sabretasche in the facing colour with crowned cypher 'FWR' and edging in the regimental lace. Waistcoat in the facing colour.

	a (facings)	b (OR's lace)	c (officers' lace)
1st Graf Henckel	a red	b white with three red stripes	c silver
2nd von Beeren	a crimson	b crimson (white on the waistcoat)	c silver
3rd Leib regiment	a dark blue	b dark blue with white stripes	c gold
4th von Wagenfeld	a black	b white and dark blue checks	c gold
5th Bailliodz	a light blue	b white and light blue diced	c gold
6th von Quitzow	a light brick red	b white with light brick red pattern	c gold
7th von Reitzenstein	a dark blue	b white with two dark blue stripes	c silver
8th von Holzendorf	a dark crimson	b white with three crimson stripes	c gold
10th Gensdarmes	a red	b red with a wide gold stripe	c gold
11th Lieb-Karabiniers	a light blue	b white with a light blue chain design	c silver
12th von Bunting	a dark orange	b orange with white stripes	c gold
13th Garde du Corps	a red	b red with silver stripes	c silver

Prussian Kürassiers 1808–15
Behind the titles of the newly formed regiments are the numbers of those

old regiments which contributed troops to them:

	a (facings)	b (buttons)
1st Kürassiers (Schlesisches) (K 4, 8, 9, 10, D 13)	a black	b yellow
2nd Kürassiers (Ostpreussisches) (D 6, 9, 10)	a light blue	b white
3rd Kürassiers (Garde du Corps) (K 13 (Garde du Corps))	a red	b yellow
4th Kürassiers (Brandenburgisches) (K 10 (Gensdarmes), 2, 3, 6, 7 and 11) (In 1815 3rd Kür Brand)	a red	b white

The uniform consisted of a black leather helmet with combe and short black horsehair crest, yellow chinscales and front plate with a star badge for the Garde du Corps, an eagle for the other regiments; white tunic with two rows of buttons on the chest, facings shown on collar, Swedish cuffs and piping to shoulder straps and turnbacks; white belts, grey breeches, no Kürass. Trumpeters had a red crest. During 1813 a dark blue Litewka with white shoulder straps and regimental facings on the collars was also worn.

In 1810 the 4th Regiments' facings became light blue (but the Litewka collar stayed red). The Garde du Corps received white lace loops to collars and cuffs in 1810 and in 1812 officers wore fringed epaulettes. French Kürasses were adopted in 1814–15 as were French Kürassier swords. In 1813 the 3rd Kürassiers was removed from the line and became 'Garde du Corps' and the 4th became the new 3rd Regiment. On 7 March 1815 a new 4th Kürassier Regiment was raised.

Prussian Dragoons 1792–1806

Large bicorn with white plume, light blue tunic and turnbacks, facing shown on collar, lapels, Swedish cuffs and turnback edging. White belts, gauntlets and breeches, high black boots. On the right shoulder an aiguillette in the button colour.

REGIMENTAL DISTINCTIONS 1806

	a (facings)	b (buttons and aiguillette)	c (officers' lace)
1st König von Bayern	a black	b yellow	c gold
2nd von Prittwitz	a white	b yellow	c gold
3rd von Irwing	a pink	b white	c silver
4th von Katte	a buff	b white	c silver
5th Regiment der Königin	a dark crimson	b white	c silver
6th von Auer	a white	b white	c silver
7th vacant von Rhein	a scarlet	b yellow	c gold
8th von Esebeck	a scarlet	b white	c silver
9th Graf von Herzberg	a scarlet	b white	c silver
10th vacant von Manstein	a orange	b white	c silver
11th vacant von Voss	a lemon yellow	b white	c silver
12th vacant von Brüsewitz	a black	b white	c silver
13th vacant von Rouquette	a crimson	b yellow	c gold
14th von Wobeser	a buff	b yellow	c none

Prussian Dragoons 1808–15

	a (facings)	b (buttons)
1st Dragoner (Königin) (Regiment der Königin & D 5)	a crimson	b white
2nd Dragoner (1st Westpreussisches) (K 1, D 2, 6, 9, 10 & 11)	a white	b white
3rd Dragoner (Littauisches) (D 7)	a red	b yellow
4th Dragoner (2nd Westpreussisches) (D 8, 9, 10)	a red	b white
5th Dragoner (Brandenburgisches, 'Prinz Wilhelm von Preussen') (K 5, D 1)	a black	b yellow
6th Dragoner (Neumärkisches) (D3, 4)	a light red	b white

Uniform was a shako reinforced with leather; white plume, black within white pompon over an eagle and cords in the button colour, chinscales in the button colour were later added.

The light blue double-breasted tunic showed regimental facings on collar, Swedish cuffs, shoulder straps and piping to the light blue turnbacks, on the chest two rows each of eight buttons, white belts, grey buttoned overalls. Initially the old straight sword in brown leather sheath was carried but by 1813 this had been replaced by the lighter sabre in steel sheath.

On 23 February 1813 the Leichte-Garde-Kavallerie-Regiment was raised from the Normal-Dragoner-Eskadron (8 April 1813 Garde Dragoner Eskadron), the Leib-Ulanen-Eskadron (see section on Lancers 1808–15 p 208), from the Garde-Kosaken-Eskadron and from the Normal-Husaren-Eskadron.

In March 1815 the 7th (Rheinishes) a—yellow, b—white and the 8th (Magdeburgisches) a—white, b—yellow were raised.

On 21 February 1815 the Garde-Dragoner-Regiment was raised from the dragoon squadron of the Leichte-Garde-Kavallerie-Regiment, two squadrons of the Pommersches National-Kavallerie-Regiment and from the Leib-Eskadron of the Dragoner-Regiment Königin No 4.

Hussar Regiments 1806

	a (dolman)	b (collar and cuffs)	c (lace and buttons)	d (pelisse)	e (sash)
1 Von Gettkandt	a dark green	b red	c white	d dark green	e red and white
2 von Rudorff	a red	b dark blue	c white	d dark blue	e dark blue and white
3 von Pletz	a dark blue	b yellow	c yellow	d dark blue	e yellow and white
4 Prinz Eugen	a light blue	b red	c white	d light blue	e yellow and white
5 von Prittwitz*	a black	b red	c white	d black	e red and white
6 von Schimmel-fennig von der Oeye	a dark brown	b yellow	c yellow	d dark brown	e yellow and white
7 von Kohler	a lemon yellow	b light blue	c white	d light blue	e light blue and white
8 von Blücher	a dark crimson	b black	c white	d dark crimson	e red and white
10 von Usedom	a dark blue	b straw yellow	c white	d dark blue	e crimson and blue
11 von Bila	a dark green	b red	c yellow	d dark green	e red and yellow

* This regiment had a white skull and crossbones on their headdress

Most regiments still had Mirlitons but some wore the newly introduced felt shako with pompon and cockade in the colours of the pelisse and the lace (outer), regimental loop and button, high white plume and regimental cords, Breeches were white, the hussar boots untrimmed, leatherwork white and the sabretasche bore the royal cypher ('FWR'). The 5th Regiment wore a white skull and bones on their Mirlitons. The 9th Regiment was the 'Towarczys', see under Lancers p 209.

Prussian Hussars 1808–15

Uniform was a leather-reinforced shako with white plume (red for trumpeters), black within white pompon, regimental loop and button and black within yellow cockade; cords in the regimental lace colour, brass chinscales.

Dolman, pelisse, collar, cuffs, lace and buttons as shown below; red and white sash, black belts, grey button overalls, sabretasche in red with crowned cypher ('FWR') and edging in the lace colour. Sabre in steel sheath. Black sheepskin saddlecloth with red edging, black Hungarian harness.

	a (dolman and pelisse)	b (collar and cuffs)	c (buttons and lace)
1st Leib-Husaren (the old 5th Husaren)	a black	b red	c white
	skull and bones badge to shako, plain black leather sabretasche		
2nd Leib-Husaren (the old 5th Husaren)	a black	b black	c white
	skull and bones badge to shako, plain black leather sabretasche		
1st Brandenburgisches (the old 2nd and 11th Husaren)	a dark blue	b red	c white
2nd Brandenburgisches (Schill)	a dark blue	b red	c yellow
Pommersches (Blücher) (the old 8th Husaren)	a light blue	b black	c yellow
Oberschlesisches (the old 1st, 4th, 6th, 7th and 10th Husaren)	a brown	b yellow	c yellow
Niederschlesisches (the old 3rd Husaren)	a green	b red	c white

The 2nd Brandenburg regiment was disbanded in 1809 after Schill's unauthorised invasion of Westfalia; the Pommersches regiment changed its uniform in that year to a and b—dark blue c—yellow.

In 1811 the Normal-Husaren-Kompagnie was raised which in 1815 became the Garde-Normal-Husaren-Eskadron and then the Garde-Husaren-Regiment (a—dark blue b—red c—yellow).

By 1815 the regiments were numbered as follows: Garde; 1st (1st Leib); 2nd (2nd Leib); 3rd (1st Brandenburg); 4th (1st or Oberschlesisches); 5th (Pommersches); 6th (2nd or Niederschlesisches) and new regiments were raised, numbered and dressed as below:

	a	b	c
7th (Westpreussisches)	a black	b red	c yellow
7 March 1813 8th (1st Westfälisches)	a dark blue	b light blue	c white
and 9th (Rheinisches)	a cornflower blue	b cornflower blue	c yellow
25 March 1813 10th (1st Magdeburgisches) from the Elbe-National-Kavallerie Regt.	a green	b light blue	c yellow
5 December 1813 11th (2nd Westfälisches—the old Lancers of Berg)	a green	b red	c white
12th (2nd Magdeburgisches) the old Saxon hussars	a cornflower blue	b cornflower blue	c white

Prussian Lancers 1792–1806

The 9th Hussars was the Bosniaken regiment raised 1745 and in 1798 had the following uniform: colpack with white plume and cords, long red coat with dark blue collar and cuffs, long, wide red trousers, white belts. They were then replaced by the 'Towarczys' raised from the lesser Polish nobility of the Provinces taken by Prussia in 1795 at the time of the dissolution of Poland. They wore a peakless shako with white plume on the right side, yellow cords, cockade; dark blue tunic of dragoon cut but with Polish cuffs, poppy red collar, cuffs, lapels and turnback edging, red 'Passgürtel' (waist sash) with white edging, white belts and small clothes, yellow buttons and hussar boots. The front rank were armed with lances with pennants in the squadron colour.

There was also an independent battalion of Towarczys with the same uniform but with white buttons.

Prussian Lancer Regiments 1808–15

1st Ulanen (1st Westpreussisches) (D 9, 10, H 1, Towarczys 9)
2nd Ulanen (1st Schlesisches) (D 9, 10, H 1, Towarczys 9)
Raised 1809
Leib-Ulanen-Eskadron (H6) later Garde-Ulanen-Eskadron then regiment.
3rd Ulanen (Brandenburgisches)
Raised 1811
Normal Eskadron 1st Company was dragoons, 2nd hussars. In February 1813 it became the Leichte-Garde-Kavallerie-Regiment.

Uniform in 1808 was a leather reinforced shako, black plume (red for trumpeters), black within white pompon, yellow cords, black within white cockade, yellow loop and button. Dark blue, Prussian-style tunic with red collar and Polish cuffs, red piping to dark blue turnbacks, yellow buttons, shoulder straps according to seniority (1st—white; 2nd—red; 3rd—yellow). Red piping to front of jacket. Black bandolier, dark blue waist belt (Passgürtel) edged red, grey overalls. Lance pennants were dark blue over the shoulder strap colour. Black sheepskin saddle cloths edged red.

The Leib-Ulanen-Eskadron (raised 1809) wore dark blue czapkas with black plume, dark blue kurtka with red collar, lapels, Polish cuffs, turnbacks and seam piping; white buttons and woollen epaulettes, white Passgürtel with two black stripes. Officers wore dark blue overalls with red side stripes, the men grey. Lance pennants red over white.

In 1810 they were re-named the Garde-Ulanen-Eskadron, the czapka received yellow edging and cords, the red lapels were removed, buttons were yellow, the epaulettes white with yellow half moons. Yellow guards' lace was added to collar and cuffs and the Passgürtel became dark blue edged red. In the field all Ulanen wore dark blue Litewkas with red collars and regimental shoulder straps. In February 1813 they became part of the Leichte-Garde-Kavallerie-Regiment.

The Garde-Kosaken-Eskadron was raised in 1813; its uniform was a black colpack, red bag, white plume and cords, completely blue uniform with white epaulettes and guards lace to the red-piped collar and Swedish cuffs, white buttons, black belts, lances with no pennants. In 1815 it became the Garde-Kosaken-Regiment.
The facings in 1815 were as follows:

	a *(shoulder straps)*	b *(buttons)*
Garde-Ulanen-Regiment	a red epaulette fields	b yellow
1st (1st Westpreussisches)	a white	b yellow
2nd (Schlesisches)	a red	b yellow
3rd (Brandenburgisches)	a yellow	b yellow

4th (Pommersches)	*a* light blue	*b* yellow
5th (Westfälisches)	*a* white	*b* white
6th (2nd Westpreussisches)	*a* red	*b* white
7th (1st Rheinisches)	*a* yellow	*b* white
(raised from Saxon Ulans and Hellwig's Cavalry)		
8th (2nd Rheinisches)	*a* light blue	*b* white

(raised 25 March 1815 from 1st and 2nd Hussars of the Russian German Legion)

Landwehr Cavalry 1813–15

As for Landwehr infantry but usually shakos (sometimes of straw within a black oil cloth cover) and grey button overalls, black belts, lances with pennants in the provincial colours.

Freikorps and National Cavalry Regiments

The Freikorps of 1806–7 were usually formed in great haste during the campaign from stragglers and thus had little formal dress regulation.

In 1813 new units were raised as follows:

Lützows—shako in oilskin cover, black Litewka, red piping to collar, Swedish cuffs and shoulder straps, yellow buttons, black trousers (button overalls for cavalry) and belts. The hussars wore black dolman and pelisse with black lace and fur, the lancers wore the shako and Litewka, red over black pennant to the lance. The Tyroler-Jäger-Detachment wore Austrian Corsican hats with green plume, grey tunics with green collar, Polish cuffs, lapels and turnbacks, white buttons, grey breeches and black belts. The infantry later became the 25th Regiment.

Ausländer-Bataillon (Foreign Battalion) von Reuss—line infantry uniform but with light blue facings. It later became the 26th Infantry Regiment.

Ausländisches-Jäger-Bataillon von Reiche—line Jäger uniform with light green shoulder straps edged red. It later became the 27th Infantry Regiment.

Hellwig's Freikorps (Infantry)—shako with white hunting horn badge, dark green tunic, black collar, Polish cuffs, shoulder straps and shoulder rolls, white piping, three rows of white buttons on the chest, grey breeches.

Cavalry

Black colpack with white drooping plume on the left and dark blue bag, red dolman and pelisse, dark blue collar and cuffs, white lace and buttons (gold for officers) black fur, red and yellow sashes, grey overalls, black sheepskin saddle covers. The front rank carried lances with blue over red pennants. The infantry later became the 27th Regiment, the cavalry the 7th Ulanen.

National Cavalry Regiments

Ostpreussisches—raised 12 February 1813, became part of Leib-Garde-Husaren-Regiment on 21 February 1815—all leatherwork black, shako with cockade, yellow eagle and cords, dark blue Litewka with red collar and Polish cuffs, yellow lacing on the chest and white shoulder straps, dark blue breeches with double red piping down each leg. Lance pennants varied for each squadron: 1st—white; 2nd—white over red; 3rd—white over blue; 4th—white over green. The elite company wore colpacks with red bag and brass scale epaulettes.

Pommersches—raised 27 March 1813, became part of Garde-Dragoner-Regiment 21st February 1815—shako with green cords, cockade, green tunic of dragoon style, white collar and Polish cuffs, yellow buttons, light green Passgürtel edged red, grey overalls. Elite company wore brass scale epaulettes.

210

Schlesisches—raised 17 February 1813, became part of Garde-Ulanen-Regiment 21 February 1815—Hussar shako with cords, all black hussar uniform later with red collar and cuffs, red lace.

Elb National Husaren—as for line hussars, green with light blue facings and yellow laces, became 10th Husaren (Magdeburgisch) on 25 March 1815.

THE PRINCELY HOUSES OF

Reuss

(Cockade black within red within yellow)

Prior to joining the Confederation of the Rhine on 13 April 1808 the five houses of Reuss (Gera, Greiz, Ebersdorf, Lobenstein and Schleiz) had maintained only company-sized units of palace troops. From 1807 until November 1813 the princely houses were to band together to produce a contingent of 450 men who served as part of the 2nd Battalion, 6th Regiment of the Confederation of the Rhine (the principality of Waldeck made up the rest of the 2nd Battalion; the two principalities of Schwarzburg made up the 1st Battalion).

The contingent was dressed as follows: French style shako with oval brass plate bearing an 'R', cockade, red plume, red, black and yellow mixed cords, white, single-breasted tunic with light blue collar, round cuffs and turnbacks, yellow buttons. Light blue Hungarian breeches with red, black and yellow cord decoration to thighs and sides, short black gaiters. White belts and shoulder straps. French rank badges.

Officers carried sabres on white baldrics and wore gold epaulettes, shako trim and sabre knot; they wore hussar style boots with gold trim and tassel.

Plate 41   The Contingents of Reuss and Schwarzburg 1809
(*l to r*) Schwarzburg – fusilier private (red plume and facings, dark green coat, yellow buttons, grey breeches), officer (as above but with gold epaulette and collar loops and dark green breeches); Reuss – officer (white uniform, light blue facings, gold buttons and epaulette), corporal (as above but yellow shako trim, yellow rank bar over cuff, light blue breeches), private (as for corporal but white trousers). *Augsburger Bilder*.

Battle History

1807—Siege of Glogau (Prussia); 1809—Tyrol; 1809–11—Spain; 1812—Russia as part of 2nd Brigade, 'Division Princiére'; 1813—besieged in Danzig.

IMPERIAL

Russia

(Cockade black within orange within white)

Rulers

Catherine the Great until 1796, Paul Petrowitsch until 11 March 1801 then Alexander I.

Catherine the Great
In 1786 Catherine the Great had introduced a uniform designed by Prince Potemkin which was simple, practical, very advanced in concept and was applied to almost all arms except the guard, the hussars and the Cossacks. It consisted of a low-crowned black felt helmet with peak, brass front band, black front plate, a yellow woollen crest running from ear to ear over the top of the front plate, black leather chinstrap, short plume on the left side and for non-commissioned ranks, two strips of coloured cloth hanging down the back and ending in tassels at about shoulder blade level. These were designed to be tied around the ears in the winter.

The short-skirted jacket was double-breasted and the skirts were turned over only at the front corners. These turnbacks were in the coat colour. Facings were shown on collar, lapels, Swedish cuffs, turnback edgings and piping to rear of skirts. Legwear was long red trousers with black leather booting to the bottoms, closing with six buttons. They were decorated with double yellow side stripes, sometimes straight, sometimes with scalloped outer edges. Belts were white. The hair was cut to ear lobe level and was not powdered.

Paul Petrowitsch
When Tsar Paul Petrowitsch came to the throne in 1796 he put the sartorial clock back ten years and reintroduced all the powder, queued hair and pomp of the bygone era. Also in 1796 rank badges were introduced for officers in the form of gold or silver stars on their epaulettes with a mixture of the regimental colour.

Officers' coats had no turnbacks and their hats were edged in silver/gold; they wore silver waist sashes and sword knots mixed with black and orange and carried halberds. As sign of office they wore the gorget as follows: field officers—all gold; captain—gold with silver double eagle; vice captain—silver with gold rim and double eagle; lieutenant—silver with gold double eagle; ensign—silver.

In November 1797, following the Peace of Campo Formio, the French Emigré corps of the Prince of Condé (Grenadier Regiment Duc du Bourdon, Regiment of the Prince of Hohenlohe, Noble Dragoons of the Duc du Berry, Dragoons of the Duc du Enghien and two artillery companies) were taken into Russian service until February 1800 when they passed into British service.

Alexander I

When Alexander became Tsar on 12 March 1801 he did away with his predecessor's custom of naming the regiments after their Colonels-in-Chief and reintroduced the old regional titles. The pigtails were shortened at this time and a new, shorter uniform was introduced. It was dark green, double-breasted with a high collar open at the front, Brandenburg cuffs with dark green, three button flaps. The collar, cuffs and turnbacks were in various colours for each Inspectorate, the shoulder straps were initially red and later a different colour for each regiment. Breeches were white and short boots were worn. The bicorns were very high and bore a black within orange cockade and woollen pompons one above the cockade and one in each corner.

NCOs wore yellow lace to front and bottom of collar and top of cuff, they wore only one shoulder strap, on the left, and had white gauntlets. Drummers and fifers had swallows' nests and rich decoration in white lace on the chest, sleeves and back seams.

Officers had similar uniforms but with longer skirts, gold edged shoulder straps and a black feather plume to the bicorn. They had gloves without cuffs. Sash, sword knot and gorget as before except that the crimson silk threads (which had been added to sash and sword knot when Tsar Paul became Grand Master of the Order of St John in 1799) were removed as Tsar Alexander laid down that office in 1801. Officers of horse artillery wore white plumes and all ranks of that arm wore a yellow aiguillette on the right shoulder. Field officers had leather breeches and high boots, generals also had a white feather hat edging. Grenadiers wore high, metal-fronted mitre caps, fusiliers shorter caps of slightly different design. Jäger uniforms were light green.

The Gatschina Army Detachment

Before his mothers' death Paul Petrowitsch had developed an army in miniature at his estate, Gatschina, near St Petersburg. His 'toy soldiers' were all dressed exactly as his father's army had been before the new, very practical uniform designed by Prince Potemkin had done away with all the impractical pomp.

The detachment consisted of 1 grenadier and 4 musketeer battalions each of 3 companies of 65 men, a Jäger company (35 men) a Kürassier, dragoon, hussar and Cossack regiment each of 2 squadrons of 150–170 men (the Cossack squadrons were 50–60 men) and 200 artillerymen with 59 guns. The entire corps was so perfectly drilled and dressed that they served as a model for the army when Paul came to the throne in 1796 and were absorbed into the guard. Their uniforms were in the style of 1762 with minor alterations; officers carried spontoons, NCOs halberds. The grenadiers wore brass fronted mitre caps; the Kürassiers had white tunics and polished steel Kürasses; the dragoons had green coats, yellow waistcoats and leather breeches; the hussars wore light blue with white lacing and the artillery

213

were as for the infantry but with a green shawl collar with red piping, straw yellow waistcoats and breeches.

The Guard

In 1796 the Life Hussar Regiment of two squadrons was raised; the old Chevalier Guard was disbanded and a new one raised at three squadrons which in its turn was disbanded in 1797. The Horse Guards were now in two battalions each of five squadrons and two combined grenadier battalions were organised in the guard infantry and then disbanded again. The Preobrashenski Infantry regiment then consisted of two grenadier and three musketeer battalions, the Ssemenow and Ismailow regiments each had one grenadier and two musketeer battalions.

In January 1798 the Life Cossack Regiment was raised, the Life Hussar Regiment was increased to two battalions each of five squadrons and on 11 January 1799, when the Tsar became Grand Master of the Order of St John, a new Chevalier Guard was raised.

In 1803 the guards infantry received the new infantry uniform with red cuffs and turnbacks and with collars and shoulder straps in the regimental colour as follows: Preobrashenski—red; Ssemenow—light blue; Ismailow—dark green. A new helmet was introduced, of black felt or leather, with a large double eagle of copper on the front plate which was trimmed around the top by a thick crest of horse hair. The rear headband and the bag which fell to the back were in the regimental colour (but white for Ismailow) and the tassel at the bag end was in the battalion colour. The bag was decorated around the edge and down the centre with gold braid and the chinstrap bosses were brass grenades.

NCOs had a white plume with a black and orange tip to the left side of the helmet. Officers had bicorns with plumes and the embroidery to collars and cuffs was as decreed by Tsar Paul.

On 19 October 1811 the Finland battalion was converted to the Finland Life Guard Jägers; on 7 November the Lithuanian Life Guard Regiment was raised from a battalion of the Preobrashenski regiment and other, selected troops. It had red collars.

Line Infantry 1792–6

The standard uniform with red turban to back of helmet edged yellow; the cloth strips were black with yellow tassels and the plume was black and stemmed from a white bow. Light green coat, red facings, yellow buttons. Regimental identity was shown by an epaulette in various designs and colours, worn on the left shoulder. The pouch was decorated with a round brass plate bearing the double eagle. Bayonets and sabres were worn on a white waist belt over the coat. Grenadiers had a larger front plate to their helmets and carried sabres on slings with white fist straps. Officers' helmets had no cloth strips hanging to the rear. In 1796 the old uniform of 1786 was reintroduced complete with long pigtail and powdered and curled hair. The uniform for musketeers was a bicorn with white edging, white bow, loop and button; old-fashioned light green, long-skirted coat with open front; collar, lapels, Swedish cuffs and turnbacks in the regimental facing colour; yellow buttons, light green waistcoat with red collar and green cuffs, red breeches (in summer white linen), long black gaiters, white pouch bandolier

214

and waistbelt (under the coat); a green shoulder strap replaced the epaulette. Grenadiers wore higher, metal-fronted mitre caps of the Prussian model bearing the double eagle, the imperial cypher ♔ and trophies of arms, later the crests of the cities whose names their regiments bore. Atop the pointed plate was a regimental pompon. Fusiliers wore shorter, mitre caps than grenadiers; they were similar to those worn by the Prussian fusiliers under Frederick the Great. Officers' coats had no skirt turnbacks, their silver hat edging was in vandyke style and they wore white gauntlets. NCOs had one or two gold lace edgings to collar and cuffs. In 1802 the cloth backing to grenadiers' and fusiliers' metal-fronted mitre caps was in the collar colour, the headband in the shoulder strap colour.

The first shakos were introduced in 1803 for musketeers and were decorated with a ribbon cockade, a pompon and tassel; in 1805 grenadiers and fusiliers also adopted it. Officers retained the modernised bicorn with high, black feather plume and in 1806 they adopted a single epaulette on the left shoulder. Halberds and spontoons were withdrawn and all regiments received red facings. From 1801 the now dark green coat was worn closed over with two parallel rows of yellow buttons down the chest and the turnbacks were shortened. Within each division, regiments showed their seniority by the colour of their shoulder straps: 1st red, 2nd white, 3rd yellow, 4th dark green edged red, 5th light blue. On 15 February 1807 officers' epaulettes and soldiers' shoulder straps were decorated with the divisional number and the belts were worn crossed over the shoulders instead of the sabre belt being around the waist. For winter wear, white cloth trousers with black leather bottoms closed with ten black leather buttons were introduced. In summer close-fitting trouser-gaiters in white linen were worn. Officers adopted a second epaulette in 1809 but lost the aiguillette which they had worn until then. That same year the shako was decorated with white cords. It bore a brass three-flamed grenade badge for grenadiers, a single flamed grenade for musketeers. The famous 'Kiwer' shako with its extended, scalloped top, leather trim and reinforcing bands was introduced in 1812.

The Pawlow regiment had worn brass-fronted, mitre caps since 1796 (with the imperial eagle badge since 1802). The backing cloth was red, the headband and piping white; in 1816 brass chinscales were added and even in 1914 this regiment appeared on parade in these caps. The coat collar, worn open until late 1812, was now closed.

Infantry equipment was a cylindrical, black leather valise until 1807 when a more conventional rectangular black leather pack replaced it. Pouch badges were round brass plates bearing the double eagle until 1809 and grenadiers had additionally four corner grenades. In 1809 the pouch badge was the same as the Kiwer badge—a brass three-flamed grenade for grenadiers, a single flamed grenade for others.

Organisation
In 1795 each line infantry regiment consisted of 2 grenadier, 8 musketeer and 2 depot companies each of 159 men.

In 1796 the line infantry strength was: twelve regiments of grenadiers— Life Regiment, Tauride, Jekaterinoslav, Little Russia, Kiev, Siberia, Phanagora, Astrakhan, St Petersburg, Chersson, Moscow and Caucasus; fifty-five infantry regiments—Old Jngermannland, Moscow, Troizk, Vladimir, Nowgorod, Schlüsselburg, Kazan, Pskow, Smolensk, Asov, Woronesh, Nishegorod, Tschernigow, Rjasan, Ssusdal, Rostow, Weliki-Luki, Archangel, Perm, Wjatka, Narwa, Tobolsk, Newa, Witebsk, Wyborg, Uglitsch, Kexholm,

Ladoga, Bjelosersk, Muromsk, Apscheron, Shirvan, Kabardinsk, Nascheburg, Nisow, Tiflis, Stary-Oskol, Bjelew, Rjaschki, Ssjewersk, Jelez, Tambow, Orel, Brjansk, Kursk, Koslow, Alexopol, Reval, Polozk, Dnjeprowski, Tula, Sewastopol, Ssophia, New Jngermannland and Jaroslaw.

There were also twenty 'Field Battalions'—Jekaterinburg, Ssenispalatinsk, 3rd–6th Siberian, 1st–6th Orenburg, 1st–8th Moscow, which in 1796 were converted to six musketeer regiments: Butyrk, Ufa, Rylsk, Jekaterinburg, Sselenginsk and Tomsk.

On 20 August 1798 it was decreed that all regiments, with the exception of the Life Grenadiers, were to be known by the names of their colonels in chief and six new regiments were raised: Pauluzki, Brandt, Müller I, Marklowski, Berg and Leitner. In 1800 the Senate Regiment was raised (later called Uschakow) from the Senate Battalion; the 1st Jäger Regiment was disbanded and two new divisions (Karkow and Brest) were organised. In 1807 all regiments received again their old geographical titles and the new regiments were redubbed as follows: Scherbatow (formerly Acharow)— Tenginsk; Runitsch (formerly Pawluzki)—Nawaginsk; Nesswetafew (formerly Leitner)—Saratow; Kaschkin (formerly Brandt)—Olonez; Müller I— Kolywan; Anikejew (formerly Maklowski)—Poltawa; Baklanowski (formerly Berg)—Ukrain; Uschakow—Lithuania.

Russian Army Organisations

Early in 1812 the Russian army was organised into various Armies, Corps and Divisions as shown below:

1st Army of the West (General-lieutenant Barclay de Tolly)
1st Infantry Corps (Graf von Wittgenstein)
5th Infantry Division: 1st Brigade: Ssjewski Grenadier (formerly a musketeer regiment) and Kaluga, infantry regiments; 2nd: Perm and Mohilew Regiments; 3rd: 23rd and 24th Jägers.
14th Infantry Division: 1st Brigade: Tula and Nawaginsk Regiments; 2nd: Estland and Tenginsk; 3rd: 25th and 26th Jägers.
Cavalry: Riga and Jamburg Dragoons, Grodno Hussars, three regiments of Cossacks.
Artillery: 9 companies, 2 pontoon and 1 pioneer companies.
2nd Infantry Corps (General-lieutenant Bagohofwud)
4th Infantry Division: 1st Brigade: Krementschug and Minsk Regiments; 2nd: Tobolsk and Wolhynia; 3rd: 4th and 34th Jägers.
17th Infantry Division: 1st Brigade: Rjasan and Bjelosersk Regiments; 2nd: Wilmannstrand and Brest; 3rd: 30th and 48th Jägers.
Cavalry: Jelissawetgrad Hussars.
Artillery: 7 companies.
3rd Infantry Corps (General-lieutenant Tutschkow)
1st Infantry Division: 1st Brigade: Life Grenadiers, Grenadier Regiment Graf Araktschejew; 2nd: Pawlow Grenadiers, Jekaterinoslav Grenadiers; 3rd: St Petersburg and Tauride Grenadiers.
3rd Infantry Division: 1st Brigade: Reval and Muromsk Regiments; 2nd: Koporje and Tschernigow; 3rd: 20th and 21st Jägers.
Cavalry: Life Guard Cossacks, one other Cossack regiment.
Artillery: 8 companies.
4th Infantry Corps (General-lieutenant Graf Schuwalow)
11th Infantry Division: 1st Brigade: Kexholm and Pernau Regiments;

2nd: Polozk and Jelez; 3rd: 1st and 33rd Jägers.
Cavalry: Isum Hussars.
Artillery: 6 companies.

The Reserve

5th Infantry Corps (Grand Prince Constantin Pawlowitsch)
Guards Division: 1st Brigade: Preobraschenski and Ssemenow Life Guards; 2nd: Ismailow and Lithuanian Life Guards; 3rd: Life Guard Jägers and Finland Life Guard Jägers.
Guard Equipage: marines.
Combined Grenadier Division: 26 grenadier battalions.
Cavalry: Life Kürassiers Emperor, Life Kürassiers Empress, Kürassier Regiment Astrakhan.
Artillery: 4 foot companies, 2 horse batteries, 1 pioneer company.

6th Infantry Corps (General Dokturow)
7th Infantry Division: 1st Brigade: Pskow and Moscow Regiments; 2nd: Libau and Ssophia; 3rd: 11th and 36th Jägers.
24th Infantry Division: 1st Brigade: Ufa and Schirvan Regiments; 2nd: Butyrk and Tomsk; 3rd: 19th and 40th Jägers.
Cavalry: Ssumy Hussars.
Artillery: 7 companies.

1st Reserve Cavalry Corps (General-lieutenant Uwarow)
Kasan and Njeshin Dragoons, Polish Ulans, 1 artillery company.

2nd Reserve Cavalry Corps (General-major Baron von Korff)
6th Cavalry Brigade: Pskow and Moscow Dragoons.
7th Cavalry Brigade: Kargopol and Jngermannland Dragoons, 1 artillery company.

2nd Army of the West (Prince Bagration)

7th Infantry Corps (General-lieutenant Rajewski)
12th Infantry Division: 1st Brigade: Smolensk and Narwa Regiments; 2nd: Alexopol and New Jngermanneand; 3rd: 6th and 41st Jägers.
26th Infantry Division: 1st Brigade: Ladoga and Poltawa Regiments; 2nd: Nishegorod and Orel; 3rd: 5th and 42nd Jägers.

8th Infantry Corps (General-lieutenant Borosdin)
2nd Grenadier Division: 1st Brigade: Crimea and Moscow Grenadier Regiments; 2nd: Astrakhan and Phanagora; 3rd: Siberia and Little Russia Grenadiers.
3rd Grenadier Division: 22 combined grenadier battalions.
2nd Kürassier Division: 2nd Brigade: Jekaterinoslaw and Military Order Regiments; 3rd: Gluchow, Little Russian and Nowgorod Regiments.
Artillery: 5 companies.

4th Reserve Cavalry Corps (General-major Graf Sievers)
12th Cavalry Brigade: Karkow and Tchernigow Dragoons.
13th Cavalry Brigade: Kiew and New Russian Dragoons, Lithuanian Ulans.
Artillery: 1 company, 1 pontoon and 1 pioneer company.

3rd (reserve) Army (General Tormassow)

Corps of General Markow
9th Infantry Division: 1st Brigade: Nascheburg and Jakutsk Regiments; 2nd: Apscheron and Rijashk; 3rd: 10th and 38th Jägers.
15th Infantry Division: 1st Brigade: Koslow and Witebsk Regiments; 2nd: Kura and Kolywan; 3rd: 13th and 14th Jägers.
Cavalry: Alexandrija Hussars.
Artillery: 7 companies.

Plate 42　Imperial Russia: Jägers 1802–1804
Batallion drummer (*left*) and hornist Lifeguard Jäger Regiment. Note the drummer's NCO pompon (quartered white and black and orange) and collar and cuff lace edging. Wiskowatow.

Plate 43　Imperial Russia: Lifeguard Hussars 1801–1802
Officer status is indicated by the black plume base, the silver lace and buttons and the leopard skin pelisse as well as the black and silver sabre strap. The elaborate Polish harness was only worn for parades. Wiskowatow.

Corps of General-lieutenant Graf Kamenski
18th Infantry Division: 1st Brigade: Vladimir and Tambow Regiments; 2nd: Kostroma and Dnjeprowsk; 3rd: 28th and 32nd Jägers.
Combined Grenadier Division: 18 battalions.
Cavalry: Pawlograd Hussars.
Artillery: 4 companies.

Corps of General-lieutenant Baron von Osten-Sacken
36th Infantry Division (composition unknown).
11th Cavalry Division (composition only partially known).
Lubny Hussars.
Artillery: 2 companies.

Reserve Cavalry Corps (Graf Lambert)
5th Cavalry Division: 15th Brigade: Starodub and Twer Dragoons; 16th: Zhitomir and Arsamass Dragoons; 17th: Tartar Ulans, Vladimir, Taganrog and Sserpuchow Dragoons, 9 regiments of Cossacks, 1 pioneer and 1 pontoon company.

The Russian forces in Finland, on the Turkish border and in Grusinia are shown below.

218

Finland (Baron Steinheil)

6th Division: 1st Brigade: Brjansk and Nisow Regiments; 2nd: Uglitsch Regiment and 35th Jägers; 3rd: Asov Regiment and 3rd Jägers.

21st Division: 1st Brigade: Petrowsk and Podolia Regiments; 2nd: Newa and Lithuania; 3rd: 2nd and 44th Jägers.

25th Division: 1st Brigade: 1st and 2nd Marine Regiments; 2nd: 3rd Marines and Woronesh Regiment; 3rd: 31st and 47th Jägers.

Turkish Border (General Kutusow)

8th Division: 1st Brigade: Ukrain and Archangel Regiments; 2nd: Schlüsselburg and Old Jngermannland; 3rd: 7th and 37th Jägers.

10th Division: 1st Brigade: Bialostok and Crimea Regiments; 2nd: Kursk and Jaroslaw; 3rd: 8th and 39th Jägers.

13th Division: 1st Brigade: Galitsch and Weliki-Luki Regiments; 2nd: Pensa and Saratow; 3rd: 12th and 22nd Jägers.

22nd Division: 1st Brigade: Wjatka and Stawropol Regiments; 2nd: Olonez and Wyborg; 3rd: 29th and 45th Jägers.

26th Division: 1st Brigade: Ladoga and Poltawa Regiments; 2nd: Nishegorod and Orel; 3rd: 5th and 42nd Jägers.

Grusiania Corps (Marquis Paulucci)

19th Division: Kazan, Ssusdal, Bjelew, Sewastopol, Wologda and 16th and 17th Jäger Regiments.

20th Division: Grusinia, Chersson, Troizk, Tiflis, Kabardinsk, 9th, 15th and 46th Jäger Regiments.

28th and 29th Divisions: formed of the garrison troops of the Orenburg and Siberian Lines.

27th Division: still in process of formation and eventually consisted of: 1st Brigade: Odessa and Zhitomir Regiments; 2nd: Wilna and Ssimbirsk; 3rd: 49th and 50th Jägers.

Not included in the above organisations are the following cavalry divisions:

1st Kürassier Division: *Guards Brigade*: Chevalier Guards and Horse Guards.

1st Cavalry Division: *1st Brigade*: Life Guard Dragoons, Life Guard Ulans; 2nd: Life Guard Hussars, Ural and Tschernomor Life Guard Cossack Ssotnias.

9th Brigade (of 3rd Cavalry Division): Kurland Dragoons.

14th Brigade (of 4th Cavalry Division): Pawlograd and Achtyrka Hussars.

6th Cavalry Division: 18th Brigade: St. Petersburg and Livland Dragoons; 19th: Ssjewersk and Kinburn Dragoons; 20th: White Russian Hussars and Wolhynia Ulans.

7th Cavalry Division: 21st Brigade: Smolensk and Perejeslaw Dragoons; 22nd: Tiraspol and Dorpat Dragoons; 23rd: Olviopol Hussars and Tschugujew Ulans.

25th Brigade: Nishegorod, Narwa and Borrisoglebsk Dragoons.

27th Brigade: Finland and Mitau Dragoons.

26th Brigade: Lubny Hussars.

Apart from these forces the 30th–37th Divisions were formed from the Depot Battalions of existing infantry divisions as shown below: *30th Division* —4th and 14th Divisions; *31st*—5th and 17th; *32nd*—1st, 11th and 23rd; *33rd*—3rd and 7th; *34th*—24th and 26th; *35th*—2nd and 18th; *36th*—12th and 15th; *37th*—9th and 27th.

The 38th–47th Divisions were formed of the 4th or Reserve Battalions of existing divisions as listed below: *38th*—6th and 21st; *39th*—14th and 25th; *40th*—4th and 5th; *41st*—3rd and 17th; *42nd*—7th, 11th and 23rd; *43rd*—18th and 24th; *44th*—13th and 26th; *45th*—9th and 15th; *46th*—8th and 22nd; *47th*—10th and 16th.

In a similar manner the 9th–12th Cavalry Divisions were formed from the depot squadrons of the 1st–8th Cavalry Divisions as shown below:

9th Division: 1st Kürassier Division—4 squadrons; 1st Cavalry Division—11 squadrons; 2nd Cavalry Division—8 squadrons.

10th Division: 3rd and 4th Divisions—14 squadrons.

11th Division: 5th and 6th Cavalry Divisions—12 squadrons.

12th Division: 7th and 8th Divisions—16 squadrons.

The 13th–16th Divisions were formed of various cavalry recruit depots as follows: *13th*—24 squadrons; *14th*—10; *15th*—8 and *16th*—16.

The artillery was also increased by drawing on recruit and reserve formations: 1st Reserve Brigade—1 heavy, 4 light and 1 horse companies; 2nd—1 heavy, 4 light and 1 horse; 3rd—3 light and 3 horse; 4th—1 heavy, 3 light and 3 horse companies.

The regiment Kexholm Grenadiers was retitled 'Grenadier-Regiment Kaiser Franz I' and the St Petersburg Grenadiers were retitled 'Grenadier-Regiment King Friedrich Wilhelm III' from 19 October 1813 to commemorate the great allied victory at Leipzig (16–18 October 1813—also known as the 'Battle of the Three Emperors').

Jägers

In 1792 the Jägers wore the standard uniform as for the line infantry but with the jacket all green and with black side stripes to the green trousers, the helmet had a black crest, green front band and green cloth strips to the rear. The clock was put back in 1796 when the old fashioned style of 1786 was reintroduced.

It was a tricorn, all green coat with Polish cuffs, black hussar lacing to chest, white breeches and short boots. In 1801 the breeches became light green and collar and cuffs showed the facings of the line infantry regiment to which the Jäger detachment belonged. The long shallow black cartridge pouch was worn around the waist. The tricorn was replaced in 1802 by a 'top hat' with a horizontal brim all the way around, black cockade with orange rim, yellow button, loop and pompon topped with a tuft showing battalion and company colour. In 1807 this was replaced by the shako. In 1806 the cartridge pouch was reduced in size; leatherwork was black and on the pouch was worn the battalion number in brass.

Coat style variations were as for the line infantry but collar and cuffs were dark green piped red, battalion identity was shown on the shoulder strap.

Organisation

In 1795 each Jäger battalion had four field companies and a depot company and in 1796 there were ten corps (totalling forty battalions): Kuban, Caucasus, Tauride, Bug, White Russia, Finland, Livonia, Jekaterinoslav, Estonia and Lithuania. There were also the three Jäger battalions: 1st and 2nd Siberia and Olonez. In 1796 the Jägers were reorganised into twenty battalions numbered 1–20.

The Jäger battalions were each increased to regiments in 1796, each of two battalions of five companies and in 1798 the 1st Jägers was disbanded. In 1801 all regiments were renumbered 1–19 to fill this gap and the new cut of uniform was introduced but still in light green with similar trousers,

Plate 44 Imperial Russia: Officer of Lithuanian Tartars 1801–1803
Dark blue kurtka and overalls, crimson czapka top, facings and overall stripes, silver buttons and epaulettes; saddle furniture dark blue and crimson with silver piping and cypher; silver, black and orange sash and sabre knot. Wiskowatow.

Plate 45 Imperial Russia: Horse Artillery 1804–1807
Trumpeter (*left*) and trumpet-major. Red crests (white front with twin orange stripes for trumpet-major) dark green coats, black facings piped red, yellow buttons, white lace and trumpet cords. Note NCO lace to trumpet-major's collar and cuffs and his black and white sabre knot wreath. Wiskowatow.

different facings for each regiment and the trousers had a piping in the collar colour. Officers wore green plumes, but discarded the gorget and sash. Dark green uniforms were introduced in 1801.

Artillery

Foot Artillery 1972
Standard uniform with white helmet crest, red coat and trousers, black facings, yellow buttons and trouser stripes. In 1796 the old uniform of 1786 was reintroduced: bicorn with white edging and bow, green coat with black facings and yellow buttons.

In 1801 the black facings were piped red and the coat followed all the alterations laid down for the line infantry. In 1807 the shako with black cockade edged orange, yellow button and loop, red pompon and tuft was introduced. Subsequent alterations as for the infantry but the badge was a grenade over crossed cannon barrels; cords were red.

In early 1796 the foot artillery consisted of the Bombardier Regiment

221

(for the manning of howitzers and mortars), two Gunner Regiments, two Fusilier Regiments and three Bombardier battalions. A wide reaching reorganisation occurred in the November of that year when the foot artillery was converted into ten field battalions and three siege battalions. Each field battalion had five companies of twelve pieces: four ½ Pudige Unicorns (1 Pud = 16.32 kg), four medium 12 pdrs and four light 12 pdrs. Each siege battalion had five companies with four heavy 12 pdrs, four 1 Pudige Unicorns and two 1 Pudige mortars. Count Araktschejew reorganised the siege artillery and equipped each company with three 24 pdr, three 18 pdr cannon, one 5 Pudige, one 2 Pudige and two 1 Pudige Unicorns and eight Coehorn mortars. In 1800 those light artillery pieces hitherto attached to each infantry battalion were withdrawn and concentrated into the field artillery proper, which now had eight regiments. Equipments were modelled on the Prussian example and not the more modern French or Gribeauval system.

Horse Artillery (raised 29 September 1794)
Standard uniform in foot artillery colours but with a round-brimmed civilian hat with the left side turned up and bearing a white tape cockade and white feather plume; two black cloth strips with yellow tassels to the rear. In 1796 as for the foot artillery; 1803 they adopted the Kürassier style black leather helmet and wore it until 1815.

Officers wore the same uniform but with velvet facings and on the right shoulder a gold aiguillette, on the right a shoulder strap with the imperial cypher.

Organisation
In 1795 there were six companies each with seven ¼ Pudige Unicorns, seven 6 pdr cannon, 380 men and 219 riding horses and in 1796 these were gathered into a horse artillery battalion. (A unicorn was a lighter-chambered cannon using a lower powder charge and having a shorter range than conventional cannons.)

Engineers 1792
Standard uniform as for the foot artillery but with white buttons and trouser stripes. 1796 as for the foot artillery but with white buttons.

Kürassiers 1792–1815

Standard uniform in 1792 with white helmet crest and brass front band as broad as that of infantry grenadiers. The back binding in the regimental facing colour, yellow cloth strips hanging to the rear. Light yellow coats with facings and trousers varying with the regiment. On the right shoulder was an aiguillette in the regimental colour. No Kürasses were worn and the crossed, white bandoliers supported carbine and pouch while the waist belt held the heavy, straight-bladed sword. In 1796 the old uniform of 1786 was reintroduced: tricorn with white bow and plume, buff tunic with green collar and cuffs, green waistcoats, buff breeches, high cuffed boots. The tunic was trimmed on the front in green and white lace. Only the front plate of the black Kürass was worn. They carried sabretasches in green with white border and yellow cypher ₮ .

In 1801 the tunic became white and grey button overalls were worn for daily duties. A black leather helmet with black leather combe, brass front plate with the double eagle, which was the Star of the Order of St George for the Military Order regiment, and a huge black woollen sausage crest was introduced in 1803. NCOs had white fronts to their crests with double vertical orange stripes, trumpeters all red and officers all white crests.

Within a short time this crest was replaced by a short, bristly black horsehair crest (red for trumpeters). This uniform was retained until 1846 with only minor alterations.

The Leib-Kürassier-Regiment in 1790 consisted of thirty squadrons and included the regiment of the Military Order, the Kazan Kürassiers and the two Carabinier regiments Twer and Ssophia. Saddle furniture was in the facing colour, edged in the button colour. It bore the imperial cypher (eight-pointed Guards' Star for the regiments Emperor and Empress).

Organisation

In 1796 there were five regiments: Life Regiment (1796 Empress' Life Regiment); Crown Prince (1796 Emperor's Life Regiment); Military Order (1796 Little Russia); Kazan and Potemkin (1796 Jekaterinoslaw). Each regiment had five squadrons and ten new regiments were added to this arm by converting Carabiniers and Chevau Légers regiments (see pp 225/226 for details).

In 1798 the regiment Zorn was raised and in 1801 retitled Twer. In 1800 the existing regiments Ssophia, Njeshin, Jamburg and Rjasan were dis-- banded.

Russian Kürassier Regimental Distinctions 1807

	a (facings)	b (buttons)
Emperor's Life Regiment	a light blue	b white
Empress' Life Regiment	a raspberry	b white
Military Order	a black	b yellow
Little Russia	a dark green	b yellow
Gluchow	a dark blue	b white
Jekaterinoslaw	a orange	b white
Kazan	a raspberry	b yellow

Dragoons 1792

Standard uniform in infantry colours but with yellow shoulder straps, aiguillette to right shoulder and buff gauntlets. Crossed bandoliers as for Kürassiers. In 1796 the 1786 pattern uniform was reintroduced: tricorn with white edging and bow; loop and button, light green coat with short skirts, white breeches and boots or grey button overalls. They were armed with the heavy, straight sword and a musket and bayonet. In 1803 they adopted the black leather Kürassier helmet with its huge woollen crest and in 1804 changed this for the short, black horsehair bristles.

Organisation

In 1796 there were eleven regiments: Astrakhan, Vladimir, Smolensk, Taganrog, Kinburn, Nishegorod, St. Petersburg, Orenburg, Siberia, Irkutsk and Pskow; the Kinburn regiment was disbanded but six new regiments were added from the Carabiniers. Each regiment now had five

Plate 46   Imperial Russia: Grenadiers 1808
The huge plumes had white tips with double orange vertical stripes for NCOs; they were replaced shortly after this date by thinner plumes. The method of wearing the straps over the shoulder, under the rolled greatcoat, is somewhat obscured. Wiskowatow.

Plate 47   Imperial Russia: Pontoniers 1805–1809
Junior NCO (*left*), note cuff edging, and senior NCO with extra edging to collar as well. The extremely long sleeves seem to have been popular in Prussia as well at this period.   Wiskowatow.

squadrons. In 1798 the regiment Schreiders (later Müller II and in 1801 Kinburn) was raised. In 1800 the existing regiments Rostow and Astrakhan were disbanded and six others were combined into three—Vladimir and Taganrog into Obrjeskow (later Schepelew); Narwa and Nishegorod into Puschkin (later Portnjagin) and Irkutsk and Siberia into Sacken II (later Skalon). This concentration was reversed in 1801 and the original six regiments reappeared.

Regimental distinctions in 1803 were as follows:

	a *(collar)*	b *(cuffs)*	c *(buttons)*
Life Guard	a red with yellow laces	b red with yellow laces	c yellow
(this regiment also had red lapels)			
Riga	a red	b red	c yellow
Jamburg†	a green, piped red	b red	c white
Kazan	a crimson	b crimson	c yellow
Njeshin§	a green, piped light blue	b light blue	c yellow

224

Regiment	a	b	c
Pskow‡	*a* orange	*b* orange	*c* yellow
Moscow	*a* pink	*b* pink	*c* white
Kargopol	*a* orange	*b* orange	*c* white
Jngermannland	*a* black	*b* black	*c* white
Kurland	*a* light blue	*b* light blue	*c* yellow
Orenburg†	*a* black	*b* black	*c* yellow
Siberia†	*a* white	*b* white	*c* white
Irkutsk*	*a* white	*b* white	*c* yellow
Charkow	*a* deep yellow	*b* deep yellow	*c* yellow
Tschernigow§	*a* blue	*b* blue	*c* white
Kiev	*a* crimson	*b* crimson	*c* white
New Russia	*a* light blue	*b* light blue	*c* white
Starodub‡	*a* red	*b* red	*c* white
Twer	*a* blue	*b* blue	*c* yellow
Zhitomir†	*a* red, piped white	*b* red	*c* white
Arsamass§	*a* green, piped light blue	*b* light blue	*c* white
St. Petersburg	*a* pink	*b* pink	*c* yellow
Livonia§	*a* red, piped white	*b* red	*c* yellow
Sjewersk§	*a* deep yellow	*b* deep yellow	*c* white
Kinburn	*a* yellow	*b* yellow	*c* white
Smolensk	*a* yellow	*b* yellow	*c* yellow
Perejeslaw§	*a* green, piped crimson	*b* crimson	*c* white
Tiraspol§	*a* green, piped red	*b* red	*c* yellow
Dorpat§	*a* green, piped yellow	*b* yellow	*c* white
Vladimir†	*a* green, piped white	*b* white	*c* yellow
Taganrog†	*a* green, piped pink	*b* pink	*c* yellow
Serpuchow†	*a* green, piped yellow	*b* yellow	*c* yellow
Nishegorod	*a* green, piped white	*b* white	*c* white
Narwa	*a* green, piped pink	*b* pink	*c* white
Borissoglebsk	*a* green, piped crimson	*b* crimson	*c* yellow
Finland	*a* white, piped red	*b* white	*c* yellow
Mitau	*a* white, piped red	*b* white	*c* white

* converted to Hussars on 10 November 1812
† converted to Ulans on 10 November 1812.
‡ converted to Kürassiers on 10 November 1812
§ converted to Mounted Rifles on 10 November 1812

Saddle furniture was green edged in the cuff colour, harness black with brass fittings.

Carabiniers (Regiments Twer and Ssophia) 1792–1796 (Part of Leib-Kürassier-Regiment since 1790)

Standard uniform with white helmet crest, dark blue coats, red facings and trousers, yellow buttons, white trouser stripes, no aiguillette.

In 1796 there were sixteen regiments: Riga*, Narwa†, Rjasan*, Kargopol†, Rostow†, Moscow†, Jamburg*, Jngermannland†, Ssophia*, Gluchow*, Twer, Kiev*, Sjewersk†, Tschernigow*, Njeshin*, and Starodub*. All Carabinier regiments were converted or disbanded in 1796; nine to Kürassiers (those

225

marked *) and six to dragoons, those marked †). The regiment Twer was disbanded.

Chevau Légers 1792–6

As for Carabiniers but white buttons and aiguillette. In 1796 there were eleven regiments: Marupol†, Pawlograd†, Alexandrija†, Chersson‡, Poltawa‡, Ostrogoschk‡, Achtyrsk†, Ssumy†, Karkow*, Isum† and Ukrain‡. In 1796 the Karkow regiment was converted to Kürassiers (*), six others (marked †) to hussars and named after their colonels in Chief. The other four regiments (marked ‡) were disbanded.

Hussars 1796

There were only two hussar reigments (Olwiopol and Woronesch) in the Russian army from 1788 until 1796 when six Chevau Légers regiments were converted to this arm. In 1802 they were clad in black Mirlitons with cockade and white plume, dolman and pelisse in regimental colours and gery button overalls. Bandoliers were of buff suede leather for the pouch, white for the carbine. Headgear was a black felt shako with black cockade edged orange, button loop and pompon, white cords around the top. The sabretasche bore the imperial cypher ⚟ until 1801 thence ⚟ . Weapons were a steel hilted sabre in steel sheath, carbine and pistols. Shabraques were in the dolman colour with vandyke edging in the lace colour. In the long rear corners was the imperial cypher.

Rank was indicated by gold/silver lacing to cuffs. The hair was worn in two plaits in front of the ears and a pigtail until 1806 when all three disappeared. In 1796 each regiment consisted of two battalions each of five squadrons.

Regimental distinctions were as follows:

	a (dolman)	b (collar and cuffs)	c (pelisse)	d (lace and buttons)
Alexandrija	a crimson	b crimson	c crimson	d white
Pavlograd	a green	b light blue	c light blue	d yellow
Mariupol	a white	b yellow	c light blue	d yellow
Oliwiopol	a green	b green	c green	d white
Jelisabethgrad	a yellow	b red	c yellow	d yellow
Sumski	a yellow	b light blue	c light blue	d white
Isum	a red	b dark blue	c dark blue	d white
Achtyrsk	a brown	b yellow	c brown	d yellow

The shako style altered as for the infantry and in 1813 the regimental distinctions were as follows:

	a (dolman)	b (collar and cuffs)	c (pelisse)	d (lace and buttons)	e (fur trim)
Alexandrija	a black	b red	c black	d white	e white
Pavolgrad	a green	b light blue	c light blue	d red lace, yellow buttons	e white
Mariupol	a blue	b yellow	c blue	d yellow	e white
Oliwiopol	a green	b red	c green	d white	e white
Jelisabethgrad	a grey	b grey	c grey	d red lace, yellow buttons	e black
Sumski	a grey	b red	c grey	d white	e white
Isum	a red	b blue	c blue	d white	e white

Achtyrsk	_a_ brown	_b_ yellow	_c_ red	_d_ yellow	_e_ white
Lubenski	_a_ blue	_b_ yellow	_c_ blue	_d_ white	_e_ white
Bjeloserk	_a_ blue	_b_ red	_c_ brown	_d_ white	_e_ black

In 1800 the Moscow police hussars were combined into the Achtyrsk regiment and in 1801 the regiment Tsarewitsh von Grusien (later Schepelew) was raised.

Jäger zu Pferde 1792–6

Standard uniform but with green Mirlitons and black plumes, all green coat and trousers, white buttons and aiguillette, black bandoliers and waist sash. In 1796 there were four regiments: Perejeslaw, Jelisabethgrad, Kiev and Tauride, each of ten squadrons and they were all disbanded that same year.

Jäger zu Pferde (mounted rifles) 1813–15

In 1813 certain dragoon regiments were converted to mounted rifles regiments with the Kiwer, green cords, dark green tunics, similar collars and breeches (the latter with double side stripes in the regimental colour); all regiments had white buttons.

The regimental facings, shown on collar piping, shoulder straps, cuffs, turnbacks and trouser stripes were: Njeschin—turquoise, Tschernigow—blue, Arsamass—light blue, Ssjewersk—orange, Livland—crimson, Perejeslaw—pink, Tiraspol—yellow, Dorpat—light red.

Lancers 1803–15

The first regiments were raised in 1803; the uniform was traditional Polish costume: czapka with the top part coloured according to regiment, dark blue kurtka and breeches or grey button overalls. In 1812 the regimental distinctions were as follows:

	a (collar)	_b (lapels, cuffs, piping and trouser stripes)_	_c (buttons and epaulettes)_	_d (czapka top)_
Life Guards	_a_ red, with two yellow laces	_b_ red	_c_ yellow	_d_ blue
Polish	_a_ crimson	_b_ crimson	_c_ white	_d_ crimson
Lithuanian	_a_ blue	_b_ crimson	_c_ white	_d_ white
Tartar	_a_ blue	_b_ crimson	_c_ white	_d_ crimson
Volhynia	_a_ crimson	_b_ crimson	_c_ yellow	_d_ crimson
Jugujew	_a_ red	_b_ red	_c_ white	_d_ red

Light cavalry, dark blue saddle furniture and black harness. The front rank were armed with lance, sabre and pistols; the rear with carbine, sabre and pistols.

Cossacks

These dressed, very roughly, according to the army to which they belonged; those of the Don, Urals and Arenburg wore light blue coats and trousers, those of the Volga and Jugujew red and that of Astrakhan brown. The bags of the fur caps were also in the army colour. On 13 June 1792 the Army of Loyal Cossacks of the Black Sea was settled on the Taman peninsula and in 1793 the Jugujew, Little Russia and Potemkin's Cossack Escort become the 1st, 2nd and 3rd regiments of Jugujew.

In 1796 there were the following armies: Don, Black Sea, Siberia, Orenburg, Urals, Astrakhan and Jekaterinoslaw. Apart from this there were nine regular cossack regiments: 1st – 3rd Jugujew, 1st – 3rd Orenburg, Astrakhan, Mosdok and Ufa. There were also the following 'settlers' Cossack regiments: Grebnisch, Terek, Semeinyje-Choper, Volga and the Stawropol baptised Kalmucks. In 1796 the 3rd Jugujew regiment was disbanded; two new cavalry regiments—the Lithuanian Tartars and the Polish Cavalry were raised and the Jekaterinoslaw army was disbanded. The two Jugujew regiments were combined into one in 1800.

Battle History

1794—against Poland; 1798–1801—against France in Italy, Switzerland and the Low Countries; 1805—against France in Austria (✗ Austerlitz 2 December 1805); 1806–7—against France (✗ Preussisch Eylau, Friedland); 1806–12—against the Ottoman Empire; 1807–12—against Britain; 1808–9— against Sweden; 1812–14—against France in Russia, Germany and France; 1813–14—against Denmark.

KINGDOM OF

Sardinia

1792 – 1815

(Cockade cornflower blue)

Line Infantry 1792

French style uniform, bicorn edged white, dark blue coat with facings shown on collar, cuffs, lapels and turnbacks, white belts and breeches, tall black gaiters. Grenadiers wore bearskin bonnets. In 1803 a very strong Austrian flavour was felt when antique helmets with cornflower blue crest and brass fittings, and the then current Austrian (German) infantry pattern tunic and breeches, both in dark blue, were introduced. In 1814 facings were:

	a (collar & cuffs)	b (turn-backs)	c (buttons)	d (remarks)
Grenadier Guards (bear-skin caps)	a red	b red	c white	d nine white laces across the chest, three over each cuff
Savoia	a black	b red	c yellow	d None
Piemonte	a red	b red	c yellow	d None
Aosta	a dark red	b yellow	c white	d None

228

Cuneo	*a* crimson	*b* white	*c* white	*d* None
La Regina	*a* white	*b* dark red	*c* white	*d* None
Sardegna	*a* red	*b* red	*c* white	*d* laces as for Grenadier Guards

Foot Artillery

Infantry uniform, yellow hat edging, dark blue coat, small clothes and turn-backs, black facings, yellow buttons. Officers' hats had wide scalloped gold edging, alternate gold and silver lace button holes.

Engineers

As for artillery but white buttons, crimson facings, yellow turnbacks and white small clothes.

Cavalry 1792

Large bicorn edged yellow, dark blue coat with brass shoulder scales, facings on collar, and Swedish cuffs, red turnbacks, buff small clothes, high cuffed boots, white belts, heavy, straight sword, carbine and pistols. White sheepskin shabraque, dark blue holster covers with Sardinian badge and white edging with blue worm; black harness.

The regiments' facings were : Piemonte red, yellow buttons; Savoia black, (no lapels) white buttons.

Battle History

1792–6 War against France; December 1798 war against France.

Saxony

Electorate until 1807 thence kingdom

(Cockade white until 1813 thence green within white)

Rank Badges 1792

Generals

Cocked hats with cockade, gold loop and button, dark blue frock coat with gold buttons and embroidery according to rank, red waistcoat and breeches, silver and crimson sash and sword knot, high cuffed boots. Cavalry generals also had white plumes.

Officers

Cocked hats edged in the button colour, white cockades, simple loop, regimental button; silver and crimson waist sash and sword knot, gold gorgets with silver cypher ('FA') on crimson velvet ground, malacca canes, no halberds (grenadier officers wore bearskin and carried carbines). Cavalry officers had white plumes with black bases.

Plate 48   Electorate of Saxony: Leib-Grenadier-Garde
(*l to r*)   Private, parade dress (brass cap plate, yellow backing, red tunic, yellow facings, white buttons), private, drill order (as above but white waistcoat faced red), NCO (rear view), (as for private in parade dress but red and silver bearskin cords, epaulettes, silver buttons, crimson and silver sabre knot). *Augsburger Bilder.*

Plate 49   Electorate of Saxony: Infantry 1800–1810
(*l to r*)   Musketeer 'Prinz Anton' (dark blue facings, white buttons), NCO and officer 'Prinz Friedrich August' (light green facings, yellow buttons), officer, 'von Oebschelwitz' (light blue facings, yellow buttons). (*Background*) men 'von Niesemeuschel' (purple facings, white buttons). *Augsburger Bilder.*

NCOs

Infantry sergeant-majors and sergeants—spontoons, silver/gold hat edging, silver and crimson sabre knot, spontoon and pistol (infantry) or no carbine (cavalry), malacca cane. Corporals—as above but with hazelnut sticks, crimson and white sword straps, with simpler spontoons. Cavalry NCOs had white plumes with black tips and no spontoons. Musketeer privates had white hat edging and a hat pompon in the facing colour over white.

Infantry

Saxon uniforms had changed only very slightly since 1763:

Leib-Grenadier-Garde

Bearskin bonnets with brass plates bearing the electoral cypher 'FA' under a cap and within laurels (the enamelled crests of Saxony and Poland added for officers), yellow top patch with white cross and cords; red coat, yellow facings, white buttons. Privates wore two white epaulettes, NCOs one or two in red and silver according to rank, officers two in silver; drummers wore yellow coats and light blue facings as did musicians (who also wore silver edged bicorns). Small clothes white, gaiters black with yellow buttons. White belts. Other ranks wore moustaches.

Line Infantry

White belts, coats and small clothes, black gaiters. From 1806 officers wore boots. Facings and changes of title were as follows:

	a (facings)	b (buttons)
1st Kurfürst; 1806—'König'; 1813—'Provisional Guards Regiment'; 1815—Guards Regiment:	a red	b yellow
2nd 1794—'aus dem Winkel'; 1798—'von Sänger'; 1808 'von Cerrini'; disbanded 1810:	a red	b white
3rd 'Prinz Anton'; 1813—'1st Provisional Line Infantry Regiment'; 1815—'Prinz Anton':	a dark blue	b white
4th 'Prinz Clemens'; 1812—'von Steindel'; disbanded 1813:	a dark blue	b yellow
5th 'Prinz Max'; 1813—'2nd Provisional Line Infantry Regiment; 1815—'Prinz Max':	a yellow	b yellow
6th 1794—'von Nostitz'; 1802—'von Thümmel'; 1808—'von Burgsdorff'; disbanded 1810:	a yellow	b white
7th 'Prinz Friedrich August'; 1813—'3rd Provisional Line Infantry Regiment'; 1815—'Prinz Friedrich August':	a light green	b yellow
8th 'von Low'; disbanded 1813:	a light green	b white
9th 'Prinz Xaver'; 1806—'von Oebschelwitz'; disbanded 1810:	a light blue	b yellow
10th 1791—'von der Heyde'; 1800—'von Braune' and then 'von 'Ryssel'; 1805—'von Bünau'; 1806—'von Bevilaqua'; 1808—'von Dyherrn'; disbanded 1810:	a light blue	b white
11th 'von Niesemeuschel'; 1810–13 vacant;	a purple	b white
12th 1786—'von Lindt'; 1801—'von Rechten'; disbanded 1813:	a purple	b yellow

Grenadiers wore moustaches and had bearskin caps with top patches in the facing colour, white cross and cords, pompon in facing colour over white, brass plate with 'FA' under a cap (from 1806 a crown).

In 1810 the French style shako, rank badges and inter-company distinctions were introduced. The shako had a company pompon over a white cockade over brass shield bearing the crowned 'FA', brass chinscales; cords and plume (if appropriate) for parades. The style of the coat was also modernised. In 1813 the cockade became black within green within yellow and in 1815 green within white. Officers' shakos had silver top bands in clover leaf design, NCOs two or one gold or yellow bands. Drummers had red plumes and cords, white swallows' nests edged in green, yellow and black.

231

Plate 50 *Kingdom of Saxony: Heavy Cavalry 1810–1815*
(*l to r*) Trumpeter, Garde du Corps (red plume and tunic, dark blue facings, yellow, red and blue lace), officer, Garde du Corps (buff tunic, dark blue facings, gold lace), trooper, von Zastrow Kürassiers (buff tunic, yellow facings, yellow lace with black and white edges). Note that this plate is wrong in showing Kürass backplates being worn. (*Background figures*) Leib-Kürassier-Garde (buff tunics, red facings, yellow lace edged red). *Augsburger Bilder.*

Plate 51 *Kingdom of Saxony: Light Cavalry 1810–1815*
(*l to r*) Officer and trooper (mounted) 'Prinz Johann' Chevau Légers (red coats, black facings, yellow buttons), trooper, 'Prinz Clemens' Chevau Légers (seated), (red coat, canary green facings, yellow buttons), trooper, 'von Polenz' Chevau Légers (red coat, light blue facings, yellow buttons), trooper, hussars (light blue dolman and breeches, black facings, white buttons and lace, white and crimson sash, light blue and white sabretasche). *Augsburger Bilder.*

In 1809 the 1st and 2nd Schützen-Bataillon were raised and converted in 1810 to the 1st and 2nd Leichte Infanterie-Regimenter. Uniform and small clothes dark green, no lapels but two rows of yellow buttons, black facings and belts, green plume and cords, otherwise as for the line.

A Jäger-Corps (one battalion) was also raised in 1809, uniform as for the Leichte Regimenter but brass hunting horn shako badge, white cords; black facings piped red (black patches to green collar).

Garrison Infantry—as for the line but black facings and white buttons.

Heavy Cavalry

Large bicorn edge white or yellow (silver/gold for NCOs, wide scalloped silver/gold for officers) white cockade and plume, regimental button. Buff 'Kollets'—single-breasted, hooked together on the chest, no buttons and edged in regimental lace, white belts and breeches, high boots, carbines, pistols and heavy, brass hilted sword in brown leather sheath. Only the front plate of the Kürass was worn and this was black with red leather edging, and officers wore the crowned cypher 'FA' in gold at the top below the neck. Saddle furniture was in the facing colour, edged in regimental lace, harness black with brass fittings.

	a (facings)	b (officers' lace)	c (men's lace)
Kurfürst Kürassiers (1806 'König'; 1807—'Leib-Kürassier-Garde'; 1813—'Kürassier-Regiment'; 1815 — 'Leib-Kürassier-Garde'): The coat became white in 1810.	a red	b gold	c yellow, red edges
Karabiniers (disbanded 1810):	a red	b gold	c yellow, with red and black striped edging
Garde du Corps (destroyed in Russia 1812):	a dark blue	b gold	c yellow, red and blue striped
Kochtitzky (1808—'von Zastrow'; 1813—combined into 'Kürassier-Regiment'): The coat became white in 1810.	a yellow	b silver	c yellow with black and white edges

In 1810 the bicorns were replaced by brass helmets with brass combe, white crest and plume, brown fur turban (circled with gold oak leaves for officers), brass chinscales. Brass epaulettes edged in the facing colour were worn.

Chevau Légers

Bicorns as before, red coats, yellow buttons, buff waiscoat, white breeches and belts, high cuffed boots. Officers wore two gold epaulettes. Red saddle furniture with yellow edging, black harness with brass fittings; carbines, pistols, curved sabres with brass hilt in brown leather sheaths.

1st Regiment (1796 'von Dehn-Rothfelser'; 1799 'Prinz Clements'; converted to Uhlans in 1811)
Until 1813 facings were canary green then costume became traditional Polish in light blue with black facings piped red, in 1815 this changed to red with light blue facings and the shako.
2nd (1778 'Prinz Albrecht'; destroyed in Russia 1812) facings dark green.
3rd (1790 'von Gersdorff'; 1804 'Prinz Johann'; destroyed in Russia 1812) facings black.
4th (1793 'von Rossler'; 1801 'von Polenz'; 1810 vacant; destroyed in Russia 1812) facings light blue.
The shako replaced the bicorn in 1810.

Hussars (raised 1791)

Mirliton (black with light blue wing edged white, white plume and cords on top left side), white dolman and pelisse, white buttons and lace, light blue collar and fur, crimson and white sash, white belts and breeches, hussar boots, light blue sabretasche and shabraque edged white, black harness with brass fittings. Unpowdered hair worn in three plaits, moustaches. In about 1806 the dolman became light blue with black facings and the shako was introduced in 1810.

Heavy cavalry trumpeters wore no Kürasses and had red crests and plumes, silver trumpets with blue and white cords, red tunics in the Garde du Corps, reversed colours in the Kürassier regiments. In the Chevau Légers they had red shakos with gold top band, red plumes, tunics in reversed colours (buff faced red for Prinz Johann) red and white trumpet cords to brass trumpet. Hussar trumpeters had light blue shakos, red plume, red dolman and pelisse, light blue trumpet cords. All trumpeters rode greys.

Foot Artillery

Bicorn with gold edging, black plume; dark green coat, red facings, yellow buttons, buff waistcoat and breeches; NCO's collar, cuffs, and lapels were edged in gold.

Horse Artillery

As for foot artillery but uniform of Chevau Léger style, white breeches and low, hussar boots. Trumpeters had reversed colours and green shakos, red plumes.

Train

Light blue coats, black facings edged red, white buttons.

Engineers

Bicorn with double silver edging for officers, single for other ranks, dark green coat, red facings, white buttons, red small clothes. Other ranks had facings edged silver.

Battle History

1806—Jena as Prussia's allies; 1807—Danzig and ✕ Friedland as French allies; 1809—Linz, ✕ Wagram, Poland and Saxony as IX Corps; 1812—Russia as VII Corps (detached units also in IX Corps); 1813—Saxony as VII Corps.

THE

Saxon Duchies

(Cockade black within yellow)

Together the Saxon duchies (Coburg-Saalfeld, Gotha-Altenburg, Hildburg-hausen, Meiningen and Weimar) joined the Confederation of the Rhine on

15 December 1806 and each contributed a contingent to form the three-battalion strong 4th Regiment of the Confederation.

Individual contingents were as follows (French badges and distinctions):

Coburg (400 men)

French shako with brass rhombic plate bearing a hunting horn, white cords, company pompon (grenadiers had bearskins), red cords and plumes, red epaulettes, officers initially wore bicorns, later shakos. Dark green, Prussian-style coat with two rows of white buttons on the chest, dark green cuff flaps, yellow collar and cuffs, red turnbacks, three white lace buttonholes on the square cuff flaps; light blue Hungarian breeches with yellow thigh and side lacing, short black gaiters with a point at the front, white belts.

Gotha (1,100 men)

In the 1790s Gotha's infantry regiment wore bicorns with cockade and white edging, dark blue, single-breasted coats with red collar, cuffs, stock and waistcoat; white breeches and belts, black gaiters.

The uniform of the contingent of the 4th Confederation Regiment (Gotha and Meiningen provided two of the battalions between them) was a white-edged bicorn with black, gold edged cockade, loop, button and company pompon, dark blue coat, red collar, lapels, round cuffs and turnbacks, yellow buttons, belts and small clothes, black gaiters. Grenadiers had red plumes, light companies green.

By 1812 the bicorn had been replaced by the French shako with crowned, oval brass plate bearing the Saxon crest, company cords and pompon or plumes according to the French system, black within yellow cockade, royal blue coat with similar cuff flaps, red collar, lapels, cuffs and turnbacks (and pipng to fusiliers' blue shoulder straps), yellow buttons, white belts and small clothes, short black gaiters.

Hildburghausen (200 men)

See Weimar.

Meiningen (300 men)

Until 1807 Meiningen had a Jäger-Corps in Austrian-style black leather kaskets, dark green coats, red facings, white buttons, green trousers, black belts and gaiters. After joining the Confederation of the Rhine they wore the same uniform as described for Gotha except that until about 1811 they had black belts and retained the old, Prussian coat style with a double row of buttons on the chest. In 1812 they were dressed as for the Gotha contingent.

Weimar (1,100 men)

In 1788 Duke Karl August raised a Jäger-Bataillon which in 1790 was entitled Scharfschützen and had the following uniform: black, Corsican hat with red headband and loop, green plume on left hand (turned-up) brim; dark green tunic with similar collar, cuffs and cuff flaps, yellow patches, each bearing a yellow button, to collar front, yellow turnbacks, Prussian-style double rows of buttons on the chest. Red stock, white breeches, short black gaiters, buff belts. In 1796 the belts became black and the pouch was worn at the front of the waistbelt.

In 1806 the pouch was again carried on a black bandolier and the headgear was the then current Prussian grenadier cap with high black leather front plate with brass front band, black peak, black woollen edging to front plate, green plume on left side, Trousers were now dark green.

In 1807 the headgear changed to a yellow edged bicorn with a brass shield badge at the front centre and above it a green plume. Leatherwork was now buff, other details as before. In 1809 the French shako replaced the bicorn; on the front was a hunting horn in brass, cockade, yellow pompon and chinscales. Tunic as before but now worn with the collar closed, white trousers or pantaloons, black belts.

The Hildburghausen contingent served as part of the Weimar battalion which was the light battalion of the 4th Regiment.

In January 1813 Napoleon demanded that the Saxon dukes raise another battalion as the remnants of the 4th Regiment were besieged in Danzig. The unit, known as the 'Thuringian March Battalion' wore Weimar shakos, dark blue Litewkas with red collars and light blue cuffs, grey trousers. They went over to the Allies at Altenburg on 20 April 1813 and fought against the French, being reuniformed in dark blue British coats with light blue facings.

Napoleon demanded (and received) yet another contingent from the unfortunate Saxon dukes, this time a whole regiment which was dressed in the 1812 uniform.

Battle History

1806—✂ Jena (on the Prussian side); 1807—siege of Colberg; 1809—Tyrol (almost destroyed in the Sachsenklemme); 1809–11—Spain (Gerona and Manresa); 1812—Russia as part of the 2nd Brigade of the 'Division Princiere'; 1813—besieged in Danzig; 1813—(newly raised regiment) Saxony.

PRINCIPALITIES OF
Schwarzburg-Rudolstadt,
AND
Schwarzburg-Sondershausen

(Cockade dark blue within white)

In 1792 Schwarzburg had raised an infantry battalion to fight the French; its uniform was a bicorn with white edging and company pompon (colours unknown), double-breasted blue coat with blue lapels edged red, red collar, cuffs and turnbacks, yellow buttons, white belts and small clothes, black gaiters.

On 13 April 1807 the princely houses joined the Confederation of the Rhine and provided a contingent of a battalion (650 men) known as the 1st Battalion 6th Regiment of the Confederation (in 1808 they also raised two companies for the 'Bataillon des Princes' which served, and was destroyed, in Spain).

Uniform was a French shako with brass front plate (rhombic with 'FSR' under a crown for Rudolstadt, octagonal with 'FSS' under a crown for Sondershausen), cockade, company pompons and cords, brass chinscales. Dark green double-breasted, Prussian-style coats with green shoulder straps; red collar and turnbacks, yellow buttons. Plain round red cuffs for Rudolstadt, red with green cuff flaps for Sondershausen. Black belts, grey breeches, short black gaiters.

French rank badges. Officers had gold shako trim, cords and epaulettes, silver and crimson sword knot, gold trim and tassel to hussar boots, long dark green coat turnbacks and a narrow red side stripe to grey breeches.

Battle History

1807—siege of Glogau (Prussia); 1809—Tyrol; 1809–11—Spain; 1812—Russia as part of 2nd Brigade, Division Princiére; 1813—besieged in Danzig.

KINGDOM OF THE

The Two Sicilies

1792 – 1806 and 1814 – 15

(Cockade red)

All uniform details very much as for Austria and Spain. In 1806 Napoleon took the mainland portion of this state and created the Kingdom of Naples (see p 167) for Joachim Murat. The island of Sicily remained under allied control, with the help of the Royal Navy, and in 1814 the kingdom was reunited at which time uniforms with much British flavour were introduced with red tunics, shoulder wings, white lace and buttons for the guard; similar details but with dark blue, single-breasted coat for line infantry. Officers' sashes were red and silver.

Battle History

1793–6 war against France, 1798–1801 war against France. 1805–15 the island part of the kingdom was at war against France.

KINGDOM OF

Spain

(Cockade red)

Officers wore fringed epaulettes in the button colour and had wide hat

Plate 52   Spain: Officer of Hussars, Regiment Maria Louisa
Red plume and cockade, white cords, red dolman, light blue collar, cuffs and breeches, white buttons and lace; red and light blue sash. From Goddard and Booth *Representations of the Principal European Armies* (*Courtesy National Army Museum.*)

edgings in the button colour if in cavalry regiments; sword knots were gold and red, sashes and gorgets were not worn.

NCOs had red sabre knots and carried sticks; drummers had red and white edging to collar and cuffs, brass drums with black hoops; drum majors had large elaborate sashes in red, heavily embroidered in the button colour, red, white and yellow feather plumes to their hats, brown staffs with knob, tip and chains in the button colour. Musicians had swallows' nests in the facing colour. Pioneers wore large fur colpacks with brass front plates, bags in various colours, aprons either black or buff with ornate decoration according to regiment, axes, adzes and carbines. They appear to have been no more hairy than any other Spanish soldiers of this period.

Line Infantry

In 1793 the uniform consisted of a plain bicorn with cockade and pompon, white coats (the foreign regiments wore light blue), with white turnbacks edged in the lapel colour, white small clothes and belts, high black gaiters. Grenadiers wore tall bearskin caps with no front plates and with long cloth bags hanging to the rear in the facing colour and covered with intricate designs. Regimental distinctions were worn on collars, Swedish cuffs, lapels and buttons. In 1806 rectangular cuff flaps in the cuff colour, piped white

238

were introduced. The scheme went as follows (all coloured parts were piped white and vice-versa):

	a (collar)	b (cuffs and later cuff flaps)	c (lapels)	d (buttons)
Regiment Rey	a violet	b violet	c violet	d yellow
Reyna	a violet	b violet	c violet	d white
Principe	a white	b violet	c violet	d yellow
Soria	a white	b violet	c violet	d white
La Princesa	a violet	b violet	c white	d white
Saboya	a black	b black	c black	d yellow
La Corona	a black	b black	c black	d white
Africa	a white	b black	c black	d yellow
Zamora	a white	b black	c black	d white
Sevilla	a black	b black	c white	d white
Granada	a light blue	b light blue	c light blue	d yellow
Valencia	a light blue	b light blue	c light blue	d white
Toledo	a white	b light blue	c light blue	d yellow
Murcia	a white	b light blue	c light blue	d white
Cantabria	a light blue	b light blue	c white	d white
Cordova	a red	b red	c red	d yellow
Guadalaxara	a red	b red	c red	d white
Malorca	a white	b red	c red	d yellow
Leon	a white	b red	c red	d yellow
Aragon	a red	b red	c white	d white
Saragoza	a green	b green	c green	d yellow
España	a green	b green	c green	d white
Burgos	a white	b green	c green	d yellow
Asturia	a white	b green	c green	d white
Fixo de Ceuta	a green	b green	c white	d white
Navarra	a dark blue	b dark blue	c dark blue	d yellow
America	a dark blue	b dark blue	c dark blue	d white
Malaga	a white	b dark blue	c dark blue	d yellow
Jaen	a white	b dark blue	c dark blue	d white
Las Ordines Militares	a dark blue	b dark blue	c white	d white
Estremadura	a crimson	b crimson	c crimson	d yellow
Voluntarios de Castilla	a crimson	b crimson	c crimson	d white
Voluntarios de Estado	a white	b crimson	c crimson	d yellow
Voluntarios de Corona	a white	b crimson	c crimson	d white
Voluntarios de Borbon	a crimson	b crimson	c white	d white
Irlanda*	a yellow	b yellow	c yellow	d yellow
Hibernia*	a light blue	b yellow	c yellow	d white
Ultonia*	a yellow	b yellow	c light blue	d yellow
Neapolis*	a yellow	b yellow	c yellow	d white

(* foreign regiment, light blue coats with yellow turnbacks)

In 1800 the cut of the coat had been altered so that it closed to the waist and had straight lapels. Also in this year the fusiliers' bicorn was replaced by a mitre cap in the regimental button colour bearing the royal arms in the centre, edged in regimental lace and with a red pompon and tuft at the top. This cap was withdrawn again shortly afterwards and the bicorn readopted with button, loop and red cockade. By 1806 the coat skirts of soldiers were shortened to rump length, officers retained long skirts. In each corner of the turnbacks was a heart-shaped patch in the lapel colour; the white shoulder straps were edged in the facing colour and the oblong

239

Plate 53 *Spain: Artillery, Infantry and Dragoons*
(*l to r*) Artillery (red tuft, dark blue coat, red facings, yellow buttons, red piping
and waistcoat), fusilier, 1st Regiment of Estremadura (crimson facings and hatband
(fatigue cap), yellow buttons), trooper, Zamora Dragoons (?) (There was no dragoon
regiment of this name, two regiments had black facings, Numantia and Lusitania.)
From Goddard and Booth (*Courtesy National Army Museum.*)

cuff flap had four buttons. The black gaiters were now below knee length
and the pigtail was still worn.

The shattering defeats at French hands in the campaigns of 1808–12
allowed little attention to be paid to dress but in 1812 Great Britain delivered
stocks of new clothing which was issued to most units. It consisted of the
conical shako with red cockade and badges and trim to bottom and sides
of the shako as follows: grenadiers—brass grenade, red trim; fusiliers—brass
lion and white trim; light companies—brass hunting horn and green trim.
The coat was dark blue, single-breasted with red collar, Polish cuffs, piping
and turnbacks, yellow buttons. On the sides of the collar were the yellow
initial letters of the regiment's name. Fusiliers had blue shoulder straps
edged red, grenadiers additional blue wings with red fringes, light companies
blue wings and green fringes. Belts were white, trousers grey and worn
over short black gaiters; British packs of dark blue painted canvas were
carried.

In 1815 bearskin caps with no front plates, red plumes and cords were
introduced for grenadiers, the tunic was turquoise, long skirted with Swedish
cuffs and lapels widening at the tops. Turnbacks were red and regimental
facings were worn on collar lapels and cuffs; buttons, buttonholes and lace
edging were again in regimental colours. Fusiliers and light companies wore

240

shakos with wide tops, the elite companies retained the British-style fringed shoulder rolls. Bourbon lilies were worn on collars and turnbacks, elite companies apparently also wore grenades or hunting horns in red/green above the cuff. Belts and breeches were white and long; black gaiters were worn.

Light Infantry

In 1793 their uniform was a bicorn, green coats with red cuffs and lapels, white small clothes, brown leather gaiters to the knee, white belts and blue greatcoats carried slung over the left shoulder. In 1800 the coat was blue with red facings and the greatcoat green. In 1802 they were re-equipped with black, low crowned leather helmets with red turban and cockade on the left side, green plume, black fur crest with an oval brass plate at the front centre bearing the coat of arms. They wore a dark green dolman with red collar and cuffs and yellow lace and buttons, red sash, black pouch at the front of the waist, white breeches and long black gaiters.

By 1806 this uniform was replaced by a costume of line infantry style but in dark blue. The waistcoat had a double row of buttons and the greatcoat was now brown. Individual regimental distinctions were as follows:

	a (collar)	b (cuffs and cuff fllaps)	c (lapels)	d (buttons)
Primero de Voluntarios de Aragon	a red	b red	c red	d white
Primero de Voluntarios de Cataluña	a dark blue	b yellow	c yellow	d yellow
Taragona	a yellow	b yellow	c dark blue	d yellow
Voluntarios de Gerona	a yellow	b yellow	c yellow	d white
Primero de Barcelona	a yellow	b yellow	c dark blue	d white
Secundo de Barcelona	a dark blue	b red	c red	d yellow
Cazardores de Barbastro	a red	b red	c dark blue	d white
Voluntarios de Valencia	a crimson	b crimson	c crimson	d white
Voluntarios de Campo Major	a dark blue	b crimson	c crimson	d white
Voluntarios de Navarra	a crimson	b crimson	c crimson	d white

The 'British' uniform of 1812 was as for that of the line but with dark blue collar, white turnbacks edged dark blue. In 1815 they had wide-topped shakos, short, dark green tunics and trousers, crimson collars and red cuffs and piping.

Artillery
Uniform of line infantry cut in dark blue with red facings and yellow buttons; yellow grenade badge to the collar.

Engineers
As for artillery (but with light infantry helmet in 1806), black facings, white buttons and piping on the collar and white tower badge.

Heavy Cavalry

Prior to 1800 the coat had been white, in this year it was changed to dark blue with red turnbacks. Headgear was a large bicorn with regimental button, loop and edging. Long-skirted coat with facings shown on collar, lapels, Swedish cuffs, buff small clothes, white belts. Dark blue saddle furniture edged in the button colour, black harness. Arms were a straight bladed heavy sword and a brace of pistols. High, cuffed boots were worn. In the collar corners were white rampant lions (yellow for the 4th Regiment) and on the cuffs three white lilies (yellow for the 4th).

Regimental distinctions were as below:

	a (collar)	b (cuffs)	c (lapels)	d (buttons)	e (remarks)
1st Rey	a red	b red	c red	d yellow	e white edging; yellow buttonholes on the lapels
2nd Reyna	a light blue	b light blue	c light blue	d white	e red piping; white buttonholes on the lapels
3rd Principe	a red	b red	c red	d white	e white piping; white buttonholes to lapels
4th Infanta	a white	b white	c white	d yellow	e yellow piping; yellow buttonholes to lapels
5th Borbon	a red	b red	c red	d white	e white piping
6th Farnesio	a red	b red	c red	d white	e yellow piping
7th Alcantara	a red	b red	c light green	d white	e red piping to light green facings, light green to red
8th España	a yellow	b crimson	c crimson	d white	e yellow piping
9th Algarbe	a yellow	b yellow	c light blue	d yellow	e red piping
10th Calatrava	a red	b light blue	c light blue	d white	e red piping
11th Sanjago	a crimson	b crimson	c crimson	d white	e red piping
12th Montesa	a crimson	b crimson	c white	d white	e white piping

During the rest of the Napoleonic wars the uniform changed according to what was available and it was not until late in 1815 that new uniform regulations could be realistically applied. These are outside the scope of this book.

Dragoons 1806
Large bicorns with white edging, loop, button and red cockade, yellow long-tailed coat of infantry cut. Yellow waistcoat and breeches, white belts, high cuffed boots, yellow saddle furniture edged white, heavy, straight sword

in brown leather sheath, muskets and a brace of pistols. Black harness. In the corners of the collars were white badges of crossed sabre and a palm frond. Facings were shown on collar, pocket flap piping, lapels, cuffs and four-button cuff flaps; all turnbacks yellow and all facings were piped white and on the lapels were white lace buttonholes. The 4th, 6th and 8th regiments had yellow collars. The other regiments had collars in the facing colour. 1st Rey crimson; 2nd Reyna light red; 3rd Almansa light blue; 4th Pavia red; 5th Villaviciosa light green; 6th Sagunto light green; 7th Numantia black; 8th Lusitania black.

Chasseurs à Cheval 1806
Black shako with white top and bottom bands, white cords and front plate, red cockade and plume to left side; dark brown dolman, breeches and shabracque with white lace, buttons and trim. Facings were shown on collar, Polish cuffs, trouser stripes, thigh knots and saddle furniture edging. Regimental distinctions were: Olivencia red facings, red and light blue barrel sash; Cazadores Voluntarios de España light blue facings, white and light blue sash. In the collar corners white sabre and palm frond badge.

Hussars
Shako and uniform detail as for Chasseurs à Cheval, but with a pelisse as well. Regiments were: Maria Luisa red dolman with light blue collar and cuffs, light blue pelisse with red collar and cuffs, black fur, white buttons and lace, light blue breeches and shabracque with white trim; Españoles as for Maria Luisa except light green dolman, light blue collar and cuffs, light blue pelisse with light green collar and cuffs, black fur, white buttons and lace, light blue breeches and saddle furniture both trimmed white. In 1808 this regiment wore black helmets with black fur crests, brass front plate and fittings and red plumes and cockades. The barrel sash was light green with white and red striped knots.

Army of King Joseph 1808–14

This army was in 'French' service and fought against the old regiments loyal to the Junta.

Grenadiers of the Guard, Tirailleurs and Fusiliers of the Guard
As for their counterparts in the Imperial Guard except: red and yellow cockade.

Hussars of the Guard
Brown fur colpack, red bag edged yellow, red plume with yellow tip; red dolman and pelisse with sky blue collar and cuffs, yellow buttons and lace, black fur edging to pelisse. White breeches with gold lace decoration, hussar boots with gold trim and tassel. Light blue saddle furniture edged yellow. French light cavalry harness and equipment.

Chevau Légers
Brass helmet of French Chevau Lègers model with black turban and crest, red plume; dark green coat with yellow collar. Polish cuffs and turnbacks, dark green lapels and shoulder straps edged yellow, yellow

buttons and seven yellow buttonholes to each lapel. White breeches, hussar boots with gold trim and tassel. Officers had white plumes; trumpeters had red crests and white plumes, yellow coats faced red. Dark green saddle furniture edged yellow; French light cavalry equipment.

Artillery of the Guard and Sappeurs of the Guard
As for Imperial Guard but yellow and red cockade.

Infantry of the Line
Seven regiments all with French shakos with red carrot-shaped pompon over red and yellow cockade, yellow loop and button, brass lozenge plate bearing a crowned 'JN'; yellow cords and chinscales.

Dark brown, short-tailed coats (long skirted for officers) with regimental facings shown on collar, shoulder straps, lapels, Swedish cuffs and turnbacks, yellow buttons, white small clothes, black gaiters, white belts. French badges of rank and inter-company distinctions. Facings: 1st Regiment (Madrid) white; 2nd (Toledo) light blue; 3rd (Seville) black; 4th (Soria) violet; 5th (Granada) medium blue; 6th (Malaga) dark blue; 7th (Cordova) red.

Light Infantry
As for line infantry except: light green pompon with red tip, light green facings all edged red, dark brown breeches, short, black 'hussar' gaiters with red trim and tassel.

Regiment 'Joseph Napoleon'
Uniform as for the line infantry but white coats, light green facings, yellow buttons; brass eagle plate to shako.

Line Cavalry
Six regiments and two squadrons of lancers. General uniform style as for the old Spanish heavy cavalry but without badges to collar and cuffs. Yellow edging, loop and button to bicorn, red and yellow cockade; red plume with yellow tip. Dark brown coat with facings on collar, lapels, Swedish cuffs and turnbacks, yellow buttons and seven yellow buttonholes to each lapel; yellow trefoils on each shoulder. White small clothes, high cuffed boots. White belts, brown saddle furniture with wide yellow edging having a narrow red central piping. French heavy cavalry equipment. Trumpeters wore red coats faced yellow, yellow plumes with red bases and red and yellow trumpet cords. Facings: 1st Regiment red; 2nd white; 3rd light blue; 4th pink; 5th black; 6th green. Lancers red (they wore black leather helmets with green crest, red plume, brass fittings, coats as above but yellow collar having red collar patches, red shoulder rolls piped yellow, dark brown overalls piped red with yellow buttons). Dark green saddle furniture edged yellow with black outer scallops piped red; yellow grenade badges in the front corner, yellow '7' in the rear. Lance pennants were red with a yellow central stripe.

Artillery
As in France but with yellow and red cockade and dark brown coat and trousers.

Engineers
Bicorn with gold edging, loop and button, yellow and red cockade, dark brown infantry coat, black facings, yellow buttons and edging to collar, yellow epaulettes.

Battle History

(Spanish National Army) 1793–5 war against France; 1804–8 war against Britain; 1808–14 Spanish insurrection and war against France; 1809–14 war against Denmark.

KINGDOM OF

Sweden

(Cockade blue within yellow)

Information as to the uniforms of this army in the Napoleonic era is sparse, contradictory and confusing.

Rank Badges

Generals
Bicorn with gold edging, loop and button, blue over yellow plume; single-breasted dark blue coat with gold buttons and rank shown by gold embroidery to collar and cuffs: general—three rows; lieutenant-general—two; major-General—one. Gold waist sash with gold front buckle having the blue and gold national crest in its centre. Buff breeches and gauntlets, high cuffed boots. Gold and blue sword strap and tassel, gold epaulettes.

Field officers
As above but instead of the heavy gold collar and cuff embroidery they had gold stars and buttonholes to the collar only: colonel—three; lieutenant-colonel—two; major—one.

Junior officers
As for senior officers but only buttonholes to the collar and stars on the epaulettes (captain—an epaulette on the right, contre-epaulette on the left; lieutenant and subaltern—epaulette left, contre-epaulette right). Stars were: captain—three; lieutenant—two; subaltern—one. Officers wore a white brassard on the upper left arm and carried canes. Senior NCOs had long coat skirts, like the officers, yellow and blue sword knots and in 1792 they carried halberds and canes.

In 1814 Sweden and Norway were at war which ended with Norway becoming constitutionally part of Sweden.

245

Plate 54   Kingdom of Sweden: Guards Infantry 1812
The Kusket is shown here but the crest should run diagonally over the crown; brass hatband, dark blue coat, white lace, buttons and epaulettes. (*left*) Private Konungens Andra Lif Garde; two privates Konungens Svea Lif Garde (yellow facings, white buttons). (*Background*) two officers in walking out dress, Svea Lif Garde (*left*) and Andra Lif Garde. Private unidentified regiment. *Augsburger Bilder.*

Swedish Infantry

In 1806 each guards regiment had two battalions each of six musketeer companies, there was then a Jäger company attached to each regiment. All companies were 100 men strong. The line regiments each consisted of two battalions each of four companies of 150 men. Within each company a certain number of the best shots were designated 'Jägare' and distinguished by a green tuft and pompon. In action they were brigaded together and employed as specialist companies and were armed with rifles.

Inter-company distinctions were worn in the form of hat pompons: 1st red; 2nd white; 3rd blue; 4th yellow; 5th white within red; 6th yellow within blue; 7th blue within red; 8th yellow within red. From 1807 to 1810 (when all line regiments wore grey uniforms with blue facings) the individual regimental identity was shown by a round cockade bearing an upright Teutonic cross.

In 1792 the line infantry wore a black 'top hat' with yellow head band, the extended left brim held up by a button and loop under the company pompon and a plume; double-breasted, dark blue coat with facings shown on collar, lapels, Swedish cuffs and turnbacks; white breeches and belts, high black gaiters. The large black pouch was plain; the sabre was worn on a waistbelt over the coat.

In 1807 the hat was augmented by a wide brass hat band with an oval central extension bearing the provincial crest. Above this was the round regimental cockade with its vari-coloured Teutonic cross. The tunic was grey and single-breasted with dark blue collar, Swedish cuffs and turnbacks; a yellow waist sash with two dark blue stripes was worn and only NCOs carried sabres. Breeches were grey.

By 1810 the coat was dark blue, Prussian style and most regiments had red facings; the cuffs were now Brandenburg style with dark blue flaps, the turnbacks yellow. The breeches were full length, grey, with Hungarian-style thigh knots and side stripes in red or yellow. Belts were now white again but the yellow and blue waist sash was still worn. The short black gaiters were worn under the breeches. Following the 1812 campaign the Russian Kiwer shako with yellow fittings and white cords replaced the top hat. Guard infantry wore a bicorn edged in the button colour in 1802, white lace decoration to collar, lapels and cuffs, yellow small clothes. In 1807 the 'Kusket' or crested, round-topped version of the top hat was introduced. The black hair crest (white for 2ᵉ Garde) ran diagonally from rear left to front right and the brass front band bore the Swedish crest. White epaulettes and plumes were worn. In 1812 the guards wore old-fashioned, dark blue tunics with high collars, lapels hooked back and open from the breast bone (thus showing the waistcoat and breeches), white epaulettes and lace to collar, lapels and cuffs. Small clothes were yellow with white belts and high white gaiters with brass buttons.

In 1815 the line wore shakos (either the Russian 1812 Kiwer or a newer, flat-topped model) with white plume over company pompon (red for grenadiers, white for centre companies, green for Jägers), white cords, chin-scales and front badge. Dark blue coat with facings to collar, Swedish cuffs, turnbacks and lapels (apparently the latter were buttoned on to the coat for parades only); epaulettes in the pompon colour, dark blue trousers for winter, white trouser-gaiters for summer. Drummers had eight white chevrons, point up on each sleeve.

Senior NCOs were distinguished by a yellow woollen shako cockade, long tunic skirts and carried a sword with yellow and blue silk strap and tassel. Corporals wore two silver chevrons on the upper sleeve. Officers wore white feather plumes, silver pompons, yellow silk cockades behind the silver shako star with central provincial badge in coloured enamels, gold and blue cords; long-tailed coats, epaulettes in the button colour with stars and crowns as rank badges, yellow and blue silk waist sash (for parades) and light blue, long breeches with silver side stripes and thigh decoration. For every day wear they had grey overalls with a silver side stripe.

The colour code in the following table gives first the background then the vertical arm of the cross and finally the horizontal arm.

Infantry 1792

Konungens Svea Lif Garde (known as the 'Fleetwoodska' regiment from 1800–9) a (coat)—dark blue, b (facings)—yellow, c (buttons)—yellow, d (lace)—white, e (remarks)—yellow and dark blue plumes. 1802 white plumes, yellow pompon. 1803 (Jägare Bataljon) a—dark green, e—dark green plume,

Plate 55   Kingdom of Sweden: Artillery 1807
(*l to r*) Officer, Finska regiment (dark blue coat, red facings, yellow plume and buttons), officer, Vendes regiment (as above but white collar with yellow laces, white plume). (*Background*) men of both regiments. *Augsburger Bilder*.

yellow pompon, white buttonholes, yellow collar and piping to lapels and cuffs; black belts, white decoration to dark green trousers. Officers and NCOs had dark green crests, privates black. 1807 a—dark blue.

Konungens Andra Lif Garde (known as Svenska Gardet until 1809) a—dark blue, b—pink, c—yellow, d—white, e—yellow plume, band and button, white pompon and loop. 1798 b—pink and white, piped red, e—white crest. 1806 b—yellow piped red, e—white plume, yellow and dark blue hat badge. 1813 b—red, e—black plume, yellow and dark blue cockade.

Konungens Finska Garde a—blue, b—yellow collar and cuffs, red lapels and turnbacks, c—yellow, d and e—not known. This regiment was disbanded in 1808.

Kongl. Lif Regementets Grenadier Corps a—dark blue, b—white with red lapels and cuffs, c—yellow, d—red, e—not known. 1807 e—yellow epaulettes, yellow and red lace, yellow and dark blue sash, yellow grenade hat badge, bow, loop and button, white plume.

Kongl. 1ˢᵗᵃ Lif Grenadier Regemente a—dark blue, b and c—yellow, d—white, e—not known. 1798 b—red, c—white, red and dark blue hat badge. 1807 b—white collar and turnbacks piped red, red lapels and cuffs piped white, e—bearskin cap with red top patch, white plume on left and yellow cords. 1813 e—Kusket with white plume.

Kongl. Andra Lif Grenadier Regemente a—dark blue, b—red, c—yellow, d—none, e—yellow plume. 1798 c—white, e—white plume, red bag.

Drottningens Lif Regemente a—dark blue, b—yellow, c—white, d—white. 1813 e—Russian 'Kiwer' shako, white epaulettes, cords, pompon and plume

Plate 56   Kingdom of Sweden: Light Cavalry 1807
(*l to r*)   Officer, Dragoons (rear view), (dark blue tunic, red facings, yellow scale epaulettes and buttons), officer, Lif Regemente Dragon Corps (gold and light blue hat shield, dark blue coat, white facings, yellow buttons), officer, Lif Regemente Husar Corps (dark blue dolman and pelisse, white cuffs, yellow buttons, white lace and fur, yellow and blue sash). *Augsburger Bilder.*

for musketeers, red for grenadiers, green for Jägers. Passed into Prussian service as Regiment No 34 in 1815.
Kongl. Westgotha Regemente a—light blue, b and c—yellow, d—none, e—yellow and light blue plume. 1802 e—white plume, 1807 a—dark blue, b—red, c—yellow, d—white, e—white plume, red pompon, yellow and blue cords.
Kongl. Smålands Grenadier Bataljon 1812 a—dark blue, b and c—yellow, d—none.
Kongl. Uplands Regemente a—dark blue, b and c—yellow, d—white, e—plumes were yellow, white and dark blue. 1798 b—yellow but collar now white, d—no lace, e—yellow plumes. 1807 e—cockade white with a blue cross. 1815 b—red, d—red.
Enkedrottringens Lif Regemente a—dark blue, b—pink with white piping, c—yellow, d—none. In 1808 this regiment was disbanded and absorbed into the Andra Lif Garde.
Kongl. Skaraborgs Regemente a—dark blue, b and c—yellow, d—white, e—plumes yellow and dark blue. 1798 e—plumes all yellow. 1807 e—cockade yellow with blue and white cross.
Kongl. Sodermanlands Regemente a—dark blue, b and c—yellow, d—white, e—plumes yellow, dark blue and white. 1798 e—plumes yellow. 1807 e—cockade yellow with a blue cross.

Kongl. Kronobergs Regemente a—dark blue, b—red, c—yellow, d—none, e—plumes yellow, red and dark blue. 1798 b—red with yellow lapels and shoulder straps and white turnbacks. 1807 a—grey, b—dark blue, e—yellow plume, yellow cockade with light blue cross. 1810 a—dark blue. 1815 b—red, c—yellow, d—none.

Kongl. Jonkopings Regemente a—light blue, b—red, c—yellow, d—none, e——plumes yellow and light blue. 1798 b—red with yellow lapels and shoulder straps, e—yellow plumes. 1807 a—red cockade with blue cross. 1815 b—red.

Kongl. Dahl Regemente a—dark blue, b and c white, d—none, e—plumes yellow and dark blue. 1798 b—white with red collar and cuffs, c—yellow, e—yellow plume. 1807 e—yellow cockade with black cross. 1815 b—red.

Kongl. Helsinge Regemente a—dark blue, b—white, c—yellow, d—none, e—plumes white and yellow. 1798 b—white, e—yellow plume.

Kongl. Elfsborg Regemente a—dark blue, b, c and d—yellow, e—yellow plumes. 1798 b—yellow with white collar turnbacks and cuffs, d—none, e—yellow plume, white pompon. 1807 a—grey, b—dark blue, c—yellow, d—none, e—yellow cockade with red cross. 1810 a—dark blue, b—yellow.

Kongl. Westgotha-Dahls Regemente a—dark blue, b and c—yellow, d—none, e—yellow plume. 1798 e—yellow plume. 1807 a—grey, b—dark blue, c—yellow, e—yellow plume, red and yellow cockade. 1810 a and b dark blue.

Kongl. Bohus-Lams Regemente a—light green, b and c—yellow, d—none, e—plumes yellow and light green. 1798 a—dark blue, b—yellow with red collar, e—yellow plumes. 1806 a—grey, b—dark blue, e—yellow plume. 1810 a—dark blue, b—red.

Kongl. Westmanlands Regemente a—dark blue, b—yellow piped white, c—white, d—none, e—plumes yellow, white and light blue. 1798 c—yellow, e—yellow plume. 1807 e—red cockade with white and blue cross. 1815 b—red.

Kongl. Norrbottens and Kongl. Westerbottens Fält Jägare Corpser a—dark blue, b—white, c—yellow, d—none, e—plumes white, yellow and dark blue. 1798 b—facings white, collar red, e—yellow plumes. 1815 b—red.

Kongl. Calmare Regemente a—dark blue, b—red, c and d—yellow, e—plumes red, dark blue and yellow. 1798 b—red with yellow lapels and shoulder straps and white turnbacks, d—none, e—yellow plumes. 1807 a—grey, b—dark blue, c—yellow, e—yellow cockade with blue and red cross. 1810 a—dark blue, b—red.

Kongl. Nerikes Regemente and Kongl. Wermlands Regemente a—dark blue, b—red, c—yellow, d—white (red piping), e—plumes red, yellow and white. 1798 e—yellow plumes. 1807 b—yellow piped white.

Kongl. Norra Skånska Regemente and Kongl. Sodra Skånska Regemente No data given prior to 1811; a—dark blue, b—red, c—yellow, d—none, e—yellow plume.

Kongl. Wermland Fält-Jägare Regement a—dark green, b—black piped white, c—yellow, d—white, e—dark green plume and crest to helmet. No data given after 1794.

Artillery
Finska Regemente a—dark blue, b—red, c—yellow, d—none, e—yellow plume, white within red pompon. No further data given.

Vendes Regemente a—dark blue, b—dark blue, white collar, c—yellow laces to collar, d—none, e—white plume, yellow bow and loop.

Finnish regiments passing into Russian service after the 1808 war were:
Abo-Lans   a—dark blue b—dark blue c—yellow d—none
1807   a—grey e—red cockade with white cross
Adlercreutz   a—dark blue b—dark blue piped yellow c—yellow d—none
1807   a—grey
Bjorneborg   a—dark blue b—light blue c—yellow d—none
1807 a—grey e—white cockade with black cross
Kajana   a—dark blue, b—dark blue c—yellow d—none
1807 a—grey
Nyland   a and b—dark blue c—yellow d—none
1807 a—grey
Osterbottens   a—dark blue b and c—yellow d—none
1807 a—grey
Savolax   a—dark blue b and c—yellow d—none
1807 a—grey b—grey collar piped yellow, yellow facings
Tavastehus   a—dark blue b—dark blue piped red c—yellow d—none
1807 a—grey
Karelska Jägare   a—dark green b—dark green piped yellow c—yellow
d—none
Nyland Jägare a—grey b—grey piped dark blue c—yellow d—none
Savolax Jägare   a—grey b—dark green piped white c—white d—none

Cavalry

Until 1796 infantry style uniform, from then the dragoons wore the large
bicorn with pompon and plume in regimental colours. The Lif Kürassiere
had a black, Greek-style helmet with brass combe, peak, front plate and
neck shield and black crest, buff tunic (with no facing colour), and breeches,
white belts and gauntlets, black Kürass edged red, high cuffed boots. All
cavalry carried sabretasches in light blue with yellow edging and three crown
emblem.

In 1807 most cavalry regiments adopted the 'Kusket' as for the foot guards
but with regimental differences. Uniform regulations changed rapidly and
great confusion now reigns as to what actually was worn.

Konungens Lif Garde til Hast   a—white, b—dark blue, c—white, d—none,
e—white plume, yellow hat crown; red, dark green and white cords. 1803
a and b—dark green, c—white, e—white plume and crest, dark green band,
white star badge. 1807 a—dark blue, b and c—white, e—white plume, dark
blue pompon, red cords with dark blue tassels; white star badge and loop.
Sabretasche light blue with yellow edging and three crowns; light blue
shabraque edged white, black harness with steel fittings. 1813 a—white,
b—light blue.

Kongl. Lif Regemente Dragon Corps   a—dark blue, b—white, c—yellow,
d—none, e—white plume and pompon, yellow loop and button, dark blue
sabretasche with three yellow crowns.

Kongl. Lif Regemente Husar Corps   a—dark blue, b—white, c—yellow,
d—white, e—red hat cords and pompon, yellow and blue sash.

Kongl. Smålands Husar Regemente   a—dark blue, b, c and d—yellow,
e—dark blue and yellow plumes. 1799 e—white plume, red pompon, yellow
fittings.

Kongl. Skånska Husar Regemente   a—buff, b—dark blue, c—yellow, d—
red lace on collar, otherwise yellow, e—white plume, red tassels, white
within red pompon.

Kongl Skånska Dragon Regemente a—dark blue, b and c—yellow, d—none, e—white plume and pompon, yellow cords and tassels.
Kron-Prinsens Husar Regemente a—dark blue, b, c and d—yellow, e—red shako cords and rosette. 1806 e—pompon white within red, red shako cords.
Kongl. Jemtlands Hast-Jägare Corps a—dark blue, b and c—yellow, d—none, e—yellow plume, yellow and blue cords, white star badge. 1803 a—dark green, b—black, c—yellow, e—dark green plume, red cockade.

Battle History

1805–10 war against France and her allies; 1806–7 war against Prussia; 1808–9 war against Russia; 1808–9 war against Denmark; 1810–12 war against Britain; 1813–14 war against France and her allies; 1814 war against Norway.

Switzerland

During the period under review each Swiss canton maintained its own militia and there was only a very small 'standing army' called the Helvetian Legion which served the needs of the whole republic. This system is rather like that which exists today.

In 1800 the Helvetian Legion (1798–1804) consisted of infantry, Chasseurs à Cheval and artillery. Uniform colours were based entirely on the red-green-yellow tricolour flag of the republic.

The Chasseurs à Cheval wore a black Mirliton with red flame edged yellow and with a yellow tassel and yellow over red over dark green plume at the top left side. Dark green dolman and breeches, red collar, cuffs, waistcoat and sash, yellow buttons and lacing to all three garments, white bandoliers, black hussar boots with yellow trim. Black sabretasche and harness with brass fittings, white sheepskin shabrack with scalloped red edging; brass hilted sabre in brass and black scabbard, white leather fist strap, carbine and pistols. Hair was unpowdered but worn in three plaits (one before each ear, one to the rear), all ranks wore moustaches. In 1804 the Chasseurs à Cheval were absorbed into the 19e Chasseurs à Cheval of the French army.

The infantry wore bicorns, dark green coats faced red with yellow buttons, white belts and breeches, black gaiters.

United States of America

(Cockade black and white)

Rank Badges

Generals

Large bicorn with black and white cockade, silk binding and gold tassels, dark blue, double-breasted coat with buff collar, lapels and round cuffs, gold buttons, buff small clothes, short, straight-topped boots. Rank was indicated by silver stars on gold, fringed epaulettes as follows: Major-general—two, brigadier—one. In 1813 a new uniform was introduced —the bicorn was much larger than before and a gold eagle was added to the centre of the cockade. The coat became plain blue, single-breasted with ten gold, ball buttons and black 'herringbone' embroidery across the chest and in four chevrons (from four gold buttons) on each forearm and one on each side of the collar. High cuffed boots were now worn.

Senior officers

Colonel, Lieutenant-colonel and major—bicorns, two gold, fringed epaulettes.

Junior officers and NCOs

Captain—a bullion epaulette on the right. Lieutenant—a similar epaulette on the left. Sergeant—red waist sash, two yellow epaulettes. Corporal—one epaulette on the right. Captains, lieutenants and NCOs carried spontoons.

In 1782 an attempted standardisation of dress regulation ordered that all uniforms should be dark blue with red facings and white buttons but not until 1796 was any general acceptance of this noticeable.

In 1799 the cockade became black with a white eagle in the centre and in 1802 the tricorn was replaced by a black crested helmet with coloured turban, peak and white plume to left side.

Army reorganisation

In 1794 General Wayne had reorganised the army into a 'Legion' of four sub-legions each consisting of two battalions of line infantry, one of rifles, a troop of dragoons and a company (battery) of artillery—a remarkably practical and modern system. There were no guards units in the army.

Infantry 1794

Beaver hat with brim bound in the sub-legion colour (1st white; 2nd red; 3rd yellow; 4th green) and having a crest of bearskin over the crown (sub-legion turban and black plumes on the left side were added for parades); dark blue coat with red collar, lapels and round cuffs, white turnbacks, buttons, belts and small clothes.

Plate 57   USA 1810–1821
(*l to r*) Infantry private 1810–1813 (the dark blue uniform is still showing the red facings discarded in 1813 and the man wears the old fashioned beaver 'top hat'), general in the new, all dark blue uniform, infantryman 1813–1821 (here the new shako with brass eagle plate, black cockade with white eagle and white cords and plume can be seen; the dark blue coat is piped and buttoned white), cavalry trooper 1813–1821 (the helmet has brass front plate and fittings, white over dark blue plume, white horsehair crest, piping, buttons and epaulettes are white; coat and holster covers dark blue, the latter edged white), rifleman 1813–1821 (cockade as before, brass horn shako badge, green plume and cords, brass chinscales, grey coat and trousers, yellow buttons), foot artilleryman 1813–1821 (red plume, yellow cords, yellow piping to dark blue collar). A plate by Knotel. (*Courtesy Kosmos Verlag, Stuttgart*)

Cavalry

British style, bearskin-crested, light dragoon leather helmets with cockade and black plume to left side; sub-legion turban. Coats as for infantry but with short skirts; short, straight-topped boots.

Artillery

Cocked hat with red plume and yellow edging, dark blue coat faced and lined red, yellow buttons, white or dark blue breeches. Musicians wore reversed colours.

Engineers

As for artillery but with black velvet facings and with yellow lace bars to chest (8), forearms (3) and collar (1).

The flat buttons bore the eagle under the motto scroll and at the top 'USI' (infantry) or 'USC' and at the bottom the regimental number '13 REG'.

In 1808 a horse artillery regiment was raised (the 'Regiment of Light Artillery') dressed in a slightly bell-topped shako with large brass front plate, white under red plume and cockade on the left side, yellow cords, all blue uniform with collar decorated in yellow lace, yellow buttons and white belts. Officers wore white breeches.

Prior to 1812 the infantry coat became shortened into a coatee, in 1813 the red facings were replaced by blue (with white lace edging and two loops to each side of the collar) and the cocked hat was replaced by a shako initially wider at the crown than at the bottom but later more conical and with a raised and rounded front plate, white cords and plume and octagonal brass plate bearing the eagle. This latter shako was very similar to the British 'Belgic' model. Long white trousers replaced the knee breeches.

Rifle battalions wore the 'light artillery' shako with a green plume and a round brass plate at top front bearing a bugle horn; cockade on top left side and green cords. For dress wear they had a grey coatee and breeches, in the field they wore green, fringed tunics with fringed cape shoulders and green breeches. Musicians had black facings to their grey tunics. Many units wore grey kersey fatigue coats at this time due to the shortages of the blue cloth.

In 1814 the cavalry regiments added yellow lace to their uniforms.

Battle History

1792–4—Florida, Indiana, Kentucky and Ohio against the Miami and other Indians; 1812—the war against Britain; 1813–14—war against Britain; 1811 —Tippecanoe (Indian war); 1812—the Great Lakes; 1815—⚔ New Orleans; (burning of the White House in the summer of 1814).

PRINCIPALITY OF

Waldeck

(Cockade black within red within yellow)

Waldeck joined the Confederation of the Rhine on 13 April 1807 and provided a contingent for Napoleon of 400 men in three companies as part of the 2nd Battalion, 6th Regiment of the Confederation and also as part of the 'Princely Battalion' (contingents of Waldeck, Schwarzburg–Rudolstadt, Lippe–Detmold and Reuss) which was rapidly destroyed in Spain.

Uniform consisted of French shako with brass chinscales and rhombic plate bearing the Waldeck crest, company cords and pompon, white tunic with dark blue collar, lapels, round cuffs, turnbacks and shoulder straps, yellow buttons, white belts. Grey breeches, short black gaiters, brass pouch badge of a crowned, eight-pointed star between the letters 'F and W' (Fürstentum Waldeck). French rank badges; officers had gold shako trim, epaulettes and sword knots, hussar-topped boots.

Battle History

Until 1798 there was a regiment of Waldeck troops in Batavian (Dutch) service. 1807—Siege of Glogau (Prussia); 1809—Tyrol; 1809–11—Spain; 1812—Russia as part of 2nd Brigade, Division Princiere; 1813—besieged in Danzig.

KINGDOM OF

Westfalia

(Cockade dark blue within white)

Napoleon created this state in November 1807 from the old Electorate of Hanover, the Duchy of Brunswick, the Electorate of Hessen-Kassel and minor parts of Prussia.

All badges of rank and inter-company distinctions were after the French system as were weapons, equipment, tactics and discipline.

Guards

All guards units' buttons bore the Westfalia eagle holding a shield with 'JN'.

Garde du Corps
Steel helmets with brass trim and combe, black crest, white plume to left side. Crowned 'JN' on front plate, brass chinscales. White tunic and breeches, royal blue collar, lapels and cuffs edged red with gold buttonholes and buttons, gold contre-epaulettes, white gauntlets, high black boots. Trumpeters wore white crests, red plumes, red tunics faced blue.

Grenadier-Garde
Bearskin bonnet, red cords, plume and top patch with yellow grenade, brass chinscales. White tunic, breeches, gaiters and belts, long skirts, red collar, lapels, cuffs and turnbacks bearing yellow grenades. Red sabre knots and epaulettes, gold buttons and buttonholes. Pouch badge a rhombus with crowned 'JN' and four corner grenades all brass.

Jäger-Garde
Shako with white eagle plate, cords and chinscales, cockade, white plume. Dark green coat, lemon yellow collar, round cuffs, turnbacks

and piping to dark green lapels. White buttons and face to collar, cuffs and lapels, green epaulettes, green breeches with white Hungarian thigh knots, hussar gaiters trimmed white, white belts, white bugle pouch badge, green sabre knot.

Chevau Légers Garde
Black helmet, brass combe, fittings and chinscales, black fur crest, red plume. Short, dark green tunic and trousers, red collar, cuffs and turnbacks, yellow trefoil epaulettes and bars of lace to collar, chest and cuffs, yellow Hungarian thigh knots and side stripes, buff leatherwork, hussar boots with yellow tassel. Trumpeters—reversed colours, brown fur colpacks with red cords, white plume and bag, yellow tassel.

Füsilier-Garde
As for the line infantry but with white lace bars to collar, lapels and cuff flaps.

Jäger-Carabiniers-Bataillon
Shako with red-tipped green plume, red cords, yellow eagle plate, all green tunic and breeches, red lace to collar and cuffs, red half moons to epaulettes, red piping to collar, cuffs, jacket front and turnbacks, red Hungarian thigh knots and side stripes; black leatherwork, red trim to hussar-style gaiters and yellow buttons.

Husaren-Garde (raised 1813, transferred to French service)
Red shako, white plume, yellow top band, cords, chinscales and crowned shield bearing 'JN', black peak. Red dolman, blue pelisse and breeches with yellow buttons and lace, red and white sash, white leatherwork, black sabretasche with crowned 'JN'.

Artillery of the Garde
Shako with red cords, plume and pompon, yellow lozenge plate and chinscales. Dark blue coat, red collar, cuffs, epaulettes and turnbacks, seven red lace bars across the chest, yellow buttons. Blue breeches with red Hungarian thigh knots and side stripes; hussar boots trimmed red, buff gauntlets and bandolier.

Infantry

Line Infantry
Shako with company trim (Grenadiers of the 1st Regiment initially wore bearskins), brass lozenge plate with crowned Westfalian eagle over the pierced regimental number; white coats, yellow buttons with facings shown on collar, lapels, round cuffs and turnbacks. From 1807–10 the facings were as follows: 1st and 2nd Regiments—dark blue; 3rd and 4th—light blue; 5th and 6th—yellow. After this they were all dark blue and the only distinction was the number raised on the button. White breeches and belts, black gaiters. In 1812 the centre companies adopted dark blue epaulettes with white half moons in place of their previous white shoulder straps edged dark blue. By 1812 there were eight line regiments.

Light Infantry (three battalions)
As for the line infantry but initially in cornflower blue with dark green

facings (soon changed to orange) and white buttons. By 1809 the uniform was dark green with light blue collar, cuffs, cuff flaps, turnbacks and piping to single-breasted front, white buttons, dark green breeches, black leatherwork. The shako bore a white eagle plate and chinscales.

Artillery
Shako, red pompon, plume and cords, yellow lozenge plate bearing crowned crossed cannon barrels, yellow chinscales.

Dark blue coat and trousers, red epaulettes, collar, cuffs, cuff flaps, turnbacks and piping to dark blue lapels, yellow buttons, white belts.

Train
Shako with red pompon, white lozenge plate with crowned 'JN', white chinscales; grey tunic with white buttons, red collar, round cuffs and piping to lapels and turnbacks, red waistcoat laced white, grey shoulder straps edged white, grey breeches with white Hungarian trim, plain hussar boots, buff belts.

Cavalry

Line Cavalry
1st Kürassiers (1806–12) French Kürassier helmet, with black crest, brass combe, front shield (with crowned 'JN'), chinscales and peak trim, white plume, brown fur turban. White tunic, crimson collar, lapels, round cuffs and turnbacks all piped white, white buttons, breeches, gauntlets and belts; heavy, cuffed boots.

In 1810 French-pattern steel Kürasses with red and white trim and brass shoulder chains were issued. The coat changed to single-breasted dark blue in 1812.

2nd Kürassiers Dark blue coat with orange facings, otherwise as for 1st Regiment.

1st Chevau Légers Helmet as for Chevau Légers of the guard but with white fittings, dark green coat, orange collar, pointed cuffs, turnbacks, piping and Hungarian trim to dark green breeches; white buttons and trim to hussar boots, buff belts. Dark green saddle furniture edged orange. Trumpeters wore black fur colpacks, green bag, white plume, light blue coats faced red. In 1811 lances with dark blue and white pennants were issued but later withdrawn. A 2nd Regiment was raised in 1812; its uniform was as for the 1st but with buff facings.

1st Hussars Shako with white eagle plate and chinscales, green plume, white cords, green dolman, pelisse and breeches, white buttons and lace, black fur, red and white barrel sash; black sabreasche with white '1'; white belts. Trumpeters wore red.

2nd Hussars As for 1st Regiment but light blue dolman, pelisse and breeches, red collar and cuffs, white or grey fur; '2' on the black sabretasche. Trumpeters wore reversed colours. Saddle furniture was in the dolman colour edged white; black Hungarian harness with white fittings.

Gendarmerie As in France but with dark blue within white cockade.

Battle History

1808–13—in Spain as part of the German Division; 1809—in Saxony as part of the IX Corps; 1812—Russia as VIII Corps; 1813—Saxony as VII Corps.

Württemburg

Duchy until 1803, electorate until 1806 thence kingdom

(Cockade red within black within yellow)

Rank Badges

Generals
As in the French army but with national cockade and silver, red and yellow waist sashes and sword knots, red collar and cuffs, gold embroidery.

Field Officers
Sashes and sword knots as above, two epaulettes in the button colour with heavy bullion fringes, brown cane with gold knob. Captains—as above but with thin fringes. Lieutenant—fringed epaulette on right shoulder, contre epaulette on the left. Second-lieutenant—as above but epaulettes reversed.

NCOs
Sergeant-major—gold or silver (button colour) lace to front and bottom of colour, top and back of cuffs and around lapels, brown cane with gold knot, silver and red sabre tassel. Sergeant—as above but as lapel lace. Corporal—as for sergeant but red and white tassel and hazelnut stick.

Infantry

Line Infantry
Prior to 1799 the uniforms were very Prussian both in colour and style with similar systems of rank badges. Headgear was the bicorn with regimental edging and regimental pompon, dark blue coat with red turnbacks; facings shown on collar, lapels and round cuffs. The belts and small clothes were white, the long gaiters black. The infantry in 1798 were organised into independent battalions named after their 'Inhaber' as follows:

	a (collar, cuffs, lapels)	b (buttons and hat edging)	c (shoulder straps)
Mylius	a yellow	b yellow	c yellow
Obernitz	a light blue	b white	c light blue
Seeger	a red	b white	c white
Beulwitz	a pink	b white	c pink
Perglas	a white	b white	c white

In 1799 a low-crowned, black leather helmet with black leather combe was introduced to replace the bicorn. It had a brass front plate extending between the chinstrap bosses and rising to a point to cover the front of the combe. Along the combe was a crest of black horsehair falling to the rear and at the front of the combe was a pompon in battalion colour. In all, this helmet closely resembled the Rumford kasket which the Bavarian army had worn from 1790–9.

259

Plate 58 Duchy of Württemberg: Line Infantry and Jägers 1800
(*l to r*) (*standing figures*) Private, Infanterie-Bataillon 'von Seeger' (dark blue coat, red facings, white buttons), private, Infanterie-Bataillon 'von Mylius' (as above but yellow facings and buttons), officer of Jägers (dark green coat, black facings, white piping and yellow buttons, silver, red and yellow sash). *Augsburger Bilder.*

At the same time the coat was remodelled, having half lapels in regimental colour and very short skirts—once again reminiscent of Rumford's uniform. Drummers had swallows' nests in the facing colour, edged and decorated with regimental lace, brass drum, yellow and black striped hoops, red plume.

In 1806 a new form of kasket was introduced, it was higher in the crown and the pompon and drooping horsehair crest were replaced by a black woollen 'sausage' crest. The brass front plate bore the crowned Württemberg crest over a front band terminating in the chinstrap bosses; on the left side was a white plume. By 1812 all regiments wore this headgear and lapels were no longer in the facing colour but were in the dark blue of the coat.

During 1812 the helmet began to be replaced by a bell-topped shako with brass, rhombic front plate bearing the crowned cypher 'FR' (Friedrich Rex), brass front band and 'V' shaped side struts springing from the chinstrap bosses. At the top left side was the cockade, the chinstrap was black.

In 1814 those regiments with members of the royal household as their Colonel-in-Chief received white/yellow lace decoration to the collar and cuffs.

Prior to 1798 Württemberg had provided an infantry and a cavalry regiment (the 'Kreis-Regimenter') as their contribution to the Holy Roman

Empire's wars against France. In 1798 a complete reorganisation took place and the following infantry battalions were raised:

1 Grenadier-Bataillon von Zobel (from grenadiers of the Kreis-Regiment and the Regiment von Hügel)
2 Musketier-Bataillon von Obernitz (2nd Bn Kreis-Regiment)
3 Musketier-Bataillon von Mylius (1st Bn Kreis-Regt)
4 Musketier-Bataillon von Seeger (musketier-Bn Regt von Hügel)
5 Musketier-Bn von Beulwitz (musketier-Bn Regt von Hügel)
6 Grenadier-Bataillon von Perglas (Grenadiers Kreis-Regt and von Hügel)

Light Infantry and Jägers

In 1799 a company of Jägers was raised; their uniform was a black Corsican hat with front brim extended and turned up; on this was the white cypher 'F II' and a green plume. Dark green tunic of contemporary infantry cut with black facings edged white, yellow buttons, dark green breeches, black belts and gaiters; small pouch at the front of the waist with white cypher 'F II', rifles and sword bayonets.

In 1801 it was increased to a battalion and its Chef was von Romann; the Corsican hat was then replaced by a cylindrical black felt shako with dark green turban, green pompon and plume. Buglers had black swallows' nests decorated in yellow lace and red tips to their plumes.

Two battalions of light infantry were raised in 1805; they wore line infantry uniform but in dark green with light blue facings, white piping and yellow buttons, buff belts, kasket with black crest, white breeches. In 1807 they were issued with cylindrical shakos having green turban and red plume; 1811 bell-topped shako with rhombic brass plate and fittings, cockade and no plume. They were disbanded in 1817.

In May 1811 the line infantry regiments were numbered and their facings were as shown below:

1st 'Prinz Paul' (previously Musketier-Bataillon 'von Mylius', from 1805 'Herzog Paul') a (collar, cuffs, turnbacks)—yellow, b (buttons)—white, c (piping)—yellow.

2nd 'Herzog Wilhelm' (1798–1805 'von Seeger'), a and c—orange, b—white.

3rd 'von Phull' (previously Füsilier-Regiment 'von Neubronn' raised in 1806) a, b and c—white.

4th 'von Franquemont' (1798 Musketier-Bataillon 'von Beulwitz'; 1804–7 'von Romig') a—pink, b and c—white.

5th 'Prinz Friedrich' (1798 Musketier-Bataillon 'von Obernitz', 1804–8 'von Lilienberg') a—light blue, b and c—white.

6th 'Kronprinz' (raised February 1803 on Musketier-Bataillon 'Erbprinz'; April 1803—January 1806 'Kurprinz') a—white, b—yellow, c—red.

7th 'von Scharffenstein' a and c—red, b—yellow.

8th 'von Etzdorff' a and c—straw yellow, b—yellow.

Jägers 1799 'Fussjäger corps'; 1801 Fussjägerbataillon 'von Romann'; 1805 'von Romann Nr 1'; 1806 'von Hügel Nr 1'; 1807 'König Nr 1' a—black, b—yellow, c—white (dark green coat, black belts).

1805 Fussjägerbataillon Nr 2 'von Scharffenstein' raised; 1808 'von Neuffer Nr 2'; 1812 'von Scheidemantel Nr 2' a—black, b and c white.

In 1813 both Jäger battalions were combined as 'Leichtes-Infanterie Regiment Nr 9'. 'König', and yellow laces were added to collar and cuffs; buttons were yellow.

Plate 59   Duchy of Württemberg: Foot Artillery 1800–1804
Brass helmet plate, light blue coats, faced black, yellow buttons; the officer (rear view) has silver, red and yellow sash and yellow turnbacks edged black. *Augsburger Bilder.*

Light Infantry

Two battalions were raised in 1805; 'von Neubronn Nr 3', (later 'von Wolff Nr 3') and 'von Brüsselle Nr 4' (later 'von Stockmeyer Nr 4') a—light blue, b—yellow, c—white. These two battalions were combined in 1813 as the 'Leichtes-Infanterie-Regiment Nr 10'.

Foot Artillery

In the 1790s they wore a bicorn trimmed yellow, light blue coat of infantry style with black facings and yellow buttons, white belts and small clothes, boots. The kasket replaced the bicorn in 1799 and was replaced itself in 1804 by a Bavarian style Raupenhelm with black 'sausage' crest, brass front plate bearing the Württemberg crest, brass chinscales and side struts, white plume on the left side. Lapels were now light blue and short black gaiters were worn. Drummers as for the infantry.

Horse Artillery (1st Battery had guards status)

As for foot artillery except: black waist sash, white buttons and shoulder scales, white piping, one white lace bar to collar, two to cuffs, yellow turnbacks with wide black edging, light blue breeches, boots.

2nd Battery

As for 1st Battery but no lace to collar and cuffs, yellow buttons and lace.

Train

Shako, no plume, single-breasted, light blue coat, black collar, round cuffs, turnbacks and shoulder straps (the latter edged yellow), yellow buttons, grey breeches, boots.

In 1813 the new bell topped shako with rhombic plate and cords, front and rear peaks was issued; its fittings were white for the 1st Horse Artillery Battery, yellow for line artillery and train.

Cavalry

Leibgarde

This unit had been disbanded in 1794 but was re-raised in 1799 at four squadrons which dressed as Grenadiers à Cheval when parading together (each squadron had its own uniform for solo appearances). The regimental uniform consisted of a bearskin similar to that worn by the Grenadiers à Cheval of the Imperial Guard, dark blue (dark green for the 1st Squadron), single-breasted tunic with yellow collar, cuffs and turnbacks, white buttons and epaulettes, steel Kürass, white breeches, belts and gauntlets, high jacked boots.

A mounted Feldjäger corps (military police) had been raised in 1782; it had the Kasket, dark green tunic breeches and waistcoat, red facings, white buttons and black belts. Later the facings became black and the Bavarian-pattern Raupenhelm was worn.

Line Cavalry

In 1798 there was a regiment of Chevau Légers which in 1807 was titled 'Herzog Heinrich', 1811 'Prinz Adam Nr 1' and in 1813 it became the 'Leib-Kavallerie-Regiment Nr 1'. A second regiment was raised in 1805 and titled 'Leibchevaulègers Kurfürst'; 1811 'Leibschevaulègers Nr 2'. It was disbanded in 1813 for going over to the Allies. In 1805 two Jäger-Regimenter zu Pferde (Chasseurs à Cheval) were raised; the first was 'Prinz Paul' (1807) 'Herzog Louis', 1811—Nr 3; 1813 'Herzog Louis Nr 2'). The second was the Jäger zu Pferde 'König', 1811 Nr 4 'König'. This regiment was disbanded in 1813 for going over to the Allies. In 1809 a dragoon regiment was raised; 1811 'Kronprinz Nr 5', 1813 'Kronprinz Nr 3'.

Two new regiments of Jäger zu Pferde were raised in 1813 from the men of the disbanded 2nd and 4th regiments. They were: Nr 4 'Prinz Adam' and 'Nr 5'.

Uniforms

1st Chevau Légers Black low crowned helmet for the men with black leather combe, yellow over black crest, white metal front plate and band. Dark blue tunic with yellow half lapels, yellow collar, cuffs, piping and buttons, yellow turnbacks, steel shoulder scales, yellow waist sash, white belts, gauntlets and breeches, high boots. By 1811 the lapels were dark blue piped yellow. Officers wore Bavarian Raupenhelme with high crowns, black bearskin crests and the full Württemberg coat of arms on the front; to the left was a high, white plume.

2nd Chevau Légers As above except: falling black horsehair crest to troopers' helmets, white helmet fittings and buttons, brick red facings and waist sash. A single white button and lace to each side of the collar.

3rd Jäger zu Pferde As for Chevau Légers except: helmet crest yellow over dark green, white helmet fittings, yellow shoulder scales, dark green coat, collar, lapels and breeches, white buttons, yellow piping to collar and lapels, yellow turnbacks, black belts and gauntlets, hussar boots.

4th Jäger zu Pferde As above except: green helmet crest, pink collar, white piping.

5th Dragoons Infantry shako with white rhombic plate and cords, dark green tunic with white collar, turnbacks, buttons and piping, steel shoulder scales, black gauntlets, white belts and breeches, high boots. Saddle furniture was in the coat colour, edged in the facing colour with the crowned cypher 'FR' in the rear corners (and front for officers). Harness was black with steel fittings.

In 1814 all cavalry regiments received the shako and the 2nd–5th wore dark green uniforms.

Battle History

1793–7—against France; 1806—against Prussia (sieges of Glogau, Breslau, Schweidnitz, Neisse and Glatz); 1807—against Russia and Prussia; 1809—against Austria; 1812—Russia as 25th Division, III Corps; 1813—Saxony against the Allies; 1814 and 1815—against France.

Würzburg

Bishopric until 1805 thence Grand Duchy until 1815 when it was absorbed by Bavaria

(Cockade blue within red within yellow)

Infantry

In 1795 the Würzburg infantry wore bicorns with white edging, blue coat with red collar, cuffs and turnbacks, white buttons and small clothes, black gaiters. This regiment was reorganised into three battalions in 1801 and the coat changed to white, Austrian pattern with red facings for the 1st Battalion, blue for the 2nd and green for the 3rd. Grenadiers wore bearskin caps, fusiliers black leather Kaskets with black combe and crest and brass fittings; both items of Austrian pattern. White belts and breeches, black gaiters.

Würzburg joined the Confederation of the Rhine on 30 September 1806 and the infantry became the 1st Regiment of that Confederation. Uniform as before but grenadiers had a red helmet plume on the left side, the light company a green one; they also had red and green epaulettes respectively. In 1809–11 the French shako replaced the kasket and although the uniform colours were retained, the style was completely French with red lapels, cuffs and cuff flaps as well as collar and turnbacks. Badges of rank and inter-company distinctions were completely on the French pattern. The brass, rhombic shako plate bore an 'F' (Ferdinand) under a crown. Officers had gold gorgets with silver crest, gold, red and blue sabre knot (with gold, red and blue sash for parades).

Artillery

1806: As for infantry but reddish brown coat faced red, yellow buttons and brass scale epaulettes. When the shako was introduced it had a red topband, plume and cords.

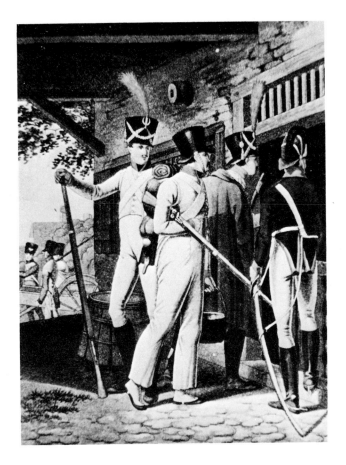

Plate 60   Grand Duchy of Würzburg: 1801–1806
(*l to r*) three privates, 2nd Infantry Battalion, three privates 1st Infantry Battalion; trooper, Chevau Légers. *Augsburger Bilder.*

Cavalry

1806: Austrian pattern cavalry kasket with brass front plate bearing a crowned 'F', red over black plume on the left side, dark green, single-breasted Austrian Chevau Légers pattern tunic with red facings and yellow buttons; white belts and breeches, short boots.

In 1811 the shako replaced the helmet; it was of infantry style but with red pompon and black plume with red tip. Red epaulettes were added to the shoulders.

Battle History

1806—Berlin, Stettin with the Grande Armée; 1807—Danzig and Stralsund; 1808–13—Spain; 1812—Russia as part of the 1st Brigade of the Division Princiére; 1813—Saxony.

Würzberg left the Confederation of the Rhine in November 1813 and as a result of the Congress of Vienna in 1815 was absorbed by Bavaria. The infantrymen were taken into the 12th Bavarian Line Infantry Regiment and the Chevau Légers into the Bavarian Lancer Regiment.

265

Appendix:
Alphabetical list of major clashes and battles 1792-1815

The italicised commanders' names are the victors in the battles. Indecisive battles are shown by neither commanders' name being italicised. The present day countries of the battle locations and the nationalities involved in the battles are indicated by the code letters after place names and commanders' names.

A—Austria; B—Belgium; BAV—Bavaria; BG—Bulgaria; CH—Switzerland; CZ—Czechoslovakia; D—Federal Republic of Germany; DDR—German Democratic Republic; DK—Denmark; E—Spain; EG—Egypt; F—France; FB—Bourbon French Loyalists; GB—Great Britain; GE—German Empire; GR—Greece; H—Hungary; I—Italy; IRL—Ireland; N—Norway; NA—Naples; NL—Netherlands: Batavian Republic, Kingdom of Holland; NV—Naval battle; P—Portugal; PL—Poland; PR—Prussia; R—Russia (Imperial); S—Sweden; SF—Finland; SX—Saxony; SY—Syria; T—Turkey; USA—America; USSR—Present day Union of Soviet Socialist Republics.

Abensberg, D; 20 April 1809	*Bonaparte* (F) vs Erzherzog Ludwig (A)
Abukir Bay, EG; 1 August 1798 (NV)	*Nelson* (GB) vs Bruyes (F)
Abukir, EG; 25 July 1799	*Bonaparte* (F) vs Said Mustapha (T)
Alba de Tormes, E; 25 November 1809	*Kellermann* (F) vs Duke of la Parque (E)
Albuferra, E; 16 May 1811	*Beresford* (GB and P) vs Soult (F)
Aldenhoven, D; 2 October 1794	*Jourdan* (F) vs Clerfayt (A)
Alexandria, EG; 21 March 1800	*Abercrombie* (GB) vs Menou (F)
Almonacid, E; 11 August 1809	*King Joseph* (F) vs Venegas (E)
Amberg, D; 24 August 1796	*Erzherzog Karl* (A) vs Jourdan (F)
Andujar and Menzibar, E; 20 July 1808	Dupont and Wedel (F) vs *Castanos* and *Redding* (E)
Antrain, F; 20 November 1793	*Jacqueline* (FB) vs Rossignol (F)
Arcis sur Aube, F; 20 March 1814	*Schwarzenberg* (A) vs Bonaparte (F)
Arcole, I; 15, 16, 17 November 1796	*Bonaparte* (F) vs Alvintzy (A)
Aspern-Esslingen, A; 21–22 May 1809	*Erzherzog Karl* (A) vs Bonaparte (F)
Auerstädt, DDR; 14 October 1806	*Bonaparte* (F) vs King of Prussia (PR)
Austerlitz, CZ; 2 December 1805	*Bonaparte* (F) vs Tsar Alexander I (R) and Kaiser Franz II (A)
Bailén, E; 19 July 1809	*Castaños* (E) vs Dupont (F)
Barossa (or Chiclana), E; 5 March 1811	*Graham* (GB) and La Peña (E) vs Victor (F)
Bassano, I; 8 September 1796	*Bonaparte* (F) vs Wurmser (A)
Batin, BG; 7 September 1810	*Kamenskoi* (R) vs Kuschanz Ali (T)
Bautzen and Würschen, DDR; 20–21 May 1813	Bonaparte and Duroc (F) vs *Blücher* (PR) and *Wittgenstein* (R)
Bayonne, F; 9–13 December 1813	*Wellington* (GB, E, P) vs Soult (F)
Bazardžik, BG; 3 June 1806	*Kamenskoi* (R) vs Pechlivan Khan (T)
Belchitte, E; 18 June 1809	*Suchet* (F) vs Blake (E)
Beresina, USSR; 28 November 1812	*Wittgenstein* (R) vs Dukes of Belluno and Reggio (F)
Berg Tabor, SY; 16 April 1799	Bon (F) vs Abdullah Pasha (T)
Bergara, E; 28 November 1794	Moncy (F) vs Ruby (E)
Bergen, NL; 19 September 1799	*Brune* (F) vs Duke of York (GB and R)
Bergen, NL; 2 October 1799	*Abercromby* (GB and R) vs Brune (F)
Biberach, D; 2 October 1796	*Moreau* (F) vs La Tour (A)
Biberach, D; 9 May 1800	*St Cyr* (F) vs Kray (A)
Bladensburg, USA; 24 August 1814	*Ross* (GB) vs Winder (USA)
Borodino, USSR; 6–7 September 1812	*Bonaparte* (F) vs Kutusow (R)
Boulou, F; 30 April 1794	*Dugomier* (F) vs de la Union (E)

Braga, P; 20 March 1809 — Soult (F) vs Eben (P)
Brienne, F; 29 January 1814 — Blücher (PR and R) vs *Bonaparte* (F)
Brzesc-Litowski, USSR; — Suworow (R) vs Kosciusko (PL)
  18–19 September 1794
Bussaco, E; 25–27 September 1810 — *Wellington* (GB and P) vs Elchingen
  and Esslingen (F)

Caldiero, I; 12 November 1796 — *Alvinczy* (A) vs Bonaparte (F)
Caldiero, I; 29–31 October 1805 — *Erzherzog Karl* (A) vs Massena (F)
Camperdown, NL; 11 October 1797 — *Duncan* (GB) vs De Winter (NL)
  (NV)
Campmany, E; 17–20 November 1794 — *Dugommier* (F) vs de la Union (E)
Cardedeu, E; 16 December 1808 — *St Cyr* (F) vs Vives (E)
Cassano, I; 27 April 1799 — *Suworow* (R and A) vs Moreau (F)
Cassina Grossa, I; 20 June 1799 — *Moreau* (F) vs Bellegarde (A)
Castalla, E; 13 April 1813 — *Murray* (GB and E) vs Suchet (F)
Castiglione, I; 5 August 1796 — *Bonaparte* (F) vs Wurmser (A)
Castricum, NL; 6 October 1799 — *Brune* (F, NL) vs Duke of York
  (GB, R)
Cateau Cambrésis, F; 26 April 1794 — *Prince of Coburg* (GE) vs Pichegru (F)
Charleroi, B; 3 June 1794 — *Prince of Orange* (A, NL) vs
  Desjardins (F)
Chollet, F; 17 September 1793 — *Lechelle* (F) vs Gigot de Elbée (FB)
Corunna, E; 16 January 1809 — *Moore* (GB) vs Soult (F)
Dennewitz, DDR; 6 September 1813 — *Bernadotte* (S) vs Esslingen (F)
Deutsch-Wagram, A; 4–6 July 1809 — *Bonaparte* (F) vs Erzherzog Karl (A)
Diersheim, D; 20 April 1797 — *Moreau* (F) vs Sztaray (A)
Dresden, DDR; 26–27 August 1813 — *Bonaparte* (F) vs Schwarzenberg (A)
Dürrenstein, A; 11 November 1805 — *Kutusow* (R) vs Mortier (F)
Eckmühl, D; 22 April 1809 — *Bonaparte* (F) vs Erzherzog Karl (A)
Egmond and Beverwyk, NL; 2 October — Brune (F) vs *Duke of York* (GB)
  1799
Emmendingen, D; 19–20 October 1796 — *Erzherzog Karl* (A) vs Moreau (F)
Engen, D; 3 May 1800 — *Moreau* (F) vs Kray (A)
Entrames, F; 27 October 1793 — *Jacqueline* (FB) vs Westermann (F)
Espinosa, E; 11 November 1808 — *Dukes of Danzig and Belluno* (F) vs
  Romana and Blake (E)
Etsch River (or Legnano), I; 26 March — *Kray* (A) vs Scherer (F)
  1799
Ettlingen (or Malsch), D; 9 July 1796 — *Moreau* (F) vs Erzherzog Karl (A)
Eylau—see Preussisch Eylau
Famars, F; 23–24 May 1793 — *Prince of Coburg* (GE) vs De la
  Marche (F)
Figueras, E; 17–19 November 1794 — *Dugomier* (F) vs Dela Union (E)
Finisterre, E; 22 July 1805 (NV) — Calder (GB) vs Villeneuve and Gravier
  (F)
Fleurus, B; 16 June 1794 — *Prince of Orange* (A, NL) vs Jourdan
  (F)
Fleurus, B; 26 June 1794 — *Prince of Coburg* (A, NL) vs Jourdan
  (F)
Fontana Fredda (or Sacile), I; — *Erzherzog Johann* (A) vs Eugene (F)
  16 April 1809
Fontenay-le-Conte, F; 25 May 1793 — *de Lescare* (FB) vs Chalbos (F)
Friedberg, D; 24 August 1796 — *Moreau* (F) vs La Tour (A)
Friedland, PL; 14 June 1807 — *Bonaparte* (F) vs Bennigsen (R)
Froschweiler (or Wörth), F; — *Hoche* (F) vs Hotze (A)
  22 December 1793
Fuentes d'Onoro, P; 4–5 May 1811 — *Wellington* (GB and P) vs Duke of
  Esslingen (F)

Gamonal and Burgos, E; 10 November 1805 — *Duke of Dalmatia* (F) vs Castanos (E)

Genola, I; 4 November 1799 — *Melas* (A) vs Championnet (F)

Gibraltar and Cadiz, E; 12–13 July 1801 (NV) — *Saumarez* (GB) vs Mureno (F)

Gorodeczna (or Podubnie), USSR; 12 August 1812 — *Schwarzenberg* (A and SX) vs Tormassow (R)

Gross-Beeren, DDR; 23 August 1813 — *Bülow* (PR and R) vs Oudinot (F and SX)

Gross-Görschen or Lützen, DDR; 2 May 1813 — Bonaparte and Bessieres (F) vs *Blücher* (PR) and *Wittgenstein* (R)

Hanau, D; 30–31 October 1813 — *Bonaparte* (F) vs Wrede (BAV)

Heilsberg, PL; 10 June 1807 — *Bennigsen* (R and PR) vs Bonaparte (F)

Heliopolis, EG; 20 March 1800 — *Kleber* (F) vs Grand Vizier (T)

Herrenalb—see Malch

Herzogenbusch (or Boxtel), NL; 14 September 1794 — *Pichegru* (F) vs Baron Dalwigk (GE)

Hohenlinden, D; 3 December 1800 — *Moreau* (F) vs Erzherzog Johann (A)

Hollabrunn, A; 3 December 1800 — *Bonaparte* (F) vs Erzherzog Karl (A)

Hondscoote, NL; 6–8 September 1793 — *Houchard* (F) vs Duke of York (GB, NL, A)

Jakubowo, USSR; 30–31 July and 1 August 1812 — *Wittgenstein* (R) vs Oudinot (F)

Jemappes, B; 5–6 November 1792 — *Dumourier* (F) vs Herzog Albrecht (A)

Jena (and Auerstädt), DDR; 14 October 1806 — *Bonaparte* (F) vs Duke of Brunswick (PR)

Kaiserslautern, D; 27–29 November 1793 — *Duke of Brunswick* (PR) vs Hoche (F)

Kaiserslautern, D; 23 May 1794 — *Möllendorf* (PR, A) vs Ambert (F)

Kargali-Dere, T; 23 July 1810 — Jussuff (T) vs Langeron (R)

Katzbach (stream), DDR; 26 August 1813 — *Blücher* (PR) vs Macdonald (F)

Kenzingen and Emmendingen, D; 19–20 October 1796 — *Erzherzog Karl* (A) vs Moreau (F)

Killala (or Tory Island), IRL, 12 October 1798 (NV) — *Warren* (GB) vs Bompard (F)

Kobryn, USSR; 12 August 1812 — *Tormassow* (R) vs Klengel (SX)

Kopenhagen, DK; 2 April 1801 (NV) — *Nelson* (GB) vs Fisher (DK)

Krasnoi, USSR; 15–19 November 1813 — *Kutuzow* (R) vs Bonaparte (F)

Kulm, CZ; 30 August 1813 — *Barclay de Tolly* (R, A, PR) vs Vandamme (F)

La Fère Champenoise, F; 25 March 1814 — *Schwarzenberg* (A) vs Marmont (F)

La Rothière and Brienne, F; 1 February 1814 — Bonaparte (F) vs *Schwarzenberg* (A) and *Blücher* (PR)

Landen and Neerwinden, B; 18 March 1793 — *Prince of Coburg* (A) vs Dumouriez (F)

Lâon and Coucy, F; 9–10 March 1814 — Bonaparte (F) vs *Blücher* (PR, A, R)

Lautern and Weissenburg, D; 14 October 1793 — *Wurmser* (A) vs Carlen (F)

Lautern and Weissenburg, D; 26–27 December 1793 — *Hoche* (F) vs Wurmser (A) and Duke of Brunswick (PR)

Le Mans, F; 13 December 1793 — *Kleber and Marceau* (F) vs Jacqueline (FB)

Leipzig (including Wachau and Möckern), DDR; 16–18 October 1813 — Bonaparte (F) vs *Tsar Alexander I* (R), *Kaiser Franz I* (A), *King Friedrich Wilhelm III* (PR).

Lemnos (Island), GR; 22 June 1807 (NV)	*Siniavin* (R) vs Said Ali Pasha (T)
Ligny, B; 16 June 1815	*Bonaparte* (F) vs Blücher (PR)
Lissa, YU; 13 March 1811 (NV)	*Hoste* (GB) vs Dubourdieu (F)
Loano, I; 23 November 1795	*Scherer* (F) vs Devins (A)
Lodi, I; 10 May 1796	*Bonaparte* (F) vs Beaulieu (A)
Lonado, I; 3 August 1796	*Bonaparte* (F) vs Quosdannovich (A)
L'Orient (Quiberon Bay), F; 23 June 1795 (NV)	*Vice Admiral Lord Bridport* (GB) vs Villaret-Joyeuse (F)
Luciensteig, CH; 14 May 1799	*Hotze* (A) vs Mesnard (F)
Lübeck, D (storm of); 6 November 1806	*Pontecorvo* (F) vs Blücher (PR)
Luçon, F; 14 August 1793	*Tuncq* (F) vs Gigot d'Elbèe (FB)
Lützen—see Gross-Görschen	
Lyon, F (storm of); 19 March 1814	*Bianchi* (A) vs Castiglione (F)
Madcziewicze, PL; 10 October 1794	*Fersen* (R) vs Kosciusko (PL)
Magnano, I; 5 April 1799	*Kray* (A) vs Schérer (F)
Mainz, D; 29 October 1795	*Clerfayt* (A) vs Schaal (F)
Malch (or Herrenalb), D; 9 July 1796	*Moreau and St Cyr* (F) vs Erzherzog Karl (A)
Malo-Jaroslawetz, USSR; 24 October 1812	*Bonaparte* (F) vs Kutusow (R)
Mantica (La Favorita), I; 16 January 1797	*Bonaparte* (F) vs Wurmser (A)
Marengo, I; 14 June 1801	*Bonaparte and Dessain* (F) vs Melas and Zach (A)
Marthartey (Heliopolis), EG; 20 March 1800	*Kleber* (F) vs Grand Visier (T)
Medellin, E; 28 March 1809	*Duke of Bellano* (F) vs Cuesta (E)
Medina de Rio Secco, E; 14 July 1808	*Duke of Istria* (F) vs Cuesta (E)
Millesimo, I; 13–14 April 1796	*Bonaparte* (F) vs Beaulieu, Argenteau and Colli (A)
Mincio, I; 24–26 December 1800	*Brune* (F) vs Bellegarde (A)
Mincio, I; 8 February 1814	*Eugene* (F, I) vs Bellegarde (A)
Molins-del-Rey, E; 21 December 1808	*St Cyr* (F) vs Caldagues (E)
Mondovi and Vico, I; 22 April 1796	*Bonaparte* (F) vs Beaulieu and Argenteau (A)
Montebello (or Casteggio), I; 9 July 1800	*Lannes* (F) vs Ott (A)
Montenotte, I; 21 April 1796	*Bonaparte* (F) vs Beaulieu and Argenteau (A)
Montmarte, F; 30 March 1814	*Blücher* (PR) vs Mortier (F)
Montmirail, F; 8 February 1814	*Bonaparte* (F) vs Osten-Sacken (R) and Yorck (PR)
Moskwa, USSR; see Borodino	
Mösskirch, D; 5 May 1800	*Moreau* (F) vs Kray (A)
Nantes, F; 29 June 1793	*Canclaux* (F) vs Cathelineau (FB)
Neerwinden and Landen, B; 18 March 1793	*Prince of Coburg* (GE) vs Dumouriez (F)
Neresheim, D; 11 August 1796	Erzherzog Karl (A) vs *Moreau* (F)
New Orleans, USA; 8 January 1813	*Jackson* (USA) vs Pakenham (GB)
Newied, D; 18 April 1797	*Hoche* (F) vs Werneck (A)
Nivelle, F; 10 November 1813	*Wellington* (GB, E, P) vs Soult (F)
Novi, I; 15 August 1799	*Suworow* (A, R) vs Joubert (F)
Ny Carleby, SF; 24 June 1808	Adlerkreutz (S) vs Jankowitsch (R)
Occaña, E; 19 November 1809	*Duke of Treviso* (F) vs Ariezaga (E)
Oporto, P; 29 March 1809	*Soult* (F) vs Bishop of Oporto (P)
Oporto, P; 11 May 1809	*Beresford* (GB) vs Duke of Dalmatia (F)

Orivas, SF; 14 September 1808	*Kamenskoi II* (R) vs Klingspor (S)
Orthez, F; 27 February 1814	*Wellington* (GB) vs Duke of Dalmatia (F)
Paris, F; 30 March 1814	*Blücher* (PR) and *Schwarzenberg* (A) vs Dukes of Ragusa and Treviso (F)
Pirmasens, D 14 September 1793	*Duke of Brunswick* (PR) vs Moreau (F)
Podubnie—see Gorodeczna	
Polozk, USSR; 16–18 August 1812	*St Cyr* (F, BAV) vs Wittgenstein (R)
Polozk, USSR; 18–20 October 1812	*St Cyr* (F, BAV) vs Wittgenstein (R)
Ponta della Priula, I; 8 May 1809	*Prince Eugene* (F) vs Erzherzog Johann (A)
Preussisch Eylau, DDR; 7–8 February 1807	*Bonaparte* (F) vs Bennigsen and Lestocq (R)
Pultusk, USSR; 26 December 1806	*Lannes* (F) vs Bennigsen (R)
Pyramids (The), EG; 21 July 1798	*Bonaparte* (F) vs Grand Vizier (T)
Pyrenees, E; 25 July–2 August 1813	*Wellington* (GB, P, E) vs Soult (F)
Quatre Bras, B; 16 June 1815	Ney (F) vs Prince of Orange (NL, G)
Raab, H; 14 June 1809	*Prince Eugene* (F) vs Palatin (A)
Ramanie, EG; 19 April 1801	Hutchinson (GB) vs Menou (F)
Rawka, USSR; 6 June 1794	*de Favrat* (PR) and *Denisow* (R) vs Koscuiszko (PL)
Rivoli, I; 14–16 January 1797	*Bonaparte* (F) vs Alvintzy (A)
Roliça, P; 19 August 1808	*Wellesley* (GB) vs de Laborde (F)
Roveredo, I; 4 September 1796	*Bonaparte* (F) vs Davidovich (A)
Rustschuck (storm of), BG; 4 August 1810	*Turks* (*defenders*) vs Kamenskoy II (R)
Rustschuck, BG; 4 July 1811	*Kutusow* (R) vs Grand Vizier (T)
Sacile, I; 16 April 1809	*Erzherzog Johann* (A) vs Prince Eugene (F)
Sagunto (or Murviedro), E; 25 October 1811	*Suchet* (F) vs Blake (E)
Salamanca, E; 22 July 1812	*Wellington* (GB) vs Duke of Ragusa (F)
Salzburg, A; 14 December 1800	Lecourbe (F) vs Erzherzog Johann (A)
San Giorgio (nr Mantua), I; 15 September 1796	*Bonaparte* (F) vs Wurmser (A)
San Giorgio (nr Mantua), 1; 16 January 1797	*Bonaparte* (F) vs Wurmser (A)
Savona (nr Genoa), I; 14 March 1795 (NV)	*Hotham* (GB) vs Martin (F)
Schiumla, BG; 23–24 June 1810	*Kuschanz Ali* (T) vs Kamenskoi (R)
Schiumla, BG; 8 August 1810	*Kamenskoi* (R) vs Kuschanz Ali (T)
Schlingen, D; 24 October 1796	*Erzherzog Karl* (A) vs Moreau (F)
Sedymann, EG; 7 October 1798	*Dessaix* (F) vs Murad Bey (T)
Smolensk, USSR; 17–18 August 1812	*Bonaparte* (F) vs Barclay de Tolly (R)
Smoljäntzi, USSR; 14 November 1812	*Wittgenstein* (R) vs Victor (F)
Somosierra, E; 30 November 1808	*Duke of Belluno* (F) vs Montblanc (E)
Spremont, B; 18 September 1794	*Scherer* (F) vs La Tour (A)
St Giovanni—see Trebbia	
St Vincent (Cape of), F; 14 February 1797 (NV)	*Jervis* (GB) vs Cordova (E)
Stockach and Liptingen, D; 25–26 March 1799	*Erzherzog Karl* (A) vs Jourdan (F)
Tabor (mount), SY; 15 April 1799	*Bonaparte* (F) vs Ibrahim (T)
Tagliamento, I; 16 March 1797	*Bonaparte* (F) vs Erzherzog Karl (A)
Talavera, E; 28 July 1809	*Wellesley* (GB) and *Cuesta* (E) vs King Joseph and Jourdan (F)
Tartaritza, BG; 22 October 1809	*Pechlivan Khan* (T) vs Bagration (R)
Tolentino, I; 2–3 May 1815	*Bianchi* (A) vs Murat (NA)
Toulouse, F; 10 April 1814	*Wellington* (GB) vs Soult (F)

Tourcoing, F; 17–18 May 1794 — Souham (F) vs Prince of Coburg (GE)
Tournay, B; 22 May 1794 — Prince of Coburg (GE) vs Pichegru (F)
Trafalgar (Cape) E; 21 October 1805 (NV) — Nelson and Colingwood (GB) vs Villeneuve (F) and Gravina (E)
Trebbia or St Giovanni, I; 17–19 June 1799 — Suworow (R, A) vs Macdonald (F)
Truillas, F; 22 September 1793 — Don Ricardos (E) vs Dagobert (F)
Tudela, E; 23 November 1808 — Conegliano and Montebello (F) vs Palafox (E)

Ucles, E; 13 January 1809 — Victor (F) vs Venegas (E)
Ulm, D; 14–15 October 1805 — Bonaparte (F) vs Mack (A)
Ushant, F; 1 June 1794 (NV) — Admiral Lord Howe (GB) vs Villaret Joyeuse (F)

Utznach, CH; 25 September 1799 — Soult (F) vs Hotze (A)
Valeggio, I; 9 February 1814 — Bellegarde (A) vs Prince Eugene (F, I)
Valutina-Gora, USSR; 19 August 1812 — Tutschkow I (R) vs Ney (F)
Vals, E; 25 February 1809 — St Cyr (F) vs Reding (E)
Vera, E; 31 August–1 September 1813 — Wellington (GB, E, P) vs Soult (F)
Verona and Legnano, I; 30 March 1799 — Kray (A) vs Serrurier (F)
Verona and Magnano, I; 5 April 1799 — Kray (A) vs Scherer (F)
Vimiero, E; 21 August 1808 — Wellesley (GB, P) vs Duke of Abrantes (F)

Vittoria, E; 21 June 1813 — Wellington (GB, P) vs King Joseph (F)
Voltri, I; 18 April 1800 — Melas (A) vs Massena (F)
Waterloo, B; 18 June 1815 — Wellington (GB), Prince of Orange (NL), Blücher (PR) vs Bonaparte (F)

Wattignies, F; 15–16 October 1793 — Prince of Coburg (GE) vs Jourdan (F)
Wörth—see Froschweiler
Würschen (see Bautzen)
Würzburg, D; 2–3 September 1799 — Erzherzog Karl (A) vs Jourdan (F)
Znaim, CZ; 11–12 July 1809 — Bonaparte (F) vs Erzherzog Karl (A) (battle undecided)

Zürich, CH; 4 April 1799 — Erzherzog Karl (A) vs Massena (F)
Zürich, CH; 25 September 1799 — Massena (F) vs Korsakow (R)

Select Bibliography

Main sources used in the preparation of this work; regimental histories are not quoted as they would be too numerous

The Army List. London 1815.
Abbildung der Chur-Hannoverschen Armee-Uniformen. Hanover and Leipzig 1791.

An officer of the Staff. *Costumes of the Army of the British Empire According to the Last Regulations 1814.* London 1815.

Bezzel, Oskar. *Die Geschichte des Kurpfalz-Bayerischen Heeres.* (8 volumes) München 1930.

Bredow-Wedel. *Historische Stamm und Rangliste des Deutschen Heeres.* August Scherl, Berlin 1905.

Gayda, M. and Krijitsky, A. *L'Armé Russe sous le Tsar Alexandre 1er de 1805 à 1815.*

Grouvel, Vicomte. *Les Corps de Troupe de l'Emigration Française 1789–1815.* Paris 1962.

Kling, C. *Geschichte der Bekleidung, Bewaffnung und Ausrüstung des Königlich Preussischen Heeres.* (3 volumes) Weimar 1912.

Knötel, R.	*Mittheilunzen zur Geschichte der Militarischen Tracht.* Rathenow 1896–1920.
Knötel, R., Knötel, H. and Sieg, H.	*Handbuch der Uniform Kunde.* Helmut Gerhard Schulz, Hamburg 1966.
Kraft, H.	*Die Württemberger in den Napoleonischen Kriegen.* Stuttgart 1953.
Lienhart and Humbert.	*Les Uniformes de l'Armée Française depuis 1690 jusqu'a nos Jours.* (5 volumes) Leipzig 1895–1906.
Lünsmann, F.	*Die Westfälische Armee 1807–1813.* Berlin 1935.
Malibran, A. and Chelminski, J.v.	*L'Armée du Duché de Varsovie de 1807 à 1812.* Paris 1913.
Muller and Braun.	*Organisation der Königlich Bayerischen Armee 1806–1906.* München 1906.
Pietsch, Paul.	*Uniformierungs-und Organisations-Geschichte des Preussischen Heeres.* Berlin 1911 and 1913.
Scharnhorst, G. von, Generallieutenant.	*Handbuch für Officiere in den Angewandten Theilen der Kriegs-Wissenschaften.* (3 volumes) Hannover 1792 and 1815.
Schermer, F.	*Nec Aspera Terrent!* Hannover 1929.
Schuster, O. and Franke, F. A.	*Die Geschichte der Sächsischen Armee.* Leipzig 1895.
Sichart von.	*Geschichte der Königlich Hannoverschen Armee.* (6 volumes) Hannover 1866–1898.
Stein, F. von.	*Geschichte des Russischen Heeres von den Ursprunge desselben bis zur Thronbesteigung des Kaisers Nikolai I Pawlowitsch.* Leipzig 1895.
Weiland, C. F.	*Darstellung der Stärke und Organisation der Kaiserlich Französischen Armee und Ihrer Allierten im Jahre 1807 und 1812 nebst 148 Kupfern die Uniformen derselben darstellend.* Weimar 1807 and 1812.
Wiskowatow.	*A History of the Uniforms of the Russian Army.*

Zeitschrift fur Heereskunde—a periodical published by the Deutsche Gesellschaft für Heereskunde e.V. Berlin.

In addition to printed works, documents, plates and items of uniform in the following museums and archives were also consulted:

Austria:	Heeresgeschichtliches Museum, Vienna
France:	Musée de l'Armee, Paris
Netherlands:	Leger und Wapensmuseum, Leiden
Federal Republic of Germany:	
	Museum für Preussische Kulturbesitz; Lipperheide Kostumsammlung – Berlin
	Wehrhistorisches Museum, Rastatt
	Historisches Museum am Hohen Ufer, Hannover
	Bomann Museum, Celle
	Bayerisches Armeemuseum, Ingolstadt
	Archives in the following cities: Berlin, Düsseldorf, Braunschweig, Hamburg, München
German Democratic Republic:	
	Museum für Deutsche Geschichte, Berlin
United Kingdom:	British Library
	Victoria and Albert Museum
	National Army Museum
	Ministry of Defence, Library